Apple Pro Training Series

Encyclopedia of Color Correction

Alexis Van Hurkman

Apple
Certified

Apple Pro Training Series: Encyclopedia of Color Correction
Alexis Van Hurkman
Copyright © 2007 by Alexis Van Hurkman

Published by Peachpit Press. For information on Peachpit Press books, contact:

Peachpit Press
1249 Eighth Street
Berkeley, CA 94710
(510) 524-2178
Fax: (510) 524-2221
http://www.peachpit.com
To report errors, please send a note to errata@peachpit.com
Peachpit Press is a division of Pearson Education

Series Editor: Nancy Peterson
Production Coordinator: Laurie Stewart, Happenstance Type-O-Rama
Editor: Linda Laflamme
Technical Editor: Robbie Carman
Technical Reviewers: Brendan Boykin, Michael Wohl
Copy Editor: Darren Meiss
Media Reviewer: Eric Geoffroy
Compositor: Chris Gillespie, Happenstance Type-O-Rama
Indexer: Valerie Perry
Interior Design: Mimi Heft
Cover Illustration: Kent Oberheu
Cover Production: Chris Gillespie, Happenstance Type-O-Rama

ISBN 0-321-43231-2
9 8 7 6 5 4 3 2 1
Printed and bound in the United States of America

Contents at a Glance

Table of Contents

Getting Started

Color correction is a complex activity that weaves together the disciplines of color reproduction, photography, cinematography, videography, optics, physics, art, and innumerable other bits of science and trivia in the pursuit of idealized (or stylized) imagery.

If that sounds a bit daunting, relax.

Instead of dwelling on color theory for its own sake, *Apple Pro Training Series: Encyclopedia of Color Correction* presents a wide variety of hands-on, practical color correction techniques supported by both real-world and technical details. In other words, the *why* is presented alongside the *how*. In addition, the book will pull back the curtain on video engineering standards and practices, enhancing your ability to deliver an accurate image to your audience.

Although the *Encyclopedia of Color Correction* focuses on color correction for broadcast, the techniques are applicable to other types of programming, as well, such as standard and high definition video postproduction for independent digital features. Whether you're delivering your program to a terrestrial, cable, or satellite broadcaster or submitting it to a film festival for video screening, the methods presented in this book will help you to maximize your program's image quality and precisely control its "look."

A guiding philosophy of this book is to focus on getting the job done using the tools you have. Color correction inside of Apple's Final Cut Pro is a fast and flexible solution for many projects, and the *Encyclopedia* will show you how you can customize the application's familiar filters in countless ways to accomplish completely different tasks.

Although this Apple Pro Training Series book uses Final Cut Pro to demonstrate its techniques, keep in mind that you can apply the methods described using *any* application with color-correction tools that include three-way (shadows, midtones, and highlights) primary color correction and secondary color correction with HSB qualifiers.

> **NOTE** ▸ If you're interested in a more thorough series of Final Cut Pro tutorials that walk you through using the video scopes, making basic contrast and color adjustments, and performing scene-to-scene color correction, consider *Apple Pro Training Series: Advanced Color Correction and Effects in Final Cut Pro 5* by Alexis Van Hurkman and DigitalFilm Tree (Peachpit Press).

> **NOTE** ▸ The focus of this book is on fast, efficient color correction techniques, rather than special effects, For information about more complex compositing and effects techniques, see Damian Allan and Brian Connors' excellent *Encyclopedia of Visual Effects* (Peachpit Press).

The Methodology

The *Encyclopedia of Color Correction* is divided into two sections. In short, the Encyclopedia section is a collection of hands-on techniques and articles concerning the examination, manipulation, and correction of your program's images, and the Fundamentals section discusses concerns common to all techniques and colorists.

Fundamentals

In the Fundamentals section, you'll find what you need to know to get started and work efficiently.

Chapter 1 walks you through the important considerations when setting up a room for doing color correction. Whether you're designing a dedicated suite or simply pulling together a spare room to work on a personal project, this chapter will show you how to create an environment conducive to the accurate evaluation of your images.

Chapter 2 presents ideal workflows for importing projects, capturing media, and outputting your program to maximize image quality in Final Cut Pro.

Encyclopedia of Techniques

Each entry in the Encyclopedia section is a self-contained article or lesson covering a particular aspect of the color correction process. Most of the entries have exercises that help you learn the procedure by doing it. That doesn't mean that the method presented is the only or definitive way to grade your shots. They are starting points, guidelines for you to study, experiment with, and even expand. Each example and exercise illustrates flexible and customizable solutions that you can apply to your own unique situations.

Where relevant, third-party filters that relate to a particular technique are referenced at the end of that entry, along with the Web site at which they're available.

> **NOTE ▶** It's difficult to present examples of color in three completely different gamuts; invariably, print, onscreen, and broadcast representations of the same image all look dramatically different. If possible, perform the example lessons with a broadcast monitor. If not, be aware that your results will certainly vary from the illustrations in the book.

Copying the Lesson Files

Apple Pro Training Series: Encyclopedia of Color Correction includes a DVD containing the files you'll need for working through some of the techniques. Each technique identifies the filename and location of the relevant content.

> **NOTE ▶** Most of the included media is standard definition, but a few of the exercises use high definition clips.

Installing the Lesson Files

1   Insert the Apple Pro Training Series: Encyclopedia of Color Correction DVD into your computer's DVD drive.

2   On the desktop, double-click the DVD icon, titled **APTS_CycCC**, to open it.

3   Drag the Book Media and Exercises folder to your Macintosh HD icon or dedicated media drive. Eject the DVD.

4   Open the Book Media and Exercises folder from your hard drive, and then open the **Color Correction Exercises for FCP** project file that corresponds to your version of Final Cut Pro. There is a exercise file for version 4.5 (HD), 5.0, and 5.1.

The main project file that accompanies the media is in Final Cut Pro 5.1.2 format. If you have an earlier version of Final Cut Pro, you can import one of the XML versions of the project instead. Use the File > Import > XML command and look for the files in the **For XML Import** folder inside the APTS_CycCC folder.

Companion Web Site

Every effort has been made to make this book current. However, new versions, whether dot releases or full-blown point releases, may introduce changes that subtly affect the detail-oriented operations described herein.

This book has a companion Web site: www.peachpit.com/title/0321432312. From time to time, the author may post additional content on this site. Please check periodically for revised lessons, new content, or trial software.

Apple Pro Certification Program

Apple Pro Training Series: Encyclopedia of Color Correction is both a self-paced learning tool and part of the official training curriculum of the Apple Pro Training and Certification Program, developed by experts in the field and certified by Apple Computer. The series offers complete training in all Apple Pro products, and are the approved curriculum for Apple Certified Training Centers worldwide.

For a complete list of Apple Pro Training Series books, see the course catalog at the back of this book, or visit www.peachpit.com/applebooklet.

Contact the Author

You can reach Alexis Van Hurkman at encyclopedia@vanhurkman.com, or visit his Web site at www.alexisvanhurkman.com.

Referenced Works

Throughout this book reference is made to additional works covering specific aspects of video engineering, color theory, and postproduction in greater detail. Among the most relevant of these are Charles Poynton's *Digital Video and HDTV Algorithms and Interfaces* (Morgan Kaufman), Keith Jack's *Video Demystified, 4ᵗʰ Edition* (Newnes), Maureen Stone's *A Field Guide to Digital Color* (AK Peters Ltd.), Ansel Adams' *The Negative* (Bulfinch), David K. Lynch and William Livingston's *Color and Light in Nature* (Cambridge), and Jane Campsie's *Marie Claire Hair & Makeup*.

Three other excellent, and more generalized, works on color correction are Steve Hullfish and Jaime Fowler's *Color Correction for Digital Video: Using Desktop Tools to Perfect Your Image* (Focal Press), Stuart Blake Jones' *Video Color Correction for Non-Linear Editors: A Step-by-Step Guide* (Focal Press), and Jack James' *Digital Intermediates for Film and Video* (Focal Press).

Special Thanks

The author would like to gratefully acknowledge the following people for contributing their knowledge and time to this project: Eric Graves, Dave Black, Robbie Carman, Grant Petty and Victoria Battison of Blackmagic Designs, David Smith of NOMAD: post, and Graeme Nattress.

The following filmmakers generously contributed the clips used throughout this book:

- ▶ Paul Darrigo (actor/producer) *FBI Guys*
- ▶ Natasa Prosenc (producer/director) *Souvenir*
- ▶ Chris Purcell and Zac Petrillo (producers/directors) *Impunity*
- ▶ Kaylynn Raschke (producer/director) *Sleep Tight—A Bedtime Story*
- ▶ Jeremy Workman (producer/director) and Robert Lyons (cinematographer) *One Track Mind*
- ▶ John Dames, Crime of the Century, and coreaudiovisual for *Branded Content for Maserati Quattroporte*

Finally, special thanks to Kaylynn Raschke for contributing the numerous photographic examples referenced throughout this book.

Fundamentals

1

Techniques

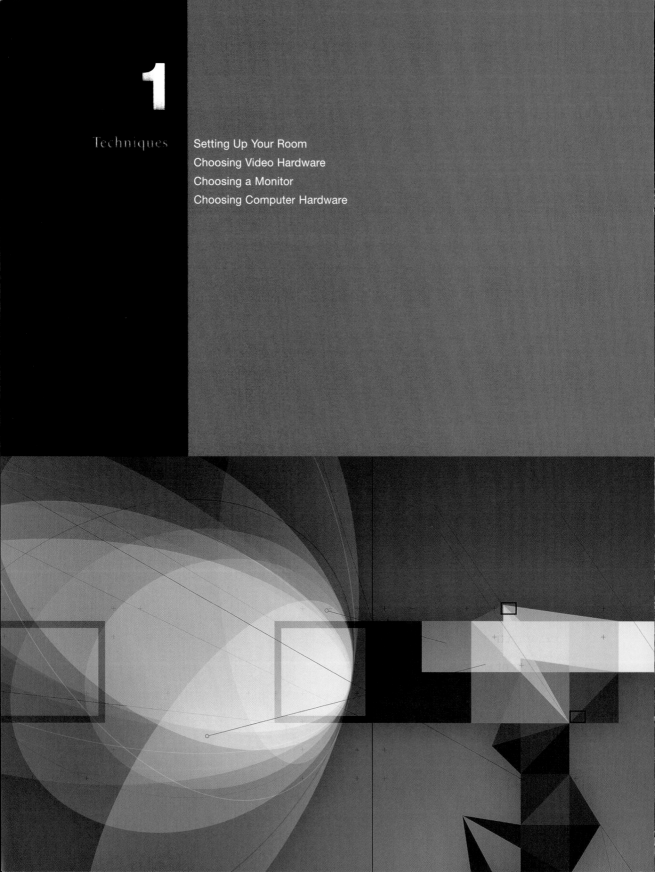

Chapter 1

Setting Up a Color Correction Environment

Before you begin color correcting anything, you need to take stock of the room in which you're working. Successful color correction requires careful setup of your room, much more so than editing, compositing, or broadcast design typically requires (although those disciplines also benefit from the same attention to your environment).

This chapter suggests ways in which to set up your room and choose equipment so that you can work quickly, comfortably, and most important, accurately.

> **NOTE** ▶ Although the advice in this chapter is most applicable to larger facilities that are willing to spend the time and money to convert existing edit suites into color correction rooms, many of the suggestions are certainly feasible even for individual operators with smaller rooms or home editors who are temporarily setting up rooms in which to color correct their video shorts.

Best practices for room setup can be accomplished in many ways; the important point is that you understand why wall color, lighting, and careful equipment selection and placement are important. Once you do, you then can decide how far to go to set up your color correction environment to meet your needs.

Setting Up Your Room

The environment in which you're looking at your program has almost as big an effect on how the picture is perceived as the monitor you're looking at. If you're making critical color evaluations of video, it's vital to make sure that your viewing environment and monitor are up to the task.

> **NOTE ▶** Much of the information in this section is referenced from Sony's booklet, *The Basics of Monitor Technology*, available online at www.sony.ca/luma. This is an excellent reference.

Wall Color

The room in which you're working should be desaturated overall. In particular, the visible area behind the monitor should be a neutral, desaturated gray. The color may be a bit darker or lighter than 50 percent gray, according to your taste, but it should be completely desaturated (not slightly bluish or reddish, as some paints can be). Sony recommends the neutral gray area be more than eight times the monitor screen area, but it's basically a good idea to paint enough of the wall to fill your field of view while you're looking directly at the monitor.

This does two things. First, by making sure that the wall isn't any particular hue, it ensures that you'll be able to evaluate the colors of your image without outside influence. Because our eyes judge color relative to other surrounding colors, having an orange wall behind your evaluation monitor would influence your color perception, potentially causing you to overcompensate and make inaccurate corrections to the video.

Second, the contrast of images on your reference monitor is also going to be influenced by the brightness of the wall surrounding it. If the wall is either white or black, you risk misjudging the lightness or darkness of the image on your monitor as a result.

Lighting

The lighting in your color correction room should be tightly controlled. You do not want mixed lighting in your room (light sources with two or more color temperatures in the same room), so if you have an outside window, it's best to completely darken it out using a light-blocking material. Duvetyne or other blackout fabrics work well, but whatever material you select, make sure that it blocks *all* the light, otherwise you risk allowing a bit of light into the room that's filtered to a different color, which is potentially even worse!

Once you've blocked all outside light, the interior lighting of your room should be set up very specifically. Here are some guidelines:

▶ In most North and South American and European countries, all studio lighting fixtures should have a color temperature of 6500K (D65, see Color Temperature). This matches the color temperature for noon daylight and is also the color temperature to which your broadcast monitor and computer displays should be set. One of the easiest ways to make sure your lighting is exact is to use color-balanced fluorescent lighting. You can easily obtain D65-rated tubes, and the newer electronic ballasts give instant turn-on, as well as eliminating the flicker of older fluorescent lighting fixtures.

▶ In some Asian countries including China, Japan, and Korea, the standard color temperature for broadcast monitors and studio lighting is 9300K (D93, see Color Temperature), which is a "bluer" white.

▶ All lighting in the room should be *indirect*, meaning there should be no light bulb within your field of view. It's common for lighting to be bounced off of the wall behind the monitor.

▶ Sony recommends that the indirect lighting behind (visually surrounding) the monitor be no more than 12 cd/m^2 (candela per meter squared, a standard unit of measurement). In other words, the ambient lighting should be about 10 percent of the illumination from a 100 IRE white signal displayed on your monitor. A more general rule of thumb is that the ambient lighting should be no more than 10 to 25 percent the brightness of your monitor displaying pure white.

> **NOTE** ▶ This formula is intended for CRT monitors; other display technologies may benefit from different lighting ratios. Sony points out that CRT displays have higher perceived contrast with lower lighting, but LCD-based displays have higher perceived contrast with higher ambient lighting.

▶ Because the ambient lighting in the room has a significant effect on the perceived contrast of the image, some colorists recommend that your room's lighting match the ambient lighting of the intended audience's environment. In other words, if you're color correcting a program that will be watched in an average living room, then brighter ambient lighting is appropriate. If you're color correcting a program intended for an audience in a darkened theater, consider working in a darker room.

▶ There should be *no* light that reflects off of the front of your broadcast monitor. Any light that spills onto the face of a CRT-based broadcast monitor will lower its apparent contrast, making critical evaluation of contrast difficult. This is another reason for indirect lighting.

Have a White Spot

Many colorists set up a *white spot* in their room. A white spot is basically a pure, desaturated area of white on the wall, illuminated with D65 temperature lighting. Think of this as a videographer's white card for your eye. Its purpose is to give you a pure white reference point with which to "rebalance" your eye. As you work, your eye fatigues, and your sense of white may drift. Glancing at the white spot lets you regain a sense of neutral white.

Set Up Your Furniture for Comfortable Viewing

You want to set up your working surface to be as comfortable as possible, with the height of your seating, typing/mousing surface, and monitors ergonomically adjusted to avoid back pain and wrist fatigue. You're going to be sitting there a lot, so you'd better be physically relaxed in order to focus on the work. Your chair should be durable, comfortable, and adjustable (you can't spend too much on a good chair). And make sure that the client has a comfortable chair, too.

To go along with the need for a desaturated enviroment, the color of your furniture should also be desaturated. Black is a good color for the desktop, and your desk surface should be nonreflective to prevent light spill on your monitors.

Monitor Placement

Unlike an editing suite, in which the broadcast monitor may be more for the client than for you, the reference broadcast display in a color correction room should be placed for the comfortable, ongoing viewing of both you and your client, because you're both going to be staring at it throughout every session.

For your own sanity, it's best to have a single color display to which both you and the client refer during the session. Although there are situations in which multiple displays are advantageous (for example, an extremely high-quality video projector and a smaller reference monitor for yourself), there should be only *one* display that the client refers to when describing desired changes. Otherwise, you risk having the client point at another monitor with completely different display characteristics and asking, "Can you make it look like that one instead?"

> **NOTE** ▶ Trust me, it'll happen. It's not infrequent for a client to point at the Canvas on the computer monitor and say, "Can't you make the image look more like that?" Although this is a perfectly reasonable request, it can be difficult to explain why clients shouldn't be looking at your computer's monitor.

If you've got a small room and a small monitor, placing it to one side of your computer displays is a perfectly reasonable setup.

If the size of your room (and your budget) permits, get a larger reference monitor and place it above and behind your computer's displays. This helps to prevent the light from the computer displays from creating glare on the broadcast monitor.

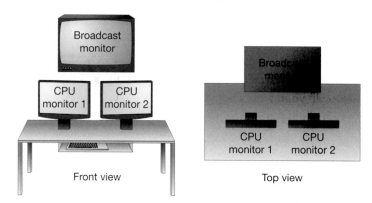

Ideal placement of the reference monitor; above, for easy viewing by both you and the client, and behind the computer monitors to prevent light spill from causing unwanted glare. The distance from the reference monitor to you should be four to six times the vertical height of the image.

In either case, you want to make sure that your reference monitor is positioned such that you're not constantly turning your head left and right and up and down every time you switch between looking at the broadcast monitor and your computer's display.

Sony recommends that the ideal distance of a viewer from the reference monitor is four to six times the vertical height of the monitor's viewable screen area.

▶   A 14-inch monitor (with a picture 8 inches in height) should be 32 to 48 inches away from you.

▶   A 20-inch monitor (with a picture 11 inches in height) should be 44 to 66 inches away from you.

▶   A 32-inch monitor (you lucky, lucky person, a picture 14 inches in height) should be 56 to 84 inches away from you.

As you're arranging your room, don't forget about your clients. They need to see the reference monitor just as much as you do. Ideally, you'll have a monitor that's big enough for them to comfortably view from a client area behind you (replete with comfy leather furniture, a working desk, Internet access, magazines, candy, and Legos to distract them from paying too much attention to you).

If your budget doesn't allow for either a huge monitor or expansive client area, then you'll need to create room for your client somewhere beside you, so you can both sit there and evaluate the image together.

Choosing Video Hardware

When putting together a room for color correction, be very careful about the equipment you select. Because you are the last word in the quality of the video program, you need to have the cleanest, highest-quality video interface and reference monitor you can afford.

Your Video Output Interface

You can use a variety of video output interfaces to output the program's video signal from your computer to a broadcast monitor. Rather than go into each available product in a changing marketplace, this section presents each video interface standard employed by the various video interfaces out there, as well as suggesting which might be appropriate for your application.

▶   S-Video is a four-pin analog prosumer video interface designed as a higher quality video interface for consumer equipment. It runs the luma and chroma of a signal separately, connected with S-Video connectors. S-Video interfaces are most commonly found on FireWire-to-DV interfaces with digital-to-analog conversion. This is not a recommended interface for professional use, but if you're working on a short program with a limited budget, it's better to use S-Video to output video to your broadcast monitor than it is to use composite.

▶ Y'PbPr is a three-cable professional analog video interface (as opposed to Y'CbCr, which is the standard for digital component video signals). It outputs each video component (luma and each of two color difference components) over separate pairs of wires, connected using BNC connectors (British Naval Connector). This is the highest-quality analog video signal that's typically used for professional video monitoring applications, and it's a perfectly respectable way of monitoring video for any professional application.

▶ SDI (Serial Digital Interface) is typically used for digital, uncompressed, standard definition video input and output. SDI is the highest-quality digital signal you can use for monitoring.

▶ HD-SDI (High Definition Serial Digital Interface) is the high definition version of SDI.

▶ Dual-Link SDI is designed as the interface for high definition uncompressed 4:4:4 video (as used on Sony's HDCAM SR equipment).

You want to make sure that, as you color correct your project, you're looking at the highest-quality image possible. If you're working on a standard definition program, either Y'PbPr or SDI would be good choices for connecting your computer's video output to a reference broadcast monitor, with SDI being the better of the two. If you're working on a high definition project, then HD-SDI is the appropriate choice. Dual-Link SDI is only necessary if your video format requires it.

To successfully monitor the picture, both the video interface connected to your computer and the video monitor must have the same interface. Most professional video monitors are expandable, so that you can purchase the appropriate interface cards for whichever format you intend to monitor.

Choosing a Broadcast Monitor

Your broadcast monitor is your primary tool for evaluating the picture of your program. This is probably the single most important piece of equipment you will own and quite possibly the most expensive. Depending on the size of your operation, your budget is going to dictate, in large part, which monitor you'll be

Display technologies are advancing at a furious pace, so it's difficult to make recommendations that will still be valid six months later. However, when you evaluate different monitoring solutions, you should keep the following in mind:

▶ Contrast ratio—For color correction work, this is one of the most important metrics of any display technology. If your monitor won't display a wide range of contrast, including deep blacks and vibrant whites, you won't be able to make a proper evaluation of the image. The continued dominance of CRT displays for grading is owed to the extremely high contrast ratios they're capable of, which translates into very deep, rich blacks (in a proper viewing environment) and bright, pure whites. If you're evaluating a properly calibrated monitor for purchase and the blacks look gray, you should probably look elsewhere.

▶ Accurate color—Whichever display you choose should be capable of supporting the full gamut (range of colors) required for NTSC, PAL, or HD video imaging. For CRT displays, the phosphor coatings on the tube itself in part determine the color gamut of which the monitor is capable. The two current standards employed by professional NTSC displays are the SMPTE-C phosphors, and P-22 phosphors (which are slightly brighter, encompassing a *slightly* different gamut). Newer, more expensive monitors tend to use the SMPTE-C standard. One of the biggest advantages of the SMPTE-C standard phosphors is that it's easier to match the color of a group of monitors that all use SMPTE-C, which is a consideration if you're a facility with multiple suites. However, there's nothing wrong with using a high-quality monitor that conforms to the P-22 standard in a single-monitor environment. PAL monitors, and NTSC monitors in Japan, use the EBU (European Broadcasters Union) standard; however, most high-end professional monitors support gamuts for both NTSC and PAL. Color for HD monitors is supposed to conform to the Rec. ITU-R BT.709 standard, although many CRT-based HD studio monitors seem to use SMPTE-C phosphors; the monitor's electronics process the color space as appropriate.

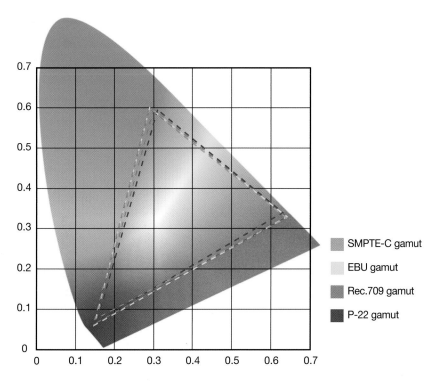

Comparison of the minute variations in gamut for each display standard currently in use, when plotted against the standard CIE chromaticity graph (a visualization of color space in two dimensions, approximated by the colored gradient in the background). The corners of each triangular gamut represent the assignment of each gamut's primaries.

▶ Resolution—You want a reasonably high-resolution image so that you can properly see the detail in the image you're correcting. Most high-end CRT monitors advertise 800 to 1000 lines of resolution. Other digital display technologies have fixed resolutions, based on the construction of the screen or the chip being used to create the image.

▶ Adjustability—You want to make sure that the monitor has the appropriate manual adjustment controls and menu settings so you can properly calibrate and set up your display for your room. At the least, a monitor should have: degaussing (for CRT displays), blue only (for calibration), under scan (for evaluation of action safe areas), bright/chroma/phase/contrast adjustments (for calibration), user selectable color temperature (with options for D65, D93 for setup), and adjustable setup/black level and component level (for setup of analog monitoring).

▶   Size—This is one of the biggest factors affecting the price of your monitor. Ideally, you'll want a monitor large enough for both you and your client to be able to sit back and watch the picture from a comfortable distance, but display technologies larger than 20 inches tend to be rather expensive (especially CRTs).

▶   Interface compatibility—Make sure that the monitor you purchase is capable of supporting (or being upgraded to) the highest-quality video signal output by your video interface.

In general, high-end CRT displays remain the favored choice for color correction work. Unfortunately, as other display technologies are taking over the consumer space, fewer and fewer manufacturers are continuing to invest in this time-honored technology. Sony, JVC, and Panasonic are three manufacturers who are still sell broadcast-quality, CRT-based products.

A few companies are developing higher end LCD display technologies in an effort to make color-critical LCD monitors. At the time of this writing, Cine-tal, Frontniche, and E-Cinema are three vendors at the vanguard of this effort.

Another option, albeit at the time of this writing a considerably more expensive one, is to outfit your room with a high-end video projector. Video projectors have the advantage of producing a huge image for viewing, and higher-end monitors are capable of very high contrast ratios when properly installed. Be forewarned that there's a significant difference in both price and quality between projectors available for the home video enthusiast and those intended for digital cinema viewing applications. Vendors you might want to investigate include JVC, Sony, Barco, Christie, and Projection Design.

As mentioned previously, some colorists are experimenting with dual-display setups, with a smaller, inexpensive CRT-based display for color-critical viewing, and a larger display of some sort for comfortable client viewing. The key to making this work is to make sure that both displays are calibrated to be as identical as feasible and that accurate calibration is maintained.

Sanity-Checking Monitors

Another option is to have an extra set of deliberately low-quality monitors available, so that you can check to see how your programs hold up on an average television.

Some colorists also like to have a small monitor that only shows a monochrome version of the picture. This can be helpful for evaluating the contrast of the image. Because there's no color in the picture, clients are unlikely to pay much attention to it.

Hardware Scopes vs. Final Cut's Scopes

Anyone needing to do broadcast-legal color correction in Final Cut Pro versions 5.1 and earlier pretty much needed to have a hardware scope to make a comprehensive evaluation of the video signal. These versions of Final Cut Pro didn't sample every line of video, and the software scopes presented only an approximation, useful for general adjustments, but not so good for catching every little superwhite pixel.

Starting with Final Cut Pro version 5.1.2, the video scopes are capable of sampling every single line of video, making it less necessary to have a set of hardware scopes for daily use. However, hardware scopes still have abundant uses. In particular, they're a terrific diagnostic tool for determining the state and quality of your video at various points in the signal chain. Most commonly, attaching a set of hardware scopes to the final output of your video interface allows you to sanity check the readings of Final Cut Pro's software scopes against the actual output. If there are any discrepancies, you can start working on discovering the cause, such as an incorrect setting or problem with your video interface.

Even in regular use, some hardware scopes have a wider variety of settings, options, and displays than are available with Final Cut Pro's video scopes. Furthermore, when it comes time to do a QC (quality-control check) of your program, many hardware scopes have the ability to log QC violations, along with the timecode at which they happen, in an automated fashion as you play the program through.

Bottom line, it's a very good idea to have a hardware scope available to you in your room. See Video Scopes, QC (Quality Control), Broadcast Legality.

Video Legalizer

Video legalizers are hardware video processors that clamp or compress parts of an incoming video signal that fall outside of user-programmable limits (in other words, luma or chroma that's too high or too low) before sending the video signal out to a video deck during print-to-tape or edit-to-tape operations.

These are not intended to replace the color correction process, because it's better to adjust an out-of-range signal manually than it is to simply clip it off. Instead, these are meant to be a final wall of defense against broadcast illegality, protecting you from the occasional stray pixel, and freeing you to focus on the creative aspects of your color correction adjustments.

This is by no means a required item, but if you don't have one, you'll need to be extra careful about legalizing your programs.

See Broadcast Legality, Broadcast Safe Filter.

Choosing Computer Hardware

If you're planning on doing color correction with Final Cut Pro, all the standard rules for choosing hardware to run Final Cut Pro apply. You'll want a good, fast computer with lots of RAM, and as much hard drive space as you can afford. Make sure in advance that the video interface you want to use is compatible with the computer model you're looking at getting.

If you're planning on mastering programs using uncompressed video, you'll need fast, accelerated hard drive storage. If your computer supports one or more ATA or SATA internal hard drives, this can be a good option. If you need more space, there are also fibre-channel based arrays such as the Xserve RAID from Apple, or one of a variety of eSATA (external SATA) array solutions.

> NOTE ▶ For much more information on setting up a Final Cut Pro workstation, see *Optimizing Your Final Cut Pro System* by Sean Cullen, Matthew Geller, Charles Roberts, and Adam Wit (Peachpit Press).

Input Devices

Final Cut Pro is not currently compatible with any of the third-party color correction interfaces available for other color correction applications. However, there are a handful of input devices that you can use to make your job easier:

▶   A mouse with a scroll wheel is an absolute must. You can use the scroll wheel to make fine adjustments to any slider in Final Cut Pro simply by moving the pointer over the slider you want to adjust and rolling the wheel.

▶ A set of keyboard shortcuts enables the use of a trackball with Final Cut Pro's color corrector. It's not the same as having a three-trackball interface, but because the color balance controls are essentially virtual trackballs, you might find this an interesting way to work. For the specific commands, see Color Balance Controls.

▶ A variety of USB shuttle interfaces on the market are useful for navigating the Timeline. In particular, they usually have custom buttons that you can map to the Show Next Edit, Show 2nd Next Edit, Show Previous Edit, Show 2nd Previous Edit, Show In Point, and Show Out Point keyboard shortcuts to help you flip between shots as you work.

Now that you've set yourself up with a nice little room, it's time to examine how you might approach the workflow of your project.

2

Techniques

Chapter **2**

Managing Your Color Correction Workflow

The workflow you choose—your methods of capture, importing, adjusting, and outputting media—is vital to the success of your project. Such simple decisions as which type of online/offline process to use, which type of media to capture, which codec to use, how to set up your sequences, and even which command to use to output your program's final master all have a critical effect on the quality of the finished product.

This chapter outlines each step of the typical Final Cut Pro–based color correction workflow, presenting which options are available to you, and which make the most sense depending on your project.

Importing a Project to Correct

Before you can start color correcting anything, you need to prepare the program's project file and its media. Depending on how the program was originally edited, a project might be delivered to you several different ways.

Starting with a Final Cut Pro Project

In the fastest and easiest scenario, you'll be provided with a Final Cut Pro project file and its accompanying media at its highest quality (depending on the original format of the media). In this case, you can simply open the project and get right to work.

You could also be given a project, but with its media files in a highly compressed, offline format. In this case, before you start working you'll need to recapture all of the clips at the highest available quality from the source tapes, or relink to the original high-resolution media files if you're using a tapeless workflow. You should never color correct offline clips, *especially* if they're in the OfflineRT format, because you can't guarantee that the corrections will match once the clips have been recaptured using the online codec.

In either case, working from a Final Cut Pro project is the most convenient way to get started, because it allows you to work on superimposed effects clips and titles along with edited alternate takes that might still be in the Timeline. And the client can retain all transitions, motion effects, and filters that might have already been applied to the sequence, sparing you from needing to recreate these a second time.

Here are a few things you can do to prepare a Final Cut Pro project for a smoother color correction session:

► Make a duplicate of the edited sequence with which to do your color correction pass. Then you always have the originally edited sequence to refer to if your work causes an unintended change.

► Collapse all superimposed clips that aren't deliberate effects onto a single video track, and delete any disabled clips that are hanging around. Doing so helps you keep track of what you're doing, and you can quickly open any clip into the Viewer for correction by moving the playhead over it and pressing the Return key (as opposed to double-clicking each clip and risking accidentally dragging it out of sync). You can also use the Open Playhead Sync mode to automatically open up every clip the playhead intersects in the Timeline into the Viewer, ready for adjustment, if that's how you prefer to work.

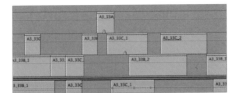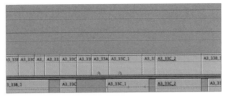

Collapsing an edited sequence. The sequence to the left uses superimposed clips as an editorial technique. Collapsing all of these clips down to a single track, as seen in the sequence to the right, makes it easier to keep track of everything as you color correct.

▶ Lock and disable all audio tracks. Locking all of the audio tracks (Shift-F5) is one more step you can take to prevent accidentally dragging clips out of sync while you work. Disabling the audio tracks lets you free up processor cycles for video processing. Besides, you don't necessarily want to subject your client (or yourself) to endless snippets of repeating audio while you're making your color corrections (although this is more a matter of preference, some people want to hear the audio play back).

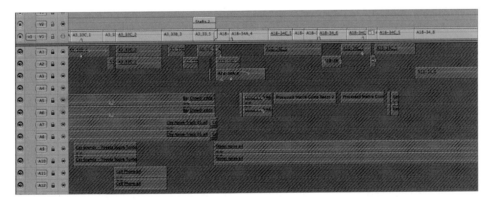

▶ If you're going to remove any previously existing color correction filters in preparation for your own work (often, just starting from scratch is easier), be careful not to also remove effects filters that are necessary for the program.

▶ If you're consulted prior to the actual edit, one thing that can speed up the eventual color correction session is if the source media is named smartly. The Find command is a powerful tool for identifying and selecting multiple clips to which you might apply an identical correction, but the Find command that's available from the sequence is only capable of searching for criteria inside of clip names, markers, and timecode values.

Logging clips with a consistent, detailed nomenclature makes using this command a lot easier. Using the right naming conventions can help you automatically find all instances of clips from a particular angle (master, reverse, over) or with a particular framing (LS, MS, CU) within a scene, or with a specific actor's name, location, or type of location (INT, EXT) throughout the program.

Importing EDLs and Other Project Formats

You might also be given an EDL, in which case you'll need to choose File > Import > EDL to create a project file from the EDL you've been provided, complete with edited sequence and offline master clip. When the project is created, you can recapture all necessary clips at the highest available quality.

This typically happens when a program has been edited using another application. Most editing applications export EDL files to facilitate onlining in other environments, and you can import most popular EDL formats in to Final Cut Pro.

The advantage of the EDL formats is that they're pretty universal (there are several EDL formats, and Final Cut Pro supports the most popular ones), and most software and hardware editing environments support one type of EDL or another. The disadvantage of most EDL formats is that they were originally designed to exchange relatively simple editing data. As a result, only two tracks of video (including superimposed video) and four tracks of audio are typically supported. The only video transitions that can be described by most EDLs are those found on the standard SMPTE transitions list, and other effects such as filters, motion settings, audio mixing data, and other keyframed effects are usually not included.

> **NOTE** ▶ One way of importing projects with multiple tracks of video using EDLs is to export each video track separately as its own EDL. You can then import each EDL into Final Cut Pro, and copy and paste each track into a master sequence for further work.

Another option for importing projects from Avid is Pro Import FCP, by Automatic Duck. This software is capable of translating Avid project files into the Final Cut Pro project format, in the process preserving additional project information such as multiple superimposed audio and video tracks, and compatible compositing operations. For more information, see www.automaticduck.com.

Working with Master Tapes and Files

A program may also be edited and finished in its entirety *prior* to color correction, with the mastered program either fully output to tape or saved as a self-contained media file (or image sequence). In either case, you should ideally ask for a version of the program with no superimposed titles. They'll interfere with your color correction pass, and you can easily add them later, in the process guaranteeing that they're broadcast legal.

If you're given a single master tape with the entire program on it, you'll need to capture the whole thing at the highest available quality. Alternately, if you're given a QuickTime movie file that serves as the digital master for the entire program, be sure to ask for it to be encoded with an uncompressed Y'CbCr codec, such as the Apple Uncompressed 8- or 10-bit 4:2:2 codecs.

After you import the QuickTime master file into a sequence, you can prep the file for color correction a few different ways:

▶ You could manually "notch" the entire file, adding edits at each cut point in preparation for adding separate color correction operations to each shot of the program. Be sure to match all existing transitions in the program with Final Cut Pro transitions of the same duration to ensure that the new color corrections dissolve or wipe from one shot to another appropriately. As you insert your cut points using the Add Edit command (Control-V), make sure the playhead always sits on the frame *to the right* of each transition (the incoming frame), because the cut is made at the frame boundary to the left of the playhead.

▶ If the client can also provide an EDL for the program, you could use the third-party application EDL Mirror (www.digital-heaven.co.uk) to automatically notch the QuickTime movie file to match the EDL. Of course, if you have an EDL, you could also choose to recapture all of the source media from scratch, but simply working from the notched master file is often more time-efficient.

▶ If you don't have an EDL, another third-party utility that might be helpful is Recut (http://videotoolshed.com), which uses automatic scene detection with adjustable parameters to scan through the clip, finding the cut points. It then exports an XML file with all of the edits, which you can import into Final Cut Pro and link to the original source file.

▶   If the program is fairly short, or if you don't have the time to notch it in advance, you
     could also choose to color correct the entire program with a single color correction
     filter, keyframing different correction settings at each edit point. See Animating Color
     Changes.

Capturing and Importing Project Media

After you've been provided with a project file, you may also have to recapture the source
media. If the editors worked with an offline format, or if you were provided with an EDL
that requires you to recapture from the source tapes, you must choose a format with
which to capture your media.

The quality of your final output, whether to tape or to disk as a master QuickTime file,
will only be as high as the quality of your source media. Video compression, while convenient in terms of hard drive space, processor speed, and choice of video format, almost
always sacrifices quality to a greater or lesser degree. One of the biggest advantages of
high-end color correction systems is that they typically work with minimally compressed
or uncompressed media from start to finish. If you've been provided with uncompressed
media in the course of onlining a program in Final Cut Pro, you'll benefit from a similar
advantage.

Of course, you're not always going to have a choice. For programs shot on video, the
amount of compression applied to the video signal is dictated by the format chosen for
the shoot. For example, programs shot using the DV/DVCPRO-25 or HDV formats are
more highly compressed than those shot with Digi-Beta, DVCPRO-50, or DVCPRO HD
because that's how those formats are encoded. The visual data lost was lost when the
media was recorded, is gone forever, and you can't do a whole lot about it short of minimizing whatever artifacts may have been introduced as a result.

Fortunately, this lost data isn't always as terrible as it sounds, at least from the perspective
of the audience. With the current generation of video technology, even the most highly
compressed formats produce video that looks quite good to the average viewer. Although
there are definitely disadvantages in the color correction process when using highly compressed media (for example, expanding the contrast of 4:1:1 and 4:1:0 subsampled media
results in a noisier image than when working with 4:2:2 subsampled media), they are not
insurmountable obstacles, and you'll generally be able to output programs of high visual

quality regardless of the format. What's more critical is the quality of exposure and color balance that was achieved during the shoot, which will enhance or hinder your work regardless of the source format.

The Advantages of Uncompressed Media

On the other hand, if you have a choice, you always want to use a format that applies the least possible amount of compression. If you're importing from a video format such as Beta SP, Digi-Beta, or HDCam, where you're capturing media via Y'CbCr or SDI/HD-SDI using your choice of codec, capturing the media using the Uncompressed 8- or 10-bit 4:2:2 codecs provides the best starting point for color correction.

> **NOTE ▶** The driver software for third-party video capture interfaces from AJA and BlackMagic also come with their own video codecs, which may provide various advantages depending on your workflow. Check with the vendor for more information.

In so doing, you're preserving as much of each color component of the image as possible, which provides superior color rendition and ultimately higher quality when making adjustments. Using a codec with 4:2:2 color sampling also makes it considerably easier to pull secondary keys—for the same reasons that chroma keying 4:2:2 media is easier than chroma keying 4:1:1 media (see Limit Effect Controls).

Capturing 8- or 10-bit Media

When you're choosing an uncompressed codec to use when capturing video, you generally have two choices: 8- or 10-bit encoding. The difference is fairly simple. Video encoded using 8-bits per channel has 220 values with which to represent each of the luma and chroma components that make up a video signal. (It's not the full 256 range of values because of the way that digital video is encoded, see Color Encoding Standards.) This can result in banding artifacts appearing in areas with smooth gradations of color, such as skies or walls.

Video clips encoded with 10 bits per channel have 876 values with which to represent each signal component. This results in significantly smoother transitions from one color to another. 10-bit video is especially advantageous when you start adding effects like vignettes, where banding at 8-bit resolution can be more apparent.

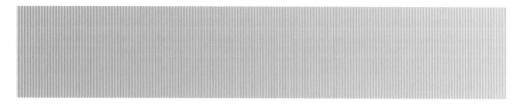

> **NOTE ▶** Despite these limitations, the dithering effect of video noise or film grain may reduce the visibility of such banding artifacts in your program.

Given a choice, you almost always want to do the final export of your program with 10-bit color. You can also work with 10-bit color while you color correct the program, but be aware that this is a more processor-intensive format, and you may not be able to play back as many real-time effects as you're used to.

Make sure that, if you're working with 10-bit media, your entire Final Cut Pro environment is set up for 10-bit video, which includes two key steps:

▶ Make sure your sequence is set to either Render 10-bit Material in High-Precision YUV or to Render All YUV Material in High-Precision YUV in the Video Processing tab in the Sequence Settings window.

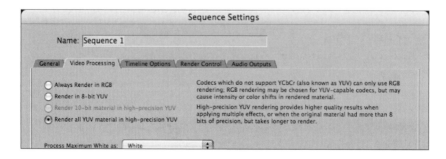

▶ Make sure that Final Cut Pro's Video Playback (options vary depending on the video interface you're using to monitor your output) is set to a 10-bit output option.

If either of these options is not properly set, you won't be able to monitor your program at full quality. Furthermore, if your video output device isn't capable of outputting 10-bit video, you simply won't be able to see it.

> **NOTE** ▸ The Canvas does not display 10-bit video in the same way as Final Cut Pro's video output. As a result, you'll still see banding artifacts on your computer display even though the video output is showing beautifully smooth, continuous tones.

Working with Compressed Media

Despite the compromise in color quality, working with highly compressed media does have its advantages. Because the file sizes are smaller, you don't have to have as much hard drive space at your disposal as when working with uncompressed media, and your hard drive's throughput doesn't need to be nearly as fast to keep the video data flowing. Furthermore, many of the videocameras and decks that record highly compressed formats use FireWire (IEEE 1394) as the primary video interface for capture and output. Although this doesn't exempt you from needing a high-quality video interface for monitoring, it does make pure digital capture of these formats a lot easier, and QuickTime has codecs compatible with most of the popular compressed formats that are currently in use so that you can manipulate this data natively (such as DV/DVCPRO-25, DVCPRO-50, HDV, M-JPEG captured media, and so on).

As mentioned previously, once video has been recorded using a specific format, the limitations of that format have already been imposed. Because the video quality was compromised the minute the camera operator pressed the Record button, the most important thing you can do to maximize quality is to prevent any further compression.

Some advocate recapturing, or transcoding, your program's compressed source media to an uncompressed format for purposes of color correction, which you can do in Final Cut Pro one of two ways:

▸   Recapturing compressed media from tape using a deck with an SDI interface as uncompressed media files will smooth out the Cb and Cr channels of video formats employing 4:1:1 color sampling. Although this may or may not yield a perceptible increase in visual quality, it can make the process of pulling secondary keys easier when doing secondary color correction.

▶   Re-rendering your compressed media to disk using a chroma reconstruction filter of some kind has a similar effect, but you don't have to commit to recapturing all your media using SDI. The Batch Export window is a good tool for doing this kind of operation, because it preserves superwhite and excessive chroma values that may be in the uncorrected source footage. On the other hand, high-quality filters for doing this, such as those by Graeme Nattress (www.graemenattress.com) are computationally intensive, so you'd better have some time set aside for the render.

In theory, recapturing is all well and good, but in practice it's probably not a necessary step for most programs, at least when preparing your media for color correction in advance. The increase in visual, perceptible image quality with either of the two methods is negligible, so if you're recompressing your media solely for the purpose of making your program look better, you probably shouldn't bother.

Final Cut Pro's Render Pipeline

Final Cut Pro's render pipeline for effects is designed to maximize image quality by processing all video as uncompressed data with 4:4:4 color sampling, regardless of the original codec. So when you're color correcting a clip in the Timeline, the following processes happen:

▶   A clip is uncompressed by the render engine in preparation for effects processing. The color space is promoted to the 4:4:4. If you've chosen one of the High-Precision YUV options in the sequence settings, the image data is also promoted internally to 32 bits. Although this doesn't inherently improve the quality of the image, it ensures that no data will be lost, rounded off, or clipped by Final Cut Pro during processing.

▶   Each filter applied to that clip processes the internal, uncompressed video data. If the clip has two filters applied to it, the first filter in the Filter tab's stack is processed, and the output from that filter is sent to the next filter to be processed, all uncompressed.

▶   If one or more clips are nested within another unrendered sequence, the resulting uncompressed data is then processed by any filters or compositing operations applied to the enclosing sequence.

   NOTE ▶ If a nested sequence has been rendered, the only case in which its render file will be used instead of processing the nested sequence's uncompressed data from scratch is if the nested sequence has no filters applied to it, and the sequence settings of the nested sequence match those of the enclosing sequence. Otherwise, if the nest is unrendered, its sequence settings don't match those of the enclosing sequence, the nested sequence is composited (superimposed with either opacity or composite modes), or has one or more filters applied to it, the nested sequence's uncompressed data will be rendered from scratch to produce the highest quality.

After processing from filtering and other compositing operations is complete, how the image data is output depends on whether you're monitoring or exporting the data:

▶ If you're monitoring or outputting an unrendered sequence in real time using a video interface capable of outputting uncompressed video (Y'CbCr or SDI), the final uncompressed video is sent to the video interface connected to your monitor, regardless of what the sequence settings are. However, what is output depends on whether or not the sequence or clips have been rendered. Before rendering, the uncompressed video data is output to video. After rendering, the compressed version of the video is sent out, instead.

▶ If you're monitoring or outputting your sequence using FireWire, the processed video is recompressed using the codec specified by the enclosing sequence and digitally sent to your FireWire interface for recording, or for analog output by that device's own digital-to-analog circuitry.

▶ If you're rendering a QuickTime movie using the Export QuickTime Movie command, the video is recompressed using the codec specified by the enclosing sequence and written to disk. Regardless of the sequence settings that were originally used, you can change the codec used by the sequence in order to write the internal uncompressed video to disk, preserving all of the high-quality processing that Final Cut Pro has been doing (more on this in a bit).

In short, whether you decompress your video all in advance, or you let Final Cut Pro decompress your video as part of the rendering process, it's still being done only *once*. At the end of the process, it's your choice whether or not to recompress the resulting data (see the upcoming section "Exporting Media from Final Cut Pro").

One last note: the advantage of smoother secondary keying posed by uncompressed media is admittedly useful. However, the improvements to the types of keys that are generally pulled for purposes of secondary color correction may not be worth the time or hassle of the recapture or rerendering process. Furthermore, you *do* have the option of specifically adding chroma smoothing filters to only the clips that really need it, without having to rerender every clip in your program, speeding up processing times (which is always a concern).

Working with HDV Footage

Like all other highly compressed media, HDV can be color corrected perfectly well in its native format. If your color correction pass is going to be fairly simple (restricted mostly to primary correction, with occasional secondary corrections here and there), this may be the most efficient way to work.

Because HDV is an MPEG-2 based codec, it uses temporal compression to further reduce the storage requirements of high definition video, which means that not every frame has all of the image data necessary for display, because data is shared bi-directionally among groups of frames (GOPs). Final Cut Pro lets you work with these clips natively by reading as many frames as are necessary to reconstruct the frame at the position of the playhead, but this process is more processor-intensive during general use, and the resulting reduction in real-time functionality may be unacceptable if you're doing more complex work. In this case, recapturing or reencoding these clips to an uncompressed format is probably a good idea.

Furthermore, HDV encodes video using 4:2:0 chroma subsampling (similar to the PAL versions of DV/DVCPRO-25). Although the Apple Intermediate codec has been provided as a fast, space-efficient, non-temporally compressed codec in which to transcode your HDV video, it's also highly compressed, and it keeps the 4:2:0 chroma subsampling.

For more information, see the HD and Broadcast Formats document, available from the Final Cut Pro Help menu.

Mixing Formats

If your program uses multiple video formats (for example, mixing DV with Digital Betacam footage), pick a single preferred format and codec, and then either recompress the clips into that format, or dub the tapes that don't match to that format with cloned timecode (if possible). Doing so will ultimately make the finishing process much easier.

Working in High Precision

Even if your program uses 8-bit source media, there's still a good reason to change your sequence's Video Processing settings to Render All YUV Material in High-Precision YUV. When you render a sequence that's set to High-precision YUV, you enable higher mathematical precision (similar to Float space in Shake) as the filters applied to your clips are processed. This eliminates the clipping and quantization that can occur when processing images in 8-bit YUV.

▶ Clipping happens when the results of one filter's image processing calculation is limited to a maximum value prior to handing off the data to another filter. For example, if one filter (for example, a glow filter) boosts the luma of a clip well above 100 percent, the processed result will be clipped before it's fed to the next filter, potentially flattening regions of the picture.

▶ Quantization happens when the results of one filter's image processing calculation is rounded off prior to handing off the data to another filter. An illustration of this effect would be if you considered the output of the first of two filters processing in 8-bits to be "9.0 + 0.3 = 9.0" (the result is quantized) and the next filter then processes "9.0 - 0.6 = 8" (the result is quantized again). The same calculation in high-precision would be "9.0 + 0.3 = 9.3" and then "9.3 - 0.6 = 8.7" (all data is preserved). Even though the final result may be rounded off to 9 when you export to an 8-bit codec, there is still a difference between both sets of calculations. 8-bit quantization as one filter hands off data to another can cause subtle, banded artifacts.

In both cases, the results are not always easy to see. Noise, grain, and moving subjects mask many kinds of artifacts. However, the advantage of high-precision rendering can often be seen as higher-quality glow and blur effects that preserves more subtle detail when processing in high-precision.

Furthermore, high-precision rendering is a huge benefit when you use vignettes and gradients as part of your color correction pass. In 8-bit YUV, vignettes and gradients often exhibit banding, which can be eliminated by promoting your sequence to high precision, and then rendering it using a 10-bit codec.

High-precision YUV has greater processor requirements than 8-bit, so you may want to keep your sequence set to Render in 8-bit YUV while you work. Then, when you're ready to render, switch your sequence's Video Processing settings over to high precision to get the benefit of higher quality.

Exporting Media from Final Cut Pro

After you've finished color correcting your video, adding filters, superimposed generators, and all of the other compositing operations necessary to complete the program, chances are a large part (if not all) of your program will require rendering. There are two ways you can deal with this.

The first way is to render all of the clips within the sequence in preparation for outputting to tape. Even though the Print to Tape and Edit to Tape commands render your project prior to output, rendering the sequence directly in the Timeline before using these commands guarantees the rendered clips stay rendered after the operation.

You can also choose to export a self-contained QuickTime movie file for use as your master. This solution has many advantages. It provides you with a single, prerendered deliverable that you can copy to a hard drive and give to the client to walk away with. Creating a single file with no dependencies on source media, graphics, and render files is also an excellent way to back up your program in a way that's easy to restore and easy to output to tape.

There are a few ways you can render out a self-contained QuickTime movie of your program. Which one you choose depends entirely on what you need to export, and it's vital to make sure that you pick the right one.

Preparing Your Sequence for Rendering

If you've finished color correcting a program using highly compressed media, you can use the Export QuickTime command to re-encode the program to an uncompressed format.

The trick is that, once you've finished editing your program, you should change your sequence's settings to use the uncompressed codec you want to write out to (typically Apple Uncompressed 8- and 10-bit 4:2:2). If you've nested your edited sequence inside of another sequence to apply additional filters for video legalization (such as the Broadcast

Safe filter; for more information, see Broadcast Legality), make sure that the export sequence's settings use the desired uncompressed codec.

When you do so, the Export QuickTime command uses the rendered data that Final Cut Pro generates internally, bypassing the recompression stage that happens when the sequence is set to the originally used codec. The result is a file that contains the cleanest possible output.

Another step you can take to maximize quality during rendering is to set the Video Processing tab in the Sequence Settings to Render All YUV Material in High-Precision YUV.

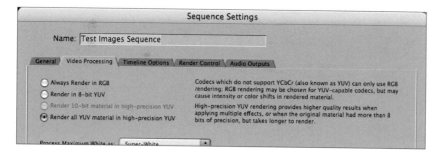

The Export QuickTime Command

If you're exporting a self-contained QuickTime .mov file of your program for delivery to a client, archival backup, or any other purpose, use the Export QuickTime command.

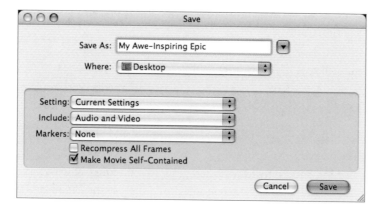

Aside from the convenience of outputting using the current sequence's settings by default, its main advantage is that it maximizes image quality by bypassing QuickTime and using the Final Cut Pro image processing engine to render your program, and by writing the output directly to a QuickTime file. This has two important implications:

▶   Superwhite luma and chroma levels, if present, are preserved if you export using the appropriate Y'CbCr-compatible codec.

▶   10-bit image data is written out at the highest quality.

Basic Options in the Save Dialog

Although the Save dialog window, which lets you choose the movie's output type, defaults to the settings of the sequence you've selected for output, you can choose any of the currently available sequence setups from the Setting pop-up menu. You can also choose Custom (at the bottom of the list) to pick your own settings from the Sequence Preset Editor window.

You also have the option to pick which tracks to export from the Include pop-up menu. By default you export Audio and Video, but you can choose to export either the Audio or Video tracks separately.

The Markers pop-up menu lets you embed specific types of sequence markers (clip markers are not included) in the exported QuickTime file. Two other options bear specific explanation:

▶   Recompress All Frames—By default, this option is turned off. If it's left off, frames from clips that don't have any filters or other effects applied to them are copied directly from the source media into the newly written QuickTime file as is, bypassing the render process altogether. This is useful if you're outputting a program using uncorrected compressed media in its original format, because it prevents double-compression.

Turning on this option forces Final Cut Pro to run every single frame through the render engine, even if no effects are applied. Turn this option on if you're outputting an uncompressed final master of a color-corrected program that still contains clips with no effects applied to them, in order to clip any blacker-than-black (less than zero percent) camera noise that might be lurking in the uncorrected clips (see Video Scopes). Any clip that requires processing will have this superblack noise automatically clipped. This is a good precautionary measure, and it should have a negligible effect on the render times of programs with color correction filters on nearly every clip.

▶ Make Movie Self-Contained—This option, turned on by default, ensures that the QuickTime file that's generated contains every frame of the program. Ordinarily, this is what you want, so that when you copy the resulting file to give to a client, you copy the entire program. Because the entire program is self-contained, the resulting QuickTime file is bound to be rather large.

Turning off this option results in the creation of a *referencing movie,* a much smaller QuickTime file that doesn't contain all of the image data itself, instead linking to the source media on disk and the render files for previously rendered effects that are used by that sequence. Any effects that weren't previously rendered are rendered and embedded inside of the referencing movie, as is the mixed-down audio from the project. This option is useful when you want to create a movie file to process with another application on your computer, because it lets you export your program without duplicating its media. On the other hand, it's not particularly useful if you're exporting a file to give to someone else, because you'd also have to provide all of the source and render media to go along with it.

Other Export Options

Final Cut Pro has several other methods for exporting QuickTime files. Each has its own advantages and disadvantages, summarized in the following sections.

Export Using QuickTime Conversion

The Export Using QuickTime Conversion command, unlike Export QuickTime, uses the QuickTime image processing engine to process the video data output by Final Cut Pro. The advantage is that it gives you access to all of the formats that QuickTime supports, including AVI, DV Stream, MPEG-4, still image formats, and audio-only formats.

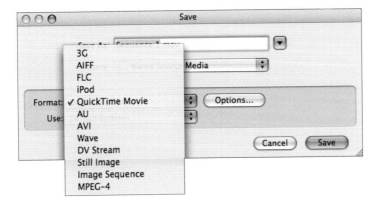

Despite this convenience, there are three important disadvantages:

▶ Export Using QuickTime Conversion doesn't preserve superwhite and high-chroma levels.

▶ 10-bit uncompressed data is not written out as cleanly as with the Export QuickTime command.

▶ A gamma adjustment is made to the output file, even if you're outputting using the Apple Uncompressed 8- and 10-bit codecs. See Gamma (Imported and Exported Media in Final Cut Pro 5.1 and Earlier).

As a result, this command is only really useful for quickly generating highly compressed test renders, still image, or audio files.

Export Using Compressor

The Export Using Compressor command lets you use Compressor to render out an entire sequence. Because it works closely with Final Cut Pro and receives image data straight out of the Final Cut Pro image processing pipeline, it preserves superwhite and high-chroma levels, renders 10-bit video beautifully, and doesn't apply any automatic gamma operations.

Although Compressor is probably most often used for multipass rendering of extremely high-compressed formats for distribution, such as MPEG-2 and H.264, it's also an excellent tool to use for high-quality format conversion, due to its support of adaptive image analysis for retiming, deinterlacing, and resizing video.

Export Using Media Manager

The Media Manager is not actually intended to export a sequence as a self-contained movie file. Instead, it's a tool for managing all of the individual clips used in a project or sequence.

The first pop-up menu in the Media section of settings lets you choose an operation with which to manage your clips—copying, moving, or recompressing the clips in the selected range of media. Of these, two operations bear further explanation:

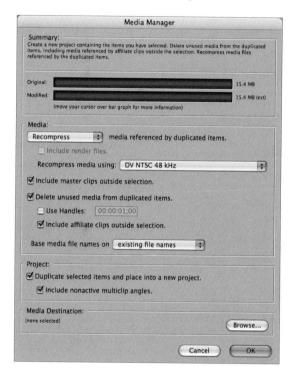

▶   Copy, when used in conjunction with the Delete Unused Media from Duplicated Items checkbox, lets you create duplicates of the media used in your sequence while eliminating all of the media that's unused by your project. True to its name, this option merely duplicates the existing image data, preserving superwhite and high-chroma data if present.

▶ Recompress gives you the option to create copies of the existing media that are compressed using a different codec. This option is generally used to create offline media from online source material, and it is best used to downcovert your media to a highly compressed format for editing. Do not use the Media Manager to upconvert media to a less compressed or alternative format, because the Recompress option *does not* preserve superwhite or high-chroma data.

Export Using FCP Batch Export

The Batch Export command adds selected sequences or clips to the Export Queue window, and it allows you to queue up multiple clips or sequences for export. It's extremely flexible, allowing you to organize your export jobs with multiple folders, if you like. It has many uses:

▶ You can let multiple sequences render overnight, one after another.

▶ You can render a single sequence using multiple settings (for example, an uncompressed master file and a highly compressed H.264 file for sending to the client via the Internet).

▶ You can queue up multiple clips for format conversion.

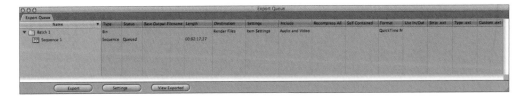

Choosing a folder, sequence, or clip in the Export Queue window and clicking the Settings button opens the Batch settings window, where you define how to process the selected items.

If you use the QuickTime Movie setting in the Format pop-up menu (which appears by default), the Batch Export mechanism outputs video identically to using the Export QuickTime command, providing all of the same advantages and options.

If you use the QuickTime (Custom) command, or any of the other options listed in the figure below, the output is identical to using the Export Using QuickTime Conversion command.

Exchanging Media with Other Applications

There has been much confusion with regards to Final Cut Pro's luma and chroma handling when importing images from other applications, or when exporting images to other applications. The following explanation should help clear things up.

Luma Handling

As described earlier, if you're exporting QuickTime .mov files using an RGB-based codec such as the Animation codec, any superwhite levels above 100 percent will be clipped. If you export a QuickTime file using a Y'CbCr-compatible codec using an export method that supports superwhite levels, levels above 100 are preserved.

However, if you import any QuickTime file into an RGB compositing application such as Shake, Motion, or After Effects, superwhite levels will be clipped regardless of the codec used to encode that file. This is due to the Y'CbCr to RGB gamut conversion that's done to re-encode the color values from one standard to another.

In the following image, a Gradient generator has been edited into a sequence set to use the Apple Uncompressed 10-bit 4:2:2 codec, and with the Process Maximum White setting in the Video Processing tab of the Sequence Settings set to Super-White. Although the Canvas is not capable of displaying the gradient as smooth as it really is (you should see a perfectly smooth ramp if your video output interface is capable of 10-bit output), the Waveform Monitor shows a linear progression from 0 to 110 percent, in other words, all the way through superwhite.

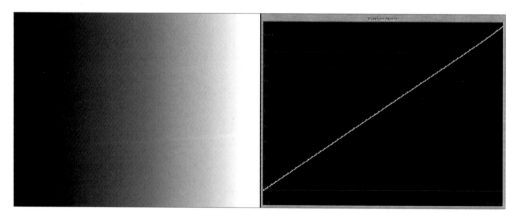

Importing the clip into Shake, and using the PlotScanline viewer script to analyze a single line of the image, reveals a smooth, linear progression from 0 percent black all the way up to 100 percent white, but the superwhite level is clipped off, as shown by the flattened shelf at the top-right of the superimposed graph. If there was highlight detail in that portion of the image, it would be lost, because all values *above* 100 percent would be set *to* 100 percent (in other words, clamped, or clipped).

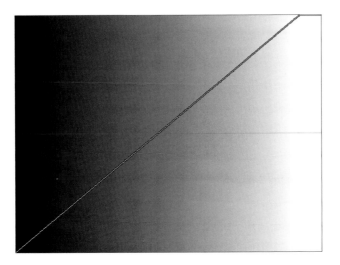

If you're dealing with an 8-bit image (for sake of simplicity), 0 percent black in Final Cut Pro is mapped to digital 0,0,0 in RGB space, and 100 percent white in Final Cut Pro is mapped to digital 255,255,255 in RGB space. In other words, the legal video range of the clip in Final Cut Pro is stretched to fit the full numeric range of RGB values. See Color Encoding Standards.

When you export a clip from Shake, Motion, or After Effects, the resulting full range RGB image is simply written out if you're exporting a QuickTime file using the Animation codec. If you're exporting a QuickTime movie using a Y'CbCr-compatible codec such as Apple Uncompressed 8- or 10-bit 4:2:2, the full range RGB data is scaled to fit within the standard encoding range of Y'CbCr data, which is 16 to 235 for 8-bit video, or 64 to 940 for 10-bit video.

What this means, practically speaking, is that when you import a QuickTime movie that was exported from an RGB-processing application, maximum white is mapped to 100 percent, and maximum black is mapped to 0 percent, as seen in the Waveform Monitor.

You can see this in the following image of a clip that was generated in Shake. The gradient at the very top runs from 0,0,0 to 255,255,255 in 8-bit color as measured by Shake. It corresponds to the diagonal part of the graph running from 0 percent at the lower-left corner to 100 percent at the upper-right corner.

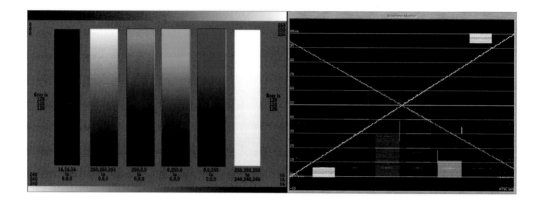

NOTE ► The other diagonal line corresponds to the gradient on the bottom, which runs from 16,16,16 to 240,240,240. This shows you that deliberately limiting the tonal range of your image to the Studio RGB range within your paint or compositing application will only result in blacks at 5 percent and whites at 95 percent.

Luma Handling for Still Images and RGB Clips

The tonal mapping of still image files is handled differently than it is for QuickTime movies. How black and white is mapped depends on the Process Maximum White As setting in the Video Processing tab of the Sequence Settings:

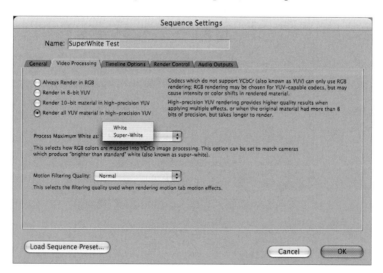

▶ If your sequence is set to White (the default), an image using the entire tonal range will be mapped from 0 percent to 100 percent as measured in the Waveform Monitor. This is the recommended setting if you're legalizing your program to the 100 percent maximum standard.

▶ If your sequence is set to Super-White, an image using the entire tonal range will be stretched from 0 percent to 110 percent as measured in the Waveform Monitor. This is only recommended if you're grading your program to occupy the maximum possible tonal range, including the superwhite range. This way, the maximum white of your image matches the superwhite levels appearing in your program. Otherwise, they could be as much as 10 percent lower than the other images.

Because the Process Maximum White As setting stretches the entire tonal range of the image, an image edited into a sequence set to Super-White will be brighter than the same image edited into a sequence set to White.

Using the same test image from the previous example at the end of the Luma Handling section, the image below shows the waveform of the test pattern in a sequence with its Process Maximum White setting set to White. The neutral gray background is represented by the flat line appearing at 50 percent.

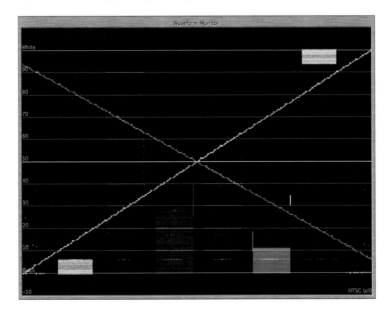

The next image shows the waveform of the same clip, with the sequence's Process Maximum White setting changed to Super-White. You can see that the tonal range has been linearly stretched to put the white level at 110 percent, which in the process has moved the neutral gray background up to 55 percent, and you can also see the various peaks of the other gradients have also been stretched upward relative to their original lightness. The entire image has been brightened, although the black level remains at 0 percent.

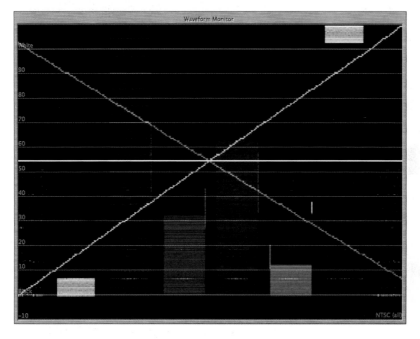

If the Process Maximum White As sequence property is incorrectly set, you can change it at any time.

Chroma Handling

Chroma values in images that are either generated or manipulated by an RGB-processing application such as Shake, Motion, or After Effects and exported to QuickTime using *any* codec have their maximum chroma values limited by the maximum range allowable by the RGB color space, which is 0 to 255 for 8-bit encoded images.The test image in the following example was rendered out of Shake using the Apple Uncompressed 10-bit 4:2:2 codec. When edited into Final Cut Pro's Timeline and viewed in the Vectorscope, you can see the boundaries of the chroma that was output by Shake's RGB processing when rendering a QuickTime file.

NOTE ▶ The Waveform Monitor graph in the following two sets of figures has been artificially brightened for print.

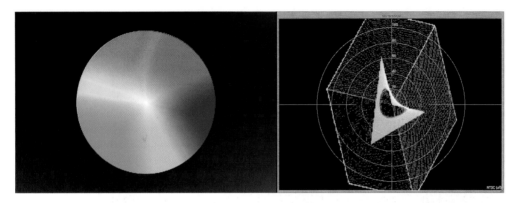

To prove the point, the chroma of the same image was tripled, obviously clamping the values at the same maximums.

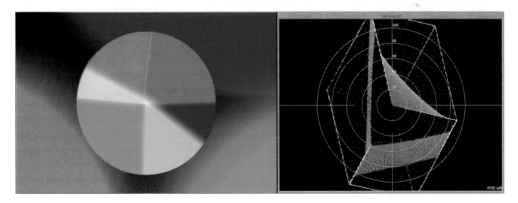

Final Cut Pro, on the other hand, is capable of internally generating and preserving more highly saturated values. The following image is Final Cut Pro's Particle Noise generator, with a Color Corrector 3-Way filter further pushing the saturation all the way to Final Cut Pro's maximum limits. (These levels are patently illegal for broadcast.)

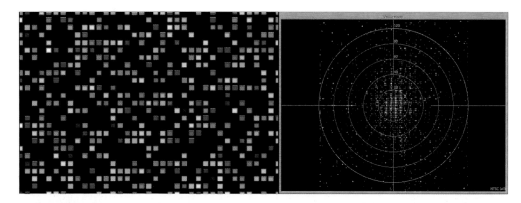

Increasing the saturation of a Final Cut Pro generator shows the maximum chroma limits that Final Cut Pro is capable of sustaining.

If you export a movie with such high saturation using a Y'CbCr-compatible codec using one of the export commands capable of preserving superwhite levels, these high chroma values will be preserved. If you export using an RGB-compatible codec, these levels will be clipped.

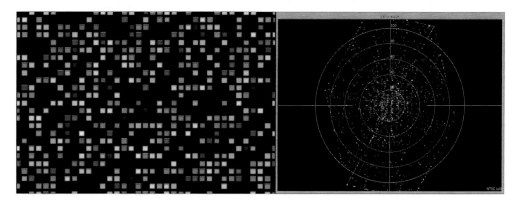

Out-of-gamut chroma levels clipped after rendering a QuickTime movie using the Animation codec.

Gamma Handling

Gamma handling is, unfortunately, a complicated topic that is covered more comprehensively within the related entries.

In short, QuickTime movies that are encoded using an RGB-encoded codec (such as Animation) are imported with an automatic gamma adjustment of approximately 1.22. See Gamma (Imported and Exported Media in Final Cut Pro 5.1 and Earlier). You can see this in the image that follows. The curved diagonal lines in the Waveform Monitor show that a gamma adjustment has been applied to the linear gradients in the test image (which was exported from Shake as a QuickTime movie using the Animation codec).

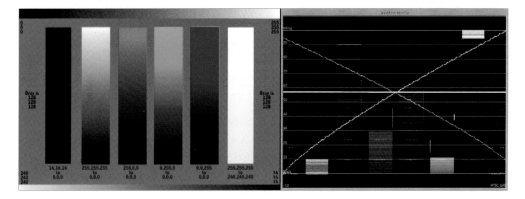

Still images (such as .tif and .jpg image files) in Final Cut Pro 5.1 and earlier also had this 1.22 gamma adjustment applied. However, Final Cut Pro 5.1.2 introduced an Imported Still Gamma setting in the Editing tab of the User Preferences that lets you determine the gamma handling for imported images. In addition, each Still Image clip has an adjustable Gamma Level property that you can change at any time. See Gamma (Imported and Exported Media in Final Cut Pro 5.1.2).

On the other hand, QuickTime movies encoded using a Y'CbCr-encoded codec (such as the Apple Uncompressed 8- and 10-bit 4:2:2 codecs, DV/DVCPRO-25, DVCPRO-50, and so on) are imported with no gamma adjustment whatsoever. In the following figure, the Shake-generated test image was rendered as a QuickTime movie using the Apple Uncompressed 8-bit 4:2:2 codec, which was imported into Final Cut Pro. The straight diagonal lines in the Waveform Monitor show that the linear gradients in the test image are being correctly processed.

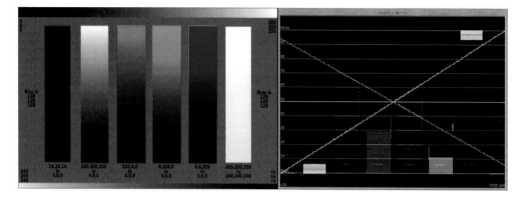

Exporting clips in Final Cut Pro version 5.1 and earlier resulted in an additional gamma operation being applied to QuickTime files rendered with an RGB-compatible codec, or to an image file or sequence when using Export Using QuickTime Conversion.

Exporting clips in Final Cut Pro version 5.1.2, on the other hand, results in no additional gamma operations being applied. The clip is exported as is. See Gamma (Imported and Exported Media in Final Cut Pro 5.1.2).

Which Codec to Use for File Exchange?

Although many third-party codecs are available for postproduction, this section covers only those codecs that accompany QuickTime and are commonly in use for file exchange. They break down into RGB-compatible codecs and Y'CbCr-compatible codecs.

RGB Codecs

The choices here are Animation and PNG. Both are 8-bit file formats and encode 4:4:4 color. For the latter reason, Animation and PNG-compressed .mov files are capable of containing alpha channels for defining areas of transparency. These codecs are a good choice for file exchange between Final Cut Pro and motion graphics and compositing applications such as Shake, Motion, and After Effects. The one limitation is that there is currently no 10-bit RGB codec available that ships with QuickTime.

Y'CbCr Codecs

Both the Apple Uncompressed 10-bit 4:2:2 and 8-bit 4:2:2 codecs encode color with 4:2:2 subsampling, which means they don't support alpha channels. On the other hand, they do support superwhite and high-chroma levels. Additionally, this is the only 10-bit solution for file exchange that comes with QuickTime, so this may be the best codec to use if you're exchanging 10-bit media with a compositing application, and quality is more important to you than the preservation of alpha channel information (as is typically the case with background plates). These codecs are good for archival, delivery for video output, and exchanging video media with other Final Cut Pro users.

> **NOTE** ▶ Compositing applications that process video in the RGB color space will always clip superwhite values from Y'CbCr encoded clips, regardless of the bit-depth.

Encyclopedia

Animating Color Changes

OVERVIEW ▶ Demonstrates methods for animating shifts in color, either for generated effects or color correction filters.

SEE ALSO ▶ animating lighting, color balance controls, color control

Methods for Animating Color Changes

You can use several methods to animate a filter or color correction from one color to another. For example:

▶   If you're changing the color of a generator, the Tint filter, Sepia filter, or another filter that uses the standard Color control, you can keyframe the Color control settings. You might try this when animating the color of a tint, vignette, composited lighting effect, or title.

▶   If you're changing the color of a clip using a Color Correction filter, you can keyframe color balance control adjustments. Consider this technique to account for a change in the color temperature of a clip's lighting; for example, someone walking from tungsten lighting inside to sunlight outside.

▶   If a keyframed color change is resulting in unwanted color shifts, you can instead try adding an edit point and dissolving between two completely different generators or Color Correction filters. This is frequently the fastest solution, although you'll want to be careful to note this as an unnecessary edit if you'll ever need to export an EDL.

Keyframing Color Control Changes

You can keyframe changes to a Color control in exactly the same way as you can keyframe any other parameter in the Controls, Filters, or Motion tab. Animated shifts in color can be a great effect for dramatically shifting a tint or gradually changing the color temperature of the image, but the results can seem confusing if you're not familiar with Final Cut Pro's method of animating the HSB values inside of the Color control.

Understanding Hue Shifts

Spending a little time with Final Cut Pro's Vectorscope will help you to better understand how color is animated and why changes between a color and its secondaries are more effective than broad leaps between primary colors.

1   Open the *01 Keyframed Color Control* sequence, located in the Animating Color Changes bin of the **Color Correction Exercises** project.

2   Choose the Color Correction window layout, and select the Vectorscope layout in the Video Scopes tab of the Tool Bench.

3   Open the Color generator in the Timeline into the Viewer, and click the Controls tab.

The color parameter of this generator has been keyframed. With the playhead at the beginning of the Timeline, you can see that the initial color is yellow, which is confirmed by the single dot inside the Y target in the Vectorscope.

4   Scrub the playhead over the duration of the color generator in the Timeline.

As you scrub the playhead, the dot of color travels in a curve around the outside of the Vectorscope.

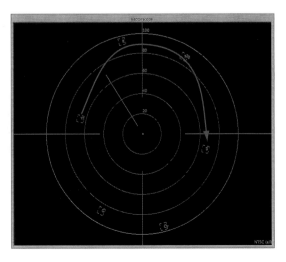

The dot takes this path because Final Cut Pro is making the animated change from one color to the next using the numerical HSB subparameters that define the color being used.

5   Click the Color parameter's disclosure triangle to reveal the HSB sliders, and scrub through the Color generator again.

When you animate significant changes in color, you end up animating the hue. As you scrub through the clip, you can see the H slider animate to match the change in color.

Because the H parameter is specified in degrees around the color wheel, animating H rotates the hue from one color to the next until arriving at the final keyframed color value. Because the Vectorscope is a visual representation of the color wheel implied by the HSB color space, you can watch the animated value as it goes from color to color about the center.

NOTE ▶ You cannot animate the H, S, and B sliders with separate sets of keyframes. All three subparameters contribute to one group of keyframes.

However, animated color corrections don't always work the way you want them to. If you're changing from a color to one of its two secondaries, for example, from red to magenta or yellow, the resulting color shift may appear perfectly natural. However, changing from one primary to another or from a primary to its complementary may result in a series of color shifts that may be too spectacular for a given effect.

On the other hand, animating only a color's saturation and brightness gives you a more natural transition, because you're only making a particular hue brighter or darker, more vivid or less.

Controlling Hue Shifts

If you intend to animate hue through a series of different colors, however, you can control which set of colors are cycled through using the Hue Direction button.

1   Still in the *01 Keyframed Color Control* sequence, move the playhead so that it sits directly on top of the first keyframe in the keyframe graph area of the Controls tab (using the Next and Previous Keyframe buttons is the fastest method), then click the Hue Direction button so that the arrow points to the left, rather than to the right.

2   Scrub through the sequence, and notice how the dot of color now moves in the opposite direction around the Vectorscope.

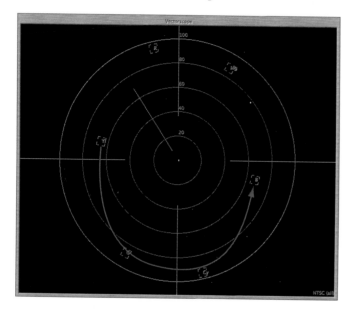

The Hue Direction button lets you alter the direction of an animated color change relative
to the color wheel, letting you choose which colors to cycle through as the hue changes.

Keyframing Color Correction Filters

If your project uses Color Correction filters, you have a choice on how you animate them.
You can work in the Filters tab as for any other filter, or you can use the keyframing controls at the upper-left corner of the Color Corrector and Color Corrector 3-Way filter's
graphical interface.

Within the Filters tab, keyframing individual parameters is much easier. However, when
you're in a hurry, adjusting keyframes directly in the Color Corrector tab can be considerably faster using the following features:

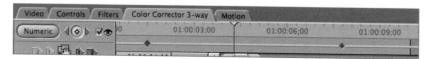

▸ The familiar Insert/Delete keyframe button appears between the Numeric interface button (which takes you to the Filters tab) and the Enable Filter checkbox. Clicking this button inserts a keyframe, at the position of the playhead, for every parameter of that Color Correction filter. Clicking this button while the playhead is directly on a previously existing keyframe deletes all Color Corrector keyframes from that frame.

▸ The Previous Keyframe and Next Keyframe buttons move the playhead to keyframes appearing to the left and right of its current position.

▸ A single-channel keyframe graph runs along the top of the Color Corrector tab. This graph displays blue keyframes at every frame where there's at least one keyframe for any parameter. If multiple parameters are keyframed at a particular frame, they'll all be represented by a single blue keyframe.

With this abbreviated interface, every animated change you make using the graphical interface is represented with a single set of keyframes. If you need a deeper level of detail, you can see and adjust each individually keyframed parameter in the Filters tab.

Hue Shifts with Animated Color Balance Controls

Keyframed changes to the contrast and saturation of an image are linear, since these controls are sliders. Animated changes to the color balance controls of the Color Correction filters, on the other hand, work the same way as the animated hue of a color control and can cause similarly undesirable hue shifts. Try this experiment:

1   Open the *02 Keyframing Color Balance* sequence, located in the Animating Color Changes bin of the **Color Correction Exercises** project.

This is a simple gray color generator that has an animated Color Corrector 3-Way filter applied to it.

2   Open the first Color generator into the Timeline, and click the Color Corrector 3-Way tab to view the graphical interface.

3   Drag the playhead from one keyframe to the next in the Color Corrector keyframe graph, and watch the behavior of the Whites color balance control.

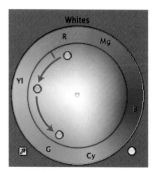

The hue shift of red to yellow to green you see is the default behavior. If you just want a shift from red to green, however, the yellow shift can be avoided by adding some extra keyframes to the animation.

Keyframing to Avoid Hue Shifts

Instead of letting Final Cut Pro automatically interpolate the animated change, you can manually force the color balance control to go to a neutral state before changing to the next hue.

1   With the playhead still over the first clip, move it to a position directly in the middle of the two keyframes.

2   Click the Whites reset control to set the Whites color balance control to a neutral state.

Because the Whites color balance control has already been keyframed, this new adjustment automatically creates a new keyframe.

Play the clip to see the change. You should notice that although the color goes smoothly from red to gray, there's still an unwanted hue shift from gray to yellow to green after the keyframe.

To eliminate the unwanted shift to yellow, you'll need to add another keyframe to a specific parameter in the Filters tab.

3   To get to the Filters tab, click the Numeric button in the Color Corrector 3-Way tab, or click the Filters tab, and click the disclosure triangle by the Color Corrector 3-Way filter to reveal its individual parameters.

Each of the three zones of color correction are grouped into Blacks, Midrange, and Highlight Controls groups. The contrast control, Level, for each zone appears at the top. The color balance controls are represented numerically by two parameters. An Angle parameter determines the hue (the position of the indicator about the center) and a Magnitude parameter that determines the strength of the correction (the distance of the indicator from the center).

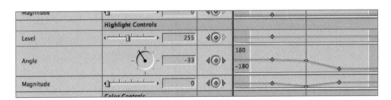

The way the Angle parameter is being animated is the reason a hue shift still occurs after you've created a third keyframe to set the color balance control to a neutral state. Although the magnitude is being animated from the initial value of 63.47 to 0, before changing to the final value of 77.93, the Angle is still being interpolated continuously from −14.94 to −152.46.

To eliminate the animated angle change that's causing the hue shift, you'll need to keyframe a one-frame transition of the Angle parameter from the initial value to the final value. One-frame changes are instantaneous.

4   Move the playhead to the last keyframe, copy the Angle value. Then move the playhead one frame forward of the middle keyframe, paste the value into the Angle parameter, and press Enter.

Final Cut Pro automatically creates a new keyframe.

5   Likewise, move the playhead to the first keyframe, copy the Angle value, then move
the playhead to the second keyframe, and paste the value into the Angle parameter.

Creating a one-frame change from one Angle value to another creates an instantaneous change, which is invisible since the Magnitude is at zero at that frame.
Scrubbing through the transition now shows a smooth transition from red to gray
to green.

Although most of your color corrections probably won't be animated, there are plenty of
times you'll want to create keyframed color corrections. There's a frequently used example
cited elsewhere in the book. See Animating Lighting.

Dissolving Between Two Color Correction Filters

If animating a single color correction filter isn't giving you the effect you're after, try deliberately adding a through edit, and then dissolving between two differently adjusted Color
Correction filters. This method is generally faster to use than the four-keyframe method
described previously.

NOTE ▶ If you're viewing this project on an external broadcast monitor, switch the monitor to 16:9 (if it is so capable). This is an anamorphic project.

1   Open the *03 Dissolving Color Corrections* sequence, located in the Animating Color Changes bin.

This sequence has four versions of the same clip. The clip is a pan following an actor who moves between two very differently lit areas that require independent color correction settings to achieve the desired look. Each clip uses a separate solution for creating the necessary animated color correction.

A continuous shot where a character moves between two completely different lighting schemes requires an animated color correction.

2   Play the first clip.

The color correction here was made for the actor as he appears at the bottom of the stairs. As he reaches the top of the stairs, and the lighting changes, the clip becomes overexposed, and the color is washed out and unpleasantly tinged. Clearly, one color correction setting will not work for the entire clip.

3   Move the playhead to the second clip and play through it.

The second clip has a keyframed Color Corrector 3-Way filter. The correction is simply animated from one look to another at the point where the man reaches the top of the stairs (indicated by a marker applied to the clip).

As you've seen with other examples of keyframed color changes, the result is a slightly magenta hue shift as a result of the Mids control going from a cool blue to a warm red adjustment.

4 Move the playhead to the position of the marker in the third clip in the Timeline.

This is an uncorrected version of the clip in its original state, and you're going to create the animated color correction in the fastest way possible, by dissolving between two different Color Correctors.

5 Create a through edit in the clip by pressing Control-V.

By splitting the clip into two parts, you've created a situation where you can apply two completely different filters to the first and second half of the same clip.

6 Open the Color Correction Presets bin, located inside of the Animating Color Changes bin, and drag the Color Corrector 3-Way Before filter onto the first half of the clip, and the Color Corrector 3-Way After filter onto the second half of the clip.

These preset filters have the same settings as the two keyframes for the animated color correction filter in clip two, so you can clearly compare the difference. If you play the clip now, you'll see a clear jump in color from one setting to the next.

7   Add a cross-dissolve to the through edit, and set its duration to 7 frames.

NOTE ► The green filter bars indicate whether or not a filter has been applied to a clip in the Timeline, and can be made visible by turning on the Clip Keyframes control.

The dissolve blends the color corrections together but without creating any undue color shifts.

This technique works best when a natural change in the lighting is already occurring in the shot, so that the visible change in color temperature is motivated. Depending on the clip, a longer or shorter dissolve may be required for the smoothest transition, but your ultimate goal is for such a color correction to go unnoticed.

Animating Lighting

OVERVIEW ► The process of changing a light level over time.

SEE ALSO ► animating color changes, day for night (classic blue look), day for night (exterior campfire), day for night (studio correction), day for night (matching video underexposure)

Animating a Lighting Change

One of the more frequent animated corrections you'll make is to account for a change in lighting that primarily affects the contrast of the image. Frequently, practical effects for lights being turned on or off don't quite look as dramatic as the director would later like, or maybe when the scene was originally shot it didn't call for a change in lighting, but now one is needed.

On the other hand, you will occasionally run into a situation where the lighting changes unintentionally, such as when the only cloud in an otherwise blue sky moves over the sun in the middle of the only close-up of the shoot, and nobody noticed until the middle of the edit.

In either instance, you can solve the problem with an animated change to the contrast of the image. The following example shows how to alter the contrast of an image to intensify the effect of a practical light being turned off:

1   Open the *Keyframing Lighting* sequence, located in the Animating Lighting Changes bin of the **Color Correction Exercises** project.

2   Play through the clip, and observe how the practical lighting looks.

About halfway into the shot, the switch is turned off, but the resulting change in lighting accentuates a hot spot shining on the wall to the right of the light switch, and the overall lighting change is pretty weak. You should also notice that the change in lighting happens over two to three frames, depending on how picky you want to be.

The first step is to make any necessary color corrections to the look of the shot at the beginning.

NOTE ▶ The second clip is the finished result, for you to use for reference.

3   Apply a Color Corrector 3-Way filter to the first clip in the sequence, open it into the Viewer, and click the Color Corrector 3-Way tab.

Assuming that the contrast level is fine, the clip is a bit yellow, due to the weak blue channel. (Take a look at the Parade scope to see this.) Looking at the Waveform Monitor, you notice that the majority of the pixels in the image lie between 20 and 80 percent, which should lead you to guess that the proper control to make this adjustment is the Mids, which exerts the most influence in this range.

4 Drag the Mids color balance control a bit towards the blue target (B). Make an even smaller adjustment to the Whites color balance control.

The adjustment to the mids takes the yellow tint out of the lighting. The whites adjustment neutralizes most of the yellow cast, although it's a particularly dingy shade of white, so you won't get rid of it all

5 Move the playhead to the first frame of the lighting change, where the finger is about to push down on the switch, and click the Keyframe button at the upper-left corner of the Color Corrector 3-Way filter.

This frame has a marker for reference. It should be the frame immediately before the first frame with a visible lighting change.

You're placing a keyframe here because this is the last frame with the original lighting scheme, and you want to lock it in place before creating the conclusion of the animated change that occurs over the next two frames.

6 Move the playhead forward to the frame where the lighting change is at its lowest level (two frames forward).

The following frame should have no change in lighting.

NOTE ▶ A good way to judge the timing of lighting changes is to look at the level of the graph in the Waveform Monitor. The top contour of the graph moves very clearly when the luma of the image is changing and can help you to pinpoint very small changes that are difficult to see.

7 Manipulate the contrast sliders to create the "darker" look for when the light is off.

How dark depends on the situation. Is someone lowering the lighting in a restaurant or an auditorium, or is the light being switched off in a house at night with nothing but the moonlight streaming through a window?

For this example, you'll create more of a night look, although you could use this example to experiment with any kind of lighting change you like.

8 Crush the blacks slightly (not too much or you'll lose detail) to account for the deeper shadows.

Crushing the blacks further accentuates the hot spot on the wall.

9 Bring down the mids to reduce the hot spot and make the entire image appropriately darker.

Reducing the mids makes the image dingier, however, so you might want to boost the whites to bring some dynamic range back into the image (even though it's thematically dark, the audience still needs to be able to see what's going on). Brightening the highlights pulls that midtone hot spot up again, so you may want to lower the mids again after you've made the whites adjustment.

10 If the color in the image really sticks out against the lowered luma, reduce the saturation until the color looks natural, given the lighting.

You can also drag the Whites color balance control to add more "midnight" blue to the image, if you prefer that kind of look.

NOTE ▶ For more information on day-for-night looks, see one of the **Day for Night** entries.

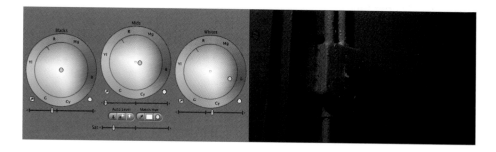

Because these parameters have already been keyframed, a second keyframe has been automatically placed at the current position of the playhead in the keyframe graph at the top of the Color Corrector 3-Way graphical interface when you adjusted these controls. This sets the values of the changes you've just made at the frame showing the off position of the light switch.

Playing back the clip shows the new animated effect.

Because the keyframed change is abrupt, over a mere two frames, the change appears fairly instantaneous. If you spaced out the keyframes more widely, however, the animated effect would happen more slowly, creating a more gradual change. Keep in mind that the distance between two keyframes that determines the duration of the animated effect.

Keyframing to Correct Auto-Exposure

Here's one last thing to consider. You can use the same method just shown to correct for the unprofessional changes in exposure that result from video footage shot with auto-exposure turned on. The trick is to identify the start and end point of each change in exposure in the clip (you can set markers to spot each section).

Next, make sure you set an *unaltered* keyframe at the beginning of each exposure shift as you correct it. When you move to the end of the unwanted exposure shift, matching the contrast levels to those at the first keyframe you created is fairly simple. You can place an In point in the Timeline at the first keyframe so you can use the Control-Left Arrow keyboard shortcut to jump between the two frames for comparison, or use the split-screen mode of the Frame Viewer.

Depending on the clip, it may be difficult to get an exact match, but you should be able to eliminate most of the shift in brightness.

Bleach Bypass Looks

OVERVIEW ▶ Methods for recreating the look associated with skipping the bleaching stage of film processing. *Related terms:* Silver-retention process.

SEE ALSO ▶ contrast adjustments

What Is Bleach Bypass?

One of the more popular looks that's achieved brand-name status is the bleach bypass. This method of film processing has been popularized by its use in films like *1984* (cinematography by Roger Deakins), *Delicatessen* (Darius Khondji), *Three Kings* (Newton Thomas Sigel), and *Saving Private Ryan* (Andrzej Bartkowiak).

Bleach bypass refers to a specific process whereby the bleaching stage—which removes the exposed grains of silver that initially formed the image—is skipped. The silver grains remain on the negative, creating greater density, which increases image contrast, intensifies grain, and reduces saturation.

Many different silver-retention processes have been developed by different film labs, mainly to manipulate contrast, deepen shadows, alter saturation, and increase grain when working with projects shot on and destined for printing and color timing on film.

When someone asks you for a bleach bypass look, ask them to describe, in simple terms, how they want the image to look. If all they want is darker shadows, higher contrast, or less color saturation, you can probably make these adjustments by simply using the Color Correction filters.

NOTE ▶ There's an excellent article on silver retention processes, "Soup du Jour," from the November 1998 issue of *American Cinematographer*, available on the ASC Web site at www.theasc.com.

If you're really looking to simulate the full-bore bleach bypass look, however, you do have a few options in Final Cut Pro.

Creating the Look in Final Cut Pro

The essence of all silver retention processes is the superimposition of a grayscale duplicate over the image. The density of the duplicate varies depending on the desired increase in contrast and reduction in saturation.

There is no one bleach bypass look. Instead, numerous variations and variables are customized to a particular project's needs. For this reason, this section presents two methods that are as flexible as possible to accommodate your own unique variations.

Method 1

The first method creates the bleach bypass look by superimposing a desaturated duplicate on top of the originating clip, combining the two images with one of several composite modes, and then color correcting the underlying clip to fine-tune the effect.

This method can play in real time on some systems (in Unlimited RT mode). Superwhite values, however, can be difficult to control, and the process of superimposing and correcting two sets of clips can be cumbersome, unless you need to create this look for only one or two clips (such as a flashback) or you're applying the effect to whole nested groups of clips.

1   Open the *Bleach Bypass, Method 1* sequence, located in the Bleach Bypass Looks bin of the **Color Correction Exercises** project.

   This is a generally well-exposed clip, with lots of saturation and contrast to go into different directions.

2 Apply a Color Corrector 3-Way filter to the first clip in the sequence. (The second group of clips is the finished correction, provided for comparison.) With the playhead over the first clip, drag the clip from the Timeline to the Superimpose overlay in the Canvas to superimpose a duplicate in track V2.

3 Open the clip in track V2 into the Viewer, and click the Color Corrector 3-Way tab to expose the graphical controls. Drag the Saturation slider all the way to the left to desaturate the image.

4 Control-click the superimposed duplicate, and choose Composite Mode > Overlay from the shortcut menu.

You've now achieved the first part of the look, as the image becomes extremely high-contrast, with dense shadows.

Overlay is an interesting composite mode to use for this effect, because it preserves the brightest values in areas of the underlying picture above 50 percent and the darkest values in areas of the underlying picture below 50 percent. Using Overlay essentially pushes the contrast by adding another layer of image density, as opposed to expanding the luma component of the image across a broader range.

You could also use other composite modes to try out variations, which may work better with clips of different exposures:

▶ In this clip, Multiply yields a darker result overall.

▶ Soft Light, on the other hand, leaves a bit more midtone detail intact and affords more control over the highlights.

The image is a bit dense, so you'll finish by making some further adjustments to the underlying image.

5   Open the clip in track V1 into the Viewer, and raise the Mids slider to bring some more detail back into the suit of the man in the middle. The highlights are rather intense, so you may want to lower them a bit, as well (in this example, don't worry about achieving a completely legal signal. Lower the Saturation slider to mute the colors, but not eliminate them.

How much you choose to lower the saturation is completely a matter of taste.

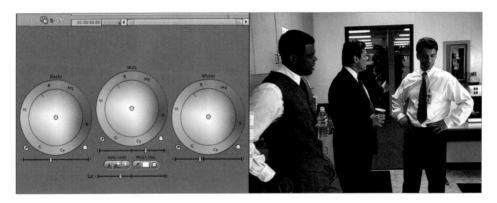

At this point, you're finished. Feel free to go back into each of the clip's filter settings to try different variations, and experiment with other composite modes to see how the layers interact.

Method 2

This method follows a similar procedure to Method 1, except it uses a Compound Arithmetic filter instead of a superimposed duplicate clip. It's slower, but this method makes it easier to control superwhite values, and two filters are easier to manage than a group of duplicated clips.

1   Open the *Bleach Bypass, Method 2* sequence, located in the Bleach Bypass Looks bin of the **Color Correction Exercises** project. Open the first clip into the Viewer, and click the Filters tab.

2   Apply a Channel > Compound Arithmetic filter to the first clip in the sequence. Leave the Layer parameter's clip control empty so that the filter uses the clip itself as the target layer, and set the Operator to Overlay.

Applying this filter has the same effect as superimposing a copy of the layer and using the Overlay composite mode to blend them together.

NOTE ▶ The Compound Arithmetic filter doesn't have all of the composite modes that are available in the Timeline. In particular, the Soft Light composite mode is missing.

3   Apply a Color Corrector 3-Way filter after the Compound Arithmetic filter. Raise the mids to add some more midtone detail to the image, lower the Whites to bring the superwhite highlights back down to 100 percent (which is much easier to do with the order of operations contained within a single clip), and finally lower the saturation to taste.

You can see here how the results (right) vary from the original (left):

Variations and Favorites

Because both of these procedures rely upon the standard Color Correction filters, you can vary the contrast and saturation to create many unique effects.

If bleach bypass is a technique you find yourself using frequently, you might consider creating a set of filter favorites. Remember, however, that these settings will have profoundly different effects, depending on the source material they're applied to.

Third-Party Filters

You can generally gauge the popularity of a particular color treatment by how many filters are available for creating that look. By this measure, bleach bypass definitely wins. Here are a few third-party choices.

Graeme Nattress

Film Effects – Nattress Film Effects

www.nattress.com

A nice Bleach Bypass filter is included in this set from Graeme Nattress.

River Rock Studios

CinemagicX

www.riverrockstudios.com/riverrock/pages/cinemagicX.html

A film-look filter from River Rock Studios that has bleach bypass options, among many other features.

The Orphanage
Magic Bullet Editors

www.redgiantsoftware.com/magicbulletfamily.html

An After Effects plug-in set developed by The Orphanage, and available from Red Giant software, that has bleach bypass settings in its list of drag-and-drop color correction.

Digital Film Tools
55mm

www.digitalfilmtools.com/55mm

This versatile set of After Effects plug-ins includes a bleach bypass filter.

Broadcast Legality

OVERVIEW ▶ Guidelines and techniques for ensuring video clips conform to broadcast standards and ranges.

SEE ALSO ▶ broadcast safe filter, titles and graphics (choosing legal colors)

What Does Broadcast Legality Affect?

It's tempting, especially if you're not used to working in a broadcast environment, to wonder what all the fuss is about with broadcast legality. Many consumer and professional videocameras are capable of recording video with superwhite levels and extremely saturated color, and nothing prevents you from capturing, editing with, and outputting such levels to tape or DVD. Furthermore, many consumer DVD and tape devices record and play such levels without issue, while consumer monitors may seem to display these levels just fine.

Despite this, keeping your program broadcast legal is of paramount importance for a variety of reasons, not the least is its eventual handoff to a terrestrial, cable, or satellite broadcaster for eventual airing on television. At the time of this writing, nearly every program handed off for broadcast is encoded as a composite signal for transmission, and any attempt to encode a signal that exceeds the broadcasters prescribed levels can create havoc with the video signal, which at the least may include occasional unwanted video artifacts, and at the worst might result in horribly clipped regions of the picture. More likely, however, it will earn you the ire (as opposed to IRE) of the broadcast engineering team responsible for that station, and will increase the likelihood of your program being rejected in their QC (quality control) process and sent back to you for recorrection. This is not something you want to risk, especially if you're on a deadline.

Even if you're not handing your program off for broadcast, keeping your video signal within legal levels guarantees a certain level of predictability with regards to how bright portions of the picture and saturated colors will look on the widest variety of displays. There are so many types of monitors available to consumers—LCD, DLP, plasma, as well as good old CRTs—and each has different methods of reencoding and displaying video signals that are fed to it. Given the wide range of playback devices, there's no telling how any particular combination of excessively high analog or digital signal components will be handled or displayed.

Illegal values are also a significant problem for analog, tape-based formats. If your luma and chroma levels are too "hot" (high), you run the risk of interference with the timing signal on the tape, which at its worst can cause a complete loss of video sync.

This entry examines the various ways in which video signals can be out of range and presents correction strategies.

White Levels

The most frequent correction you'll find yourself making in most programs is to legalize the white level of every clip in the sequence by compensating for the superwhite levels.

When discussing maximum white levels, you must understand the difference between white, which is represented by 100 percent digital (following figure, on the left), and superwhite, which is represented in the Waveform Monitor as the topmost section from 101 to 109 percent digital (following figure, on the right). (Interestingly, Final Cut Pro supports a few additional percent of luma headroom above even this level, not that you should ever use it.) Although most consumer and professional digital video cameras record superwhite levels, and Final Cut Pro happily preserves these superwhite levels if they're present in a captured clip, superwhite isn't generally allowable in broadcast programming.

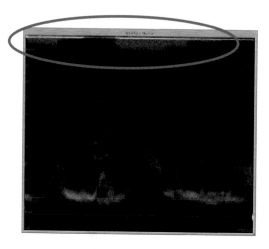
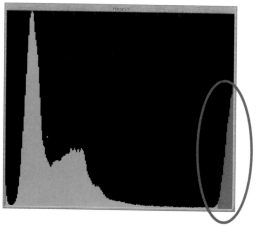

That said, limit your maximum white level to prevent unexpected clipping, even if you're simply creating a personal program to output to DVD, send to your relatives, or post on the Web, but it's not strictly necessary. Most consumer DVD players have no problem with superwhite, but you can't always be sure of any end-user's setup.

Being More Conservative

Some broadcasters are significantly more conservative with the maximum white levels they'll allow. If you know you'll be dealing with a stickler of an engineer who'll be QCing your project, you may want to consider keeping your maximum white levels down to 95 percent digital. This isn't too heartbreaking a compromise, and it will help to ensure that any stray glints or highlights stay within the 100 percent limit.

If you manually adjust the white levels of each clip in your sequence, the Broadcast Safe filter is a reliable way to compress unexpected peaks in luma. See Broadcast Safe Filter.

Analog Guidelines for Legal White Levels

When setting the white level of clips, Final Cut Pro's Waveform Monitor should always match your hardware Waveform Monitor. When comparing the two, 100 percent digital equals 100 IRE for NTSC or 700 mV for PAL.

Setting the White Level of Incoming RGB Clips

The Process Maximum White As parameter in the Video Processing tab of the Sequence settings affects the default white level of imported RGB still images and QuickTime files (such as .mov files compressed using the Animation codec), as well as the white point of Final Cut Pro generators.

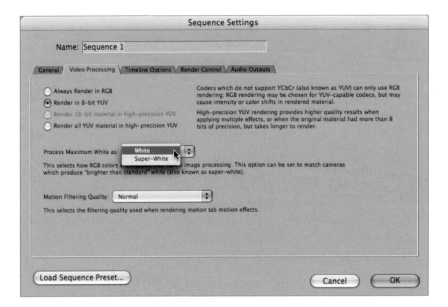

If you want the maximum white of imported RGB media to match the broadcast legal limit of 100 percent, leave this parameter set to White (the default). If you're deliberately leaving superwhite values in your program, for whatever reason, you can set this pop-up menu to Super-White so the maximum white level of imported RGB media is set to 110 percent.

If you change your mind after you've edited a bunch of RGB clips and Final Cut Pro generators into a sequence, don't worry, you can change this parameter at any time, and the white level of all RGB media and generators in your sequence is automatically updated.

In general, you are advised to leave this set to White.

Differing White Guidelines for Titles

Many broadcasters require that the peak luminance of electronically generated titles not exceed 90 IRE. See Titles and Graphics (Choosing Legal Colors).

Black Levels

Some confusion remains surrounding the standard black levels that should be output when mastering a program in Final Cut Pro. With regards to performing color correction inside of Final Cut Pro, you need only remember one simple rule: regardless of the source, once a video clip has been captured into Final Cut Pro as a digital file, absolute black is represented in Final Cut Pro as 0 percent.

When you output your program from Final Cut Pro to an analog format via a video interface such as a capture card, or a FireWire-connected video interface/video deck/camcorder, the output device determines what the analog black level will be.

Video cards usually have software that lets you set this level yourself, whereas video decks may have either hardware switches or menu settings to accomplish this. If you're using a consumer-level interface such as a FireWire converter box or camcorder, this setting may not be adjustable, and it *will* vary (either 0 or 7.5) depending on the device. If you're unsure what black level is being output by your interface, and you have a hardware Waveform Monitor, you can output a test signal from Final Cut Pro and measure it.

As you're monitoring Final Cut Pro's video output, whether or not you're using hardware video scopes, you need to make sure that your video output device and monitor are set to the same black level standard, as appropriate for your workflow. These standards are as follows:

▶ 0 percent digital when monitoring or outputting via SDI, HD-SDI, or Dual-Link SDI

▶ 7.5 IRE when monitoring or outputting NTSC video in North America via analog Y'CbCr using the Beta component standard (as when outputting to Beta SP tape)

▶ 0 IRE when outputting PAL, or NTSC in countries other than North America, via analog Y'CbCr using the Beta component standard

▶ 0 IRE when outputting any PAL or NTSC analog Y'CbCr video signal anywhere in the world using the SMPTE/N10 component standard

There are also setup considerations for your video output interface and monitor. Your video capture card should always output the black level your video deck is set to record when outputting to tape. Your monitor's setup level should always match what's being output by your video card. This is particularly true if you're monitoring an analog component signal.

If these settings aren't consistent, you risk either incorrectly crushing or washing out your blacks during output to tape or looking at a monitor with incorrect black levels, which will cause you to misjudge your corrections. In either case, the consequences will be disastrous when you later view your program on a properly calibrated monitor.

Chroma Levels

Although the guidelines for setting minimum and maximum luma levels in your program are fairly black-and-white (it had to be said), setting legal chroma levels is a considerably more complicated subject.

Both digital and analog component video equipment is capable of recording and preserving extremely saturated color values, potentially up to or even exceeding 131 IRE.

> **NOTE ▶** This capability to exceed 131 IRE is one reason why the graticules of many hardware scopes have room for excursions above white and below black of up to 40 additional units.

If present in a video signal, Final Cut Pro will dutifully capture and preserve these excessively "hot" color values.

Such high chroma values are rarely a good idea because they can cause unwanted artifacts such as loss of image detail, colors "bleeding" into one another, and buzzing noise at the border of oversaturated regions of the picture. Even *more* problems occur when such hot chroma is encoded with the luma as an analog composite signal for purposes of broadcast, and for these reasons television broadcasters have strict requirements regarding acceptable chroma saturation.

Recommended Chroma Guidelines

If you're providing a master tape for a particular broadcaster, always inquire as to their particular broadcast specifications. When in doubt, the following guidelines are a fairly conservative standard:

▶   Peak Chrominance (which should be limited only to temporary highlights and spikes of color) should never exceed 110 percent digital/IRE. Some broadcasters may allow transient peaks of up to 12 percent digital/IRE, but you should never take this for granted.

▶   Average Chrominance should be limited to 100 percent digital/IRE and under, (depending on the brightness of the area in which it appears).

Unfortunately, oversaturated chroma is exceedingly easy to create (just think of your favorite glow filter), so you need to take care whenever you increase saturation or push one of the color balance controls towards a large correction.

What Causes Illegal Chroma?

Chroma becomes illegal for three primary reasons:

▶ Any part of the chroma component of a signal exceeds the recommended maximum level. You can specifically monitor this in the Vectorscope.

▶ The combined luma and chroma components exceed the recommended maximum levels. You can monitor this in the Waveform Monitor with Saturation turned on.

▶ Some broadcasters have specific legalization requirements for the transformation of a Y'CbCr video signal into RGB, and any RGB-encoded color channel that goes above 100 percent or below 0 percent is considered to be out-of-gamut. You can monitor this in the RGB Parade scope.

These are the main causes of illegal chroma. However, they translate into the following predictable triggers of chroma illegality while evaluating and adjusting your clips:

▶ Certain hues are predisposed to becoming oversaturated. Reds are the single biggest offender, but greens and cyans also have an innate tendency to become too saturated, even when the other hues in the image are perfectly legal.

▶ The combination of high luma and high saturation in the same part of the picture (especially in portions of the picture that appear above 85 to 90 percent in the Waveform Monitor) is a recipe for illegality. This is especially vexing because it's something you'll find yourself wanting to do (adding color to a bright sky, putting color into lighting highlights), and it's difficult to detect every stray pixel using Final Cut Pro's built-in tools. (Although to be fair, this is difficult to see even when using standard hardware waveform monitors and vectorscopes.)

▶ Highly saturated values in really dark regions of the picture are also an unexpected source of illegal chroma levels. (It's technically possible to have saturation in portions of an image with low luma levels, but black is *supposed* to be completely desaturated.) Even though these sub-zero saturated regions will be clamped to 0 by the broadcast display, most broadcasters still consider this to be an illegal condition.

As you work, monitor your chroma levels with each adjustment you make.

Monitoring Legal Video Levels

Keeping the issues just addressed in mind, Final Cut Pro provides you with four tools you can use to evaluate the Saturation in your picture: range checking, the Vectorscope, the Waveform Monitor, and the RGB Parade scope. Use them individually or collectively to check the legality of uncorrected video, as well as to make sure that the corrections you're making aren't creating illegal levels in your clips.

Using Range Checking

One of the easiest ways to monitor the legality of saturation in your images is by using the View > Range Checking > Excess Chroma and View > Range Checking > Excess Luma controls.

With both commands, zebra stripes and three icons in the Canvas give you information about the levels in your clips.

An *exclamation point* icon indicates illegal levels in your clip, and red zebra stripes indicate which portions of the picture are illegal so you can quickly make the appropriate corrections:

▶   Excess luma triggers a warning for any levels above 100 percent.

▶   Excess chroma triggers a warning for any levels above 120 percent digital/IRE. (The exact trigger level increases or decreases with the luma levels of the clip.)

NOTE ▶ The Excess Chroma warning is fairly permissive, relative to the requirements of many broadcasters.

An *arrow pointing up* icon indicates luma levels that fall within the range of 90 to 100 percent digital, but no values are above that range. Green zebra stripes indicate the portions of the image with values within this range. This is a luma-only indication:

Excess Luma displays green zebra stripes in areas with luma falling in the 90 to 100 percent range.

A *checkmark* icon indicates that the entire image is completely within the legal range of either chroma or luma, whichever you're checking.

Monitoring Saturation Using the Vectorscope

You typically monitor the overall saturation of your programs using the Vectorscope. The distance of a plotted value from the center of the scope shows its degree of saturation as a digital percentage (comparable to the IRE measurement of an analog external vectorscope).

A conservative way of quickly spot-checking the legality of chroma is to imagine a boundary connecting the targets that appear within the Vectorscope. As long as the Vectorscope graph fits within this boundary, you can be fairly sure that your levels are legal.

Despite this rule of thumb, the actually permissible levels of saturation are not always so easily defined. Higher levels of saturation may be permissible in the midtones, while lower levels of saturation are permissible in highlights and shadow regions.

The Range Checking > Excess Chroma feature takes this into account, and as a result range checking triggers warnings at different levels of saturation than the Vectorscope targets indicate, depending on the specific range of luma in the image. The following chart shows how the Range Checking > Excess Chroma warnings vary with the brightness of the image, as compared to the conservative rule of thumb, which is probably a better indicator of where your saturation levels should be in most situations:

▶   The dark red, orange, and yellow dotted lines plot the outer limits of legal chroma as defined by Range Check > Excess Chroma, with an image adjusted to have varying levels of luma.

▶   The Blue solid line plots the most conservative limits of chroma legality, as defined by the outer targets of 75 percent color bars.

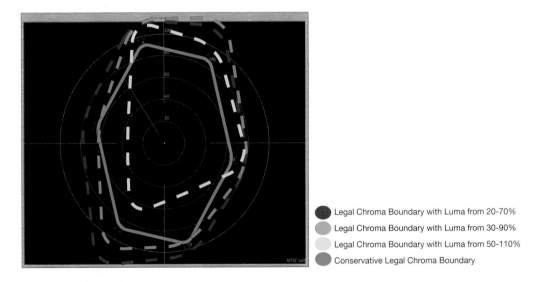

● Legal Chroma Boundary with Luma from 20-70%
● Legal Chroma Boundary with Luma from 30-90%
○ Legal Chroma Boundary with Luma from 50-110%
● Conservative Legal Chroma Boundary

The only limitation to using the Vectorscope to monitor the legal chroma limits in your program is that you can't tell which highly saturated regions correspond to areas of high or low luma. Fortunately, there is another tool you can use to make this determination.

Monitoring with the Waveform Monitor

Monitoring luma levels with the Waveform Monitor is easy, because the Waveform's scale is very straightforward.

The Waveform Monitor is an invaluable tool for monitoring the saturation of your images, as well. When you turn on the Saturation option in the Waveform Monitor, the graph plots a series of vertical bands at each luma level in the clip. Each band's height indicates the amount of saturation in that image, and the position of the bands on the graph show you whether that saturation level falls into the whites, mids, or blacks. Compare the following Waveform Monitor displays; the left image has low saturation, and the right image has identical luma values but higher saturation:

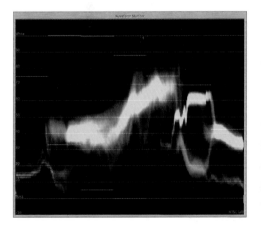 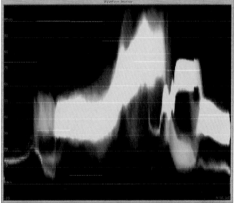

Luma only displayed in Waveform Monitor (left), Luma + Saturation displayed in Waveform Monitor (right).

This display is advantageous because it immediately lets you see illegal chroma levels in the highlights and shadows, even when the Vectorscope graph seems completely legal. For example, the following image (on the left) has oversaturated highlights, and the image on the right shows an adjustment to desaturate just the highlights made with the Desaturate Highlights filter.

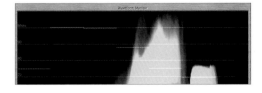 

The height of saturated values also show you the degree to which you need to make a correction (for example, using the Desaturate Highlights and Lows filter) in order to legalize these regions of your image while preserving the legal saturation falling within the midtones.

Monitoring RGB Legalization with the Parade Scope

You can use the RGB Parade scope to monitor the RGB transformation of the video signal to check for illegal RGB values above 100 or below 0 percent. Some broadcasters have this as a strict requirement, while others are more permissive of such levels.

Strictly speaking, any levels that fall below 0 percent will be clipped by the display device, be it CRT, LCD, DLP, plasma, or whatever technology is employed.

RGB levels above 100, on the other hand, are less predictable in how they'll be displayed. CRT monitors may simply run the signal a bit "hotter," while the circuitry of other types of displays may compress or clip these portions of the picture in different ways. For your own peace of mind, you may find it best to bring these levels down to the legally prescribed limits to avoid unexpected artifacts.

In the following image, you can spot illegal RGB levels in the above-white portion of the red and blue components and in the below-black portion of the red and green components.

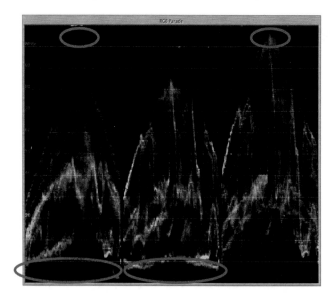

Reducing the overall saturation of the image brings the levels back into the legal range.

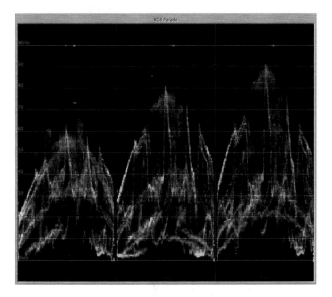

In general, you'll follow all of the same legalization steps you would when correcting the signal with the other video scopes.

Other Hardware Monitoring Options for Broadcast

Other types of displays and out-of-gamut warnings are available in hardware scopes from various manufacturers. In particular, Tektronix video scopes have two additional types of displays that are designed to make it easier to analyze how your video program will hold up in broadcast applications, where the luma and chroma are encoded together as a composite signal. These graphs are more typically used in broadcast and QC applications, but if you're lucky enough to have one available to you, they make rigorous legalization of your video signals that much easier:

▶ The Diamond Display shows two diamonds, one over the other. The red, green, and blue components of the image are represented by a graph in such a way so that legal color values fall within the diamonds, and illegal color values fall outside the diamonds. The specific side of each diamond on which the illegal values fall indicate exactly which colors are illegal, guiding you to a suitable correction.

▶   The Arrowhead Display displays a graph that's flat on the left and pointed on the
     right (similar to an arrowhead), with a scale within. The graph displays the composite
     combination of luma and chroma in such a way so that oversaturated values in spe-
     cific areas of luma cross over the scale.

For more information about these displays, see the Tektronix Web site (www.tek.com).

Legalizing Your Picture

Although you usually legalize clips individually as you perform each correction, the process of legalization can also be done in several stages, depending on the nature of the program and on the type of grades you're performing. Which approach do you take? The
following workflow may help you to organize your adjustments more efficiently.

1.   Individually legalize the white level of each clip by adjusting the contrast sliders while
     using the Waveform Monitor and Histogram as your guides. Make these adjustments
     according to the most conservative standard to which you might be submitting the
     program.

2.   Make whatever corrections and adjustments are necessary to the color of each clip
     to achieve the required look. As you make these adjustments, carefully monitor the
     resulting changes to the clip's saturation in the Vectorscope to make sure you don't
     stray outside the recommended limits. The good news is that you don't have to turn
     the saturation down on everything to legalize your picture (although this is some-
     times the fastest solution). If the chroma of a particular subject in the clip is illegal,
     but the majority of the clip is within legal limits, you can make a more targeted
     adjustment in the next two steps.

3.   Manually adjust the saturation of specific chroma values that spike beyond the legal
     limits in the Vectorscope using secondary correction. Reds, Yellows, and Cyans tend to
     be guilty of this. See Saturation (Reducing Oversaturated Hues).

4.   Use the Waveform Monitor with Saturation turned on to check for oversaturated
     highlight and shadow areas that will cause problems in composite broadcast. If neces-
     sary, you can desaturate the highlights and shadows of each clip without desaturating
     the otherwise legal midtone regions using the Desaturate Highlights/Lows filters. See
     Saturated Looks.

5. When you're finished color correcting the entire program, nest the corrected sequence inside of another, and apply a combination of the Broadcast Legal filter (set to your conservative standard of choice) and other secondary color correction operations (desaturate highlights/shadows, specific secondary hue corrections, and so on) to the overall sequence in order to catch any stray values that may have gotten by you.

NOTE ▶ If you're outputting to tape using a hardware legalizer, then step 5 is unnecessary.

Broadcast Safe Filter

OVERVIEW ▶ Guidelines for using an FXScript filter that automatically limits illegal luma and chroma values in an image by a user-selectable margin.

SEE ALSO ▶ broadcast legality, titles and graphics (choosing legal colors)

What the Broadcast Legal Filter Does

The Broadcast Safe filter (found within the Video Filters > Color Correction bin of the Effects tab) is designed to make automatic adjustments to the picture in order to limit illegal luma and chroma values. The Mode pop-up menu provides a quick list of common standards, depending on how conservatively you want to limit the chroma of the video signal, while a series of sliders below lets you customize the amount of limiting when the Mode pop-up menu is set to Custom.

Broadcast legalization is not an easy process, and although the Broadcast Safe filter tries its best, it's not meant to be used as an across-the-board legalizer for uncorrected clips. In fact, this filter works best when applied to clips that have already been corrected with other filters, and it is meant to be used as a precaution against stray values that you may have missed. As such, you'll find that the Very Conservative and Extremely Conservative settings in the Mode pop-up menu are probably the most valuable.

NOTE ► Using the Broadcast Safe filter with uncorrected clips that have very high luma and chroma values may result in insufficient adjustments or undesirable artifacts, depending on the Mode setting you're using.

Ideally, you'll have corrected your program shot-by-shot first. Then, you typically apply the Broadcast Legal filter to a nested version of your color-corrected sequence so that you can apply a single standard of legalization to every clip in your sequence, and easily change it across the board, if necessary.

How It Works

The Broadcast Safe filter is a bit tricky in how it tries to keep values in your program legal. Instead of simply clamping oversaturated and overly bright values in your image, the filter attempts to make a series of different adjustments to preserve as much detail and saturation as possible, while limiting only what it needs to:

► It compresses, rather than clamps, luma values above 100 percent when using one of the automatic modes, in an effort to preserve as much detail as possible. The resulting adjustment has a falloff from 100 to 95 percent.

► It gives you the option to darken regions of high saturation that appear above 50 percent in the Waveform Monitor, in an effort to minimize the amount of desaturation that's necessary to legalize portions of the image that are both oversaturated and bright.

► It attempts to desaturate images as little as possible, based on the brightness of the oversaturated pixels. It desaturates less in the midtones than in the highlights.

► It *does not* automatically reduce oversaturated blacks. You must do this yourself, if necessary, using the Desaturate Highlights/Lows filter.

► It *does not* do a particularly good job of desaturating illegal chroma values in the midtones of an image.

Parameters in the Broadcast Safe Filter

The Broadcast Safe filter has the following parameters:

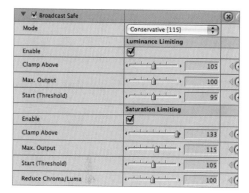

Mode

This pop-up menu offers six options. Each setting is labeled with the maximum percentage of chroma that it allows.

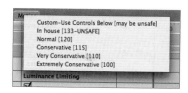

Whenever you choose one of the bottom five presets from this pop-up menu, the custom sliders in the Luminance Limiting and Saturation Limiting sections are disabled, *except* for Reduce Chroma/Luma.

> **NOTE** ▶ Even though the sliders are disabled, they don't look disabled, so you just have to be aware.

Although the amount of saturation limiting varies with the selected setting, each of these options limits luma to a maximum of 100 percent:

▶ In-house allows chroma saturation of up to 130 percent. For most broadcasters, this would allow unacceptably illegal values.

▶ Normal allows chroma saturation of up to 120 percent. For most broadcasters, this would allow unacceptably illegal values.

▶ Conservative allows chroma saturation of up to 115 percent. For most broadcasters, this would allow unacceptably illegal values.

▶ Very Conservative allows chroma saturation of up to 110 percent. This is probably an acceptable limit for more permissive broadcasters.

▶ Extremely Conservative allows chroma saturation of up to 100 percent only. In most cases, this is a good, conservative setting.

The Custom—Use Controls Below [may be unsafe] option lets you use the sliders in the Luminance Limiting and Saturation Limiting sections to create custom limiting settings. These sliders are disabled if you choose any of the automatic settings from the Mode menu.

Luminance Limiting

The parameters in the Luminance Limiting section let you customize the how the luma component of the video signal is legalized:

▶ Enable (Luminance Limiting) turns on the three sliders in this group.

▶ Clamp Above determines two behaviors. All luma values between Start (Threshold) and Clamp Above are compressed down to the Max. Output value. Any luma value above this setting is clamped to the value specified by th:e Max. Output slider, in order to limit luma values that are so bright they would prevent smooth compression. In general, compressing preserves more detail than clamping, but it affects more of the image.

▶ Max. Output specifies the maximum luma value allowed by this filter. Any luma values that are higher are either compressed or clamped, according to the value of the Clamp Above slider.

▶ Start (Threshold) specifies the percentage at which to begin compressing illegal luma. Lowering this value results in a softer falloff between the legalized and nonlegalized portions of the image, but the resulting adjustment affects more of the image as a result.

Saturation Limiting

The parameters in the Saturation Limiting section let you customize how oversaturated values are compressed or limited:

▶ Enable (Saturation Limiting) turns on the first three sliders in this group.

▶ As with the luma controls, Clamp Above determines two behaviors. All chroma values between Start (Threshold) and Clamp Above are compressed, with the maximum value determined by Max. Output. Any chroma value above this setting is clamped to the value specified by the Max. Output slider.

▶ Max. Output specifies the maximum chroma value allowed by this filter. Any chroma values that are higher are either compressed or clamped, according to the value of the Clamp Above slider.

▶ Start (Threshold) specifies the percentage at which to begin compressing illegal chroma. Lowering this value results in a softer falloff between the legalized and nonlegalized portions of the image, but the resulting adjustment affects more of the image as a result.

Reduce Chroma/Luma

Although part of the Saturation Limiting section of controls, the Reduce Chroma/Luma slider is always available, regardless of the Mode pop-up menu's setting.

Legalizing any image is going to alter it one way or another, but this slider lets you control the manner in which oversaturated portions of the image are legalized:

▶ Lowering this value desaturates illegal values more than darkening them.

▶ Raising this value darkens illegal values more than desaturating them.

If you'd like to experiment with this filter to get the hang of these settings, you can use the **Using Broadcast Safe** project, located in the Broadcast Legality bin of the **Color Correction Exercises** project.

Third-Party Alternatives

If you're not satisfied with the chroma-limiting performance of the Broadcast Safe filter, you can try a third-party alternative. Because QC specifications vary widely, however, you should try before you buy to make sure the filter you choose works for your purposes.

The Edit Doctor

"Broadcast Safe" Doctor

www.theeditdoctor.com

Developer Mike Nichols offers an easy-to-use broadcast safe filter called "Broadcast Safe" Doctor that clamps very firmly on illegal midtones values.

1z1 Screenworks

1z1 Mastering

www.1z1.at

Kurt Hennrich at 1z1 Screenworks combined chroma and luma limiting, a black lift, anamorphic handling, and letterbox cropping into a single filter. The 1z1 Mastering filter is available singly or as part of a set of useful filters called 1z1 Tools.

Further Considerations

Remember, the Broadcast Safe filter works best when you've already manually corrected each clip in your sequence, so that it only needs to make slight adjustments to the occasionally illegal values. When the Broadcast Safe filter is used on clips that significantly deviate from this filter's settings, you may get unexpected results. In short, it's always better to make your corrections manually.

If your work is usually output to tape, you may benefit more from a hardware legalizer inserted between your video output interface and your recording deck. The advantage is that you gain real-time luma and chroma limiting, and you don't have to worry too much about dealing with stray illegal pixels in your day-to-day color correction.

In addition, certain hardware video interfaces, such as the Kona cards from AJA (www.aja.com) offer hardware legalization as an option in their setup software.

Cartoon Looks

OVERVIEW ▶ Explanation of a special use technique for flattening the color in images to create a cartoon-like image.

SEE ALSO ▶ glows, blooms, and gauze looks

Flattening Color to Create a Cartoon Look

Here's a technique that's just for kicks, although you never know when you need to pull an unusual look out of your hat for a dream sequence, flashback, or music video. It uses the Darken composite mode to blur the detail in an image, flattening the color while retaining some outline detail via the underlying image.

It works best with images that are well exposed, with crisp detail, although you'll get different and interesting effects with other kinds of clips.

1 Open the *01 Flattening Color* sequence, located in the Cartoon Looks bin of the **Color Correction Exercises** project.

2 Apply a Color Corrector 3-Way filter to the first clip in the sequence. (The second group of clips are the finished correction, provided for comparison.) Open the clip into the Viewer, and click the Color Corrector tab to expose the graphical controls.

As with any other clip, you need to adjust the contrast sliders first.

3   Crush the blacks to solidify the shadows until you can just see the man's shirt darken. Then, boost the mids so that the overall image is relatively bright, and lower the Whites slider if necessary to legalize the highlights. Finally, raise the saturation until you're at the edge of legal chroma (toggle Range Check > Excess Chroma to make sure).

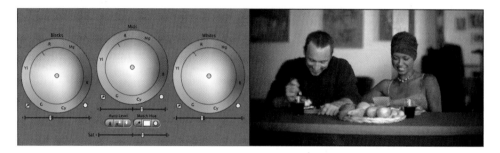

4   With the playhead over the clip you're working on, drag the **Lunch 2Shot** clip into the Superimpose overlay of the Canvas to superimpose a duplicate in track V2. Open the new clip into the Viewer, and click the Filters tab.

5   Control-click the superimposed clip in track V2 and choose Composite Mode > Darken from the shortcut menu. Apply a Gaussian Blur filter to it, and raise the Radius parameter until the color has flattened out to your satisfaction.

The Darken composite mode compares each pair of overlapping pixels, and chooses the darker of the two for the resulting output. Because blurring an image progressively reduces its contrast ratio, the shadows of a blurred duplicate layer are just a little bit lighter, and the highlights are just a little bit darker, than those in the underlying layer. The result is that the darkest sharp edge details from the bottom layer and the darker blurred highlights from the top layer are combined.

The resulting image should look like a soft, pastel version of the original, with contrasty, grainy edge detail at the darkest edges of the subjects.

6   To fine-tune the effect, you can adjust the Mids slider of the bottom layer, lowering it to add detail back into the image or raising it to further flatten the image.

You should use this example as a starting point for further experimentation. Composite modes can create many unexpected effects when used with superimposed duplicate clips with different filters applied.

Other Filters

Final Cut Pro 5.1.2 introduced some FXPlug filters that were previously available only to Motion, some of which are designed to create a more illustration-like look. The three shown in this section all work through a combination of edge detection and contrast adjustments, pulling outlines from the image and flattening midrange values to create broad expanses of color.

Line Art

Stylize > Line Art lets you create an outlined version of a clip, using edge detection to identify high-contrast borders in the original image to turn into line art.

▶ Threshold and Smoothness adjust the contrast of the filter's edge detection, which adds or removes detail in the outlines. Lost detail is flattened to the Paper Color.

▶ Paper Color determines the "background" color that appears behind the outlines the filter creates.

▶ Paper Opacity lets you adjust the "brightness" of the paper color. Values above .5 result in a positive image; values under .5 result in a negative image.

▶ Ink Color lets you choose the color for the resulting edge outlines.

Vectorize Color

Stylize > Vectorize Color lets you create a pastel-painted version of your image by flattening the tonal range of the image into four zones and rendering each zone with a single color (similar to posterization, but blurrier). The default colors can create somewhat Andy Warhol-like imagery.

▶ Resolution determines how detailed the rendering of the image is. Low values produce the most recognizable results (with shapes closest to the features in the image); high values create more abstract shapes.

▶ Smoothness softens each colored zone. High values create a more pastel-like feathering to the colors; low values result in harder edges.

▶ Curvaceousness rounds off the edges of each colored zone, creating smoother expanses of color at the expense of edge detail. Low values preserve more detail; high values create a curvier image.

▶ First-Fourth Color lets you specify which colors are used to represent each of the four tonal zones to which the filter reduces the image.

Threshold

Image Control > Threshold lets you create extremely high-contrast, black and white or duotone looks.

▶ Threshold and Smoothness adjust the contrast of the image. Threshold moves the entire tonal range up or down, clipping the whites if moved too high and crushing the blacks if moved too low. Smoothness increases or decreases the contrast of the remaining midtones.

▶ Dark Color determines the color of the darkest tones in the image.

▶ Light Color determines the color of the lightest tones in the image.

Chroma

OVERVIEW ▶ The color component of a video signal.

SEE ALSO ▶ broadcast legality, luma

What Is Chroma?

Chroma is the portion of the video signal that carries the color information, and in video applications it is typically independent of the luma (or lightness) of the image. In component Y'CbCr encoded video, the chroma is carried in the Cb and Cr color difference channels of the video signal.

This scheme was originally devised to ensure compatibility between color and monochrome television sets. Monochrome TVs simply ignore the chroma component, displaying the luma component by itself.

> **NOTE ▶** The notation for composite video varies depending on whether it's digital or analog. Y'CbCr denotes digital component video, whereas Y'PbPr denotes analog component video.

Chroma Subsampling

In most professional video formats, the chroma component of the video signal is sampled at half the rate of the luma component. This takes advantage of the fact that human vision is more sensitive to differences in brightness than to differences in color to save bandwidth (saving hard drive space in the digital world). For broadcast applications, this reduces the bandwidth required to record and transmit video without noticeably affecting the video quality. This is the source of 4:2:2 chroma subsampling, in which for every full unit of luma (4), half of the chroma is preserved (2 and 2 for each color difference channel).

Prosumer video formats, such as NTSC DV, save even more bandwidth by encoding 4:1:1 chroma subsampling, so that for every full unit of luma, one-fourth of the color is preserved. PAL DV, HDV, and MPEG-2 encode 4:2:0 chroma subsampling, which also preserves one-fourth of the color information, but in a different manner.

> **NOTE ▶** For more information about video signal components, see Charles Poynton's excellent book, *Digital Video and HDTV Algorithms and Interfaces* (Morgan Kaufmann), and Keith Jack's *Video Demystified, 4th Edition* (Newnes).

Chroma Subsampling and the Limit Effect Controls

Chroma subsampling affects how far you can adjust the contrast of your image, as well as on the resulting smoothness of your secondary keys. See Limit Effect Controls.

RGB-Encoded Video

RGB-encoded video, by comparison, encodes the lightness and color of an image together, as a set of three primary color components. Newer digital formats enable RGB 4:4:4 color sampling, so that the full amount of color in each component is preserved.

What Affects Chroma?

Chroma is affected whenever you manipulate a color balance control, adjust a saturation setting, or composite other color images over the current image.

Color Balance Controls

OVERVIEW ▶ Examination of controls in the graphical interface of the Color Corrector and Color Corrector 3-Way filters that let you remove or create color casts in an image's tonal zones.

SEE ALSO ▶ limit effect controls

How They're Used

The more you understand how the color balance controls affect the image, the better you'll be able to control your corrections, targeting them to the specific areas of the image that need adjustment.

The color balance controls in the Color Corrector filters provide a graphical interface for rebalancing the red, green, and blue color components of a video clip to remove or introduce color casts in specific portions of the image. The Color Corrector filter also has a single color balance control that adjusts color in the whites and midtones of an image.

To make an adjustment using a color balance control, the procedure is the same no matter the filter in which you find it: Click anywhere within the control (you don't have to click right on the small gray circle in the middle) and drag. The color balance indicator moves from the center into the direction you drag, and you see the correction to your clip in the

Canvas, on the video scopes, and on your broadcast monitor connected to the output of your video interface.

Color Balance Control Overlap

The color balance controls in the Color Corrector 3-Way filter are far more useful than those in the Color Correction filters because they let you make individual adjustments to the portions of an image that fall into the tonal zones described as the Blacks, Mids, and Whites.

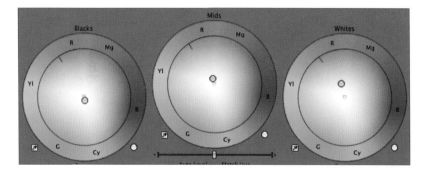

These tonal zones are defined by the luma component of the image, and changes that you make with each of the color balance controls affect the following portions of an image:

▶   The Blacks control affects regions of 0 to 90 percent brightness.

▶   The Mids control affects regions of 10 to 90 percent brightness.

▶   The Whites control affects regions of 10 to 100 percent brightness.

These regions overlap broadly, and fall off very smoothly, so you can make large adjustments without incurring artifacts such as sharpened edges or solarizing. Despite this overlap, you'd be surprised at how targeted your changes can be.

The Overlapping Zones of Correction

This exercise and the sections that follow demonstrate some of the subtleties of working with the Color Corrector 3-Way color balance controls.

1   Open the *01 Tonal Zones* sequence, located in the Color Balance Controls bin of the **Color Correction Exercises** project.

2   In the Timeline, apply a Color Corrector 3-Way filter to the Gradient clip, and open
the clip into the Viewer. Click the Color Corrector 3-Way tab.

3   Adjust the Mids color balance control, dragging it towards the red target, and examine
the effect on the gradient in the Canvas.

When adjusting any one of the color balance controls, you'll see the corresponding
region become tinted. When you drag the Mids control towards red, the portion of
the picture defined by luma values from 10 to 90 percent is tinted red. Notice how the
correction falls off gently at the edges of the correction to achieve a seamless blend.

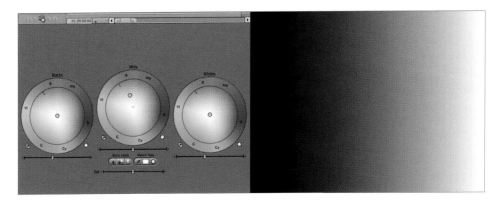

4   Adjust the Whites color balance control, dragging it towards blue, and examine the
overlapping correction.

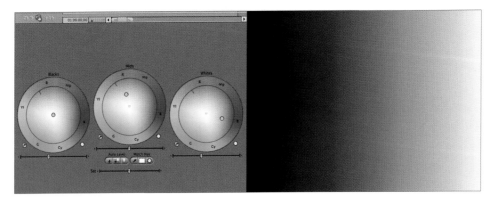

If you look carefully at the area of overlap, you may start to notice a stripe of magenta falling between the red and blue adjustments. This stripe makes sense when you remember that magenta is an even mix of red and blue.

This is an artificial example; with real-world images and subtle corrections, you won't often notice this effect. However, when you make more extreme adjustments involving two color balance controls, you may see some unexpected interactions of this sort, so keep a sharp eye out.

Color Balance Explained

When you manipulate a color balance control, you're simultaneously raising or lowering all three color channels. Every time you adjust a color balance control, you're either boosting one color channel at the expense of lowering the other two channels, or raising two channels at the expense of lowering the third. It's simply not possible to boost all three color channels, nor would you want to, because simultaneously boosting all three channels is the same as brightening the image.

To see this effect in action, give this exercise a try:

1   Open the *02 Rebalancing Color* sequence, located in the Color Balance Controls bin of the **Color Correction Exercises** project.

2   Apply a Color Corrector 3-Way filter to the Color clip in the Timeline, and open the clip into the Viewer. Click the Color Corrector 3-Way tab.

    With the playhead over the Color generator clip, the Parade scope shows a trio of flat graphs at 55 percent. Any time you see three equal graphs in the Parade scope, you know the image is completely desaturated.

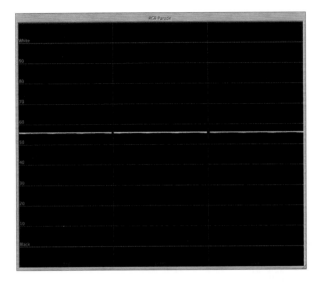

3 In the Color Corrector tab of the Viewer, drag the Mids color balance control towards red. Watch the Parade scope to see what happens.

As you make this adjustment, the reds graph shoots up towards the top, and the green and blue graphs move lower (perhaps unevenly, depending on which side of the R target you moved closer to).

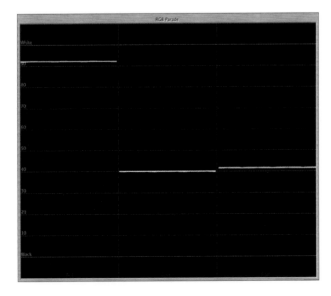

4   Drag the color balance control towards Cyan (the Cy target) to lower the red channel
     while boosting both the green and blue channels.

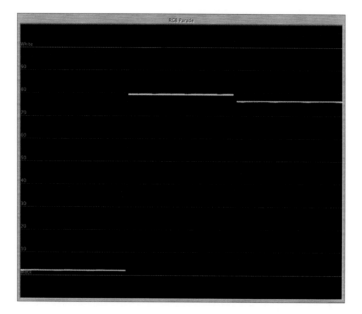

Dragging toward cyan makes sense, because cyan is the complementary color to red,
and it is made up of an additive blend of blue and green, which lie directly to the
left and right of the Cy target on the color wheel.

Reducing the Overlap of Corrections

Sometimes, you'll find that a correction made in one tonal zone is affecting portions of
the image you'd rather leave alone. In this case, you may find yourself making an opposite
adjustment to an adjacent color balance control, then wonder why you did it. The following exercise explains this phenomenon:

1   Open the *03 Reducing Overlap* sequence, located in the Color Balance Controls bin of
     the **Color Correction Exercises** project.

2   Apply a Color Corrector 3-Way filter to the Gradient clip in the Timeline, and open
     the clip into the Viewer. Click the Color Corrector 3-Way tab.

3   Make a bold correction by dragging the Whites color balance control towards blue.

As you can see, the blue correction extends well past the midtones. Fortunately, correcting this situation is simple.

4   Adjust the Mids color balance control, dragging it towards the complementary of blue, yellow, to reduce the blue cast in the midtones.

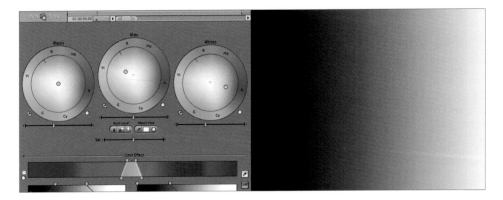

As you make this adjustment, you'll see a greater and greater portion of the midtones become a neutral gray once again, while the upper range of the whites is left with the blue correction.

Although the resulting correction in the graphical interface may seem a bit odd, it's actually an extremely common way of further targeting corrections in exactly the tonal portion of the image where you need them.

Additional Ways to Manipulate Color Balance Controls

There are several keyboard modifiers and surrounding controls that let you adjust the color balance controls in different ways.

Keyboard Modifiers

As you use the color balance controls, two keyboard shortcuts modify their operation:

▶ The Shift key lets you adjust the magnitude of the adjustment, without changing the angle. (You can't move into the complementary hue, you'll bounce back.)

▶ The Command key speeds up adjustments made using the color balance controls.

Reset Controls

The small white buttons to the right of each color balance control reset that control back to its neutral position. Shift-clicking one of these buttons resets all of the controls in the Color Corrector 3-Way filter except for the Limit Effect controls.

Adjusting Color Balance Controls in the Filters Tab

If you want to make numerical adjustments to one of the color balance controls, you can jump to a particular Color Corrector filter's parameters by clicking the Numeric button, which is in the upper-left corner of the color corrector's graphical interface.

Each color balance control is represented by three parameters in the Filters tab, which correspond to the two chroma and one luma adjustment available for each zone of influence:

▶ Angle is an angle control that changes the direction of rebalancing relative to the color wheel. It describes the balance indicator's position around the circumference of the color wheel, in degrees.

▶ Magnitude is a slider that controls the amount of the adjustment. It describes the balance indicator's distance from the center of the control.

▶ Level is the contrast adjustment slider that affects the luma component of the image for the black level, midtone distribution, and white level.

Adjusting Color Balance Controls Using a Trackball

Although Final Cut Pro isn't currently compatible with any of the third-party color correction control surfaces available, you can use a trackball to control the color balance controls one at a time, switching amongst them using special keyboard shortcuts. Because the color balance controls were designed to emulate the trackball functionality of dedicated color correction systems, using an actual trackball can provide an intuitive way to make sensitive adjustments.

These keyboard shortcuts can be cumbersome, but they were designed to be assigned to one of the optional buttons found on most trackballs. Furthermore, they work only *while the mouse button is pressed* within one of the color balance controls in the Viewer. Most trackballs have a "drag lock" option that you can assign to one of the buttons. The workflow then is to move the pointer to one of the color balance controls, press the drag lock button of your trackball, and then press the key(s) corresponding to one of the following remapped keyboard shortcuts to jump from one color balance control to the next:

▶ Tab changes focus to the next color balance control to the right, or from the Whites to the Blacks.

▶ Control-Option-8 changes focus to the Blacks.

▶ Control-Option-9 changes focus to the Mids.

▶ Control-Option-10 changes focus to the Whites.

Using Undo to Preview Individual Adjustments

Often, you'll want to see the before and after of a color control adjustment to see if it's really doing any good. Unfortunately, there are no individual on/off toggles for each control in the graphical interface, only the single filter visibility control at the top.

Fortunately, there's undo and redo. Make your change, then use the keyboard shortcuts for undo (Command-Z) and redo (Shift-Command-Z). You can also reset a color control completely, then undo to restore the correction.

Color Control

OVERVIEW ▶ Examination of a fundamental control that allows you to precisely select colors in a variety of ways and appears in many of Final Cut Pro's filters and generators. *Related terms:* Eyedropper, swatch.

SEE ALSO ▶ animating color changes, hsb color space

Using Final Cut Pro's Color Control

The ubiquitous Color control provides you with several methods of choosing and modifying colors in your projects and is embedded in many of Final Cut Pro's generators and filters. This control has many uses and almost as many hidden controls with which to make your selection.

In addition to its buttons and parameters that you use directly inside of Final Cut Pro, the Color control also provides access to the Mac OS X Colors panel (see the section "Using the Colors Panel" later in this entry), opening the door to even more ways of choosing and storing colors. For now, however, take a closer look at each of the Color control's features.

Eyedropper

To select a color from an image, click the Color control's Eyedropper button.

> **NOTE ▶** Using the eyedropper, you can only pick colors from the Canvas or Viewer.

When the Eyedropper button is highlighted, the pointer turns into an eyedropper whenever you move it into the Canvas or Viewer.

Clicking any pixel in the Canvas chooses its color, which appears in the color swatch.

After you've picked a color, the pointer reverts to whichever of Final Cut Pro's tools you were using before.

Animated Hue Direction

You can keyframe color changes the same way you keyframe any other animated parameter in Final Cut Pro. The button to the right of the eyedropper—the Hue Direction control—lets you control the method in which changes in color are animated. See Animating Color Changes.

Color Swatch

The square color swatch displays the currently selected color. Clicking the swatch opens the Mac OS X Colors panel, providing many additional methods of choosing, storing, and organizing colors.

HSB Sliders

Clicking the disclosure triangle to the left of the eyedropper button reveals the HSB sliders.

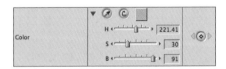

The HSB sliders provide the only numerical way to choose and modify specific colors in the Controls or Filters tabs. Together, they describe color using the HSB model, where hue, saturation, and brightness values all describe a specific color.

The HSB sliders are useful if your client has a specific shade of color that's required for the program. Even better, with these sliders you can interactively modify a color while viewing the output.

This is extremely handy when you need to fine-tune a color used as a title, in a gradient or other generator, or that's being used in a tinting operation. In fact, you can make interactive adjustments with the HSB sliders while watching the graphs update in the Video Scopes tab, just as you would while adjusting one of the color correction filters. See HSB Color Space.

Using the Colors Panel

When you click on the color swatch of any Color control, the Mac OS X Colors panel appears.

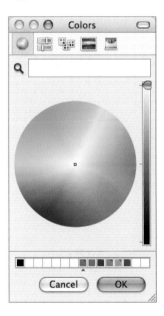

The Colors panel provides many, many different methods of choosing and saving colors. After you've chosen a color, clicking OK populates the originating Final Cut Pro Color control with the color you selected.

Magnifying Glass

The magnifying glass, which appears to the left of the current color swatch in each of the available color selection modes, works identically to the eyedropper tool in most applications. You simply click it, then click on the color you want to sample, and it appears in the current color swatch. This tool, however, lets you pick a color from anywhere on your computer display: the Finder, images displayed in preview, or in other image editing applications that are open, even the Final Cut Pro interface. Any color that appears on your computer monitors can be sampled with the magnifying glass. Once sampled, the color appears in the current color swatch.

Color Wheel

By default, the Colors panel appears showing the color wheel (with a significantly different orientation than the color wheels displayed by the color balance controls in Final Cut Pro) and its accompanying Brightness slider. This is actually a graphical representation of the HSB color model, with hue controlled by the selection handle's radius around the circle, saturation controlled by the handle's distance from the center, and brightness controlled by the separate Brightness slider to the right.

Sliders

If you need to choose a color with numerical precision, copy a color value from another application, or if you simply like the slider interface for choosing a color using different color space models, then Slider mode is the mode for you. It is particularly useful if your client has provided a very specific set of color values for a title or graphical element. No matter which color model you use to choose a color, the values will be translated into H, S, and B values when you get back to the Final Cut Pro interface.

▶ The Gray Scale slider provides a single slider that lets you choose a level of gray. Four swatches below it let you choose in 25 percent increments, and a number field to the left of the slider lets you manually enter a percentage.

▶ The RGB sliders provide both sliders and number fields for mixing red, green, and blue together to choose a color.

▶ The CMYK sliders provide both sliders and number fields for mixing cyan, magenta, yellow, and black together to create a color, which is based on the popular print model of color mixing.

▶ The HSB sliders provide both sliders and number fields for mixing hue, saturation, and brightness values to choose a color.

Color Lists

The Color Lists mode lets you use and create custom lists of colors, which is a good way to keep collections of custom colors that you use for different client's projects.

Each list consists of a scrollable collection of named color swatches. The List pop-up menu is populated by default with six premade lists of colors (Apple, Developer,

Crayons, and Web Safe Colors). Of these, one of the more notable is the list of Web-safe colors, identified by the hexadecimal code for each. A search field underneath the list lets you jump to a specific color based on its name.

You can also create your own lists:

1   Choose New from the List pop-up menu.

2   To add colors to the new blank list, either drag a color from the current color swatch into the list itself, or drag a swatch from the swatch panel at the bottom into the list.

3   To rename the new color, click it in the list, choose Rename from the Color pop-up menu underneath the list, and then type a new name into the sheet that drops down.

4   To delete a color from the list, click it, and choose Remove from the Color pop-up menu.

5   To rename your new list, choose Rename from the List pop-up menu.

The resulting list is now available from the List pop-up menu.

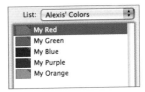

Image

The Image color picker mode lets you choose colors from a color range provided by a graphic. The default picker is a full-spectrum swatch.

You can also import an image of your own, such as a client's logo, to use as a picker when you need to match existing colors. In fact, you can import and store as many images as you like to use as palettes for future use.

To import an image to use as a color picker:

1   Create a square image file, then choose New From File from the Palette pop-up menu. (Alternately, copy a square region from any image editing application, open the Colors panel, and choose New From Pasteboard from the Palette pop-up menu.)

    No matter what the original size of your image was, it is resized to fit within the picker area. If you import a nonsquare image, it is distorted to fit.

2   To rename your new color picker, choose Rename from the Palette pop-up menu.

You can save images of actors for flesh-tone reference, pictures of skies and sunsets for creating gradients for sky reinforcement and replacement, and different types of natural images from which to grab color values for creating vignettes and overlays.

Crayons

The Crayons color picker is a whimsical interface that's always good for getting a laugh out of the client while working on an effect at the end of the day.

Swatch Panel

You can save frequently used colors for future use in the Swatch panel. By default, a single row of empty swatches appears underneath the color picker area; drag the handle underneath to reveal additional swatches.

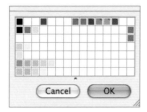

To save a color as a swatch, simply drag it from the current color swatch into any color swatch square. To choose a color swatch, click it, and that color populates the current color swatch at the top.

This is a good place to store colors for a program that uses a particular color scheme for titles, or if you have a collection of warming and cooling colors that you regularly use for creating tints.

An added benefit of storing colors in the Swatch panel is that those colors become available to any application that uses the Colors panel.

Color Encoding Standards

OVERVIEW ▶ Discussion of Final Cut Pro's adherence to the ITU-R BT.601 and 709 color coding standards, as well as the conversion of Y'CbCr clips to the RGB color space.

SEE ALSO ▶ chroma, luma

Color Standards

This entry covers some background information about how color is encoded in 8- and 10-bit Y'CbCr and RGB digital video files, and how data is converted from one color space to another. Although there are no direct controls for these settings in Final Cut Pro, it will provide some perspective when you examine equipment and software specifications relating to digital video.

Digital video software and hardware must adhere to two digital video signal standards:

▶ ITU-R BT.601 is the specification for standard definition video luma and chroma encoding.

▶ ITU-R BT.709 is the high definition color encoding specification, defining the same properties for high definition video luma and chroma encoding.

NOTE ▶ ITU stands for International Telecommunications Union, the group that negotiates international agreements on broadcast issues.

Final Cut Pro's Standards Handling

Final Cut Pro supports both standards, so that whatever your video interface is set up to capture, Final Cut Pro will correctly encode the color. Furthermore, certain codecs are specifically handled with one color standard or another. For example, clips com-pressed using DV/DVCPRO 25 are handled with the Rec. 601 standard, and clips compressed using DVCPRO HD or XDCAM HD are handled with the Rec. 709 standard.

The one exception to this neat handling of video standards are the Apple Uncompressed 8- and 10-bit 4:2:2 codecs, which accommodate either standard, depending on the source. When using the Apple Uncompressed codecs, the ITU standard used is the one the clip was captured with, depending on the hardware. Typically, any clip captured using an SD frame size will be encoded using Rec. 601, and any clip encoded with an HD frame size will be encoded with Rec. 709.

Final Cut Pro keeps track of clips encoded with one standard or another, converting clips from one color space to the other as necessary whenever you edit HD clips into an SD timeline, or vice versa, properly transforming the color gamuts.

Y'CbCr Encoding vs. RGB Encoding

As covered elsewhere in this book, the conversion of image data from RGB to Y'CbCr and back again is not always a seamless one. The more you understand about the encoding standards for 8-bit, 10-bit, and RGB encoded video, however, the smoother it will be.

The main point to remember is that Y'CbCr encoded video is essentially an attempt to recreate an analog standard within the digital domain. As a result, portions of the overall digital numeric range are allocated to specific portions of the video signal as traditionally defined in analog video. RGB encoded images have no such history to maintain, and so they typically use the full digital numeric range that's available.

8-bit Numeric Encoding

The following values describe how 8-bit video clips are encoded:

- The overall 8-bit range is 0 to 255 (counting zero).
- The blacker-than-black range is 1 to 15 (unused, except for occasional noise).
- The Y (luma) signal range is 16 to 235.
- The superwhite range is 236 to 254.
- The range of each of the two color difference channels (Cb and Cr) is 16 to 240.
- No data is permissible at 0 and 255; these values are reserved.

10-bit Numeric Encoding

The following values describe how 10-bit video clips are encoded:

▶ The overall 10-bit range is 0 to 1023 (counting zero).

▶ The blacker than black range is 4 to 63 (unused, except for occasional noise).

▶ 0 to 3 is restricted to TRS sync words.

▶ The Y (luma) signal range is 64 to 940.

▶ The superwhite signal range is 941 to 1019 (1020 to 1023 is restricted to TRS sync words).

▶ The range of each of the two color difference channels (Cb and Cr) is 64 to 960.

RGB Numeric Encoding

There are two ways that RGB color may be encoded:

▶ Full range RGB encodes color from 0 to 255 (typical for desktop video software).

▶ Studio range RGB encodes color from 16 to 235 (not typical).

Internally, Photoshop, After Effects, Motion, and Shake process image data numerically using full range RGB values.

Apple Animation is a full-range codec. Some other codecs, such as the AJA Kona 10-bit RGB codec, lets you choose which range to use.

Importing RGB Files into Final Cut Pro

When you import RGB still image files or QuickTime .mov files using RGB codecs such as Animation, Final Cut Pro maps the range of RGB values between 0 and 255 to fit into the appropriate Y'CbCr color space as follows:

▶ Luma is derived from the RGB data, and 0 is mapped to the appropriate black point (8-bit value of 16 or 10-bit value of 64), and 255 to the appropriate white point (8-bit value of 235 or 10-bit value of 940 if the sequence is set to White, and an 8-bit value of 254 or 10-bit value of 1019 if the sequence is set to Super-White).

▶ The chroma components are derived from the RGB data, with 0 mapped to the appropriate 0 percent value (8-bit value of 16 or 10-bit value of 64), and 255 mapped to the appropriate 100 percent value (8-bit value of 240 or 10-bit value of 960).

▶ All other image data between 0 and 255 is scaled to fit into the appropriate range.

Importing Y'CbCr Files into RGB-Processing Applications

When you import a Y'CbCr file into an RGB-processing application such as Motion, Shake, or After Effects, 0 percent values (16 or 64) are mapped to 0, and 100 percent values (8-bit value of 235 or 10-bit value of 940) are mapped to 255.

As a result of this transformation, any luma or chroma values in the blacker-than-black or superwhite range are clipped. As a result, if you want to export a video clip with detail in the superwhite range into an RGB-processing application, legalize the clip first, exporting a self-contained, rendered version of the clip for processing in whichever compositing application you choose. That way, you control what image data is preserved and how it is preserved.

Color Temperature

OVERVIEW ▶ Explanation of the variations in lighting color that cause color casts and guidelines for manipulation.

SEE ALSO ▶ color balance controls

What Is Color Temperature?

Nearly every lighting effect dealt with in this book is a result of the differing color of light in various circumstances. Every time you correct or introduce a color cast in an image in Final Cut Pro, you're actually manipulating the color temperature of the light source.

Color temperature is one of the most important concepts for a colorist to understand because the color temperature of the lighting in any scene changes the viewer's perception of colors and whites. Despite the human eye's adaptive nature, when the color temperature of the dominant lighting is not taken into account through the use of film stocks, filtration, or white balance, a color cast will be recorded. Sometimes a color cast is desirable, as in the case of "magic hour" lighting or sunset photography. Sometimes it's not desirable, such as when recording interior scenes with incorrectly balanced or spectrally varied light sources.

Each light source that illuminates subjects recorded by film or video has its own particular color temperature, which in many cases corresponds to how hot that light source must be to emit light. Light sources can be modeled in physics as black-body radiators, which are idealized light sources that emit pure color corresponding to their temperature. The carbon rods found in some toaster ovens are approximate black-body radiators: The hotter they get, the brighter they glow, first dark orange, then progressively lighter and lighter. The carbon rods used for arc welding are so hot that they glow a bright blue-white.

Candles, light bulbs, and sunlight operate at very different temperatures, and as a result, they emit more or less energy in different parts of the visible spectrum. Thus, comparing two different light sources (such as a household lamp next to a window on a clear morning) reveals differently colored light. Consider the following image, color balanced for tungsten, which accounts for the white quality of the interior lighting. This reveals how cool the sunlight coming in through the window is, which by comparison is a vivid blue.

The color temperature of a light source is measured in degrees Kelvin, named after William Thompson, also known as Lord Kelvin, the Scottish physicist who first proposed a scale for absolute temperature measurement. Consider how this scale matches to light sources and other illuminant standards. It's not a coincidence that the color gradient from 1600K to 10000K matches the progression in the quality of sunlight from sunrise to bright, noon-time sunlight.

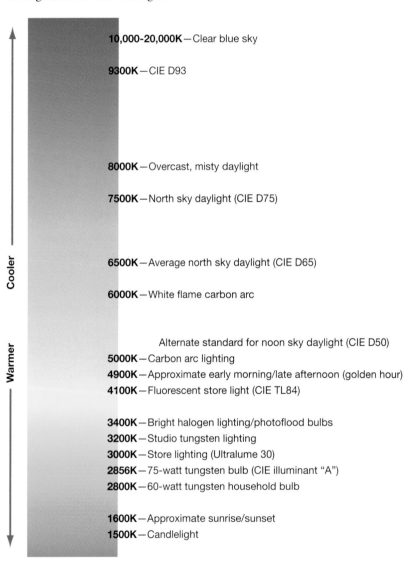

10,000-20,000K—Clear blue sky

9300K—CIE D93

8000K—Overcast, misty daylight

7500K—North sky daylight (CIE D75)

6500K—Average north sky daylight (CIE D65)

6000K—White flame carbon arc

Alternate standard for noon sky daylight (CIE D50)
5000K—Carbon arc lighting
4900K—Approximate early morning/late afternoon (golden hour)
4100K—Fluorescent store light (CIE TL84)

3400K—Bright halogen lighting/photoflood bulbs
3200K—Studio tungsten lighting
3000K—Store lighting (Ultralume 30)
2856K—75-watt tungsten bulb (CIE illuminant "A")
2800K—60-watt tungsten household bulb

1600K—Approximate sunrise/sunset
1500K—Candlelight

Cooler

Warmer

"D" Illuminants and D65

A second color temperature standard you may hear mentioned describes the so-called "D" illuminants (also listed on the preceding chart), which are defined by the Commission Internationale de l'Eclairage (CIE). The CIE defined standard illuminant graphs to describe the spectral distribution of different types of lighting. The "D" illuminants are all intended to describe daylight color temperatures, so that manufacturers of lighting fixtures can standardize their products.

Each of the CIE illuminants was developed for a specific purpose. Some are meant to be used as lighting for critical color evaluation; others are meant for use in commercial lighting.

One illuminant you should memorize is D65 (corresponding to 6500K), which is the North American and European standard for noon-time daylight. This is also the standard setting for white that broadcast video monitors use in the United States and in Europe, and is the type of ambient lighting you should employ in your color correction suite. Inconsistent lighting in your environment will cause your eyes to adapt incorrectly to the colors on your monitor, resulting in bad color decisions.

> **NOTE ▶** Incidentally, the native white point used by computer displays in Mac OS X also defaults to D65.

Broadcast monitors in China, Japan, and Korea are balanced to D93, or 9300K, which is a significantly bluer white. This should be paired with matching D93 ambient lighting.

Spectrally Varied Light Sources

The simple color temperature measurements shown on the lighting chart are good for describing light quality in general terms, and for standardizing film stocks, filter types, and camcorder white balance controls. However, the spectral distribution of real-world light sources isn't so perfect. Different light sources have unique spectral distributions that may include numerous spikes and dips.

A good example of a spectrally varied light source is fluorescent lighting, which has spikes in its spectral distribution that can illuminate other colors differently than you might expect. An average office fluorescent tube has small but significant spikes in the green and indigo-blue portions of the spectrum which, while appearing perfectly white to the human eye, may lend a greenish/blue cast to unfiltered film and improperly white-balanced videotape. For example, the image on the left is incorrectly balanced for tungsten, and the fluorescent lighting lends a greenish cast to the image (especially visible in the gray doors). The image on the right is properly white balanced.

Generalizing about the light given off by fluorescent tubes is difficult because there are many different designs, all of which have been formulated to give off different qualities of light. Some fluorescent tubes have been specially designed to eliminate these spectral inconsistencies and produce pure light.

Another spectrally varied light source is the sodium vapor lamps used in municipal street lights, which give a severe yellow/orange cast to an image.

Other spectrally varied light sources include mercury vapor lamps, which lend an intense off-red tint to shots, and metal halide lamps, which can give off either magenta or blue/green casts.

With a shot that has one of these intensely red/orange light sources as the primary source of illumination, you'll be surprised at how much of a correction you can make, assuming that the main subjects of the shot are people. Because these light sources have a strong red component, you can generally bring back relatively normal-looking skin tones. Unfortunately, other colors won't fare so well, so cars, buildings, and other colorful exterior objects may be troublesome.

Recognizing Improper Color Balances

Frequently, a tungsten-lit scene will look orange when you're using film stock that is balanced for daylight or a videocamera with its white balance set to daylight.

Aside from the obvious color cast, orange light from incandescent fixtures may lend an inadvertently theatrical look, owing to the viewer's association with artificial lighting. For example, the image on the left is incorrectly balanced for daylight, and the tungsten lighting lends a warm, orange cast to it. The image on the right is properly white balanced, with whiter highlights and truer colors throughout the scene (note the blue sunlight spill in the foreground).

Similarly, a daylight scene shot using tungsten-balanced film stock or a videocamera with its white balance set to tungsten/indoors will look bluish. If the filmmaker was not intending to portray a cold winter day, this is clearly a shot that would benefit from correction. Compare the image on left, which is incorrectly balanced for tungsten, to the properly white-balanced image on the right.

Correcting Color Casts

In any of these cases, there are two ways you can make corrections. The automatic method is to use the Select Auto-balance Color controls to identify a region of the picture that's supposed to be pure, unsaturated white, black, or gray.

Automatic Color Balancing

Once you've identified which part of the image's tonal range a color cast belongs to, you simply click the appropriate Select Auto-balance Color control, then use the eyedropper to click a feature that's supposed to be a clean, neutral white, black, or gray in your picture, and the corresponding auto-balance control is automatically adjusted.

> **NOTE ▶** Truly neutral grays are the most difficult features to find in a typical clip, so you'll want to be careful. If you don't click a feature of the midtones that's truly gray, you will introduce a completely different kind of color cast to the image.

The automatic method of color balancing is quick to use in instances where you're having a difficult time identifying the exact nature of the color cast. It can also give you a solid starting point for further manual adjustments to a particular color balance control.

Manual Color Balancing

The manual method, which is ultimately more flexible (especially if you're not planning on making a completely neutral correction), is to drag the color balance controls for the whites, blacks, and mids by hand, usually by dragging the color balance control in the direction of the color that's complementary to that of the unwanted color cast.

In the following cityscape, the lighting is obviously too blue. A look at the Parade scope predictably shows that the blue channel is far too strong. However, a closer look at the distribution of the blue channel from the shadows to the highlights indicates that not only are the colors in the whites unbalanced, but the color in the midtones is unbalanced as well, and the color in the blacks seems to line up OK.

To correct this bluish color cast, pull the Whites and Mids color balance controls towards a yellow/orange split (the complementary of the blue/cyan color cast), keeping one eye on the distribution of each color channel in the Parade scope, and the other on the image in the monitor, until you achieve the desired color balance for the clip.

The beauty of manual color balancing is that you can correct an overzealous color cast as aggressively or as gently as possible, making a deliberate choice whether to neutralize it completely, preserve part of it, or introduce a completely different one of your own.

Color Balance as a Visual Cue

You're not always going to want to correct for color casts. Color temperature can be used as an audience cue for conveying the time of day, or for the environment in which the subjects find themselves. For example, audiences fully expect a candlelit scene to be extremely warm.

You can play off of the audience's stereotypes of color temperature to change the perceived time of day, or the type of location, by deliberately throwing off the white balance and introducing a deliberate color cast.

Color casts are also used to introduce mood to a scene. How many times have you heard lighting referred to as "cool" or "warm?" In general, this is the easiest way to discuss the quality of light because it embodies the entire range of lighting we experience in our everyday lives, from the extreme warmth of tungsten bulbs to the extreme cool of overcast sunlight. It's not surprising that these descriptions also tend to dramatize light quality, with warm lighting tending towards the romantic (sunsets, candlelight), and cold lighting signifying discomfort (rainy, overcast days have *literally* cold lighting).

These, of course, are huge generalizations, and it's also fun to play lighting against type (cool lighting quality for a hot exterior shot), but it's good to develop a conscious rationale for your use of color temperature as you develop the visual vocabulary of your program.

Complementary Colors

OVERVIEW ▶ Colors that are opposite one another on the color wheel.

SEE ALSO ▶ color balance controls

What Are Complementary Colors?

Complementary colors are those that are opposite of one another on the color wheel.

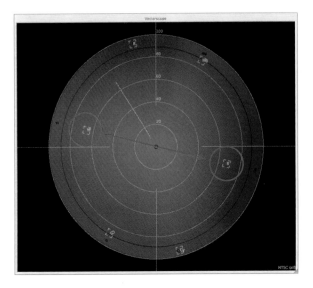

In an additive color display system such as video, combining two complementary colors results in a neutral gray.

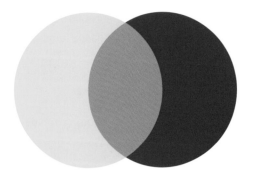

This phenomenon is what makes it possible to selectively eliminate color casts from images using the color balance controls. Drag a color balance control towards the color that's complementary to the color cast in the image, and you'll be able to neutralize it.

See Color Balance Controls.

Contrast Adjustments

> **OVERVIEW** ▶ The process of altering the highlights, shadows, and midtones of your images to fine-tune their contrast.

> **SEE ALSO** ▶ contrast and perception

The Importance of Contrast Adjustments

One of the most fundamental ways you can alter and improve video images is by manipulating the contrast between the darkest and brightest areas of the picture. Indeed, even well-exposed images benefit greatly from minor tweaks to maximize the contrast ratio, readjust the midtones, and balance different angles of coverage within a scene.

In other cases, DoPs and telecine operators may record video with deliberately compressed contrast. This means that the blacks may be well above 0 percent and the whites below 100 percent. This is done to guarantee maximum flexibility during color grading, as well as to avoid accidental overexposure and underexposure that would eliminate detail from the image.

By making simple adjustments with the Color Corrector filter's contrast sliders, you can do the following:

▶   Legalize superwhite areas of the picture with the Whites slider.

▶   Deepen muddy blacks with the Blacks slider.

▶   Brighten underexposed clips with the Mids and Whites sliders.

▶   Change the apparent time of day with the Mids slider.

▶   Improve overall image definition by expanding contrast with the Blacks, Mids, and Whites sliders together.

Contrast Affects the Color Balance Controls

The distribution of the Luma component of a clip influences which portions of the image are affected by the Blacks, Mids, and Whites color balance controls. For example, if no areas of the image are above 60 percent in the Waveform Monitor or Histogram, then the Whites color balance control won't have much of an effect. For this reason, you should always adjust a clip's contrast first, *before* correcting its color. Otherwise, you may find yourself wasting time going back and forth, making constant readjustments.

Using the Contrast Sliders

The three contrast sliders in Final Cut Pro's Color Corrector filters let you make independent adjustments:

▶ The Blacks slider (on other equipment and software, this might be called Setup when controlling a digital percentage, or Pedestal when controlling IRE) raises and lowers the black level—the darkest part of the picture. This corresponds to the left side of the histogram's graph or the bottom of the Waveform Monitor's graph.

▶ The Mids slider (sometimes referred to as a gamma function) lets you change the distribution of midtones, darkening or lightening the portions of the image that fall between the black and white levels.

▶ The Whites slider (sometimes called Picture) raises and lowers the white level—the brightest part of the picture—relative to the black level. This corresponds to the right side of the histogram's graph or the top of the Waveform Monitor's graph.

Manipulating these three controls lets you expand, compress, and redistribute the Luma component of your clips in different ways. As you make your adjustments, the Waveform Monitor and Histogram dynamically update to show how the image is being affected.

When adjusting the contrast of an image, keep in mind that the three controls interact with one another:

▶ Adjustments to the Blacks slider also affect the mids and whites (although it may take a large adjustment for this to be noticeable). For this reason, make any necessary blacks adjustments first.

- ▶ Adjustments to the Mids slider leave the black level pinned in place but change the white level, depending on the magnitude of the adjustment.
- ▶ Adjustments to the Whites slider affect the mids distribution.
- ▶ Neither the Mids nor the Whites sliders affect the black level.

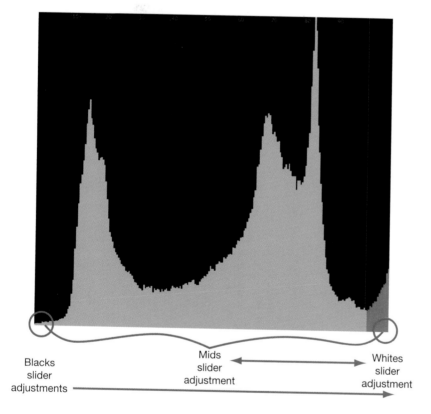

Blacks
slider
adjustments

Mids
slider
adjustment

Whites
slider
adjustment

These controls should be instantly recognizable to those of you who are familiar with the Levels controls in programs like Photoshop, and in fact they're very similar.

Expanding Contrast

Within the boundaries of broadcast legality, one of the most general guidelines for adjusting contrast is that the audience should be able to distinguish the most important subjects within the frame.

Aside from that, increases or decreases to the contrast ratio in your clips will be dictated by the content of your program, and by the look the DoP, director, and you are trying to achieve. Whatever your goals, keep in mind that maximizing the contrast of your images, whenever appropriate, gives them more "punch" (descriptors vary from client to client), resulting in a more vivid image for reasons described in Contrast and Perception.

In some images, it's appropriate to park an expanse of highlights at 90 to 100 percent, and all of the shadows down around 0 percent. In other images, a few pixels of highlights at the top of the range, and a few pixels of shadows at or near 0, are all it takes to give a bit more life to your image.

In general, contrast is expanded by lowering the blacks, raising the whites, and adjusting the mids to taste. In this example, you'll adjust the contrast of a typical on-location clip to enhance its look:

1   Open the *01 Expanding Contrast* sequence, located in the Contrast Adjustments bin of the **Color Correction Exercises** project.

2   Apply a Color Corrector 3-Way filter to the first clip in the sequence. (The second clip is the finished correction, provided for comparison.) Open the clip into the Viewer, and click the Color Corrector tab to expose the graphical controls.

A casual look at the image on your broadcast monitor reveals a generally well-exposed image, with a relatively full range of tonality. Take a moment to examine the uncorrected clip using the video scopes. The Histogram, in particular, shows an excellent profile of the clip's contrast.

In this particular clip, there are very few pixels under 10 percent, and most of those are probably just noise. At the other end of the scale, there are very few pixels above 94 percent, and those are probably also mainly video noise. Even though you don't have to, there's room to lower the black point and raise the white point in order to expand the image to the full 0 to 100 percent range.

3   Drag the Blacks slider to the left until the left edge of the Histogram just touches 0 percent.

Watch the image on your broadcast monitor as you make this adjustment to make sure the dark portions of the picture aren't becoming too dark. (No matter what the scopes tell you, the image should look good on a calibrated monitor within a suitable viewing environment.)

4   Drag the Whites slider to the right until the very tip of the average highlights in the Histogram touches 100 percent.

With this adjustment, a few pixels get pushed above 100 percent. For purposes of this exercise, assume those will get compressed by a later application of the Broadcast Safe filter.

If you look at the broadcast display, you can see that this seemingly small change makes a significant difference to the quality of the image, analogous to wiping a film of dust off of the image. That's the magic of contrast expansion.

Another look at the Histogram reveals gaps that have formed in the graph.

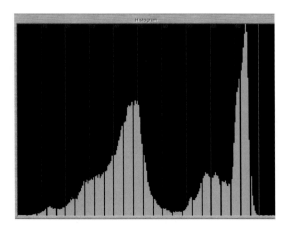

These gaps appear because you took a limited amount of image data and stretched it out to fit a greater tonal range, and they serve as a reminder that you can't get something for nothing. Most clips look perfectly fine with limited contrast expansions, but major contrast expansions can create problems due to a lack of image data. In any event, don't worry about these gaps, the image on your monitor is what's really important.

Next, you'll enhance the early-morning feel of this clip by adjusting the mids.

5   Drag the Mids slider to the left to slightly darken the midtones of the image. After you've made this change, notice how the whites are also lowered. Drag the whites slider a bit more to the right to put them back where they were.

> **NOTE** ▶ Contrast adjustments are often subtle, especially when you're working with an experienced DoP's carefully exposed footage. Whenever possible, avoid making assumptions; ask the DoP what the intended look for the footage is supposed to be.

The result should be a more vivid image, with good definition, strong shadow detail, and healthy highlights resulting from the image using the maximum broadcast legal dynamic range.

Expanding the Contrast of Underexposed Clips

The process of maximizing image contrast isn't always beer and skittles. Underexposed clips are the ultimate examples of images in which you desperately *need* to maximize contrast, but where tradeoffs in image quality become inevitable.

Past a certain point, expanding image contrast increases noise and/or grain, as well as reducing the perceived saturation.

This exercise shows the consequences of expanding the contrast of underexposed clips:

1   Open the *02 Dealing With Underexposure* sequence, located in the Contrast Adjustments bin of the **Color Correction Exercises** project.

2   Apply a Color Corrector 3-Way filter to the first clip in the sequence. (The second clip is the finished correction, provided for comparison.) Open the clip into the Viewer, and click the Color Corrector tab to expose the graphical controls.

NOTE ▶ If you're viewing this project on an external broadcast monitor, switch the monitor to 16:9 (if it is so capable). This is an anamorphic project.

This is a clearly underexposed shot, with crushed blacks, midtones that don't extend much past 30 percent, and highlights that barely reach 37 percent. The image itself is dim, and it's hard to make out the subjects.

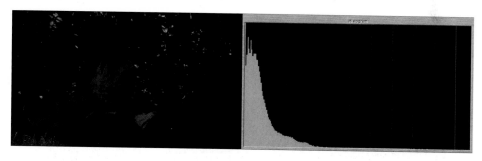

To make the task even more fun, the director wants to match this clip to a scene that's lit in noonday sun, so you're definitely going to have to brighten up this image.

3   Drag the Mids slider to the right to stretch the mids out towards the brighter end of the scale.

As you make this adjustment, keep your eye on the image in your monitor. When the highlights start to flatten out, and the image starts to look solarized, back off of the change until the picture looks bright, but more or less natural.

Because the image was so underexposed, a mids adjustment is appropriate to push these values higher. Additionally, boosting underexposed clips by raising the mids, instead of raising the whites, can minimize the exaggeration of video noise that's discussed later on in this exercise.

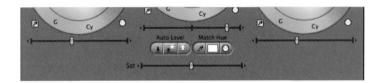

One thing you should immediately notice is that the saturation of the image, which seemed richer when the image was darker, now appears washed out. The saturation itself hasn't been reduced; instead, the act of stretching the contrast has reduced the apparent contrast relative to the brightened image. This effect is typical, although generally more subtle, and it can be hard to pin down if you don't know to look for it.

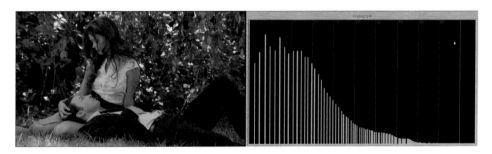

4   Raise the saturation of the image to add some richness to the colors.

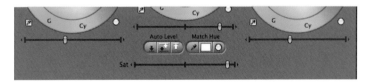

The fix is pretty simple, and the result looks quite nice. However, one problem that was introduced by the stretching of contrast isn't apparent until you play the clip.

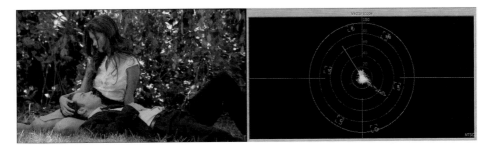

5   Play the clip, and look carefully at details in the image.

You should notice exaggerated video noise appearing over the clip, especially in darker areas of the picture.

This scenario is also typical, with more noise appearing the farther you're forced to stretch the contrast of a given clip. The exaggeration of video noise isn't just limited to clips with extreme adjustments; it also appears, surprisingly, with some clips that you're adjusting only moderately, depending on the amount of noise in the source footage.

Contrast Adjustments and Noise

Video noise is one of the biggest problems you'll face when making contrast adjustments. Some video cameras are noisier than others and respond to varying light levels differently. You'll find that every scene you work on will have different tolerances for contrast expansion, so it's important to be aware of this issue, and always play a bit of the clips you're adjusting before you move on—otherwise you might miss spotting a potential problem.

When confronted with exaggerated noise, you can try various noise-reducing techniques (see Video Noise (Supressing)). If you made the adjustment by boosting the whites, you might try a different balance of mids and whites adjustments to make the same correction.

More often than not, you'll find yourself splitting the difference between the corrected and uncorrected contrast ratios, in an effort to find a reasonable middle ground, and possibly adding noise to other clips in the scene to even out the overall look (see Video Noise (Matching)). This is one of the biggest problems associated with underexposed footage—and one of the toughest to solve.

Compressing Contrast

If you're trying to match clips shot and balanced for dusk, nighttime, or any location with faded blacks and weak highlights, or if you're creating a low-contrast look, you can also deliberately compress the contrast.

You can lower contrast in several ways. You can lower the white level while raising the mids to reduce contrast in the highlights. If you're really going for it, you can also opt to raise the black level, although you should do this with care.

In this example, you'll compress the contrast of a clip to create a faded dusk look:

1 Open the *03 Compressing Contrast* sequence, located in the Contrast Adjustments bin of the **Color Correction Exercises** project.

2 Apply a Color Corrector 3-Way filter to the first clip in the sequence. (The second clip is the finished correction, provided for comparison.) Open the clip into the Viewer, and click the Color Corrector tab to expose the graphical controls.

The clip has a wide contrast ratio to begin with, with highlights extending into the superwhite range, and blacks that extend all the way to 0 percent (most likely the clothes and car to the right). You'll begin creating the desired look by compressing the overall contrast ratio of the clip.

3   Raise the Blacks to lighten the darkest areas of the picture, but not so much that they're visibly faded relative to the expanse of pavement at the bottom of the picture (around 10 percent). Then, lower the highlights so that the brightest parts of the image become a subdued, but still bright, silver.

4   To finish the look, lower the mids slightly in order to give a bit more emphasis to the darker parts of the picture.

As discussed in Contrast and Perception, the brightness of the lightest tone in an image is relative to the darkest tone, and vice versa. Even though you're reducing the overall contrast ratio, you're not necessarily flattening out the entire image, so long as there is enough of a spread between the darkest and lightest values in the picture.

At this point, you need to adjust the color of the image to create the final silvery, muted look.

5   Because the image is all midtones now, drag the Mids color balance control towards blue until you just neutralize the yellows from the image.

You don't want to make the image blue, just cool it off.

6   Reduce the saturation to mute, but not eliminate, the overall color.

The result is a silvery tone across the entire tonal range of the image.

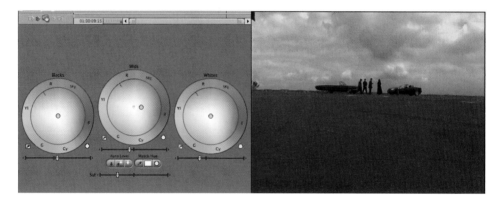

Take Care When Raising the Black Level

Raising the black level works best when the blacks aren't crushed to begin with, and have a lot of detail that will emerge from such an adjustment. If there were large areas of black in the original image, raising the black level creates flat gray areas that won't look particularly good.

Raising the black area can also result in unexpected color appearing in the shadows of the image, which may creep in from a mids adjustment. Such problems may not be apparent until you see the video on a display that's inappropriately bright, at which point it may be too late. If you do catch a problem like this, you might try using the Desaturate Lows filter to remove some of the color in the shadows.

Controlling Contrast Within a Specific Range

One of many nice things about Final Cut Pro's Limit Effect controls is that you can isolate a specific portion of an image's tonal range and manipulate the contrast in just that area. Other applications allow this sort of operation with a curves interface. Final Cut Pro lacks curves, but you can attain a semblance of this functionality, if somewhat indirectly.

This is a powerful technique, but make sure you don't overdo such corrections or you'll solarize the image (creating lighter areas where they should be darker, and vice versa, for an early '80s music video look).

In this example, you'll make a low-contrast adjustment to the background of the picture, but you'll use the Limit Effect controls to boost the contrast of a man in the foreground:

1   Open the *04 Secondary Contrast Manipulation* sequence, located in the Contrast Adjustments bin of the **Color Correction Exercises** project.

   The first clip already has a Color Corrector filter applied to it. (The second clip is the finished correction, provided for comparison.) This initial correction lightened the midtones to bring some detail out of the shadows, reduced the highlights a bit, removed some of the orange from the midtones, and lowered the saturation. The result is ideal for the background, but the client wants the man in the foreground to stand out a bit more.

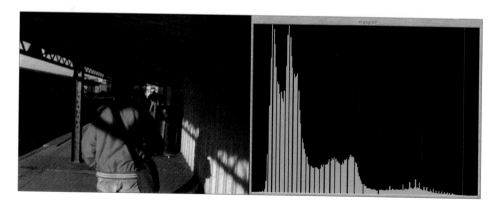

2   Add a second Color Corrector 3-Way filter to the first clip, then click the Color Corrector 3-Way - 2 tab, and open the Limit Effect controls.

3   Isolating the red jacket is pretty straightforward. Click the limit effect eyedropper, then click a middle value of red somewhere on the jacket in the Canvas.

The Hue, Sat, and Luma controls are all automatically set to that value, which serves as a starting point for further adjustments.

4   To see what you're doing as you widen the secondary key, set the View Final/Matte/ Source button to Matte (a black key against a white background). The portion of the image you're isolating will now appear as a white key against black. Drag the Luma, Sat, and Hue handles to isolate the jacket, while excluding as much of the background as possible. Adjust the top handles to isolate the base values, and then adjust the bottom handles to keep the selection narrow, but keep a small falloff around the edges of the key.

5   Drag the Softening slider to the right to soften the key, blurring the edges and preventing any buzz or chattering.

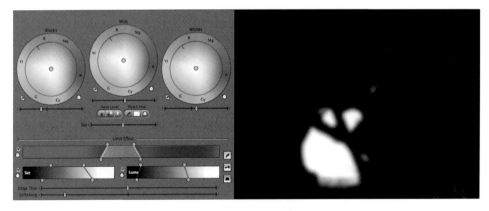

The second Color Corrector 3-Way filter with the Limit Effect settings adjusted in step 4, and the contrast adjustments from step 6.

6   Once you've isolated the brightest highlights, set the View Final/Matte/Source button to Final (a red key on a gray background). Lower the blacks and raise the whites and mids to intensify the contrast of the shadows and highlights within the jacket, but not so much so that the jacket looks odd.

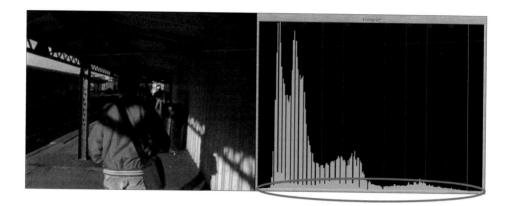

When you've finished, you can see the result of your change at the bottom of the Histogram graph. A second contour is just visible running along the bottom, within the contour of the overall image shape.

What Should My White Level Be?

Where, exactly, the white level in your video should lie is partially a matter of preference, dictated by the look you're going for and the nature of the highlights in the image. If you're going for a high-key, high-contrast image, parking your highlights at 100 percent digital is probably a good bet. On the other hand, if you're adjusting for a low-key, low-contrast look, there's no reason not to keep your highlights down at 80, 70, or even 60 percent, depending on the image.

The type of highlights has a lot to do with where you'll park them. Sun glints, reflections, a lit candle, or the sun itself should probably sit at or near the top end of the scale, otherwise you risk having these highly exposed details look dingy. For example, in this image, the highlights reflecting off of the chrome are uniformly bright and partially overexposed, and they should probably remain at the maximum exposure level.

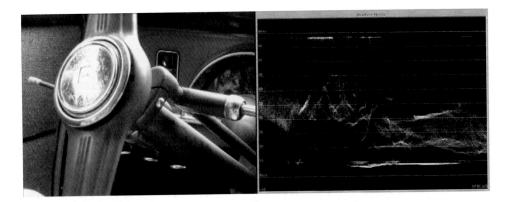

Other highlights, however, such as lit fog or smoke, white clouds, direct light falling on a white wall, or bright highlights in other features in the picture may well belong to the midtones of the image, even if there aren't any brighter highlights in the image. Consider the following image; the clouds, while sunlit, don't have to be at the maximum white level to render nicely. Lowering the blacks helps maintain healthy contrast.

Just remember that the audience's perceptions of your highlights are going to be relative to the depth of the shadows in the image. Sometimes, you'll get more results from lowering the blacks and leaving the whites alone than you will from adjusting the whites alone. The contrast in an image is entirely relative.

Also, you should make a distinction between the average highlights in an image and the peak highlights in the image. With the very brightest peak highlights sitting at the maximum level, the average highlights can and should be lower, unless you're going for a deliberately overexposed look. Here, the sun is typically overexposed, with peaks extending far above the average brightness of the highlights (seen by the bunching near the top of the waveform graph).

Choosing a Maximum White Level

Even the maximum white level you choose can vary. Technically, you should never output whites brighter than 100 percent digital or 100 IRE analog. However, some broadcasters have QC guidelines that are so strict that you may want to employ a self-imposed maximum white level of 95 percent, just to be on the safe side. You could always rely upon the Broadcast Safe filter to compress the highlights in a later step, but manually adjusting for a conservative maximum white level gives you that much more control over how the picture is processed.

Besides, letting the Broadcast Safe filter compress the highlights can result in the loss of highlight detail, which may or may not be important to you. Sometimes losing highlight detail may be desirable with a certain amount of edge feathering, such as when simulating film's tendency to softly bloom when overexposed (see Glows, Blooms, and Gauze Looks). But without edge feathering, video overexposure is generally unduly harsh, with a tendency to alias.

Maintaining Mids Levels When Legalizing Whites

You'll find yourself constantly lowering the whites of clips that were recorded on consumer or prosumer videocameras, to legalize the inevitable superwhite values that they capture. Although this is a fairly straightforward process, after the fifteenth clip in a row you may find yourself really wanting to use the Color Corrector filter's Auto Level controls.

There's nothing wrong with these controls, and they can be a real convenience if you only need to adjust the blacks and whites. Keep in mind, however, that they make their corrections based on every single light and dark pixel in the entire image. If your average brightness is at 80 percent, but there are three pixels at 108 percent, the Auto Level controls will *lower* the whites in order to legalize the clip, which darkens the midtones, too. Chances are this isn't what you wanted to do.

If all you do to correct the superwhite values in your clips is to lower the Whites slider, you're going to subtly darken the midtones, as well. A more precise correction is to immediately boost the mids a few points after pulling down the whites to compensate for this effect. This, in turn, moves the white level back up a bit, so you'll push and pull until the highlights and midtones are where you want them to be.

Don't let the midtones of your clips be held hostage by such specular highlights as sunglints and reflections. Highlights will pop up in the tiniest details, and can sometimes appear as a two-pixel twinkle in an actor's eye. Although it's important to legalize these errant pixels, you don't want to avoid making other adjustments to otherwise brighten and improve your image.

In this exercise, you'll adjust the highlights and the midtones together to brighten the image, while legalizing the whites:

1   Open the *05 Dealing with Highlights* sequence, located in the Contrast Adjustments bin of the **Color Correction Exercises** project.

2   Apply a Color Corrector 3-Way filter to the first clip in the sequence. (The second clip is the finished correction, provided for comparison.) Open the clip into the Viewer, and click the Color Corrector tab to expose the graphical controls.

   NOTE ▶ If you're viewing this project on an external broadcast monitor, switch the monitor to 16:9 (if it is so capable). This is an anamorphic project.

This is dark shot that nonetheless has numerous specular highlights (reflecting off of the car) that extend into the superwhite range. First, you'll see what happens if you try using the Auto Level controls to deal with these superwhite levels.

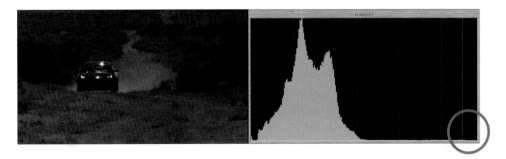

3 Click the Auto White Level control.

You should immediately see that the highlights have been legalized, but the overall image has been darkened. This is not what you wanted to happen.

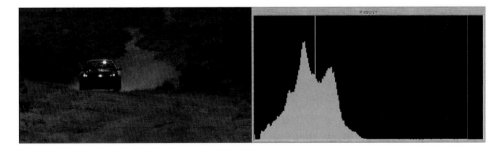

4 Shift-click any of the Color Corrector's reset buttons to reset the entire filter. Begin the correction manually by raising the mids to brighten the image.

The client wants the look of a slightly overcast day, so stop the correction before it becomes too bright.

This correction brightens the image, but it only serves to make the highlights brighter, which you don't want to happen.

5   Lower the Whites slider until the superwhite values fall just under 100 percent. This darkens the midtones of the image slightly, so raise the Mids slider a very small amount to put the mids back where they were. This may, in turn, require an even smaller adjustment to the Whites slider to lower the highlights back to 100 percent.

When you finish adjusting the contrast, you should notice that the saturation of the image seems subdued.

6   Raise the saturation to make the colors a bit more vivid.

The resulting image now has appropriately brighter contrast, a broadcast legal white level, and healthy color.

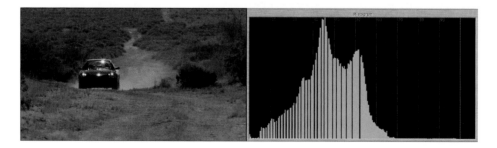

What Should My Black Level Be?

Unlike the white level, which is open to interpretation, the lowest black level you can set in Final Cut Pro is simple: 0 percent. For purposes of color correction, you can completely ignore analog NTSC video output formats that require a black signal level of 7.5 IRE, because that is an analog issue that your video output interface takes care of (when properly configured). As far as you're concerned as a Final Cut Pro colorist, the lowest tone of absolute black on the scale is 0 percent, period.

Deep shadows usually fall into the bottom 15 percent of the digital scale, with lighter shadows creeping farther up into the bottom half of the mids. As always, how dark the shadows appear to be is entirely relative to the brightest highlights in the picture, but generally speaking, deepening the shadows tends to have a bigger visual impact. A well-exposed image will have a range of shadow detail, with the bottom just touching 0 percent, if at all.

One of the biggest things you can do to impress almost any client is to lower the Blacks slider to deepen the shadows in an image. Even lowering the blacks by a few percent can give an image snap that it didn't previously have, and viewers love it.

You might ask why this is the case, even with well-exposed footage. It turns out that many videocameras record a black level that's not quite at 0 percent. The following image shows the waveform of a segment of pure black video, recorded with the lens cap on (using the Sony HDR-HC1 camcorder).

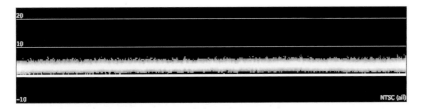

Waveform brightness exaggerated for print.

This experiment reveals two things. First, that the average black level is centered at approximately 3 percent. Second, it shows just how much random noise the recorded signal contains. As you can see, even prerecorded black can benefit from being deepened.

How Low Should I Make My Black Level?

How much you adjust the blacks depends entirely on how dark the shadows are in the original image. Well-exposed images may not have blacks that extend all the way to the bottom of the scale, giving you room to deepen them, or not, as the look you're trying to achieve dictates.

If an image already has healthy shadows, there may be no need to adjust them. The following image has extremely healthy shadows, with the black level itself sitting squarely at 0 percent:

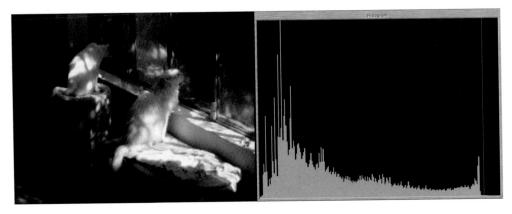

The next image, on the other hand, has plenty of room to deepen the shadows, if you wanted to. The shadows in this image bottom out at 4 percent, extending far into the mid-range of the image.

Crushing Blacks

Once you've lowered the darkest parts of your picture to 0 percent, that's pitch black, as dark as the shadows can go. However, that doesn't stop you from continuing to lower the Blacks slider to move more of the shadows in the image down towards 0 percent. Moving lighter areas of shadow down to 0 percent is referred to as *crushing* the blacks. This is most easily seen in the Waveform Monitor graph as the pixels of shadow start clumping up at the bottom.

Crushing the blacks is an easy way to jack up the perceived contrast ratio, and depending on the image, it can make it seem even "snappier," but all of this is at the expense of the loss of shadow detail. Because 0 is the lowest luma level there is, all of the pixels at 0 percent assume a uniform flat blackness. Although it's arguable whether the detail lost when crushing the blacks just a little is noticeable, if you crush the blacks too much, the shadow regions of your image will become progressively harsher, flatter, and potentially more aliased in areas of the image that make the transition from shadows to midtones.

This example shows the effects of crushing blacks in a more discernable way:

1   Open the *06 Crushing Blacks* sequence, located in the Contrast Adjustments bin of the **Color Correction Exercises** project.

The clip in the Timeline is a TIFF image where the black background is at 0 percent, and each word of the text is a couple of percent darker than the one beneath it. Because the levels used in this image are so low, you'll see the full image on a properly calibrated external broadcast display only—the Canvas probably doesn't show the top two or three words.

2   The clip already has a Color Corrector filter applied to it. Open the clip into the Viewer, and click the Color Corrector tab to expose the graphical controls.

3   Drag the Blacks control to the left.

As you lower the blacks, you'll start to see the words disappear as they merge with the black background.

This exercise also shows off the sensitivity of the contrast sliders. If you continue to lower the blacks, eventually all of the text will disappear. The detail is lost.

Try Lowering the Mids, Instead

Not every image needs to have lots of shadows down at 0 percent. The following image has only a few dark areas, and those are barely discernable:

With some shots, lowering the mids is a much more appropriate adjustment when you want to darken the shot to change the perceived time of day, whether the image looks like an interior or exterior shot, or whether the feeling of the image is bright and happy or dark and gloomy.

Although blacks and whites adjustments are very much guided by the video scopes, mids adjustments are typically eyeballed (unless you're matching a clip to another clip). There are no really firm guidelines for adjusting the mids, other than to try and make the image look right for the location and time of day, and to make sure that the clip matches the others in the scene in which it appears.

Contrast During Exhibition

There's one last important detail when dealing with black levels. Because there are so many manufacturers of videocameras, videocassette recorders, VTRs, DVD players, televisions, video projectors, and other playback and display devices, there is often confusion about the black level that any given device is set to either output or display.

Playback devices outputting analog video with one black setup level that are connected to display devices with another black setup level can cause no end of grief, either washing out or crushing the blacks unintentionally. If you're a filmmaker at a festival and this happens, it can be an excruciating experience.

Furthermore, most televisions are likely uncalibrated. If the brightness isn't adjusted correctly, the blacks may appear washed out or crushed. If the contrast isn't adjusted correctly, the overall image may be too bright or too dark.

And, if all that wasn't scary enough, many digital display devices (such as video projectors) have customizable gamma settings. Although the right gamma setting, properly matched to the environment, can maximize image quality, the wrong setting can be disastrous.

Unfortunately, the best that you, the colorist, can do in this exhibition minefield is to trust your calibrated display, give the program a test viewing on a friend's uncalibrated consumer television, and have a sit-down viewing with the client in whatever environment their audience is most likely to view the result. In this way, you're likely to catch any corrections that don't play well in those environments before wrapping up the job. It's also a good idea to warn someone who's about to march out on the film festival circuit about what can go wrong, and recommend that the filmmaker get some time before the screening to check the projection quality and make any necessary adjustments.

Contrast (Evaluating)

OVERVIEW ▶ Explanation of how to recognize and evaluate the difference between the blackest and whitest portions of an image.

SEE ALSO ▶ contrast and perception, contrast adjustments, monitor calibration

What Is Contrast?

When most people talk about contrast, they're usually trying to describe the relative amounts of light and dark in an image. Images with shadows that aren't very dark and highlights that aren't very bright are generally considered to be low-contrast.

When photographers and videographers discuss contrast, they refer to the tonal range of a photograph or video images. If you plot the entire range of tones within the luma component of the preceding image, from black to white, you'll find it's not using the entire possible range of black and white values. Instead, the tonality of the entire image lies in the middle of the scale, which gives the image its subdued appearance.

0%   100%

In this illustration, the actual black and white points from the previous image are shown in grayscale, relative to the full range of luma that's possible. As you can see, the image does not occupy the full tonal range available.

Images combining deep, dark shadows and bright highlights are considered to be high-contrast.

Plotting the range of tones in the luma channel of this image reveals that it's occupying the fullest tonal range possible. The presence of 0 percent blacks and 100 percent whites make this image more vivid.

0%   100%

In this illustration, the actual black and white points from the previous image are shown to occupy the full tonal range that's available.

Why Is Contrast Important?

Contrast describes the range and balance of tonality within an image, which is controlled by its luma component. When you adjust a clip's luma component, you change its perceived contrast, and you exert an indirect effect on the perceived color in the image, as well.

It's important to exercise careful control over the contrast of your clips to maximize image quality, keep your video signals broadcast legal, optimize the effectiveness of the Color Corrector 3-Way filter, and create the desired look of your program.

Often, you'll want to maximize the contrast found in your clips to make the images look more vivid. At other times, you'll find it necessary to lower the contrast of an image to match one clip to another that was shot at a different time or to create the impression of a particular time of day or night.

The easiest way to quantify contrast is by measuring a clip's *contrast ratio*, or the difference between the darkest and lightest pixels in that image. Your three primary tools for evaluating contrast are the Waveform Monitor, Histogram, and your broadcast monitor.

Your Environment Matters

No matter what your video scopes are telling you (so long as the signal is broadcast legal), the bottom line is that the image should look right on your monitor, so make sure that it's properly calibrated and that your room is set up for you to evaluate contrast as accurately as possible. See Monitor Calibration.

The apparent contrast that you perceive when looking at a monitor is highly dependent on the amount of light being reflected off of your monitor. Ideally, there should be no ambient light behind you to reflect off of the monitor, so you must strictly control the light in your room.

While you're controlling the light level in the room, you should also match the ambient light level of your intended audience. If you're judging contrast to be seen by an audience in a darkened theater, work in a similarly darkened environment. If you're working on a television program intended for the living room, brighter indirect ambient lighting will help you to better judge the contrast ratios that they'll be perceiving.

Finally, it's best if the surrounding color behind your monitor (the color on the wall) is a neutral gray. Make sure that it's indirectly lit such that the wall isn't forming a black frame around your monitor, because this will also distort your perception of the contrast of the image (see Contrast and Perception).

Evaluating Contrast Using the Video Scopes

Because the apparent contrast on your monitor is subject to so many variables, it's also important that you have a more objective guide as you make your adjustments, and the Waveform Monitor and Histogram are the video scopes for the job.

The Histogram is an ideal tool for evaluating the contrast of an image. It displays a graph where the brightness of every single pixel in the image is plotted against a digital scale from 0 to 110% (with 101 to 110% being the superwhite portion of the scale). An image's contrast ratio, then, can be determined by the width of the Histogram's graph, and the position and height of individual bulges in the graph make it easy to see how dense the shadows, midtones, and highlights are.

In the following image, the huge spike at the left indicates the depth and solidity of the shadows (although you should notice that there are actually very few 0% blacks right at the bottom of the scale). The bulge in the middle shows that there is a good range of values in the midtones, which taper off towards the top of the scale towards the highlights, showing that there aren't a lot of highlights in the image. One last small spike at the top of the scale represents the single biggest highlight in the picture—the sun. This is one example of an image with a high contrast ratio.

If you examine the Histogram of a low-contrast image, by comparison, the width of the graph is restricted to a far narrower portion of the scale. The following example of an underexposed image shows a huge spike in the blacks, extending all the way to 0% (perhaps indicating some crushed blacks). In other low-contrast images, the graph might be restricted to a narrow portion of the midtones, instead, but in any case it's easy to see that the Histogram's graph does not extend across the full tonal range.

You can also evaluate contrast using the Waveform Monitor, which has the advantage of making it easier to associate the features of the waveform graph with those in the originating image, so you can get a sense of which portions of the image are sitting at the bottom or top of the scale. In the Waveform Monitor, the height of the overall graph indicates the contrast ratio of the clip.

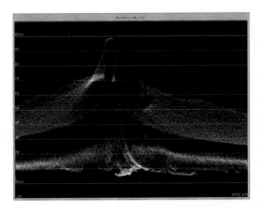 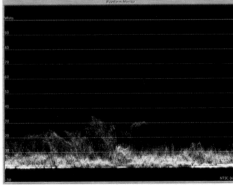

▶ The image to the left is the Waveform Monitor graph for the man walking towards the car, and you can see the shadow region running along the bottom from 0 to 30%, the sun spiking up to 100% in the middle of the graph, and the man himself clumped down between 0 and 10% at the center of the graph.

▶ The image to the right is the graph for the underexposed clip of the couple in the grass, and you can see by the shortness of the graph that the contrast ratio is quite low. The densest cluster in the graph is between 0 and 10%, with few portions of the graph exceeding 50% (except for a few faint highlights).

Once you learn to recognize contrast, you can more precisely adjust it using various filters, most importantly using the Color Corrector 3-Way filter. For more information, see Contrast Adjustments.

You will also be able to use some perceptual tricks to your advantage, as you will learn in Contrast and Perception.

Contrast and Perception

OVERVIEW ▶ Discussion of phenomena that relate to how contrast is perceived.

SEE ALSO ▶ contrast adjustments

A number of phenomena affect how people "see" contrast. You can exploit these perceptual tricks to your advantage to maximize the perceived quality of your images. The most obvious example is the surround effect.

Like color, contrast is relative, and the tone of surrounding colors affect the apparent brightness of a middle subject. In the following illustration, the pair of stars at the center of each of the boxes have exactly the same levels of gray, but appear darker against white and lighter against black.

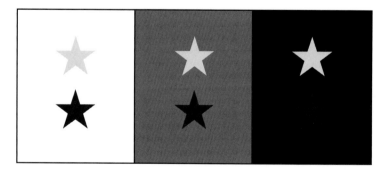

NOTE ▶ Relative contrast is why you don't typically want your broadcast monitor to be in front of a large expanse of black.

Using the Surround Effect

You can take advantage of the surround effect by adjusting the shadows of an image to boost the perceived brightness of its highlights.

The image to the left is overexposed, in an effort to make the room as bright as possible. Unfortunately, the result is a washed-out scene, with little detail in the highlights. To the right, is the same shot with the highlights reduced; by crushing the shadows (exaggerated for print) the highlights of the picture look brighter by comparison.

You can experiment with this example yourself:

1   Open the *01 Surround and Contrast* sequence, located in the Contrast and Perception bin of the **Color Correction Exercises** project.

2   Add a Color Corrector 3-Way filter to the first clip in the sequence. (The second clip is the completed example.) Open the clip into the Viewer, and click the Color Corrector tab to expose the contrast sliders.

An examination of the Waveform Monitor reveals the portions of the picture in the superwhite range that correspond to the windows and other highlights. There are shadow regions that extend down to 0%, but not many of them.

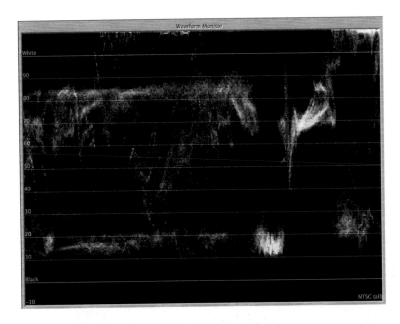

The first order of business is to legalize the whites by bringing them under 100%.

3   Drag the Whites slider to the left until the top of the waveform sits at 99%.

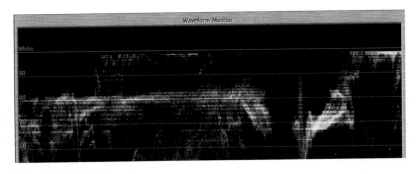

You should immediately see some highlight detail come back into the image. As long as superwhite portion of the image isn't clipped too badly, it's often possible to retrieve small patches of detail simply by manually lowering the highlights.

4   Drag the Blacks slider to the left to crush the blacks and darken the shadows, keeping your eye on details in the regions being darkened.

Once you start losing the darkest details, back off of this correction until you have a nice compromise. Use the detail in the headboard as a gauge.

You should still be able to make out these details on your broadcast monitor, even though the shadow portion of the waveform graph is showing the telltale bunching up of being crushed. See Contrast Adjustments.

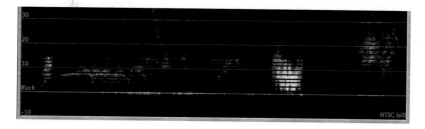

5   Drag the Mids slider to the right, boosting the mids to keep that bright, sun-streaming-in look. You may have to lower the whites a bit and perhaps crush the blacks a little more to retain the effect.

The end result is a more dynamic image, with whites that appear brighter than ever before, even though they've actually been lowered. At this point, you would ordinarily move on to make color adjustments, but the contrast is set.

Increasing Perceived Detail

One other effect of contrast manipulation is that increased contrast ratios can give the appearance of sharper detail. In the following pair, the left image has the original contrast ratio that was shot in the field. There's a full tonal range, but the bushes seem somewhat indistinct. For the right image, I expanded the contrast ratio; notice the increased appearance of detail in the same bushes.

By stretching out the contrast ratio, you're increasing the difference between the darker and lighter pixels that define the edges of subjects in your image. More contrast in the edge detail gives the appearance of greater detail, and in fact this is exactly how sharpen filters work in many popular image-editing applications (including Final Cut Pro): They increase contrast along the edges of an image. Sharpen filters are usually more targeted, detecting and adjusting contrast only in edge regions, but the general idea is the same.

It's important to realize that this is only for appearance. You're not actually adding any detail to the image, and in fact you may be eliminating detail if you need to crush the blacks of your image significantly enough to achieve this effect.

You can experiment with the effect yourself:

1   Open the *02 Contrast and Detail* sequence, located in the Contrast and Perception bin of the **Color Correction Exercises** project.

2   Follow steps 2 through 5 as in the previous example, and see how different contrast ratios affect your perception of detail in the image.

Day for Night (Classic Blue Look)

OVERVIEW ▶ The process of color grading a night scene with the classic Hollywood "blue-moonlight" look.

SEE ALSO ▶ day for night (exterior campfire), day for night (studio correction), day for night (matching video underexposure)

The Blue Night Look

One of the most classic treatments of night lighting, whether done on the set with lighting, on location via lens filtration, or in post with color grading, is the blue moonlight look. We've all seen it—it's the color of romance, of mystery, of, well, Technicolor-style night.

Many drag-and-drop, day-for-night filters fiddle with the contrast and then splash blue all over the highlights and midtones for an extreme version of this time-honored classic. With practice, however, this effect is easily and more subtly achieved using only the Color Corrector 3-Way and Desaturate Lows filters.

Before going into this particular day-for-night look, it's useful to question the conventional wisdom that forms the basis for this color treatment.

Why Is Moonlight Blue?

As sunlight reflects off of the moon towards the Earth, the reflection of moonlight is generally considered to have a color temperature of around 4000K (warmer than daylight, cooler than halogen lighting). Recording the moon via film and video reveals this warmth. In other words, moonlight isn't actually blue.

To readers living in well-lit urban environments, this is no surprise. Taking a look at the moon when there's plenty of ambient light around reveals its warmer tones.

However, this is clearly counterintuitive to decades of romantic scenes in color filmmaking, not to mention our general perceptions of moonlight. So why the discrepancy? Because when we're in the dark, moonlight does look blue. To understand why, you need a little background science.

Johannes Purkinje (1789–1869) was a Bohemian (no, he was from Bohemia) professor of physiology who first discovered what is now called Purkinje's Phenomenon, which essentially states that in low light we perceive more blue and green than we do red and yellow.

As light becomes less intense, our retinas switch from using the cones that are sensitive to color in well-lit conditions (*photopic* vision) to the rods, which provide low-light sensitivity at the expense of reduced color perception (*scotopic* vision).

In general, we are less able to resolve color in low-light conditions, so everything becomes desaturated. Specifically, longer wavelengths (red-yellow) become less visible than shorter wavelengths (blue-green), even though they may actually be of equal brightness.

As a result, even though the moon is reflecting a relatively warm quality of light, we don't perceive it with the naked eye. In moonlit conditions, away from any other ambient light (such as when you're camping or in an area otherwise free of light pollution), we experience the romance of muted, moonlight blue.

Now, the question of whether to treat your clips with the classic (or old-fashioned, depending on whom you ask) blue night look depends on your visual goals. Certainly, there are other night treatments you can apply, depending on the type of program you're working on. However, it's undeniable that after decades of film and television viewing, the average audience member is conditioned to associate blue light with night, and it doesn't hurt to take advantage of this bit of cinematic literacy. The question is not necessarily whether to use blue or not, but the intensity of the effect, and that is for you (and the client) to decide.

Other Qualities of Moonlight

To better simulate moonlight, you should be aware of a few more of its qualities:

▶   The light of the full moon provides surprisingly high-contrast light, with sharp shadows when the moon is high enough. For this reason, cinematographers shooting day for night often shoot footage with sharp shadows, with the rationale that one would only be shooting film by the brightest moonlight possible.

▶ Other, dimmer phases of the moon produce significantly softer light, with very low contrast.

▶ The blood-red moon is a phenomenon caused by dust in the atmosphere and a low position on the horizon. Depending on atmospheric conditions, a blood-red moon can have a secondary effect of throwing a reddish cast over the entire sky. (Think lunar sunrise.)

Creating a Simple Blue Night Look

In this first example, the footage was shot with a night look already. The direction and quality of the light, and the contrast ratio in general, is compatible with actual full-moonlight. The director, however, has decided to go with a more intense blue. Your job is to add it.

1   Open the *Classic Blue* sequence, located in the Day-for-Night, Classic Blue bin of the **Color Correction Exercises** project.

2   Apply a Color Corrector 3-Way filter to the first clip in the sequence (the second clip is the finished correction, provided for comparison), and then open the clip into the Viewer. Click the Color Corrector tab to expose the graphical controls.

In the Waveform Monitor, notice that there are superwhite highlights, and those should be dealt with first.

3   Lower the Whites slider until the top of the graph falls underneath 100%.

You have a bit of room to crush the blacks and stretch the mids, but there's no need to do so. The shot is very well exposed, with plenty of contrast, so why sacrifice detail?

Now, it's time to introduce some blue into the picture.

4   In the Waveform Monitor, notice that the majority of the "highlights" in the picture are between 20 and 50 percent, so drag the Mids color balance control towards a point just underneath the B (blue) target.

This adjustment rebalances those parts of the picture, while leaving the topmost white highlights and dense regions of shadow from 0 to 8 percent alone.

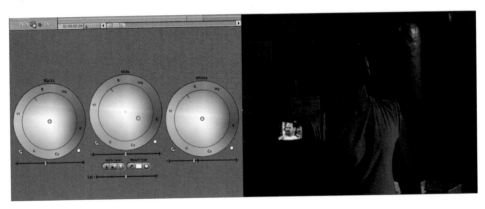

At this point, you could leave well enough alone, because this is a nice effect as is, with white highlights complementing the blue effect. If, on the other hand, a more intense blue cast is requested, you could add some blue to the whites as well.

5   Drag the Whites color balance control towards blue to intensify the effect.

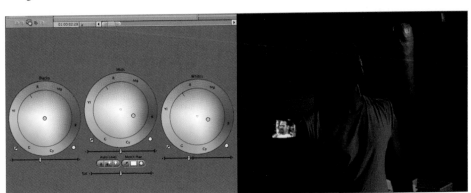

NOTE ▶ Whenever you manipulate the Whites color balance control to intensify color, check the Vectorscope and the Waveform Monitor with Saturation turned on to make sure you're not creating illegal saturation values. If you are, either back off the adjustment, use the Desaturate Highlights filter to correct the problem, or make sure you apply the Broadcast Safe filter with the appropriate settings. See **Broadcast Legality**.

At this point, you may be happy with the blue, but you should observe that the picture is pretty vivid, which may distract from the nighttime look you're going for.

6   Bring the mids down to darken the image a bit, just 3 or 4 percent. Alternately, experiment with reducing the overall saturation just a little.

Reducing the saturation after you've just hopped up your image with blue may seem counterintuitive, but the saturation adjustment uniformly mutes all of the color in the image. In this case, the overall cast is still blue, but the image is now a bit less neon.

Creating a Night Look for Daytime Clips

The previous exercise applied the blue night look to a clip that was already shot with a nighttime treatment. In this example, the clip was shot as part of a daytime scene, but you need to regrade it with the blue night look. In the process, you'll discover a few extra challenges.

1   Open the *Classic Blue From Day* sequence, located in the Day-for-Night, Classic Blue bin of the **Color Correction Exercises** project.

2   Apply a Color Corrector 3-Way filter to the first clip in the sequence (the second clip is the finished correction, provided for comparison), and then open the clip into the Viewer. Click the Color Corrector tab to expose the graphical controls.

First off, the contrast in this clip is clearly all wrong for nighttime. There's too much light overall and in the background, and his shadows are pretty light. On the plus side, there's some clear contrast available to be exploited, and throwing away light is a much higher-quality proposition than trying to boost it if there is too little.

3   Crush the blacks, mercilessly, so that the bottoms of the waveform that used to sit from 10 to 15 percent are now at 0.

This eliminates a lot of the background detail, creating darker regions that fall off to nowhere. It also boosts the contrast in his face in preparation for lowering it again by reducing the Mids level in the next step.

4 Lower the Mids slider to darken the shot, overall, reducing the highlights in the man's face to fall within 0 to 60 percent.

This is a good range for a "shot in the dark" subject. In general, subjects who've been seriously underexposed fall from 0 to 30 percent, so it's still in the perfectly visible range. It's not pretty, but it's a start. Next, you'll put some blue into this picture.

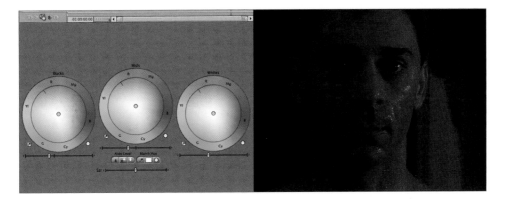

5 Drag the Mids color balance control somewhere between the blue and cyan targets until the highlights of his face are seriously blue.

If you drag the mids too close to blue, the natural reds in his face create an unpleasant magenta cast; dragging too close to cyan results in, well, too much cyan. You be the judge of what looks like moonlight to your eyes.

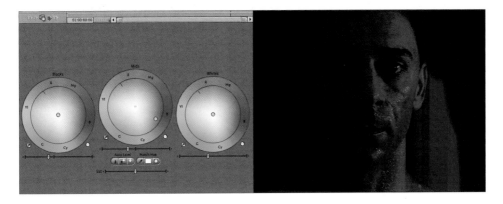

At this point, it should be pretty apparent that his face is radically oversaturated in the shadows. Aside from his general neon look, you should remember that we don't really see reds very clearly in low light conditions, and that means specifically here in the shadows. To remedy this, you'll use the Desaturate Lows filter.

6   Apply the Desaturate Lows filter to the clip, and click the Filters tab to reveal its parameters.

Its default settings are immediately apparent, as parts of his ears and hair immediately become black holes in the picture. To make this work out effectively, you need to expand the range of shadows included in the operation by using the Apply Below parameter and significantly soften the edge of the effect by using the Softness parameter.

7   Raise the Desaturate Lows Softness parameter until the black desaturated regions in the left side of the man's face are feathered out so as to be unnoticeable (around 25). Then, increase the Apply Below parameter until most of the shadowed portion of the image is desaturated (around 31).

This adjustment takes care of the neon reds, but the effect at this point is somewhat monochromatic. Now that the region to be desaturated has been defined, you can ease off of the default Amount of Desaturation parameter's value of 100 percent.

8   Lower the Amount of Desaturation parameter to reintroduce a bit of color back into the shadows, but just enough to look natural.

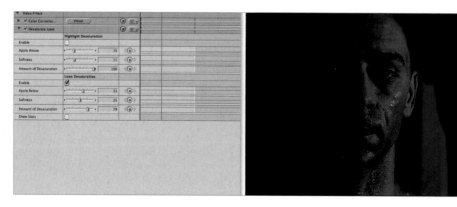

NOTE ▶ For an outer limit of how much saturation is legal to have in the blacks while you make this adjustment, turn on saturation in the Waveform Monitor, and make sure that the graph doesn't dip below 0 percent.

At this point, you're close to finished, but a few optional things would finish this shot up nicely. Now that the color and saturation for different portions of the image have been adjusted, the highlights are looking a little bright. Also, depending on the look you're going for, the image may be a bit oversaturated.

9   Switch back to the Color Corrector 3-Way filter and lower the highlights and the saturation by 5 to 10 percent to mute the image back into a somewhat more "realistic" (if less spectacular) treatment.

NOTE ▶ If you want to leave this as a richly saturated treatment, just take measures to ensure broadcast legality at the end of the project.

The image is looking great, but there's one last thing you might want to do. As it is, the man's face has a lot of red highlights. This may be fine, or it may be too much, depending on what you're going for. If you want to eliminate them, simply lowering the saturation on the Color Corrector filter won't really do what you want. Instead, lowering it will lower the color of everything in the frame, including the blue, and you've probably already reduced the saturation as low as you want it to be.

Instead, you can insert a Desaturate filter *above* the Color Corrector filter, slightly desaturating the entire image before the Color Corrector filter begins its processing.

10   Click the clip's Filters tab. Add a Desaturate filter to the very top of the filter stack, then adjust it to mute the red highlights in the man's face (10 to 20 percent).

Lightly desaturating the image before it's acted upon by the Color Corrector and Desaturate Lows filters lets you knock out some of the color from the original image, without muting the color you're adding with the Color Corrector filter. Compare the results (right) with where you started (left):

As with the other day-for-night techniques, these are highly adaptable, and you'll never use the same settings twice. Also keep in mind that you can extend the functionality of the Color Corrector filters quite a bit by careful placement of other operations in the filter stack.

Day for Night (Exterior Campfire)

OVERVIEW ► Exploration of techniques for grading an exterior clip shot in daylight to look like it takes place at night.

SEE ALSO ► day for night (classic blue look), day for night (studio correction), day for night (video underexposure match), sky corrections and enhancements, vignettes (creating shadows)

Preparing a Day-for-Night Look

The best day-for-night looks are achieved in conjunction with clever lighting on the set. Every once in a while, however, you'll be asked to regrade a shot that wasn't originally intended to be a nighttime scene. In these instances, you'll likely employ a variety of techniques to modify different aspects of the picture to match, as closely as possible, the desired nighttime look.

For example, the following image was originally shot to look like it takes place in the late afternoon, before dusk:

As is often the case, the director decided later in post that the scene would be more effective if it took place *at night*, which requires substantial modification. A quick look at the shot reveals some things working in your favor. First, the shot is fairly low contrast, with no really hard shadows, which is good. Second, the practical light thrown by the campfire will be very helpful in establishing the campfire as the dominant light source in the shot. With these two observations in mind, you can tell the director in good conscience that it's worth a try.

When you're making major adjustments (in this case, turning day into night), take a good look at the image and break it down into different zones that need to be addressed, such as this:

Darken the sky

Reinforce the campfire's light

Darken the surroundings

▶ The overall shot needs to be darker, with deeper shadows. You can accomplish this by applying the Color Correction filter.

▶ The sky needs to be darkened, and possibly tinted a deep, dark blue to emulate an early night sky. Use a typical overlaid sky enhancement here.

▶ The area surrounding the woman needs to be darkened, to simulate the area surrounding the fire gradually falling into shadow. You can easily achieve this with an oval vignette.

▶ The fire needs to become the primary source of illumination. This means that parts of the picture that naturally reflect the firelight should remain the brightest, and the subject should assume the fire-light's color temperature. A secondary or masked color correction is your best bet for this task.

Bear in mind that a correction of this magnitude typically requires several adjustments, with multiple layers. Once you've identified the parts of the shot that need to be modified, and you've created a game plan, you can proceed with the correction.

Creating the Look

In this exercise, you'll combine a number of techniques to make the campfire clip look like it takes place at night:

1   Open the *Day-for-Night Campfire Look* sequence, located in the Day-for-Night, Campfire bin of the **Color Correction Exercises** project.

2   Apply a Color Corrector 3-Way filter to the first clip in the sequence. (The second group of clips is the finished correction, provided for comparison.) Open the clip into the Viewer, and click the Color Corrector tab to expose the graphical controls.

Now you're ready to make the first correction, adjusting the overall look of the clip for a dark, nighttime look. For the initial correction, you'll be adjusting for the look of the background. Don't worry about the foreground, you'll be taking care of the highlights with another correction.

3   Using the Waveform Monitor as your guide, crush the blacks until the entire bottom of the waveform sits on the 0 percent line, then pull down the whites so that the brightest highlight is no more than 90 percent, and pull down the mids so that the average brightness of the picture is between 10 and 40 percent—a typically underexposed image.

4   With the contrast out of the way, drag the Whites color balance control up towards orange in order to add more warmth to the remaining highlights, and then reduce the saturation until the blue lean-to behind the woman is muted but still visibly blue.

While you'll typically be eyeballing this sort of correction, bear in mind that you're simulating underexposure. Although it's dangerous to generalize, video that's under-exposed typically falls under 40 percent, has a waveform that's heavily weighted towards the bottom, and has highlights that never quite manage to extend up to a full 100 percent.

You rebalanced the image to create additional warmth in the highlights generated by the campfire, just before muting the color of the entire clip. Underexposed video shares something with the eye's response to low light, which is that colors lose satura-tion in the shadows. This phenomenon is important for creating a convincing night look; boosting the color of the highlights prior to muting the entire shot lets you pre-serve the warmth while muting the background.

Next, it's time to take care of that overly bright sky with a sky enhancement.

5　Superimpose a Custom Gradient generator in track V2 over the Campfire clip, open it into the Viewer, and click the Controls tab to reveal its parameters.

6　Choose a dark blue color for the End color, and then adjust the Gradient Direction and Start point so that the gradient is angled softly across the sky in the upper-right corner of the picture.

7　To blend this gradient with the image, Control-click the Custom Gradient in the Timeline and choose Composite Mode > Multiply from the shortcut menu.

It's OK to leave a bit of light fringe along the ridge of the sky, so long as it's acceptable for this shot to be taking place after dusk rather than midnight. Evening skies are often brightest at the horizon (see **Sky Corrections and Enhancements**).

Next, it's time to create the effect of the shadowy falloff from the campfire using a vignette.

8   Superimpose an Oval shape generator in track V3, over the Custom Gradient you just created. Open it into the Viewer, and click the Controls tab to reveal its parameters.

9   To simulate a soft, shadowy falloff from the area of the campfire, adjust the Softness, Size, and Aspect parameters of the Oval Generator to create a soft, wide oval with the brightest area just surrounding the campfire itself.

Sample parameters are Size = 12%, Softness = 88%, and Aspect = 1.35.

10 To blend the oval with the rest of your growing composite, Control-click the Oval gradient in the Timeline and choose Composite Mode > Multiply from the short-cut menu.

This is a typical example of a vignette (see Vignettes (Creating Shadows)).

Well, you've certainly darkened the clip, but the woman has disappeared into the darkness. In the last few steps, you'll bring her back out by duplicating and selectively isolating the highlights from the campfire in the original Campfire clip. You'll use a Chroma Keyer filter to isolate the portion of the picture illuminated by the campfire, and a Color Corrector filter to adjust the clip for a convincing illumination effect.

11 Duplicate the Campfire clip in track V1, and superimpose it in track V4, *above* the Oval and Custom Gradient generators by Option-dragging it to track V4.

12 Open the Campfire clip in track V4 into the Viewer, click the Filters tab, and delete the Color Correction filter that was already there. Add the Chroma Keyer filter and another Color Corrector 3-Way filter, in that order.

You'll be using the Color Correction filter later, in step 17.

NOTE ▶ In this operation, you need to apply the Chroma Keyer first, to the raw image, in order to most easily isolate the necessary parts of the image.

13 Click the Chroma Keyer tab, click the eyedropper button, and then click a highlight on the woman's arm to sample that value as a starting point. To see what you're doing, set the View Final/Matte/Source button to Matte (a black key against a white background), and turn on the Invert Selection button (so that it's white against black).

The portion of the image you're isolating now appears as a white superimposition against the background layers.

14 Manually adjust the Hue, Sat, and Luma controls to isolate portions of the image that are illuminated by the campfire.

Include portions of the surrounding rocks, the fire pit, and the front of the woman.

This first adjustment won't be pretty, but you'll finesse it in the next step.

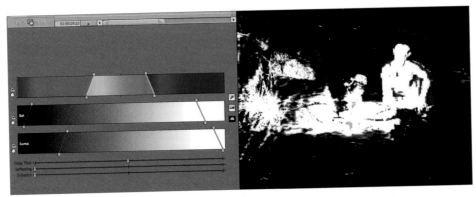

15 Raise the Softening parameter to create a nice soft key (while eliminating the small keyed bits around the edges), and then raise the Edge Thin parameter to "fill in" holes in the key, creating more solid regions of key.

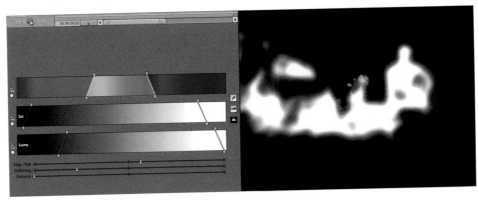

16 Set the View Final/Matte/Source button to Final (a red key on a gray background), and view the result.

Superimposed highlights held out against the corrected background. Image exaggerated for print.

What you're seeing are the highlights in the original video clip, superimposed over all of the corrections you made in the previous steps.

The highlights are too bright, and you'll take care of that in the next step, but what you want to check for is that there isn't any excessive fringing on the woman's arm or around her head that might look like a halo (a little may be OK, you just don't want too much). If there is, use the Edge Thin and Softening parameters to tighten up the key, keeping the edges soft.

17 To bring the highlights back into line, click the Color Corrector tab in the Viewer (which you added in step 12), and lower the blacks, whites, and saturation until the highlights look bright and golden, but don't stick out as too artificial.

The result should be a nice orange/gold glow illuminating the woman and parts of the background.

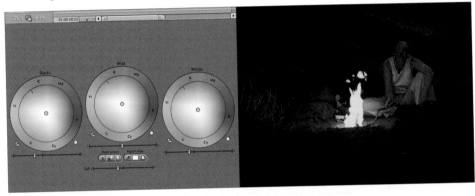

Compare where you started (left) to the results (right).

Further Considerations

As you've seen, changing a daylight shot into a night shot is a multilayer process. Ideally, you'll be working with the DoP to extend a day-for-night look that was started by the lighting on the original location. Fortunately, the example in this section was low contrast, which is a big help. You also saw how practical light coming from the campfire was instrumental to creating the desired look.

Even in less ideal circumstances, you've seen that there are options for recompositing the lighting in a shot to create a credible night look. Every situation will be different, but the techniques presented in this entry will inevitably come into play in one form or another. As always, keep in mind any and all natural night lighting that you've observed—every little adjustment helps.

Day for Night (Studio Correction)

OVERVIEW ▶ The process of converting a clip with studio lighting to a more natural moonlit look.

SEE ALSO ▶ day for night, day for night (classic blue look), day for night (exterior campfire), day for night (video underexposure look), vignettes (creating shadows)

Correcting Studio-Lit Night Scenes

From time to time, you'll be presented with a scene that was deliberately lit to look like night, but the effect isn't working to the director's satisfaction. Once you determine the reason, you can apply a fix.

The Scene Has the Wrong Color Temperature

There are many approaches for lighting a night shot. Is the primary source of illumination a bare light bulb in the garage or moonlight coming in through a window? Was there a stylized look to the original footage, such as an aggressive blue, purple, or green cast? Is it working, or is it too aggressive?

In some cases, scenes lit with professional tungsten instruments can have an overly warm, artificially lit look, especially when moonlight is called for by the director (who may have just changed his or her mind after seeing the footage edited into a scene).

Fortunately, this is an easy fix using the color balance controls of the three-way color corrector. You'll be capitalizing on the tonal-zone-specific nature of these controls to rebalance the color exactly where you need it.

The Scene Is Overlit

Despite the nighttime setting, the scene may simply be too bright. Although the director may have a furrowed brow, you should be overjoyed. You'll always get better results by cutting down excess light levels than you will by boosting underexposed clips. Most cinematographers know this, so the abundance of light may be a deliberate way to provide some flexibility in post.

In these instances, all of the standard techniques for controlling contrast are at your disposal, allowing you to reduce the highlights, darken the midtones, and either crush or boost the black level, depending on the look you're trying to create.

The Scene Is Too Evenly Lit

A different sort of problem occurs when the scene is too *evenly* lit. One of the hallmarks of nighttime locations is that light typically comes from very specific locations, such as a lamp, a bulb, or the moon through a window or doorway. As a result, light levels vary dramatically from one area of a nighttime frame to another. Furthermore, for dramatic purposes you're more likely to want the subject of the shot to have the maximum available light, while the background light levels fall off appropriately to the location.

In some instances, the director of photography may have deliberately created a lighting scheme that results in an evenly lit background with very consistent lighting. This scheme may be an attempt to save money on a low-budget shoot by creating a lighting setup that works with a wide variety of coverage. In some cases, it may also come from an instinct to avoid "too much contrast for video," based on experience with earlier generations of video recording equipment that couldn't deal with high contrast ratios.

Inappropriately even lighting is a subtle cue of theatricality. Nobody would pick it out, but it does affect the audience's perception of a scene. If your lighting is too even, you'll find yourself using vignetting techniques, masked corrections, and secondaries to selectively lower the lighting in parts of the picture.

Changing the Lighting in a Scene

In the following example, you'll use a combination of techniques to correct many of the problems just listed and to create a naturalistic, moonlit look:

> **NOTE ▶** The steps show the effects of this correction on the last frame of the clip, since the beginning is a pan up from the floor.

1   Open the *Garage Evening* sequence, located in the Day-for-Night, Studio Correction bin of the **Color Correction Exercises** project.

The director has told you that the scene takes place in a garage with moonlight streaming in through the window, so a cool look is desired. Never mind that the moon might not actually be this bright, it's the general *feeling* that's wanted.

Play through the clip, and you'll see the original clip has a very warm, tungsten color temperature and even lighting in the background. The lighting of the foreground character is probably fine, but you'll get a better sense of that when you correct the first two issues.

2 Apply a Color Corrector 3-Way filter to the first clip in the sequence (the second clip is the finished correction, provided for comparison), then open the clip into the Viewer. Click the Color Corrector tab to expose the graphical controls.

Looking at the Waveform Monitor reveals what needs to be done with the contrast of the image, usually the very first correction you'll be making. The general light level of the image is already fairly low, and light on the background wall is very even. There's a bit of wiggle-room to crush the shadows (only a few small dips in the waveform currently extend all the way to 0), and that would make the image a bit more contrasty.

3   Lower the Blacks slider until the bottom of the average black level in the Waveform Monitor just touches 0.

That puts a bit more contrast into the image, deepening the shadows while bringing the man a little more out of the background, all in preparation for the next step: cooling the color temperature to something approximating moonlight. Because the moonlight is, for all intents and purposes, the key light of the scene, you'll want to start by adjusting the whites.

4   Drag the Whites color balance control towards an area between cyan and blue, to neutralize the orange cast of the shot.

Moving the control closer to blue adds a bit more blue to the image. Keep dragging until the highlights have a cool white-blue look. You don't want the highlights looking *really* blue, just very cool.

This result looks good, but the subject is looking a bit purple/magenta, because the whites correction is extending down through the midtones, and the blue is mixing with the orange in that portion of the image to create a magenta cast. This situation is correctable by making a compensating adjustment to the mids.

5 Drag the Mids color balance control, *just a bit*, down between green and blue, to counteract the magenta hue while trying to not actually turn the man green.

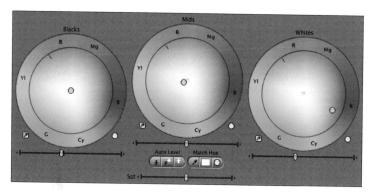

NOTE ▶ Remember, a large adjustment to the whites creates very cool lighting, and a compensating correction in the mids prevents a slight magenta cast.

At this point, the shot is looking very cool and high-contrast, but the light on the wall to the left of the man is still very even. Before fine-tuning the correction, this issue needs to be addressed so you can accurately see how further corrections will look.

6 Choose a Custom Gradient Generator from the Video tab of the Viewer, superimpose it over the Garage Evening clip in the Timeline, reopen it into the Viewer, and click the Controls tab to expose its parameters.

7 In the Timeline, Control-click the Custom Gradient, and choose Composite Mode > Multiply so you can see how the vignette you're creating affects the clip underneath as you make adjustments.

By default, the gradient is blocking exactly the wrong side of the frame.

8 Change the Gradient Direction so that the darkest part of the gradient is at the upper-left corner.

The vignette is now too small to do any good, and it's too harsh, so you'll need to adjust the Start parameter to bring the edge of the vignette closer to the man.

NOTE ▶ You may be wondering why the beginning of the shot has a pan in it. This is one of many examples of a vignette you can get away with not animating to match the camera motion. Because of the angle of the vignette, and the eventual light shade of it, it should simply look like that entire side of the room just happens to be dark once you've finished.

9   Click the Start center control, then drag within the Canvas to bring the edge of the vignette to the inside of his arm. At this point, readjust the Gradient Direction if it's cutting off his head.

The edge of the gradient should run parallel to the figure of the man sitting on the floor (around 305 degrees).

Now, the vignette is too dark at the corner.

10   Adjust the End color to be a lighter shade of gray. If you open the End color control's disclosure triangle to reveal the HSB sliders, you can adjust the B (brightness) parameter while watching the effect in the Canvas.

Another change you can make is to adjust the Gradient Width parameter to thicken the darkest part of the vignette, but don't go too far or you'll make the edge of the vignette visible.

NOTE ▶ Vignettes look darker on your computer monitor than they do on your broadcast display.

11 As an optional last step, you might choose to reduce the overall saturation of the image, no more than 10 to 15 percent.

Low-light footage is often less saturated. Depending on the look you're going for, reduced saturation might look a bit more natural. Consider this before (left) and after (right) pair.

And you're finished. As you can see, there are many ways you could modify this approach, making the color temperature cooler or warmer, making the highlights brighter or darker, or using different kinds of vignettes and varying levels of saturation.

As you consider the different steps in this exercise, see if you can match them up with your own observations of how different locations look in low light conditions.

Day for Night (Matching Video Underexposure)

OVERVIEW ▶ Techniques for matching the look of underexposed video.

SEE ALSO ▶ video noise and film grain

Matching the Look of Genuinely Underexposed Video

Every once in a while, you'll need to either match or recreate the effect of clips that were shot at night in low-light conditions, such as by candle or moonlight. In some cases, you may have to match existing shots that were intentionally recorded in those conditions. In others, you may want simply to simulate the effect of underexposed video.

To successfully create such a look, first examine footage that was already shot using the camera you're trying to match. For example, the following clip was shot by the light of a full moon with no color correction applied (available in the **Color Correction Exercises** project—open the Underexposed Video Example sequence in the Day for Night, Matching Underexposed Video bin).

Videocameras are extremely sensitive, and they're capable of great feats in underexposed conditions. Depending on the camera being used, however, mileage in low-light conditions will most certainly vary. Aside from the crushed blacks and overall dark picture you'd expect in such situations, most standard and high definition videocameras share the following characteristics in low-light situations:

▶ Increased noise—Most professional cameras have a gain adjustment that allows the shooter to amplify the signal being recorded to increase image sensitivity. Unfortunately, this almost always has the byproduct of increasing the noise in the picture (see Video Noise and Film Grain).

▶ Low sensitivity to color—The color saturation of recorded video decreases along with the amount of light.

▶ Reduced sharpness—At low exposures, the iris is typically open as wide as possible (even with the enormous depth-of-field available to videocameras with small CCDs), so the captured image has the shallowest possible depth of field. This usually results in large portions of the image being at least slightly out of focus.

You can mimic all of these characteristics easily using Final Cut Pro.

Creating an Underexposed Video Look

In this exercise, you'll combine a number of techniques to recreate an underexposed video look in the following clip:

This clip is from the same movie as the full-moon-shot night clip, and the goal is to match that earlier clip's look and feel. Fortunately, the DoP was on your side, and shot the clip low contrast to begin with, so you won't have to fight any out-of-place highlights or hard shadows. On the other hand, there's plenty of work to be done.

1   Open the Matching Underexposed Video sequence in the Day-for-Night, Matching Underexposed Video bin of the **Color Correction Exercises** project.

2   Apply a Color Corrector 3-Way filter to the first clip in the sequence. (The second group of clips is the finished correction, provided for comparison.) Open the clip into the Viewer, and click the Color Corrector tab to expose the graphical controls.

The first order of business is to mercilessly lower the blacks, mids, and whites to begin the underexposed look.

3   Lower the Whites slider until the waveform peaks at 40 percent (a typical highlight for severely underexposed video).

4   Lower the mids to compress the remaining midtones and darken the foreground (lowering the Mids further lowers the highlights, and starts to crush the blacks).

After these adjustments, there's still a bit of detail visible in the woman's shirt and in the foreground. Shadow detail in a shot like this is very much a matter of preference. Although actual low-light video may be closer to a true silhouette, it's always nice to leave a bit of detail here and there if it looks plausible. The sky is still too bright, but in order to preserve this foreground detail, you'll be darkening the sky in a secondary color correction operation.

At this point, you certainly have a low-exposure shot, but the colors, especially in the sky, have intensified to an undesirable degree.

5   Lower the Saturation until there's just a bit of color left (seen as a slight blob in the Vectorscope).

You don't want to eliminate all of the color, but you want to mute it significantly.

Now, to address the look of the sky. In this exercise, you're trying to preserve a faint amount of detail in the foreground. The only way to further darken the sky without losing the detail that's been preserved is to adjust the sky in a secondary operation.

6   Apply another Color Corrector 3-Way filter to the DayHike LS clip, and click the Color Corrector 3-Way - 2 tab to expose its graphical controls.

Because the sky is clearly lighter than the rest of the picture, you can use the Luma control all by itself to isolate this portion of the picture for more work.

7   Open the Limit Effect controls, turn on the Luma control, set the View Final/Matte/Source control to Matte (a black key against white), and then adjust the Luma controls to isolate as much of the sky as you can without including any of the foreground detail you're trying to preserve.

This is a tricky key to pull, because the darkest parts of the sky are close to the foreground areas on the ground, but once you get close so that only a faint area of the sky is showing gray, you can drag the Edge Thin slider to the right to eliminate the fringing, and then increase Softening to smooth the edges of the key.

TIP As you make these adjustments, scrub through the entire clip to see how your settings work as the camera pans and the subject moves.

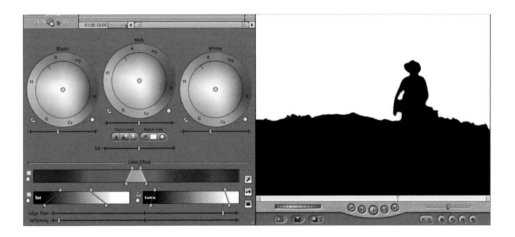

8   To adjust the sky, set the View Final/Matte/Source control to Final (a red key against gray), and then lower the Mids and Whites sliders to darken the sky.

Lower the whites more than the mids, in order to compress the contrast between the clouds and the sky. As you make this adjustment, bear in mind that you don't want to completely darken the sky—you want to simulate the faint glow of the moonlight falling across the atmosphere.

How dark this shot will ultimately be really depends on the viewing environment of the intended audience. If your audience will be primarily watching this clip in a darkened theater, you can safely create a darker clip. But if the audience will be in a well-lit environment (in a living room watching a DVD), you may want to make this a brighter shot. In this example, highlights around 20 percent are appropriate.

9   Drag the Whites color balance control towards blue to add a bit of dark blue color to the sky.

You don't want the color to be too intense, but you want it to be clear.

NOTE ▶ Depending on how your computer's monitor is calibrated, this image may look dark in the Canvas, but you should ultimately judge the results on a broadcast display.

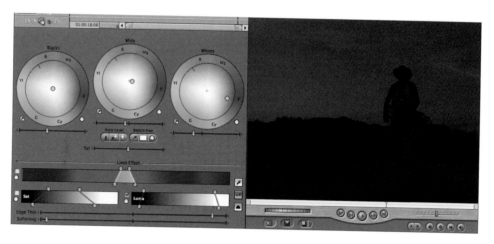

At this point, there are only two more things to add. For one thing, the edges in this clip are way too sharp for a night shot of this kind.

10 Click the Filters tab, add a Gaussian Blur filter (Video Filters > Blur bin of the Effects tab), and set the Radius to something really low, like 2.

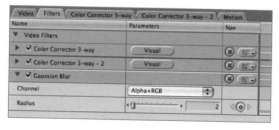

The goal is not to make the image fuzzy, just to knock some of the sharpness off the visible edges in the picture.

At this point, the only remaining step is to add some noise to the shot, to simulate a videocamera with the gain turned up (see Video Noise and Film Grain).

11 Click the Video tab. Choose Render > Noise (the first of the two Noise generators that appear) from the generator pop-up and superimpose edit the Noise generator into track V2, over the Dayhike LS clip. In the Timeline, Control-click the Noise generator clip and choose Composite Mode > Overlay.

The Overlay composite mode is ideal for blending noise into a clip to simulate camera noise, because it blends a superimposed image into both the dark and light areas of the picture.

12 The initial effect is far too grainy, so lower the opacity of the superimposed generator until the grain is at an acceptable level (somewhere between 4 and 8 should be appropriate).

Now that the grain looks right, you're probably noticing that the dark parts of the image have lightened up! This is a result of the lighter pixels of noise interacting with the darker parts of the image. Fortunately, this is an easy adjustment.

13 Open the DayHike LS clip back into the Viewer, and click the first Color Corrector tab to reveal its parameters.

14 Drag the Blacks slider to the left to darken the shadows again.

As you make this adjustment, keep your eyes on the sky, because changes you make to the contrast in this first operation may affect the secondary key you're pulling in the second Color Corrector clip.

Check out how far the clip has come (right) from where it started (left):

Further Considerations

Clearly, what's realistic is not always compatible with what looks good. Although this example is intended to simulate camera underexposure as closely as possible, the techniques used are highly adaptable, and you can create as extreme or as light a grade as you require.

What's important to remember is that while there are many possible day-for-night treatments you can create, it's useful to examine the results of actual underexposure as you come up with your own solutions.

DoP (Director of Photography)

OVERVIEW ▸ Strategies for effectively working with the member of the crew who determined how the image that you're correcting was recorded. *Related terms:* cinematographer, videographer.

SEE ALSO ▸ QC (quality control)

Who Do You Work For?

Many people get involved in the postproduction process. As a colorist, you'll find yourself working with the producer, director, and director of photography (DoP) in different proportions that are unique to every project. Although the producer and/or director usually have the final say over the creative aspect of your work, the DoP may be involved in the color correction process as well. This is usually dependent on the size and budget of the project, as well as the creative relationship of the principals. Typically the higher the budget, the more involved the DoP will be. If you're just getting started, it's important for you to have an understanding of what the DoP does and how you may work together to achieve the look of the project.

Taking into account video formats, film stocks, camera equipment, lenses, and quality of lighting, the DoP works with the director during the shoot to plan for and implement the look of the recorded program. The DoP isn't working alone, however; the art department (set design/dressing, props, wardrobe) exerts direct control over the actual range of colors that appear in each and every shot. Visually, the filmmaking process is a symphony of artists working with paint, fabric, light, and optics to create the image that is ultimately entrusted to your care. If a good range of color and contrast isn't recorded during the shoot, you won't have anything to correct; you can't really add anything that wasn't there to begin with.

Different Ways of Working with the DoP

Traditionally, a program's overall look is determined *in camera*, through careful choice of film stock, lens filtration, white balance manipulation, and lighting setups. Contrast and color is adjusted to taste in the initial exposure, according to the latitude of the recording format, and care is taken to balance each lighting setup for maximum compatibility with the other angles of coverage within the same scene.

In this way, the need for later color correction is minimized as much as possible. This is especially true for low-budget video productions for which there might never be a color correction pass, although it's also important for film productions that will be optically color timed using equipment that lacks some of the flexibility of newer digital systems.

On the other hand, with digital color correction becoming a more affordable and flexible process, some DoPs are beginning to record film and video in such a way as to sacrifice the immediate projectability of the dailies in favor of preserving maximum image data for the color correction process in post. Methods include slightly overexposing the blacks and slightly underexposing the whites in order to minimize the loss of detail due to clipping and crushing. (Telecine operators can also do the same thing when transferring film to video.) During color correction, the contrast is then easily adjusted to emphasize whichever portion of the image is necessary for the desired look.

When a program's look has been decided in camera, your job is to balance and correct according to the originally intended lighting scheme. If the image was exposed intentionally to maximize image data for later digital manipulation, the creative possibilities are considerably more open-ended and subject to reinterpretation. In either case, the DoP's involvement will be invaluable in guiding you through how everything was originally intended to look, freeing you from having to make assumptions (and the accompanying revisions) and saving you time to focus on the truly important issues.

In turn, your job includes making options available in circumstances where the DoP is considering alternatives based on changes during editing, problems with the originally recorded image, or a producer and director's ambivalence with the originally rendered image. You will also find yourself assuming the role of negotiator when conflicts between producers, directors, and DoPs occur over the look of a particular sequence.

Lastly, issues of broadcast legality must be resolved, and that is where you need to be mindful of when a requested adjustment needs to be subdued in order to maintain a legal signal. You should always discuss the quality control (QC) standard that a program should adhere to in advance, and be prepared to tactfully find alternatives for or overrule adjustments that violate those standards.

Learn to Communicate

One of the best ways you can improve your rapport with both DoPs and directors, as well as generally improve your skills as a colorist, is to take the time to learn more about the art and craft of lighting for film and video. The more you know about how color and contrast is manipulated on location through all of the tools of the cinematographer's art, the better you'll be able to analyze and manipulate each clip. Furthermore, the more you know about how a film crew works, the better you'll be able to conduct the detective work necessary to figuring out why one clip isn't matching another: Was there a wind blowing the gel in front of the key light? What time of day was that insert clip shot? Did one of your lighting fixtures become unavailable in the reverse shot?

Also, cinematography, like every discipline, has its own language. The more familiar you become with different lighting setups, film stocks, and color temperatures, and with terms such as *low-key*, *high-key*, the easier it will be to discuss and understand the DoP's goals and suggestions.

Get Your Hands on It

Certainly one of the very best ways of learning more about the interplay of light and subject is to get your hands on the filming process itself. If you haven't already, take up photography, shoot a short fictional video or documentary, or take some production classes. Any opportunity to pour light through a lens is an opportunity to learn more about color correction.

Also, develop a critical eye when it comes to watching movies. You can learn an amazing amount about light and color by examining the work of others, once you know what you're looking for.

Filters (Y'CbCr vs. RGB Processing)

OVERVIEW ▶ Description of how the different filter types supported by Final Cut Pro process images in your sequence.

SEE ALSO ▶ broadcast legality

FXScript Filters

Up until Final Cut Pro version 5.1.2, all of the filters that came with the application and appeared in the Effects bin by default were created using the FXScript plug-in scripting language that's built into Final Cut Pro. Originally intended as an accessible way for both third-party developers and enterprising end-users to extend the built-in effects capabilities, this goal has been amply served by a host of professional and shareware developers (many of whom are cited elsewhere in this book).

The important thing about FXScript filters, whether they're Final Cut Pro's default filters or third-party filters developed using FXScript, is that they're all Y'CbCr-aware. What this means is that if you apply an FXScript filter to a DV, DVCPRO-50/HD, Apple Uncompressed, or otherwise Y'CbCr-compliant codec, superwhite luma and out-of-gamut chroma values are preserved.

This concept is important, especially when you're working on a project where you need to preprocess the image, for whatever reason, *prior* to applying Color Corrector filters.

FxPlug Filters

Starting with version 5.1.2, Final Cut Pro can use FxPlug filters, paving the way for a new generation of video effects processing filters. Initially including a selection of filters from Motion, these filters dramatically extend Final Cut Pro's effects toolkit.

Although the FxPlug API supports Y'CbCr awareness, the initial plug-in architecture in 5.1.2 has an idiosyncratic behavior. When initially applied to a clip, FxPlug filters playing in real time are processed in RGB, which means that superwhite luma values are clamped after you apply the filter. In other words, all luma values *above* 100 percent are set *to* 100 percent, which results in the unfortunate loss of highlight detail in your images.

After you render a clip with one or more FxPlug filters applied to it, the superwhite values that were clipped in real time *reappear*, as long as the sequence's video processing settings are set to *Render all YUV material in high-precision YUV*. If the sequence's Video Processing is set to Render in 8-bit YUV, the clipped levels stay clipped.

Compare the Waveform Monitor displays for the original unfiltered clip (left), for the clip after you apply an FxPlug filter (center), which clamps superwhite values to 100 percent and eliminates detail, and for the clip after it's been rendered withing a High-Precision YUV sequence (right) at which point the values reappear:

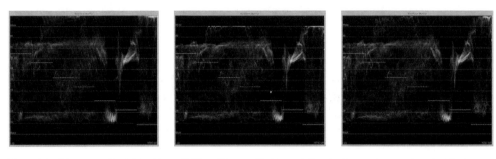

The original image to the left, with an FxPlug filter applied in real time in the center, rendered with the sequence set to High-Precision YUV to the right

If you want to avoid the hassle of superwhite levels disappearing and reappearing when using FxPlug filters, all you need to do is to legalize the clip first (see Broadcast Legality), then apply the FxPlug filter afterwards. For example, compare the Waveform Monitor graph for a clip with a Color Corrector 3-Way filter applied to legalize it (left) and then after you apply an FxPlug filter:

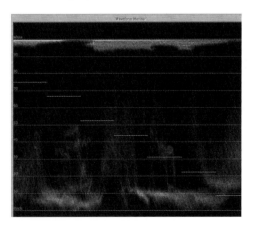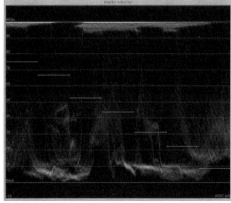

Be aware, however, that if you're applying a filter that has the effect of pushing the values of a clip higher than they already are (think glow filters), they'll still be clamped to 100 percent, unless you bring your maximum levels down in a previous color correction.

If you're going to apply numerous filters that need the headroom that superwhite provides, apply them at the top of the filter stack, prior to any non-Y'CbCr-aware (or temporarily non-Y'CbCr-aware) filters. For example, suppose you have a clip with bright highlights, and you want to apply both a third-party FXScript glow filter and the Soft Focus FxPlug filter that comes with Final Cut Pro 5.1.2. By applying the glow filter first, a Color Correction filter second to adjust and legalize the clip, and the Soft Focus filter last, you benefit from the preservation of superwhite values from the glow filter to the Color Correction filter, and you have an opportunity to legalize the image before applying the Soft Focus filter, controlling the processing of the clip.

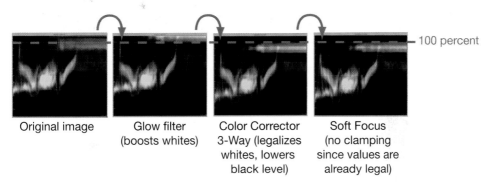

| Original image | Glow filter (boosts whites) | Color Corrector 3-Way (legalizes whites, lowers black level) | Soft Focus (no clamping since values are already legal) |

— 100 percent

After Effects Filters

Final Cut Pro supports Adobe After Effects plug-ins on PowerPC-based computers. (As of version 5.1, After Effects plug-ins are not supported on Intel-based computers.) A wide variety of After Effects plug-ins are available, but not all are compatible with Final Cut Pro. (Check with the individual developers for compatibility information.)

Of those that are compatible, know that After Effects filters are also RGB processing filters, and are not Y'CbCr-aware. Because of this, the same workflow issues outlined for FxPlug filters apply to their use as well. Just make sure you legalize your clip prior to adding any After Effects filters to ensure the greatest preservation of detail.

Gamma

OVERVIEW ▶ Explanation of the nonlinear representation of luminance on a broadcast or computer monitor.

SEE ALSO ▶ gamma correction filter (image control group), gamma (imported and exported media)

What Is Gamma?

Gamma refers to the nonlinear representation of luminance on a broadcast or computer monitor, but different monitors, cameras, and operating systems may interpret gamma differently, which has a huge effect on how your video appears. If this seems complicated, it is, but understanding what gamma means and how it's applied is essential to avoiding inconsistencies in your video, especially when you exchange media with other video editing, compositing, and color correction applications.

Gamma has its origin in the human eye's nonlinear response to light. This means our eyes have different sensitivities to the lighter and darker parts of what we see. For example, look at the following two gradients, and pick the one that seems to have the most even distribution of white to black across the entire bar.

If you picked the top gradient, you might be surprised to learn that the bottom gradient is the image that is actually a mathematically linear progression of white to black. The top image has had a gamma adjustment made to it to make it *perceptually* more even.

The human eye is far more sensitive to differences in brightness than in color, a physiological trait that informs many decisions in video standards. Partially due to this fact, video imaging specialists decided long ago that a strictly linear representation of the luminance in an image wouldn't make the best use of the available bandwidth or bit-depth for a given analog or digital video system. As a result, images are recorded with a gamma adjustment immediately applied within the video camera to retain as much perceptible detail as possible. Broadcast and computer monitors then apply a matching, but inverted, gamma correction, with the result being a more or less true representation of the image.

NOTE ▶ Broadcast monitors and televisions apply an additional gamma adjustment of 1.1/1.2 in order to create a nicer-looking image with wider contrast. Be aware, however, that different consumer televisions may apply varying gamma adjustments, whereas video projectors allow for manual adjustment (and misadjustment) of the projected gamma, causing headaches for colorists and filmmakers alike.

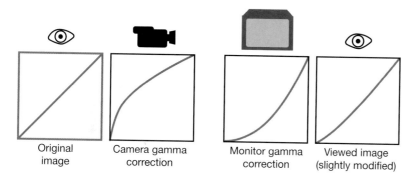

Original image   Camera gamma correction   Monitor gamma correction   Viewed image (slightly modified)

Although there is a standard for video gamma (specified as the Rec-709 transfer function), you may encounter inconsistencies if elements of your project are created or manipulated on different systems. These inconsistencies can cause much consternation when you create graphics on a computer for video output, and can be especially vexing when you combine still images and motion graphics clips that were created on different computers.

One trouble is that monitors attached to different computers might use very different gamma settings. The following chart shows the three most common gamma settings in use with computer and broadcast monitors:

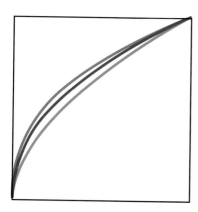

NTSC/PAL gamma average (2.5)
NTSC/PC gamma (2.2)
Mac OS X gamma (1.8)

Windows computers usually employ a gamma identical to that of the NTSC standard of 2.2; Mac OS X defaults to a gamma of 1.8 (although you can override this if you choose). There are differing standards for NTSC and PAL, depending on who you talk to. As a result, some computer graphics artists create graphics assuming a gamma of 2.5, which splits the difference between NTSC and the PAL gamma standard of 2.8.

If you render, color correct, or otherwise manipulate an image while viewing it on one kind of display, your resulting image may be either too bright or too dark when your client views it on another type of display. This is exactly what happens when graphics created on a Mac (with a default gamma of 1.8) are displayed on a Windows-compatible computer (with a default gamma of 2.2, the NTSC gamma standard): the PC image seems lighter or slightly washed-out on a Mac, and Mac images seem overly dark or murky on a PC.

Images being created or manipulated on a Mac (with a default gamma setting) for broadcast video output have an even larger discrepancy. For tips on working around these gamma discrepancies, see Gamma (Imported and Exported Media).

> **NOTE** ▶ For a more rigorous and technical explanation of gamma for broadcast, computer, and film applications, see the Gamma FAQ at www.poynton.com. The technically minded should also consult Charles Poynton's *A Technical Introduction to Digital Video* (John Wiley & Sons). For more information about human vision and digital systems, see Maureen C. Stone's excellent *A Field Guide to Digital Color* (AK Peters, Ltd.).

Gamma Handling During Video Output

When setting up your Final Cut Pro system for professional monitoring, you need to keep gamma issues in mind. The software used to control your video capture/output card may have settings for determining how the gamma of video is handled on output if RGB to Y'CbCr conversion is necessary. These settings, in conjunction with the View > Video Playback submenu within Final Cut Pro determine how the gamma is handled for the video you're monitoring and outputting to tape. If these settings are incorrect, you'll be viewing the midtones of your image incorrectly, not to mention altering the contrast of media that you output to tape.

Gamma Handling of Clips in the Canvas

One last thing: If you ever happen to notice a contrast shift in the Canvas, there is an explanation. Y'CbCr .mov files in Final Cut Pro are all assumed to have been captured from a video system employing a gamma of 2.2. As a result, Y'CbCr sequences are displayed in the Canvas with a gamma correction of .818 to "preview" how they'll look on a broadcast monitor relative to the default Mac OS X gamma of 1.8. This adjustment is used only for the onscreen display of the Canvas and is *not* applied to the sequence's video output or to exported files. Furthermore, it does not eliminate the requirement to evaluate your images on a true broadcast display.

Gamma Correction Filter (Image Control Group)

OVERVIEW ▶ Explanation of filter that enables you to use a slider to adjust the gamma of an image by a power function ($f(x) = x^a$).

SEE ALSO ▶ Luma

When to Use the Gamma Correction Filter

This filter defaults to a value of 1, which makes no change to the image. Raising or lowering this value applies a gamma correction to the image, lightening or darkening the midtones of the image. The Final Cut Pro Gamma Correction filter has one idiosyncrasy, in ~~that~~ ~~it makes~~ a slight change to the white point.

l Cut Pro's Gamma Correction filter is to make a contrast ing advantage of the gamma function's capability to leave ou might find the Mids slider of the Color Corrector 3-Way ghtforward, but if all you need to do is to make a small of midtones in your image, you can simply use the Gamma

Midtone Adjustments vs. Gamma Correction

Even though the Mids controls of the Color Correction filters and the Gamma Correction filter both allow a nonlinear adjustment of the midtones, you'll get significantly different results if you adjust the Gamma Correction filter's slider than if you adjust the Mids slider of a Color Correction filter. The Mids slider of the Color Correction filters makes a nonlinear change to the contrast of an image, altering the distribution of the midtones in an image, but the adjustment is fairly symmetric, tapering off evenly at the top and bottom of the curve.

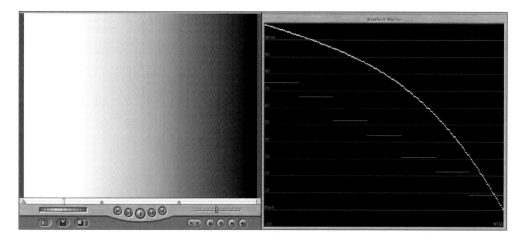

The Gamma Correction slider also makes a nonlinear change to the contrast of an image that affects the midtones, but the shape of the resulting curve is asymmetrical, affecting the darker regions of the image disproportionate to the lighter regions.

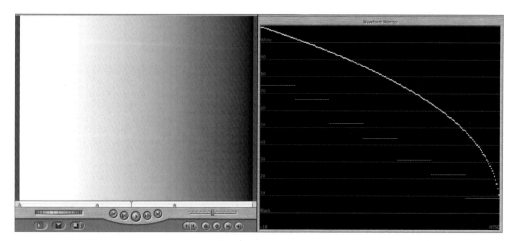

To help you understand which approach is best for your project, try the following exercise, which demonstrates both adjustments:

1   In the **Color Correction Exercises** project, open the Gamma Correction filter bin. Double-click the **Gamma vs. Mids** project.

2   With the playhead at the first clip, open the first Gradient clip into the Viewer. You'll see that a Color Corrector 3-Way filter has already been applied, so click the Color Corrector 3-Way tab.

3   Make an adjustment to the Mids slider, and observe the result to the gradient and to the graph in the Waveform Monitor.

4   Move the playhead to the second Gradient clip in the Timeline, open it into the Viewer, and click the Filter tab. You'll see that it already has a Gamma Correction filter applied to it.

5   Make an adjustment to the Gamma slider, and observe the result to the gradient and to the graph in the Waveform Monitor.

    Notice that the graph responds very differently when you adjust the Gamma slider.

6   Move the playhead to the last pair of superimposed Gradient clips in the Timeline.

    The image is a split-screen of the same gradient image. The top half has a Gamma Correction filter set to 1 (no change, as you can see by the perfectly diagonal line in the Waveform Monitor); the bottom half has a Color Corrector 3-Way filter with a Mids adjustment applied (as you can see by the curved line in the Waveform Monitor). You should see two lines in the Waveform Monitor.

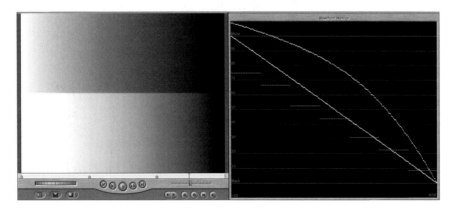

7 Open the clip in track V2 into the Viewer, and the Gamma Correction filter appears in the Filters tab.

8 Try to adjust the Gamma slider to make the bottom line in the graph match the top one, as best you can.

You'll find it's impossible to make them match precisely, but you can get the tops of both curves to line up fairly well.

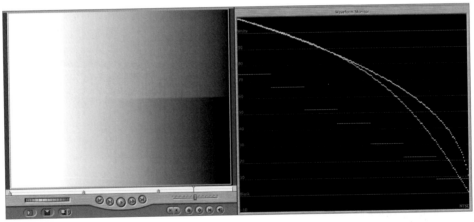

When you do this, notice the pronounced difference at the bottom of the curves in the Waveform Monitor, as well as in the blacks of the gradients of the Canvas.

As a general rule, you may find that adjustments to the Mids slider of the Color Correction filters provide more general control over the entire range of midtones, while the Gamma Correction filter is weighted to have a greater effect on the portion of the midtones closest to the blacks.

Gamma (Imported and Exported Media in Final Cut Pro 5.1 and Earlier)

OVERVIEW ▶ Explanation of how Final Cut Pro 5.1 and earlier treats the gamma of imported media files.

SEE ALSO ▶ gamma, gamma correction filter (image control group), gamma (imported and exported media in Final Cut Pro 5.1.2)

Gamma Shifts When Importing RGB Files from Another Application

Final Cut Pro versions 5.1 and earlier handle the gamma of imported RGB files differently than versions 5.1.2 and later do. In versions 5.1 and earlier, Final Cut Pro assumes that all RGB image files (for example, .tif files)and .mov files compressed using an RGB-based codec (such as the Animation codec) were created on a system employing a gamma of 1.8, which is the Mac OS X display standard.

In an effort to make these types of files appear as if they were created on a system employing a gamma of 2.2 (the broadcast gamma standard), Final Cut Pro automatically applies an automatic gamma correction of approximately 1.22 (thanks to Adam Wilt for publishing this value) when you import them. In other words, Final Cut Pro is attempting to make imported RGB graphics match the gamma setting of broadcast video.

To understand what all this means in practical terms for your production, consider the effect of this correction on some gradients. The following screen shot shows a simple linear gradient in Shake, with a PlotScanline superimposed over the image (Shake's PlotScanline function is basically a single-line Waveform Monitor). As you can see by the straight diagonal line, this gradient is perfectly linear.

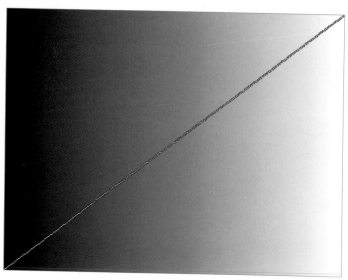

NOTE ▶ For a hands-on look at the gamma examples cited in this entry, open the projects in the Gamma, Imported and Exported Media bin of the **Color Correction Exercises** project.

When you render this image as a .tif image file and import it into Final Cut Pro, you see a very different result in the Waveform Monitor. It displays a now-familiar gamma curve resulting from Final Cut Pro's automatic 1.22 gamma correction.

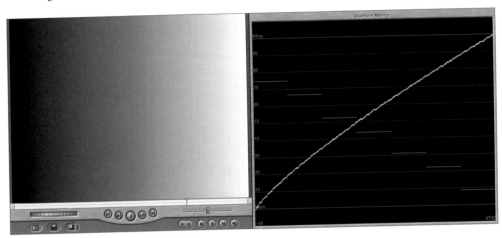

This automatic correction is applied to all RGB encoded clips regardless of whether or not any filters are applied. (You might even think of it as an invisible filter that you can't get rid of.) Although it has no effect on the source media on disk, it does affect the appearance of that clip when it's output to tape, or when rendered as a movie file using the Export QuickTime Movie, Export Using Compressor, or Export Using QuickTime Conversion commands.

Avoiding Gamma Shifts When Creating RGB Media

If you must create .mov files using an RGB-only codec (such as the Animation codec) or as a still-image sequence, there is a way you can control the eventual result in Final Cut Pro. Simply preprocess the movie clip in the application that creates it (Shake, Motion, After Effects, Combustion, and so on) *prior* to rendering it for import into your Final Cut Pro project. Apply a gamma correction of .824 (thanks to Chris Meyer of CyberMotion for publishing this value) as the very last filter or processing node to the composition you're exporting. (Every compositing application should have a gamma correction filter or node.)

> **NOTE ▶** Preprocessing the image before importing it into Final Cut Pro gives you a cleaner and more exact result than using the Gamma filter inside of Final Cut Pro afterwards, while eliminating the need for another rendered effect in your sequence.

Avoiding Gamma Shifts When Creating Still Images

If you're creating an image in Photoshop for use in Final Cut Pro, for example, you can preprocess it with an approximate gamma correction using a curves adjustment.

1   Choose Image > Adjustments > Curves.

2   Make sure Channel is set to RGB

3   Add a single point to the curve.

4   Set the Input value to *92* and the Output value to *70*, and click OK.

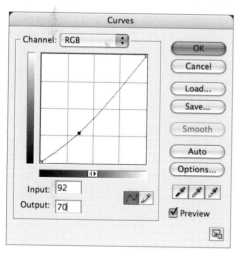

Gamma Handling of Files Exported from Final Cut Pro

Gamma isn't just a concern when you import media. There are gamma considerations involved when you export media out of Final Cut Pro as well. How Final Cut Pro handles the gamma of clips or sequences when exporting them as media files depends on two things:

▶   The type of file or codec you're rendering to

▶   The codec the sequence being exported from is using

Exporting Y'CbCr .mov Files

When you export one or more clips using a Y'CbCr-based codec, from a sequence that's also set to a Y'CbCr-based codec, the resulting media file has no gamma shift applied to it. In the following example, a linear gradient superimposed over a video image reveals the linear progression of the gradient as the diagonal line in the Waveform Monitor.

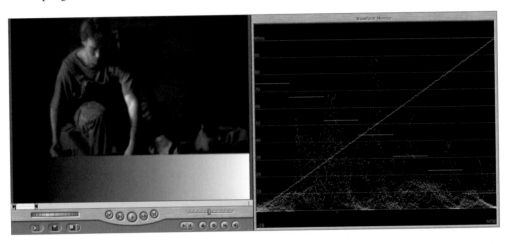

Exporting this section of the sequence as an Uncompressed 10-bit 4:2:2 .mov file using the Export QuickTime movie command, and then importing the clip into Shake and adjusting the PlotScanline function to examine the gradient shows that there is no difference in the gamma of the exported clip. This is an ideal result.

Exporting RGB Files

On the other hand, you get a very different result when you export one or more clips in a sequence using the Export Using QuickTime Conversion command. When you do so, the resulting media file (a still image, an image sequence, or a clip encoded with animation or other RGB code) has a gamma shift of .824 applied to it.

For example, suppose you exported the clip from the previous example as a .tif still image. Upon examining the result in Shake, you'll see that the image is noticeably darker, and the superimposed PlotScanline shows the now familiar gamma curve that results from the nonlinear adjustment of the midtones of the gradient below.

Import that exported clip back in to Final Cut Pro, and you'll see the same result in the Waveform Monitor.

If your intention was to export a clip for further processing in another application, this automatic adjustment is easily reversible—simply add a 1.22 gamma correction before rerendering the clip as a .mov file using a Y'CbCr codec for use in Final Cut Pro.

Gamma (Imported and Exported Media in Final Cut Pro 5.1.2)

OVERVIEW ▶ Explanation of how the gamma of imported and exported files is handled in Final Cut Pro 5.1.2.

SEE ALSO ▶ gamma, gamma correction filter (image control group), gamma (imported and exported media in Final Cut Pro 5.1 and earlier)

How Does Final Cut Pro 5.1.2 Handle Gamma Differently?

Significant changes were made to the gamma handling of clips in Final Cut Pro 5.1.2. Whereas in earlier verisons all RGB media had an automatic gamma adjustment applied during both import or export, now gamma handling is specific to the type of media you're importing.

Gamma Handling on Input

The gamma for a particular clip you import into Final Cut Pro is handled differently depending on the type of clip it is:

▶ For QuickTime movies compressed with Y'CbCr codecs, including Apple 8- and 10-bit Uncompressed 4:2:2, no gamma adjustment is applied.

▶ QuickTime movies using an RGB-based codec such as Animation have the same 1.22 gamma adjustment applied to them as in 5.1 and earlier. This gamma adjustment cannot be changed from within Final Cut Pro. See Gamma (Imported and Exported Media in Final Cut Pro 5.1 and Earlier).

▶ The gamma of TIFF images is handled according to the Imported Still Gamma setting in the Editing tab of the User Preferences window. If this is incorrectly set, you can also change this clip property at any time by changing the Gamma Level property, either in the Browser by revealing the column, or in the Format tab of the clip's Item Properties window.

Gamma Handling on Output

In a significant improvement in Final Cut Pro 5.1.2, no gamma adjustments are applied when you export a QuickTime movie or image file.

Still Image Gamma Handling

You can adjust the gamma of the following image formats:

- ► BMP
- ► QuickDraw
- ► Targa
- ► PNG
- ► TIFF
- ► SGI
- ► PlanarRGB
- ► MacPaint
- ► Photoshop

Gamma Handling Controls

Several controls are available for controlling how the gamma of imported still images is handled. A Gamma Level pop-up menu in the Editing tab of the User Preferences lets you choose what gamma adjustment is applied to imported images.

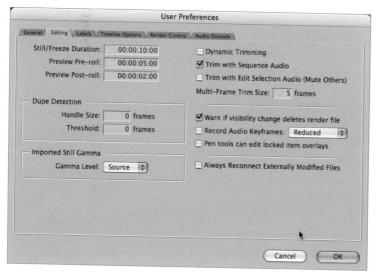

There are four options:

▶ Source makes the same automatic gamma adjustment of 1.22 as was made in previous versions of Final Cut Pro. See Gamma (Imported and Exported Media in Final Cut Pro 5.1 and Earlier).

▶ 1.80 is the default option for images generated using the standard Macintosh gamma setting.

▶ 2.20 is the default option for images generated using the standard Windows gamma setting.

▶ Custom reveals a number field with which you can enter your own gamma value.

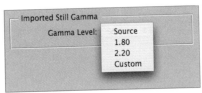

After you import a still image, you can reveal a Gamma Level column in the Browser, indicating which clips are capable of having their gamma property adjusted and how they're currently set.

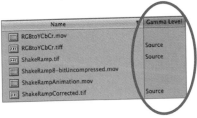

There's also a Gamma Level property in the Format tab of the Item Properties window.

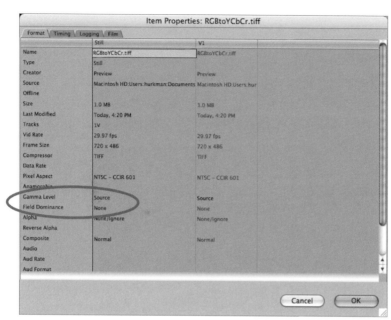

Glows, Blooms, and Gauze Looks

OVERVIEW ▶ Techniques for glowing lighting effects and softening image detail.

SEE ALSO ▶ filters (Y'CbCr vs. RGB processing)

Different Kinds of Glow Effects

Several kinds of glow effects can be useful for color grading purposes in Final Cut Pro—the key is matching the right effect to your shot:

▶ Subtle glows can simulate the way that highlights in exposed film *bloom,* rather than clip as with video. Film bloom is a soft glow that emanates from and surrounds over-exposed regions in the image, and is often deliberately induced by the DoP because of its stylized look. Adding glow to overexposed video highlights can somewhat simulate this effect, as well as take the harsh edges off. To do this, use the Limit Effect controls of the Color Corrector filters.

▶ Gauze effects are often applied to soften facial features or other image details, to lower overall image contrast, and sometimes to create a "romantic" look (although if abused this effect can make your program look somewhat dated). Although traditionally created with such time-honored techniques as using gauze, nets, pantyhose, or fog, pro-mist, and diffusion filters in front of the lens, many of these effects can be simulated using blurred and superimposed duplicates with Final Cut Pro's transfer modes, or with the Soft Focus filter.

▶ Big glow effects might include any kind of huge, fancy glow, which create really aggressive looks. These are more of a special effect, and you'll typically use one of the many third-party glow filters.

Because most glow effects deliberately boost the highlights to create their effect, they often reintroduce illegal white levels. If you add a glow filter to a clip that already has bright highlights, you'll likely have to compress the highlights even more by lowering the Whites and raising the Mids sliders.

Creating Glow Using the Color Corrector

One way of creating a controlled, subtle glow is to abuse the Edge Thin and Softening sliders of the Limit Effect controls in the Color Corrector filters. This is a very efficient and customizable technique.

1 Open the *Glow Highlights* sequence, located in the Glow Effects bin of the **Color Correction Exercises** project.

This clip already has a color correction applied to it, but you want to create a simulated film bloom effect by adding glow to the white highlights of the clip, principally the man's shirt.

2   Add a second Color Corrector 3-Way filter to the clip, then click the Color Corrector 3-Way - 2 tab, and open the Limit Effect controls. To see what you're doing, set the View Final/Matte/Source button to Matte (a black key against a white background).

The portion of the image you're isolating will now appear as a white key against black.

3   To simulate the blooming of film, isolate the desaturated highlights of the picture by turning on the Luma and Sat controls and use them to highlight the brightest whites of the man's shirt. Drag the Luma handles to isolate the brightest parts of the image, and drag the Saturation handles to isolate the least saturated parts of the image. Leave the Hue control turned off.

Here's the trick that creates the glow. Typical uses of secondary color correction necessitate minimizing the amount of soft spill around the secondary key to prevent haloing. For this effect, you're going to *deliberately* crank up the Edge Thin and Softening sliders to introduce haloing, which will create the glow.

4   Drag the Edge Thin and Softening sliders to the right until the key image looks soft and spread out.

When you're finished, the secondary key should look something like this:

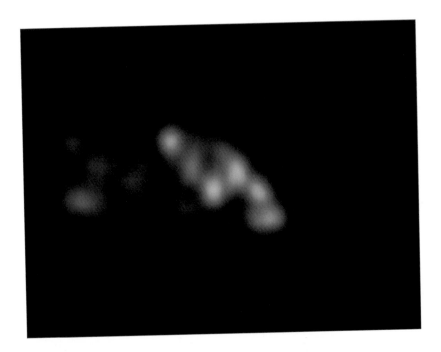

5   Set the View Final/Matte/Source control to Final, then drag the Blacks and Mids and Whites sliders up to create a bright glow. For an added bonus, drag the Whites color balance control towards a blue/cyan split to cool off the glow.

Now, the clip has a wonderful glow in the highlights, but the Waveform Monitor reveals that the highlights are too hot. To legalize this clip while retaining the glow effect, you have to compress the highlights.

6   Click the first Color Corrector tab. Drag the Whites slider to the left to lower the maximum white level, and then drag the Mids slider to the right to raise the mids distribution until the average brightness of the clip is about the same as it was before.

Compare the original shot (left) to the result (right):

One of the nice things about using the Color Corrector 3-Way filter to create glows is that you have an enormous amount of control over where the glow appears, and how it looks. Here are some pointers:

▶   Expanding and contracting the secondary key with the Edge Thin and Softening sliders lets you create wider or thinner glow effects.

▶   The Mids slider is your primary adjustment for creating a nice, soft glow within and immediately surrounding the highlights of the image. If your highlights are already close to 100 percent, you probably won't be able to safely use the Whites slider.

- ▶ The Blacks slider lets you create more aggressive glows by letting the glow seep into the shadows of the image.

- ▶ The Whites color balance control is the most useful for introducing an overall tint to the glow.

- ▶ The Mids or Blacks color balance controls can also be used to add an additional tint to the glow, giving the effect of a secondary glow coming off of the subject. For example, consider the secondary glow added to the following shot by dragging the Mids color balance control towards red:

Creating Gauzy Glows Using Superimposed Clips

You can create gauze effects by superimposing a clip over itself, blurring it with a Gaussian Blur filter, and then using one of Final Cut Pro's composite modes to blend the two layers together. The exact type of gauze effect depends on the composite mode you use, but all of these effects serve to reduce detail, soften the overall image, and subtly lower contrast.

NOTE ▶ You can buy several third-party filters that do pretty much the same thing, but within a single filter. On the other hand, the method presented here is free, fairly efficient, extremely customizable and handy if you don't have any other filters available.

By using the Mask Shape and Mask Blur filters in conjunction with this technique, you can selectively add gauzy blur to actors' faces, which is a common technique (for more information, see Masked Corrections).

1   Open the *Gauzy Glows* sequence, located in the Glow Effects bin of the **Color Correction Exercises** project.

This is a bedroom shot with bright highlights and rich colors. In short, a perfect candidate for a gauze effect. A Color Corrector filter is already applied to it for the general look; all you need to do is add the gauzy glow.

2   With the playhead over the clip you're working on, drag the Phone in Bed II clip into the Superimpose overlay of the Canvas to superimpose a duplicate in track V2. Open the new clip into the Viewer, and click the Filters tab.

3   Add a Blur > Gaussian Blur filter after the Color Corrector filter, and raise it to a value around 13.

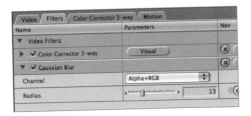

The more blurred the superimposed layer is, the softer the effect will be. How much blur you need to add depends on the frame size of the project—higher resolution projects require more blur for the same effect. For a standard definition clip, 13 is a good medium value.

4   To create the effect, Control-click the superimposed clip in track V2 and choose Composite Mode > Overlay from the shortcut menu.

You can use others, but overlay is a good, general-purpose composite mode for this effect.

5   The initial effect is likely far too strong, so click the Motion tab and lower the opacity to a value somewhere around 31.

Lowering the opacity reduces the overall effect; raising the opacity intensifies it.

You can also alter the effect by using different composite modes to combine the blurred and unblurred layers. Use the following guide to experiment with the effects of different composite modes on the preceding exercise, while viewing the effect on the image's contrast in the Waveform Monitor:

▶ Add creates an extremely hot glow that generally works best with lower opacity settings, because it intensifies highlights so much. In the preceding image, an opacity of 17 works well.

▶ Multiply darkens the overall image while softening it.

▶ Screen lightens the overall image while softening it.

▶ Overlay gives a soft overall glow, with almost no effect on the contrast of the image.

▶ Hard Light increases the contrast, raising the highlights and lowering the shadows.

▶   Soft Light gives a soft glow while reducing the contrast, lowering the highlights, and raising the shadows.

▶   Darken lowers the highlights, while leaving the shadows alone.

▶   Lighten raises the shadows, while leaving the highlights alone.

Creating Glows Using Filters

Final Cut Pro 5.1.2 offers Motion filters for creating gauze and blur effects: Soft Focus, Prism, and Light Rays.

Soft Focus

Blur > Soft Focus lets you create a gauzy blur with a single filter. It has a minimal effect on the contrast of the image, serving only to add a highly customizable gauze effect without changing the lighting.

▶   Amount adjusts the overall softness of the effect, widening or narrowing the spread of gauziness. Increasing Amount doesn't increase the blurriness of the image, it diffuses the effect.

- ▶ Strength adjusts the intensity of the blur, making the image more or less out of focus.

- ▶ Horizontal and Vertical let you adjust the width and height of the blur independently.

- ▶ Turning on Crop excludes the area outside the Canvas from the blur effect, eliminating a black border from the edges of a full-frame clip.

If all you want to do is add the gauze without changing the clip's light levels, this is the filter to use.

Prism

Blur > Prism is an FxPlug filter that creates a direction blur, then individually smears each of the color components along this axis, yielding red and green separations, similar to a prism's bending of light.

- ▶ Amount adjusts the length of the blurred streak, along which the three color components are smeared.

- ▶ Angle adjusts the direction in which the blurred streak moves.

- ▶ Turning on Crop excludes the area outside the Canvas from the blur effect, eliminating a black border from the edges of a full-frame clip.

Light Rays

A radial glow/blur filter, Glow > Light Rays creates a nice combination of effects. By centering the effect on a portion of the image you don't want to blur, you can create different vignetted blur effects.

- ▶ Amount adjusts the length of the radial blur. Raising this parameter lengthens the blurred rays.

- ▶ Center moves the center of origin from which the rays of the blur emanate. The center is also the least affected portion of the image, depending on the value of the Expansion parameter.

- ▶ Glow lets you adjust the intensity of the glow effect.

- ▶ Expansion lets you customize how much of the image is blurred. At 0, the area of the image surrounding the Center point is blurred less. At 2, the effect at the center point is exaggerated so that higher Amount values result in a more uniformly blurred image.

Third-Party Filters

For even more glow and lighting effects, you can try one of the many third-party filters to create other kinds of lighting and glow effects. A sampling of manufacturers and their offerings follows.

River Rock Studios

Chromatic Glow (free)

Cheap Lens

CinemagicX

www.riverrockstudios.com/riverrock

River Rock studios makes a variety of useful filters, among them the excellent and free Chromatic Glow, which lets you key on a portion of the clip to add a customizable glow effect. Cheap Lens provides a customizable vignetted blur that works independently on the red, green, and blue color components of the image. CinemagicX is a "make video look like film" filter that includes controls for simulating highlights and shadow bloom.

CHV

Silk and Fog (free)

www.chv-plugins.com/index1.php

CHV is giving away a very nice filter for creating gauzy effects. Five modes let you create various gauze effects, and a wide variety of options let you customize the interaction between the effect and the original image. While you're benefiting from their generosity, check out some of their other filter collections.

Stib's Filters

Colour Glow (free)

Glow (free)

Sparkle (free)

www.fxscript.org/plugins.html

Stephen Dixon is a talented and generous Australian animator who's put together a useful collection of free plug-ins (although his Web site encourages making a donation to support further development). Glow is a simple glow filter, and Colour Glow is a keyable glow. Sparkle is a keyable glow with a sort of "grain" to it.

Joe's Filters

Joe's Diffuser

Joe's Color Glow

www.joesfilters.com

The customizable Diffuser lets you do pretty much everything described in the earlier section "Creating Gauzy Glows Using Superimposed Clips" within a single filter. Joe's Color Glow is a keyable, customizable glow filter.

Eureka! Plugins

ChromaGlow – Volume 4

SilkStocking – Volume 4

Glow That Thing – Volume 5

www.kafwang.com/eureka/EurekaMain.html

Nestled among the two plug-in collections from Eureka! are ChromaGlow, a keyable glow filter, and Glow That Thing, which is simpler and non-keyable. SilkStocking is a simple-to-use, gauze-inducing filter with a variety of modes.

CGM

Silk – Vol. 3

Color Glow 8P – Vol. 2

www.cgm-online.com/eiperle/cgm_e.html

Silk is a customizable Gauze effect; Color Glow 8P combines a keyable glow with an 8-point garbage matte to limit its effect.

Genarts

www.genarts.com/sapphire-ae.html

Last, but certainly not least, Genarts has some of the prettiest, most outrageous glow effects available in their Box 1: Lighting set of filters. Unlike the other third-party filters, these are After Effects filters, with the accompanying limitations. They offer demos, so try them out to make sure they'll suit your purposes and workflow.

HSB Color Space

OVERVIEW ▶ Explanation of a method of representing color by its hue, saturation, and brightness values. *Related terms:* HSV.

SEE ALSO ▶ color balance controls, color control

What Is HSB?

The hue, saturation, and brightness (HSB) color model relates to how most people see and describe color. Each parameter of this model is easy to understand, and they can be collectively manipulated to create a predictable result.

▶ Hue describes the essential color: red, blue, yellow, magenta, and so on.

▶ Saturation describes the intensity of a color: how vivid it appears. Is it an especially intense red or a pale red? With any hue, if the brightness of a given color is at 50 percent, reducing saturation to 0 produces a neutral gray. When choosing colors for tints or titles, be aware that overly saturated colors are typically those that produce illegal chroma values.

▶ Brightness describes how light or dark a color is. Reducing brightness to 0 results in pure black, regardless of the hue or saturation of a given color.

Other color models, such as RGB or CMYK, can also be used to numerically describe color. However, the individual parameters of these are very specific to their purpose, making the models more challenging to understand.

For example, RGB describes mixes of red, green, and blue primary colors in a way that's useful for electronic imaging; CMYK describes combinations of cyan, magenta, yellow, and black inks for printing. If it's difficult for you to visualize how you'd mix cyan, magenta, and yellow to create a light orange color, you can understand why their individual parameters are not particularly intuitive when turned into controls for adjusting colors.

The standard Color control in Final Cut Pro has optional sliders that correspond to the HSB color model, letting you precisely and interactively select and adjust colors.

See Color Control.

NOTE ► HSB is also sometimes called HSV (Hue, Saturation, and Value).

HSB and the Color Balance Controls

The color balance controls in Final Cut Pro reflect two of the three parameters of the HSB color model. The angle of the colors running around the perimeter of the color wheel describes the hue, and the distance from the center to the edge describes saturation. In this two-dimensional space, you can manipulate two of the three color parameters simultaneously.

See Color Balance Controls.

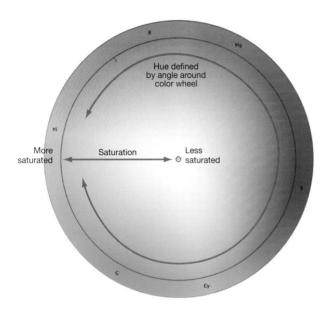

The brightness parameter is not represented by the color balance control's color wheel, but it is available in the HSB color sliders of the Color control. To visualize brightness, picture the color wheel on its side and extrapolate it into a cone. The "depth" of the cone represents the brightness of the color, with the bottom of the cone representing black.

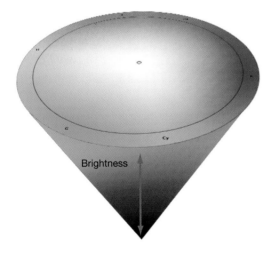

As you can see, a thorough understanding of the HSB color model makes it easier to understand and use many of the color controls available in Final Cut Pro.

IRE and Millivolts

OVERVIEW ▶ Explanation of units of measurement for NTSC and PAL monitoring equipment such as waveform monitors and vectorscopes.

SEE ALSO ▶ video scopes

What Are IRE and Millivolts?

IRE (which stands for International Radio Engineers, the organization that instituted the standard) is the unit of measurement used for NTSC test equipment. On a waveform or vectorscope with a graticule displaying IRE, the full range of a theoretical broadcast signal (including both the visible signal area and the synch portion of the video signal) is 1 volt, which corresponds to the range of −40 to +100 IRE. One IRE, then, is equal to 1/140 volts.

PAL, by contrast, is measured in millivolts (mV). In case you're looking to impress a video engineer at a dinner party, 1 IRE is equal to 7.14 mV.

When examining a video signal in a hardware waveform monitor (as shown in the following figure), you'll notice two parts of the signal. The portion of the video signal from the black level through 100 IRE (714 or 700 mV) is the picture itself. The portion of the signal extending below 0 through −40 IRE (−285 or −300 mV) is the sync portion of the video signal, which provides timing information crucial to the proper display of video. The exact levels, in millivolts, depend on the black level (setup) employed by your video capture/output interface, as you can see comparing the left and right ranges in the figure.

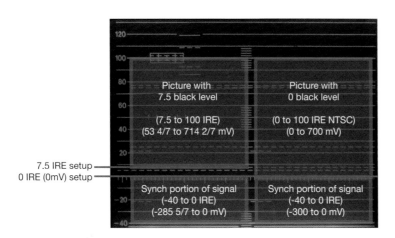

The Digital Equivalents

The IRE and millivolt units of measurement are relevant *only* when evaluating *hardware* video scopes. Final Cut Pro measures the digital video signal of your media on disk in digital percentages in the Waveform Monitor, Parade scope, Histogram, and Vectorscope.

When monitoring a video signal that extends from 0 to 100 percent digital in Final Cut Pro's Waveform Monitor, the signal should extend from whatever black level is being output by your video capture/output interface (7.5 or 0) to 100 IRE at the top of the scale. For example, compare a video output of 0 IRE on Final Cut Pro's software Waveform Monitor graph from version 5.1 and earlier (left) and a hardware waveform monitor (right). Although the hardware scope shows more detail, the general shape of both graphs should be identical.

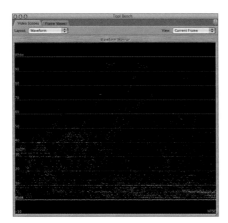 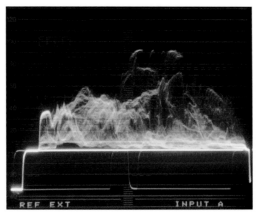

The shape of Final Cut Pro's Waveform Monitor and Vectorscope should match their hardware equivalents.

> **NOTE** ▶ In Final Cut Pro version 5.1 and earlier, hardware scopes displayed considerably more detail because Final Cut Pro's scopes were limited to analyzing only 16 lines of video, evenly distributed within the action safe portion of the image. Starting in version 5.1.2, Final Cut Pro's video scopes display every single line of video. See Video Scopes.

For more information about the specifics of digital and analog video signals, consult Charles Poyntons's *Digital Video and HDTV Algorithms and Interfaces* (Morgan Kaufmann).

Lens Vignetting

> **OVERVIEW** ▶ Explanation of a circular darkening at the corners and around the fringes of an image caused by optical or mechanical reasons.
>
> **SEE ALSO** ▶ masked corrections, vignettes (creating shadows)

What Is a Lens Vignette?

If you color correct enough programs, sooner or later you're bound to run into clips with lens vignetting, a circular darkened region that appears around the edges of a film or video image. If you understand the twin causes of this artifact, you can better target it, either for removal or to match unvignetted clips as a last resort (more on these techniques in a moment).

Vignetting in source media is typically the result of the twin phenomena of optical and mechanical vignetting:

▶   Optical vignetting is a subtle effect that's most visible in footage that was shot using lower quality wide-angle lenses that are open to full aperture; in these cases, the nature of the optics involved result in the center of the image being visibly brighter than the edges. This tends to be a more subtle effect, and it is usually at least partially reparable with a clever masked correction.

▶   Mechanical vignetting results from the edges of a lens hood, a filter attachment, or the lens barrel itself intruding at the edges of an image; this happens most frequently with zoom lenses set to their widest focal length. The result is a harder edge and a more noticeable effect, which is only correctable with aggressive digital paint techniques.

Here is a real-life example of optical vignetting:

What you do about lens vignetting depends on how drastic the effect is.

NOTE ▶ See Vignettes (Creating Shadows).

Selective Correction of Optical Vignetting

If you're dealing with a light optical vignette, you may be able to at least minimize the effect, if not eliminate it, by using a reverse masked correction, similar to the technique detailed in Masked Corrections. If you haven't read that technique yet, now's a good time to review it.

1   Open the *Fixing Optical Vignetting* sequence, located in the Lens Vignetting bin of the **Color Correction Exercises** project.

NOTE ▶ If you're viewing this project on an external broadcast monitor, switch the monitor to 16:9 (if it is so capable). This is an anamorphic project.

The first clip is the one shown above, with a very soft optical vignette that extends into the frame. This clip has already had a basic color correction applied to it. The second clip is the finished exercise for you to refer to.

2   Create a masked correction using the same methods shown in the Masked Correction entry. To summarize:

   a   Superimpose a duplicate of the clip above itself.

   b   Open the superimposed clip into the Viewer, click the Filters tab, and apply the Matte > Mask Shape, Matte > Mask Feather, and Image Control > Desaturate filters, in that order, above the Color Corrector 3-Way filter in the superimposed clip.

   c   Set the Mask Shape filter to Oval, and adjust the Horizontal and Vertical scale parameters so that the oval just hugs the *inside* of the visibly darkened area of the vignette. Use the Desaturated area as your guide while you work.

   d   When you're finished, turn the Soft parameter of the Mask Feather filter all the way up to 100.
      The mask should be extremely soft.

3   In the Mask Shape filter, click the Invert checkbox so that the outside of the oval (the area you want to correct) is masked, rather than the inside. Turn the Desaturate filter off when you're satisfied.

4 With the mask set up, click the Color Corrector 3-Way tab, and drag the Mids slider up to minimize the darkened halo around the clip.

Once the outside becomes visibly lighter, you'll know you've reached the limit.

In this image, the very corners are too dark to correct, they've already been crushed below zero. Fortunately, they're beyond the action-safe limit, so the darkest, grainiest parts probably won't be seen. Otherwise, a good portion of the vignette can be corrected. Less extreme optical vignettes would be even more successful.

If you've dragged the Mids slider up more than halfway from the center position to the right edge, and you don't see any effect, you may need to reduce the size of your mask to include more of the picture.

As you make this adjustment, use the Waveform Monitor as your guide. The Waveforms of vignetted images peak in the middle and fall off to the left and right as the image gets darker and darker. As you make this correction, you'll know you're almost there when the left and right sides come close to lining up with the center. It won't be perfect, but close is often good enough.

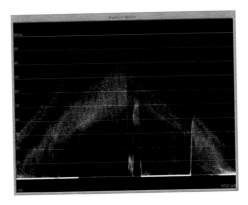 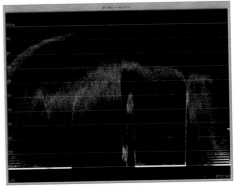

Matching Vignettes for Continuity

In cases of extreme vignetting (particularly mechanical vignetting, but also optical vignettes that are simply too dark), there's no image data to lighten—the vignetted area is simply black. In these cases, you have two choices:

▶   You can export the clip to a compositing tool such as Shake, After Effects, or Combustion, and try to digitally paint in the corners. This is not that hard to do, but it can be time consuming.

▶   You can use artificial vignetting techniques (see Vignettes (Creating Shadows)) to simply add vignettes to the other clips in the sequence that need to match. This is somewhat destructive, but it's fast, and it'll guarantee that the faulty clips don't stick out. As with noisy clips that need to be integrated with clean ones, uniformly vignetting an entire scene is better than having half of the shots sticking out.

Limit Effect Controls

OVERVIEW ▶ Explanation of the Limit Effect controls, which are used for pulling secondary keys to perform targeted color corrections. *Related terms:* qualifiers.

SEE ALSO ▶ limit effect (optimizing secondary keying operations), limit effect (splitting corrections into regions)

Using the Limit Effect Controls

The Limit Effect controls are the primary interface for doing secondary color correction in Final Cut Pro. With them, you can apply a keyed matte to isolate an area of the picture in which to perform specific color correction. Conventional uses include isolating a subject's shirt to subdue the color, the sky in order to add to or adjust its blue color, or a subject's skin to make a small adjustment that doesn't affect the background.

The Limit Effect controls are hidden by default; to expose them, click the disclosure triangle at the bottom of the Color Corrector and Color Corrector 3-Way filters. As you may notice, these controls are virtually identical to those in the Chroma Keyer filter.

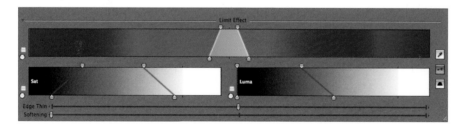

The three primary controls in the Limit Effect interface are the color qualifiers, which allow you to key on a portion of the image by making selections based on the HSB color model (more on how this works in the sections that follow).

Because you can turn these controls on and off individually, you can perform single qualifier secondary corrections. The checkbox to the left of each control (above a round white reset button) individually enables each qualifier.

Clicking a qualifier's reset button resets that individual control. Shift-clicking any reset button in the Limit Effect portion of the controls resets all of the Limit Effect controls, without affecting any of the primary controls in the Color Corrector tab.

How to Begin Defining a Secondary Key

There are two ways to begin creating a secondary key. In the first method, you click the Select Color button, then click somewhere in the Canvas with the eyedropper to select a primary Hue, Saturation, and Luma value. Depending on the HSB value of the pixel you clicked, Final Cut Pro turns on (checks), one or more of the qualifiers and sets them to the values found within that pixel. For example, if you click a white pixel, the program may turn on the Luma qualifier only. If you click a red pixel, on the other hand, all three qualifiers are likely to turn on.

The second way to begin a key is to adjust one of the qualifier controls directly, which automatically turns that control on—no need to click the checkbox first.

Either method is appropriate, although with practice you'll find that single-qualifier keys tend to be faster to pull by simply adjusting the controls, whereas keys on specific hues such as skin tones can be tricky, requiring an eyedropper selection to get started.

In either case, manual manipulation of the qualifier controls is generally the fastest way to finesse the end result.

How Much Time Should I Spend on the Perfect Key?

If you've spent any amount of time pulling blue and green screen keys to create mattes for compositing, you know how time-consuming and imperfect a process this can be. Fortunately, one of the nice things about color correction is that it's often not necessary to pull pixel-perfect keys in order to create a perfectly convincing and invisible secondary correction, although how true this is depends on how extreme a correction you're making.

If you're making a subtle adjustment to a clip's saturation or color balance, the most important things you want to watch out for are buzz and chatter in the key, both of which can be minimized by judicious use of the Edge Thin and Softening sliders. Often, it's faster and just as good to create a decent key and just soften the edges to make sure the matte isn't too animated. You just want to make sure that you don't soften the edge of the matte too much, or you'll end up with a halo around the correction.

On the other hand, if you're making more extreme corrections to color and especially to contrast, you'll want to pull a considerably tighter key to avoid visible artifacts.

In all cases, the most important thing you can do to check any secondary color correction is to render the corrected clip and play through it to make sure it's not buzzing and that the color isn't bleeding later on in the clip. These sorts of problems aren't immediately visible while you're working on a clip with playback paused. These are also just the sort of problems that ruin a perfectly good secondary.

Secondaries and Highly Compressed Footage

There are many reasons for color correcting a program's footage using the highest-quality source media possible, (preferably uncompressed, 10-bit, 4:2:2 media, if possible). Aside from general color quality considerations, secondary keying is an additional beneficiary of higher-quality media.

Because you're pulling a chroma key, highly compressed footage poses the same challenges for secondary color correction that it poses when keying to create visual effects. This is especially true when keying off of footage with limited color sampling. Keys from video formats in the 4:1:1 and 4:2:0 color spaces can suffer from blockier edges than when keying from 4:2:2 or, even more preferably, from 4:4:4 formats (which is admittedly a bit much to hope for from the average video producer). You can see the difference in the following illustration:

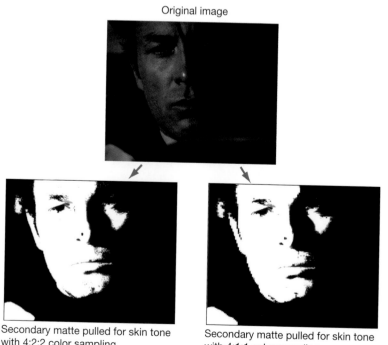

Original image

Secondary matte pulled for skin tone with 4:2:2 color sampling

Secondary matte pulled for skin tone with 4:1:1 color sampling

If you're working with highly compressed source media, you'll find yourself frequently relying upon the Edge Thin and Softening sliders to smooth off the edges of your key.

Another technique that works well when doing secondary color correction on highly compressed media is to create single-qualifier secondary keys using only the Luma controls. Because all video formats preserve the full quality of the Luma component of a color signal (Luma is the *4* in *4:1:1* and *4:2:0*), you'll find that this renders mattes with the best edge detail.

The Individual Qualifiers

Final Cut Pro's qualifier controls in the Limit Effect section are very similar to those found in many other color correction and keying interfaces. This section presents each control, along with shortcuts for its use.

When used separately, these controls allow you to perform single-qualifier secondary color correction, isolating portions of an image based on a single characteristic of the HSB color model. When used together, each control contributes to an overall chroma key, similar to those found in many other compositing packages.

Hue Control

The Hue control lets you select a portion of the color spectrum to isolate a range of color within an image. The spectrum is continuous; the blue at the right side of the control corresponds to that at the left side.

If you turn on the Hue control without turning on the Saturation control, you'll select all color values within a particular range of hues without regard to color intensity.

The two handles at the top of the control define the selected portion of the spectrum; the bottom two handles define the edge tolerance of the selection. Widening the bottom handles yields softer edges, and narrowing the bottom handles yields harder edges. All adjustments to both sets of handles are symmetrical.

Unlike the Saturation and Luma controls, the handles are always centered. To adjust the specific colors that are selected, you must drag the background spectrum gradient to the left or right.

If you're using a mouse with a scroll wheel or scroll ball, rolling up moves the spectrum gradient to the left, and rolling down moves the spectrum gradient to the right.

Saturation Control

The Saturation (Sat) control lets you select a range of saturation, or color intensity, within the image. The black end of the ramp to the left represents 100 percent saturation; the white portion of the ramp indicated by the two tick marks above and below indicate 0 percent saturation.

If you turn on the Saturation control without turning on the Hue control, you'll select all color values within a particular range of saturation without regard to the actual colors themselves.

Like the other controls, the two handles at the top of the control define the selected range of saturation; the bottom two handles define the edge tolerance of the selection. Widening the bottom handles yields softer edges, and narrowing the bottom handles yields harder edges. All adjustments to both sets of handles are symmetrical.

Unlike in the Hue control, the top handles can be moved individually to the left and right to select different ranges of saturation.

> **NOTE** ▶ Both bottom handles are locked together and move as a unit. When you adjust their width, they both widen or narrow together, centered on the midpoint between them.

If you're dragging the middle region in between both handles, then dragging moves both handles together. If you're using a mouse with a scroll wheel or scroll ball, rolling up moves both handles to the left and rolling down moves both handles to the right.

Luma Control

The Luma control lets you select a range of luma, or the lightness component of an image (the Y' in Y'CbCr). The black end of the ramp to the left represents 0 percent luma; the white end of the ramp indicated by the two tick marks above and below indicates 100 percent luma. The flat white area to the right of the two tick marks represents the superwhite range from 100 to 110 percent.

If you turn on the Luma control without turning on the Hue or Saturation controls, you'll select all areas of an image within a particular range of lightness, without regard to the color, similar to creating a luma key. This frequently yields the greatest amount of edge detail with highly compressed media.

Like the other controls, the two handles at the top of the control define the selected range of luma, and the bottom two handles define the edge tolerance of the selection. Widening the bottom handles yields softer edges, and narrowing the bottom handles yields harder edges. All adjustments to both sets of handles are symmetrical.

Unlike in the Hue control, you can move the handles to the left and right to select different ranges of saturation. They always move together.

> **NOTE** ▶ Both bottom handles are locked together and move as a unit. When you adjust their width, they both widen or narrow together, centered on the midpoint between them.

If you're using a mouse with a scroll wheel or scroll ball, rolling up moves both handles to the left, and rolling down moves both handles to the right.

Edge Thin and Softening Sliders

The Edge Thin and Softening sliders let you adjust and manipulate the matte that's created by the three controls.

Secondary color correction can be a real-time operation if you use the Hue, Saturation, and Luma controls only, but using the Edge Thin and Softening sliders increases this operation's demands on the processor to the point where real-time functionality is reduced to Unlimited RT on some machines, and even then at reduced resolution.

Edge Thin is an averaging control similar to the matte choke function found in other applications. Dragging this slider to the right expands the edges of the matte, which is useful for filling in small holes appearing in a keyed matte. Dragging to the left contracts the edges of the matte, which is useful for eliminating spurious pixels and unwanted details in the matte, as well as for shrinking the overall matte. Using Edge Thin all by itself can sometimes result in blockier edges, in which case increasing the Softening slider will smooth out the result.

Softening simply blurs the edges of the keyed matte. Dragging the slider to the right increases the amount of blur. This function is useful for eliminating spurious areas of keyed detail that you don't want affecting the final correction, as well as minimizing the visible effect of animated buzz and noise in the keyed matte.

Although these two sliders lend themselves to quick fixes, be careful not to use settings that are too aggressive. If you overdo these two filters, you'll get a halo around the area being corrected. For example, the following corrected clip has skin tones that might benefit from warming up with a secondary color correction:

Oversoftening the matte and then creating the correction could result in the same correction being applied to an area surrounding the intended subject, producing an unwanted glow where the correction is spilling onto the headrest and window to the left of the actor's face.

Select Color

The Select Color button lets you use an eyedropper to choose an initial value to create a secondary matte. It's a good way to start out if you're unsure exactly which hue you're selecting (which can be tricky), even if you plan on immediately switching to manual adjustment of the Limit Effect controls after you've found the starting point.

On the other hand, you can also use the Select Color button to expand a Limit Effect selection. After you've already clicked once to select an initial range of values, you can click the Select Color button, and then hold the Shift key down while you drag across a range of pixels in the Canvas. As you drag, the Hue, Saturation, and Luma controls will expand to include all the color vales of the pixels you dragged over.

Clicking once with the Select Color control sets the Hue, Saturation, and Luma controls to a new range of values determined by the new pixel you clicked, overriding the previous settings.

Choosing an initial value can be a tricky business. The noise and variation in detail inherent to any image can produce an extremely wide range of color even from pixel to pixel. That means that even if you think you've just clicked on a light part of the image, you might have inadvertently clicked on the one dark pixel of noise in that area, giving you a disappointing result. Don't worry, this is bound to happen, just click another pixel.

A general tip for getting started is to choose a color value that's right in-between the lightest and darkest values you're trying to key.

View Matte/Source/Final

This button lets you toggle the image that appears in the Canvas to show three different modes. Regardless of what the View Matte/Source/Final button is set to, the image displayed on the video output monitor is always the final image. You can then simultaneously adjust a secondary matte by viewing the matte in the Canvas while watching the final effect on your output broadcast monitor. The button changes to show which of the three modes is active.

A red key against a gray background displays the final image with the current secondary correction applied.

A black key against a white background displays the keyed matte that the Limit Effect controls are creating as a grayscale image. This mode lets you make manual adjustments to the matte while seeing exactly how it's being affected.

In View Matte mode, white represents the areas that will be affected by the secondary color correction operation, and black represents the areas that won't be affected. Gray areas represent areas of varying translucency.

A red key against a blue background displays the image as it appears without the current color correction. This mode lets you see the original range of colors in the image so you can make a new selection with the Select Color button. If you applied other Color Corrector filters previously, this mode shows the effect of the other filters on the image, just not the current one.

Invert Selection

The Invert Selection button lets you invert the current matte so that the selection becomes the background, and vice-versa.

Using Invert Selection is ideal if the subject to be excluded from a color correction operation is uniform enough in color and lightness to be selected with the Limit Effect controls, and you want to apply the secondary color correction to everything else.

For example, in the following clip, you want to lighten the dark portions of the image, but you don't want to affect the face.

One possible way of doing this quickly might be to use the Limit Effect controls to pull a key off of the man's face.

By clicking the Invert Selection button, you can reverse the matte, so now the face becomes the area that won't be affected by the secondary correction.

A technique that relies upon the Invert Selection control is elaborated upon in Limit Effect (Splitting Corrections into Regions).

Further Considerations

Secondary color correction is a powerful tool, and it's a good solution for many tasks. However, it's definitely a more time-consuming process than primary color correction— and more processor-intensive as well.

Many of the techniques in this book rely upon secondary color correction to make adjustments to very specific regions of the picture, but you should always verify whether or not you can make the same correction through careful manipulation of the Color Corrector 3-Way filter's primary color correction controls. It's a mistake to use the Limit Effect controls for operations that might be just as effective using the tonally specific Blacks, Mids, and Whites color balance controls. You'll be wasting time both during your correction session, and while you render the final output.

Limit Effect (Optimizing Secondary Keying Operations)

OVERVIEW ▶ Techniques for obtaining the best possible quality when pulling keys using the Limit Effect controls.

SEE ALSO ▶ chroma, limit effect controls

Improving the Key Improves the Effect

Because the Limit Effect controls are essentially a built-in chroma keyer that you use to control which parts of the image are corrected, the quality of your secondary correction is going to be dictated by the quality of the key you can pull. As with ordinary keying, this can be tricky. This entry discusses ways you can maximize the quality of your secondary corrections to prevent the noisiness and rough edges that prevent a successful correction.

Use High-Quality Digital Media

The best way to improve the quality of secondary color correction operations is to use the highest-quality video you can, ideally uncompressed media with the highest chroma sub-sampling ratio possible. High-quality video (for example, the Apple Uncompressed 8- and 10-bit 4:2:2 codecs, DVCPRO-50, and the DVCPRO HD codecs) encode video with 4:2:2 color sampling. As a result, you'll get relatively clean edge detail when pulling secondary keys when working with clips in these formats.

See Limit Effect Controls.

Apply a 4:1:1 or 4:2:2 Color Smoothing Filter

If you're correcting source material recorded with 4:1:1 color sampling (including NTSC DV and DVCPRO-25), you're stuck with as much color information as was captured, which is to say not much. Although this isn't necessarily such a severe liability with simple primary color correction, the results can be extremely blocky secondary keys.

Even 4:2:2 encoded media displays some aliasing along the edges of keys. One way to smooth these out, and potentially still some of the jitter inside of a noisy key, is to apply the Color Smoothing – 4:1:1 or Color Smoothing – 4:2:2 filters (found inside the Video Filters > Key bin of the Effects tab) to your clips prior to your color correction operations.

These filters selectively apply blurring to the Cr and Cb channels of video clips to smooth the rough edges left by the blocks of missing color information from the original encoding process. These filters were designed to improve keying operations when working with highly compressed media, and can in some cases improve the edges and lower noise of the keyed matte, usually without affecting the visible image.

Temporarily Boost the Saturation

Another strategy that sometimes helps is to boost the saturation of the overall image prior to making the secondary correction, make the secondary adjustment, and then lower the overall saturation back to the original levels in a last operation. You can think of the saturation boost as widening the difference between the colors of the subject you're trying to isolate and the areas you're trying to exclude. This can also be helpful if the initial image is fairly desaturated.

Make the Secondary Adjustment First

When you're creating a desaturated look, try boosting the areas of color that you want to adjust or maintain via a secondary color correction operation first, *before* applying primary color correction. This way you can take advantage of the pure, unadulterated color and brightness range in the image before any color manipulations that make it harder to pull secondary keys.

When you work this way, you'll need to overcompensate in the secondary color correction based on what the primary correction will be. In other words, if you know you'll be desaturating the overall image, then oversaturate by that amount in the initial secondary color correction, so the final result is correctly saturated.

In the following example, you'll adjust and boost the skin tone of the woman in the image prior to applying a desaturated look to the rest of the image:

1   Open the *Initial Secondary Overcompensation* sequence, located in the Limit Effect, Optimizing Secondary Operations bin of the **Color Correction Exercises** project.

2   Click the Filters tab, and add a Color Smoothing – 4:1:1 filter (in the Video Filters > Key bin of the Effects tab) to optimize the color channels of the clip for keying.

Later in the exercise, if you want to see how much of an effect this filter is having on your secondary key, you can toggle it on and off.

3   Apply a Color Corrector 3-Way filter to the first clip in the sequence. (The second clip is the finished correction, provided for comparison.) Open the clip into the Viewer, and click the Color Corrector tab to expose the graphical controls.

4   Open the Limit Effect controls, click the Select Color button, and click on a midtone of the woman's arm to set the Hue, Saturation, and Brightness controls. Then, either Shift-drag with the Select Color eyedropper to select more of the woman's arm, or set the View Matte/Source/Final button to Matte and adjust the handles of the limit effect handles to include as much of the woman's skin tone as possible while excluding most of the rest of the image. (You won't be able to exclude all of the rocks, but that's OK.)

5   Use the Edge Thin and Softening sliders to blur the matte to minimize noise.

There are going to be a few patches in the rocks that are included in the selection, but as long as they don't call attention to themselves in the final correction, don't worry about them.

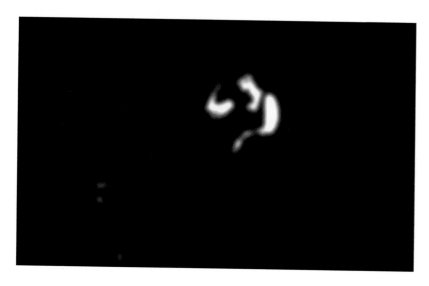

6   Once you've finished isolating the woman's arms and face, set the View Matte/Source/ Final button back to Final, and then drag the Mids and Whites color balance controls towards orange to put more color into the woman's skin. Drag the Saturation slider to the right to oversaturate the image by a significant amount.

The result is way over the top, and there are now numerous areas of rock that are unduly affected by this change, but it's only a temporary overcompensation, which will be muted in the next step.

7   Add a second Color Corrector 3-Way filter to the clip in the Viewer and click its tab. Adjust the contrast sliders to deepen the shadows, legalize the whites, and boost the mids to give a bright midday look. Finally, lower the Saturation to leech the color from the rest of the image.

Compared to the original (left), the final result (right) shows the contrast between the woman's arms and the other areas of the picture.

Third-Party Filters

A few third-party filters make the process of keying highly compressed media somewhat easier. Each of the filters from these developers uses different techniques to address the problem of low chroma subsampling ratios.

Adam Wilt

H. Chroma Blur

Chroma Offset (Y/C delay)

www.adamwilt.com/SteppyEdges.html

Adam Wilt, an authority on all things digital and video in nature, has an excellent Web site filled with useful information pertaining to DV media. The H. Chroma Blur and Chroma Offset (Y/C delay) filters provide additional control over the softening and positioning of the color channels to improve keying.

In addition to the filters, he has abundant information on what chroma subsampling is and its ramifications on your work, at the following page:

www.adamwilt.com/DV-FAQ-tech.html#colorSampling

Graeme Nattress

G Nicer – Film Effects

G Chroma Sharpen – Film Effects

www.nattress.com

G Nicer is Graeme Nattress' chroma reconstruction filter for DV video. It doesn't blur the chroma component of the image; instead, it uses various methods to interpolate the missing data from other channels.

G Chroma Sharpen uses other methods to add detail to subsampled chroma channels, and it has the advantage of also working with 4:2:0 color sampling (which includes DV PAL and HDV formats).

Joe's Filters
Joe's Channel Blur

www.joesfilters.com

An adjustable blur filter that allows you to selectively target specific channels in the Y'CbCr color space. This is a general purpose filter, but gives more customized control over exactly how you blur each channel.

Limit Effect (Splitting Corrections into Regions)

OVERVIEW ▸ Methods of using the Limit Effect controls to split an image into regions for separate correction.

SEE ALSO ▸ limit effect controls, limit effect, optimizing keying operations

You Don't Always Want to Correct Everything at Once

In many instances, you may want to apply a correction to one part of an image that will either over- or underexpose another part of the image, such as when an underlit subject is standing next to a window. Windows are notorious for being difficult to expose, and unless the crew was able to apply sheets of neutral density over the windows in the scene to balance the exterior light with the interior, they're often deliberately overexposed.

If, in a situation such as this, the extremely bright region of the picture (the window) isn't overexposed to the point of losing all visible detail, and the interior subject is underexposed (probably as a result of trying not to overexpose the window), you might feel yourself in a bit of a conundrum: How to brighten the subject without losing valuable detail in the window.

Secondary color correction is an excellent solution to these types of problems. You can use the Limit Effect controls to pull a secondary key on the brighter or darker area, and then selectively adjust the contrast of the darker subject while preserving the original values of the brighter portion of the image.

In this exercise, you'll follow this workflow to see how it's done:

1   Open the *Correcting Interior* sequence, located in the Limit Effect, Splitting Corrections Into Regions bin of the **Color Correction Exercises** project.

>   **NOTE** ▶ This is a high definition project. Although it's excellent for pulling high-quality secondary keys, you won't be able to play it out to a standard definition broadcast monitor unless you're either set up with high definition equipment, or you have a video output interface that's able to downconvert HD clips on the fly.

The clip of the man driving is well-exposed for the windows, but it has a low-key look for the interior. If the client decided that there should be more light on the man's face, you must lighten the interior of the car without making any changes to the light coming in through the window.

2   Apply a Color Corrector 3-Way filter to the first clip in the sequence. (The second clip is the finished correction, provided for comparison.) Open the clip into the Viewer, and click the Color Corrector tab to expose the graphical controls.

3   Open the Limit Effect controls, and click the View Final/Matte/Source control once to view the key while you work (a black key on a white background). Drag the handles of the Luma control all the way to the left, in order to isolate the darkest areas of the image corresponding to the interior of the automobile. Adjust the top and bottom handles until you've managed to select all of the shadows inside the car, while excluding anything outside the window. (Make sure you leave out the dark bushes running along the bottom.)

Essentially, you're performing a luma key, taking advantage of the full Luma component. Because this clip has 4:2:2 color subsampling, the results should be even sharper.

4   Raise the Softening slider a bit to blur what little aliasing there is around the edges of the mask, but don't blur the edges too much.

Because you're making a contrast adjustment to the shadows that won't also be applied to the highlights, you need to be especially sensitive to unwanted halos appearing along the edges of the correction.

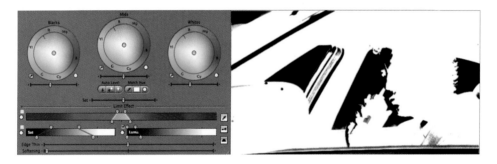

5   Click the View Final/Matte/Source control twice to view the final effect.

The button becomes a red key against a gray background.

6   Raise the Mids contrast slider, and boost the Saturation to compensate for the lack of saturation in the shadows.

Practically speaking, you won't be able to brighten the shadows too much; they were originally quite crushed, and you run the risk of overemphasizing the film grain in the image. (To be fair, this was the originally intended look of the shot.) Just bring a few of the details out of the shadows.

Final corrected clip, exaggerated for print.

This technique is effective for any clip where you have to deal with two areas that are exposed very differently.

Correcting Two Exclusive Areas

Another correction you can make, once you've isolated one area for correction, is to make a compatible correction to the inverse area by duplicating the first secondary color correction filter, using the Invert Selection button, and readjusting the primary controls.

In this exercise, you'll continue working the previous shot, this time quickly making a separate correction to the window:

1   Open the *Correcting Interior, Part II* sequence, located in the Limit Effect, Splitting Corrections Into Regions bin of the **Color Correction Exercises** project.

   The first clip is the end result of the previous exercise; the second clip is the finished effect, for comparison.

2   Make sure the playhead is directly over the first clip in the Timeline, and open it into the Viewer. Click the Filters tab, and drag the Color Corrector 3-Way filter that's already there onto the Canvas to create a duplicate of it underneath the previous filter.

   NOTE ▶ Unfortunately, there's no duplicate command that works in the Filters tab. You could copy and paste one or more selected filters, but the results end up at the top of the filter stack, which isn't always what you want.

   As soon as you duplicate the first filter, you'll notice that the image is now overexposed because you've simply doubled up the correction. This is only temporary.

3   Click the Visual button of the second Color Corrector filter to expose its graphical interface.

4   Click the Invert Selection button, and then Shift-click the Mids reset button to reset all of the primary controls to neutralize the correction while preserving the matte being generated by the Limit Effect controls.

You adjusted the contrast previously, so you'll need to make a small adjustment to the Limit Effect controls before proceeding.

5   Set the View Final/Matte/Source button to view the matte (a black key on a white background), make any necessary adjustments to make sure the matte is a continuous black in the shadows and white in the highlights and windows. Set the View Final/Matte/Source button to Final when you're done (a red key against gray).

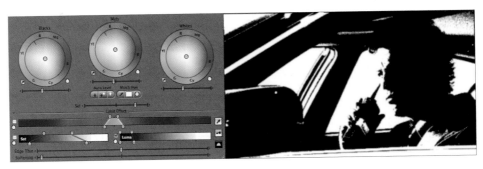

6   Drag the Mids contrast slider to the left to slightly darken the highlights, and then boost the saturation to enrich the color in the highlights and outside the window by a greater amount than the color in the shadows.

The final correction, exaggerated for print.

Breaking a shot up into multiple corrections in multiple areas isn't something you're going to do every day, but when the time is right, this is an extremely useful technique. In a way, you're using the Luma controls to define a tonal range for correction that's more customized than those defined by the Blacks, Mids, and Whites color balance controls.

Luma

OVERVIEW ▸ The component of a video signal that corresponds to light intensity. *Related terms:* Brightness.

SEE ALSO ▸ broadcast legality, gamma, chroma

What Is Luma?

Luma is the portion of the video signal that carries the monochrome portion of the image that determines brightness. In video applications, it is typically independent of the chroma (or color) of the image. In component Y'CbCr-encoded video, the luma is carried in the Y' channel of the video signal.

This scheme was originally devised to ensure compatibility between color and monochrome television sets (monochrome TVs simply ignore the chroma component, displaying the luma component by itself).

Because the eye is more sensitive to changes in luma than to changes in color, all video formats, regardless of the chroma subsampling scheme they employ, encode the full amount of luma.

NOTE ▸ The notation for composite video varies depending on whether it's digital or analog. Y'CbCr denotes digital component video, whereas Y'PbPr denotes analog component video.

Luma vs. Luminance

There is an important distinction between luminance, which is a measurement of the eye's perception of light intensity, and luma, which is a nonlinearly weighted measurement of light intensity used in video.

The human eye has varying sensitivity to each portion of the spectrum, which is represented by the luminous efficiency function. This function is approximated in the curve of the following illustration, superimposed over the visible spectrum:

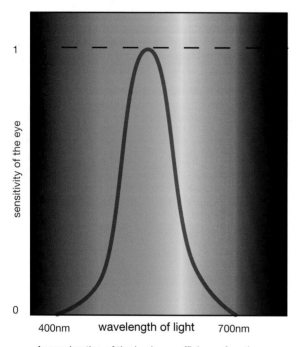

Approximation of the luminous efficiency function

As you can see, the eye is most sensitive to the green/yellow portion of the spectrum. Luminance, therefore, is a linear representation of the intensity of light, calculated by weighted sums of red, green, and blue according to a standardized model of the eye's sensitivities (as defined by the CIE). According to Charles Poynton in *Digital Video and HDTV Algorithms and Interfaces* (Morgan Kaufmann), luminance is calculated approximately 21 percent from red, 72 percent from green, and 7 percent from blue. (See the aforementioned book for much more information about luminance and luma encoding.)

This can be seen in the following image, where the measured luma of the pure red, green, and blue bars in the image is unequal, although the B value (brightness) of each bar as measured by the HSB color model is identical.

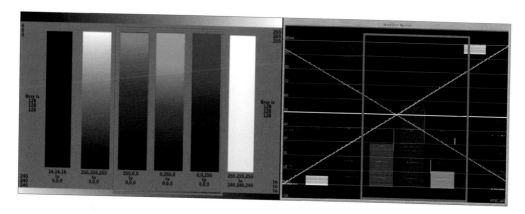

As covered elsewhere (see Gamma), the eye's perception of brightness is nonlinear. The gamma adjustment employed by video recording and display equipment takes this into consideration by making a nonlinear adjustment to the luminance calculation just described. Gamma-corrected luminance is called *luma*, designated by the Y' in Y'CbCr (the ' indicates the nonlinear transformation).

What Controls Affect Luma?

The Contrast sliders in the Color Corrector 3-Way filter directly affect the luma component of a signal, as do the controls of the Brightness and Contrast and Gamma Correction filters.

Luma and the Limit Effect Controls

Because the luma component, unlike chroma, is always sampled in its entirety, you'll get better results from luma keys than you will from chroma keys when working with 4:1:1 or 4:2:0 footage (although you'll still see some subtle aliased edges with 4:2:2 encoded video). See Limit Effect Controls.

Masked Corrections

OVERVIEW ► The process of using a shape to target a specific subject for color correction. *Related terms:* power windows, spot correction.

SEE ALSO ► masked corrections (using motion), masked corrections (using the four- and eight-point matte filters)

What Are Masked Corrections?

A masked correction is a technique using a shape, usually an oval or rectangle, to limit the effect of a color correction. Masked corrections are useful in instances where the Limit Effect controls are too cumbersome, the image is too difficult to key, or when the portion you want to affect is easily defined by an oval or rectangular shape. Consider the following before (left) and after (right) pair; the face of the man on the right was brightened with an oval masked correction to give him emphasis (exaggerated for print):

Other color correction environments refer to masked corrections by other names, such as Power Windows (Da Vinci) or spot corrections (Avid). Whatever they're called, they're indispensable tools, and with a few extra steps, you can create masked corrections in Final Cut Pro.

The Basic Components

Masked corrections in Final Cut Pro involve superimposing a duplicate of the shot you want to correct above itself, and then using filters or Motion parameters to mask off the portion of the superimposed clip you want to correct. For typical masked corrections requiring a simple shape, the fastest way to do this is using a group of three filters:

To create a masked correction, a duplicate of the clip is superimposed over the original, and then filtered.

▶ Mask Shape creates the mask, and it can be set to create a diamond, oval, rectangle, or round rectangle mask. You can customize the shape and size using the Horizontal and Vertical Scale sliders, and the position using the Center control. You also can invert the mask to create vignetted corrections, instead.

▶ Mask Feather allows you to feather the edges of any mask or alpha channel by blurring a clip's alpha channel. This filter is useful for many purposes, but here it makes up for the Mask Shape filter's lack of a feathering slider.

▶ Desaturate makes it easy to see where the shape is in the image while you're resizing and positioning it. When you're finished, turn this filter off.

After you create a mask with these three filters, you use a Color Corrector filter to actually make the correction.

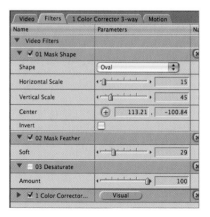

Considering all the filters involved, you've probably guessed that this isn't a real-time effect. Setting Final Cut Pro to use Unlimited RT on a fast machine will give you a low-quality preview, but you'll have to render the composite to see what it really looks like.

Compiling a Masked Correction Filter Pack

Instead of hunting down all three filters whenever you want to create this effect, you can create a filter pack (a bin in the Favorites containing multiple filters) so you can apply them all at once.

1   In the Effects tab, open the Favorites bin. Create a new bin inside of it, and name it *Masked Correction*.

2   Copy the following video filters into this bin:

   ▶ Image Control > Desaturate

   ▶ Matte > Mask Shape

   ▶ Matte > Mask Feather

3   Rename the filters to *01 Mask Shape*, *02 Mask Feather*, and *03 Desaturate*.

   Renaming the filters keeps them in the proper order; otherwise they'll become alphabetized. It's important that Mask Feather comes after Mask Shape.

Now, you can drag and drop all three filters onto a clip at once whenever you need to use this effect.

Nine times out of ten, you'll probably want to use the Shape filter set to Oval (it defaults to Rectangle), so you may want to set this up as the default in your Favorites. Customizing favorite filters is easy, just open them into the Viewer and make whatever change you want. In this case, double-click the 01 Mask Shape filter in the Masked Correction bin of your Favorites, and choose Oval from the Shape pop-up. That change sticks to the filter favorite, determining how it is applied from then on.

Creating a Masked Correction

In this example, you'll use the Masked Correction filter pack to perform a typical correction, adding highlights to the faces of a pair of actors in a shot. Afterwards, you'll learn how to animate the masks to account for camera motion in the shot.

1   Open the *Mask Shape Corrections* sequence, located in the Masked Corrections, Using Filters bin of the **Color Correction Exercises** project.

NOTE ▶ If you're viewing this project on an external broadcast monitor, switch the monitor to 16:9 (if it is so capable). This is an anamorphic project.

2   Move the playhead to the marker in the middle of the first clip (frame 01:00:05:13).

The first part of the clip has a camera dolly that you'll deal with later. The important thing to remember is that whenever you have camera motion, move to a frame where the motion has stopped (if it ever stops) so you can set up the initial effect. In this instance, the second half of the clip is locked down.

3   Open this clip into the Viewer, and click the Filters tab.

Typically, your first step would be to apply whatever color correction you wanted to the overall shot before starting in with any masked corrections. By adjusting the background first, you'll know how much latitude you'll have for subsequent corrections, saving time.

This clip already has a color correction filter applied, which is boosting the midtones and the saturation. Despite this, it's still pretty dark, but the client wanted a moody, dark tone. You'll be adding masked corrections to brighten the faces of the two actors in the shot, bringing them out of the background and making them more visible to the audience.

4   To get started, superimpose a copy of the clip above itself in track V2. There are two fast ways to do this:

▶   Option-drag the clip in the Timeline to track V2, holding down the Shift key to keep it locked to the same position on the Timeline.

▶   Drag it from the Timeline directly to the Superimpose target of the Canvas, and a duplicate will be superimposed.

Keep in mind that this duplicate also has the same color correction filter, which is important because you'll use this filter as the starting point for your masked correction.

5   Apply the Masked Correction filter pack you created before (you did create it, didn't you?) by dragging it from the Favorites bin onto the superimposed clip in track V2.

You should immediately see the desaturated area showing you the shape and position of the mask.

6   Open the superimposed clip into the Viewer, click the Filters tab, and use the parameters in the Mask Shape filter to adjust the shape and position of the mask to highlight the face of the man laying down.

7 Increase the Soft parameter of the Mask Feather filter until the shape becomes indistinct.

A successful mask is one where the viewer can't make out its shape. If the edge is too well defined, the correction will look fake because the audience can see the border of the correction. On the other hand, if the edge is too soft, you may not be able to make enough of a correction.

In the left image, the edge of the mask is too sharp, making it easy to see the correction. In the right image, the edges of the mask have been blurred to hide the effect.

In general, you want to avoid creating a halo around the feature you're trying to isolate. How much feathering, and how large a region you'll be able to successfully mask, depends entirely on the image. Since this effect simulates shining a spotlight on a portion of the image, sometimes you'll be able to get away with a lot of spill, and other times you won't.

In this exercise, a very soft border gives the best effect, and the eventual spill that results looks perfectly natural. Be thankful for shots that allow sloppy masks!

8 When you're satisfied with the shape and feathering of the mask, turn off the Desaturate filter.

You won't be needing the Desaturate filter until you perform another correction.

Now that you've defined the mask, you can make the correction. At the moment, you shouldn't be able to see any difference in the image, because the masked clip and the background clip underneath both have color correction filters with identical settings, which is by design. If you're trying to create a natural lighting effect, the masked correction needs to share the same color balance and general contrast ratio as the background.

9 Click the Color Corrector tab in the Viewer, and adjust the color correction filter to boost the luma in the mids, adding light to his face.

Raising the saturation will compensate for the apparent loss of color caused by the brightness increase, and dragging the Mids color balance control a little towards red will add a bit of health to his face, as well. Compare the original image (left) and the result (right).

As you make these adjustments, notice that there is indeed some spill from this correction on the woman's shirt and arm. In this case, don't worry about it. It looks natural, since any light falling on his face would also fall around it. More importantly, you don't want a discernable halo or shape. If necessary, you can always go back and readjust the mask to make improvements to the effect.

If you ever need to do a sanity check to see how the clip looks before and after, simply toggle the Enable Track control on and off for track V2.

Now that you've corrected his face, do the same thing for the woman, adding light to her face and shirt. To save time, you'll duplicate the man's masked correction layer and customize it for her.

10 Duplicate the clip in track V2 and superimpose it in track V3.

11 Open this new clip into the Viewer, click the Filters tab, and readjust the Mask Shape and Mask Feather parameters to cast some light on her.

Before and after.

As with the mask around the man's face, a bit of halo doesn't hurt this shot, because the light falls off into the darkness of the foliage behind her, and casting a bit of light on her arm looks natural.

So there you have it. The background remains dark and moody, but the most important subjects in the shot, the faces of the characters onscreen, are now more brightly illuminated.

If this were a locked-camera shot, you'd be done, but you shouldn't forget about the camera dolly in the first half of the shot. Fortunately, mask parameters can be animated just like any other effect in Final Cut Pro.

Animating a Mask

As nice as masked corrections are, the one problem you'll run into is when either the camera or the subject you're masking move around. If the movements are small, you might be able to get away with not animating the mask, but if the movement is significant, you'll end up with a bright (or dark) spot that's sitting somewhere it shouldn't be.

One of the nice things about using the Mask Shape filter is that its position is determined by a single parameter, the Center parameter. To match the camera motion in the current example, all you need to do is animate this one parameter to make the mask move along with the actors.

1   Start with the woman by opening the clip in track V3 into the Viewer and clicking the Filters tab.

2   With the playhead sitting on the marker that pinpoints the frame where the camera stops moving, click the Mask Shape's Center control to see where the center crosshairs are.

    If you know you need to animate a mask, one tip is to place the center of the mask over a feature of the masked subject that's easy to follow. Because Final Cut Pro doesn't have any kind of automated motion tracking, you'll have to do this by hand (don't worry, it's not hard), so having the Center control's crosshairs over an easy-to-see feature makes your job much easier. In this example, it's pretty easy to center the oval correction on the top of her shirt's collar.

3   If necessary, readjust the Mask Shape's Center parameter *before* you start creating any keyframes, to make sure you're off to a good start.

After you've made this adjustment, the crosshairs disappear; they become visible when you click the Center control again.

4   After you move the Center parameter to a feature that's easy to track, click the Center parameter's Insert Keyframe button in the Filters tab to record its position at that frame.

A keyframe appears in the keyframe graph area of the Filters tab, located to the right of the parameters. You can zoom into this keyframe graph to get greater control as you add more keyframes.

NOTE ▶ If you need to, you can also drag the Filters tab into the Timeline to get a really long view of the keyframe graph. Just remember to drag it back into the Viewer when you're finished, to avoid possible problems. Unfortunately, the Mask Shape filter's Center parameter cannot be revealed in the Timeline's keyframe editor, because it's a two-dimensional parameter.

5   Move the playhead earlier in the clip, to the first frame where that feature (the collar, if that's what you're using) just becomes visible at the far left of the frame. Click the Center control again, and move the crosshairs to the new position of her collar to reposition the mask.

Once you've started to record keyframes for a particular parameter, all adjustments you make to that parameter at other frames record additional keyframes, creating animation.

6   In order to create the smoothest motion possible, and to avoid having to add more keyframes than necessary, move the playhead to a frame directly between the two keyframes you've just created, and click the Center parameter again to see where the crosshairs are.

You now can see that the crosshairs is offset. The camera's speed isn't linear enough that Final Cut Pro's automatic position interpolation works without adjustment, but you can fix it manually.

7   With the crosshairs ready to be adjusted, reposition them onto the shirt collar.

This is the fastest way to hand-track a feature. Simply define the outer boundaries of a single continuous motion (where the subject starts, moves into a single direction, and stops), add keyframes to the first and last frame of that motion, and then check the position directly between each pair of keyframes by turning on the Center control, repositioning it to correct the motion if necessary, or turning it back off if the crosshairs are faithfully following the feature.

In this example, four keyframes are all you need to track the mask to the camera movement with a fair degree of accuracy.

Name	Parameters	Nav	01:00:12:00	01:00:15:00
▼ Video Filters				
▶ ✓ Color Corrector...	Visual	Ⓧ ☑▾		
▼ ✓ 01 Mask Shape		Ⓧ ☑▾	◆	◆
Shape	Oval			
Horizontal Scale	16	◀◉▶		
Vertical Scale	50	◀◉▶		
Center	⊕ -133.58 , -73.95	◀◉▶	◆	◆

8   When you're finished animating the woman's mask, follow the same procedure to animate the mask for the man.

When you've finished matching the man's mask to the camera movement, you need to take care of one last thing. The masks are only tracked as far as the edge of the frame, but the actors come from all the way offscreen in the first second of the clip. There are two ways you can deal with the masks:

▶   You can continue to animate them all the way offscreen, which has the advantage of looking completely natural but requires an extra couple of steps.

▶   You could also do a slow fade-in of the masked correction layers themselves using the opacity parameter. Fading them in at the frame where the subjects first appear is a quick and easy way to introduce the effect, and if you're careful, should be unnoticeable. This is the way the "after" set of clips in the *Mask Shape Corrections* sequence is set up, and you can judge the effect for yourself.

Further Considerations

Masked corrections are sometimes the fastest way of targeting a specific subject for color correction. However, dealing with animated subjects can be challenging, so make sure that the limit effect controls won't do what you need before proceeding with a masked correction.

If you're attempting to isolate a portion of the subject that's moving around a lot, you might be better off creating a rotoscoped mask using Motion. See Masked Corrections (Using Motion).

If you have Shake, After Effects, or Combustion, you could also use the motion tracking in each of those applications to try automatically matching the mask to the motion of the subject.

Masked Corrections (Using the Four- and Eight-Point Matte Filters)

OVERVIEW ▶ The process of using the Four-Point and Eight-Point Garbage Matte filters to perform masked corrections.

SEE ALSO ▶ masked corrections, masked corrections (using Motion)

Making Multi-Point Masked Corrections

Masked corrections using the Four- and Eight-Point Garbage Mattes are most useful in cases where you need to make a targeted correction to a portion of the image, but you can't easily key using the Limit Effect controls nor easily isolate using a diamond, oval, or rectangle (see Masked Corrections).

Another option, using Motion to create a Bézier or B-spline mask (see Masked Corrections (Using Motion)), may be overkill if the portion of the image you need to adjust can be isolated using a simple four- or eight-point polygonal matte. If this is the case, it's usually faster to just stay inside of Final Cut Pro.

For the following example, the client would like to eliminate the red light shining on the wall (below left). The Limit Effect controls won't work, because any amount of red that's keyed will include their faces and clothes due both to their inherent color and light spill.

The wall is an irregular enough shape to merit the use of a shape, but an eight-point isolates that area just fine, as you can see in the image on the right:

Using the Four-Point and Eight-Point Garbage Matte Filters

There are two filters available for creating polygonal mattes. Their controls are identical, except that one creates four-point mattes, and the other creates eight-point mattes. These filters were originally created to crop out the outside portion of a clip being keyed, but they are useful for any situation where you need a fast polygonal matte. The parameters for these filters are as follows:

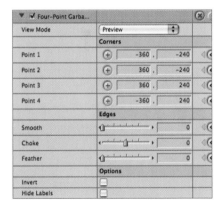

▶ View Mode—This lets you show or hide the control points and outline of the matte you're creating. As you're working, set this control to Preview to see the control points, or Wireframe to see the control points and an outline of the matte itself. When you're finished editing the effect, set this parameter to Final to hide the controls and show only the image.

▶ Point 1 through Point 8—These controls let you individually adjust the position of each point of the matte. The easiest way of using these is to click the point control for the parameter you want to adjust, then click and drag within the Canvas to interactively move the point around. In some cases, depending on the frame size of your clip and the percentage at which the Canvas is zoomed, the control point you're adjusting may be offset from the actual position of your mouse. (This is a known issue.)

▶ Smooth—Increasing this parameter rounds the corners of the polygon, creating smooth shapes instead of sharp angles. The more you increase this parameter, the rounder your shape becomes, shrinking at the same time to accommodate the new form:

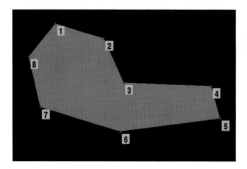 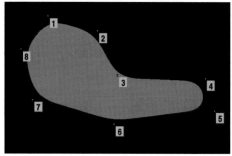

▶ Choke—This parameter lets you increase or decrease the overall size of the matte without having to move all of the points. The following figures show what happens to the same Eight-Point Garbage Matte with a high Choke value, Choke set to 0, and a low Choke value:

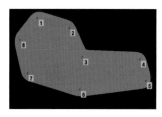 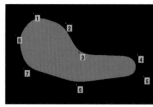 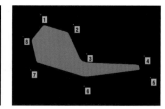

▶ Feather—This lets you blur the edges of the matte, creating a softer blend between the background and the isolated area:

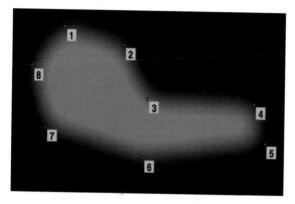

▶ Invert—If you select this option, you can create a matte using the outer area, rather than the inner area, of the shape.

▶ Hide Labels—Select this option to hide the numbers, while leaving the control points visible when View Mode is set to Preview.

How to Make Multi-Point Masks

Using the Four-Point and Eight-Point Garbage Matte filters (located in the Matte bin) to make masked corrections is similar to making masked corrections using the Mask Shape filter, although it requires fewer filters to create the effect. The preview modes eliminate the need to desaturate the center of the masked area while making adjustments, and the built-in Feather parameter eliminates the need for the Mask Feather filter.

1 Open the *Masked Corrections, Using 4- and 8-Point Masks* sequence, located in the 8-Point Masked Correction bin of the **Color Correction Exercises** project.

   NOTE ▶ If you're viewing this project on an external broadcast monitor, switch the monitor to 16:9 (if it is so capable). This is an anamorphic project.

The first clip is the one shown earlier, with red spill light on the wall that needs to be eliminated. This clip has already had a basic color correction applied to it. The second clip is the finished exercise for you to refer to.

2   Superimpose a duplicate of the clip above itself, the same way you would when making a masked correction.

3   Add the Eight-Point Garbage Matte to the superimposed clip, open the clip into the Viewer, and click the Filters tab to reveal the Garbage Matte's parameters.

4   Using the Point 4, 5, and 6 controls, isolate the portion of the wall to the left of the actors. Set View Mode to Wireframe if that helps you to see what you're doing.

When using the Garbage Matte filters, you'll quickly learn that adjusting only the points you need to is faster than readjusting the entire shape..

5   Change the View Mode to Final when you're finished adjusting the matte shape.

6   Click the Color Corrector tab. (This is a duplicate of the Color Corrector filter that's also applied to the clip underneath.) Lower the saturation until the red light on the wall goes away.

This correction also catches the forehead of the man on the right, so if you'd like, you can go back to the Filters tab and increase the Smooth parameter.

Rounding the corners also shrinks the matte slightly, in addition to edging the matte away from the sharper angles, which is exactly what you want to do here.

NOTE ▶ For extra-bonus credit, an oval masked correction was added to one side of the face of the man sitting down, subtracting color and giving him a similar lighting ratio as the man standing up. This appears in the finished version.

As you can see, the Garbage Matte filters provide a fast way of making simple masks to isolate odd areas. If one of the actors were to move, you can take advantage of the capability to individually animate each of the control points to do some simple rotoscoping.

If the shape you need to isolate is much more complicated, however, or the subjects are moving quite a bit, you may find it simpler to use Motion to make your mask. For more information, see Masked Corrections (Using Motion).

Third-Party Garbage Matte Filters

A number of third-party filters extend and improve upon the functionality of Final Cut Pro's two Garbage Matte filters.

Eureka
Trackable Matte

www.kafwang.com/eureka/EurekaMain.html

This is a free 8-point garbage matte. It's identical to the Final Cut Pro filter with one notable exception: it has a Mask Offset parameter that lets you animate the position of the entire matte with one set of keyframes. This is ideal when the region you need to isolate is moving, but its shape isn't changing.

Artmetric
16-Point Matte – Essential Box

www.artmetic.com/plugins

This plug-in package includes a 16-point garbage matte filter for those really hard-to-isolate areas.

CGM
Bezier Matte 20P – Volume 3

Selective Color Correction 4P and 8P – Volume 2

www.cgm-online.com/eiperle/cgm_e.html

This filter package includes a 20-point garbage matte filter, as well as some multi-point color correction tools that combine masking and specific color correction controls in a single filter.

CVH
Bezier Garbage Matte Pro

www.chv-plugins.com

This filter package includes the Bézier Garbage Matte filter, ingeniously creating Bézier curves within Final Cut Pro, with up to 40 control points.

Masked Corrections (Using Motion)

OVERVIEW ▶ The process of using Motion to create masks for selectively color correcting regions of clips in Final Cut Pro. *Related terms:* user-selected shapes, power windows.

SEE ALSO ▶ masked corrections, masked corrections (using the four- and eight-point matte filters)

Why Use Motion to Create Masks?

Although there are many techniques for making masked corrections right in Final Cut Pro, sometimes its Matte filters may prove too limited. If you need to isolate a portion of the image that has a very irregular shape and is animated, you can create a mask using Motion's superior drawing tools for use in your Final Cut Pro project.

Motion's interface is well suited for drawing and animating shapes and masks. Its interface lets you use two different types of shapes for creating masks:

▶ Bezier shapes—These work similarly to the drawing tools in many other applications, such as Freehand or Illustrator. Individual control points connect together with line segments to form sharp angles, and control points with Bezier handles create curves. Every control point lies directly on the surface of the shape.

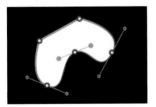

▶ B-spline shapes—The individual control points of these lie to either side of the surface of the shape they create, influencing the shape of a curve based on their proximity both to the shape surface, and to other control points contributing to the shape. More control points let you create more complicated curves; fewer control points result in simpler curves.

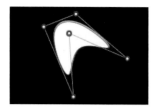

Shapes can be filled, colored, outlined, feathered, and rendered solid, opaque, or transparent. Additionally, you can create groups of intersecting shapes that work together to create extremely detailed masks. For complicated masked corrections, these tools are extremely powerful.

Motion and Final Cut Pro Workflow

Although Motion has superior masking features, it processes images in the RGB color space. If your Final Cut Pro project uses one of the Y'CbCr codecs (such as DV, HDV, or 8-bit Uncompressed 4:2:2), the Y'CbCr-to-RGB conversion that results from sending a clip from Final Cut Pro to Motion may clamp high luma and chroma values in your media. In particular, superwhite values will be clamped to 100 percent, meaning a potentially significant loss of image detail in the highlights.

Additionally, you'll find that Final Cut Pro's color correction tools are more sophisticated than those found in Motion, which are geared to compositing tasks in RGB. If you're accustomed to the power of the Color Corrector 3-Way filter, there is no direct equivalent in Motion.

Fortunately, there's an easy way you can use Motion's strengths in mask creation, and still retain Final Cut Pro's ability to color correct in the Y'CbCr color space. Simply follow this workflow:

1   Send a clip to Motion.

2   In Motion, trace the necessary part of the clip using one or more shapes, and then turn off the background clip so the image is white against black.

3   Use the resulting white-against-black Motion project clip as a Matte layer in a superimposed Travel Matte - Luma operation inside of Final Cut Pro.

4   Color correct the matted layer.

Here you use only Motion to create a matte layer, with which Final Cut Pro limits the effect of a Color Correction filter on a superimposed layer using the Travel Matte - Luma composite mode. As a result, all of the original values in the Y'CbCr space are preserved.

Rotoscoping Round-Trip: Final Cut Pro to Motion and Back

In theory, the workflow takes only five steps; in practice you need to do a little more work along the way. In the following sections, you'll prepare a clip, send it from a Final Cut Pro project to Motion, and isolate the background with an animated shape there. Afterwards, you'll use the animated shape as a matte layer in Final Cut Pro to create the final color correction.

Prepare Before Sending a Clip to Motion

A bit of preparation prior to sending a clip from Final Cut Pro to Motion eliminates steps and frustration later.

1   Open the *Masking With Motion—Start* sequence, located in the Masked Corrections, Using Motion bin of the **Color Correction Exercises** project.

   NOTE ▶ If you're viewing this project on an external broadcast monitor, switch the monitor to 16:9 (if possible). This is an anamorphic project.

The Desk Reverse 2-shot A clip has already been color corrected. In this hypothetical situation, however, the client wants the wall behind the two actors to be darker.
Because this is such an irregular region, the actors shift around a bit, and there is no
significant quality of lighting or color on which to base a secondary key, this is a good
situation in which to use a masked correction. Creating a rotoscoped mask in Motion
is one of the fastest ways to accomplish this task.

2   To set up the shot for the correction you're about to make, create two duplicates of
this clip, superimposed over the original, in tracks V2 and V3.

This isn't necessary for sending a clip to Motion, but the duplicate layers in tracks V2
and V3 will be used in later steps, so it's best to set this up now.

3   To create the actual mask, Control-click the middle clip in track V2, and choose
Send > To Motion.

4   When the Export Selection to Motion Project window appears, type a name into the
Save As field (such as *Desk Reverse Mask*), and specify a location for saving the resulting Motion project file. The location defaults to your Documents folder, but make
sure you keep your Motion projects in the same location as the other project and
graphics files used for your program. Leave the two bottom checkboxes selected, and
click Save.

Final Cut Pro creates a new Motion project using the clip you selected in Final Cut Pro. If Motion is installed on your computer, it automatically opens the new project file.

The new Motion project automatically matches the duration of the clip (or clips) that you selected in Final Cut Pro, as well as the resolution, frame rate, and aspect ratio. In case you were wondering, no new media is created, the new Motion project references the same media on disk as the original Final Cut Pro clip.

Notice that one thing is missing from the clip when you view it in Motion: The color correction you applied to it in Final Cut Pro. Final Cut Pro filters are not brought over into Motion projects, nor are they applied to the .motn project clip that has replaced the original clip in the Final Cut Pro Timeline.

Instead, the original clip, along with every filter applied to it, appears in a new sequence created in the Browser. This new sequence serves to preserve the original state of the clip that's been replaced and has the same name as the Motion project file you created.

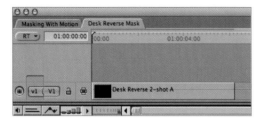

A new sequence is created whenever you send one or more clips to Motion, which contains the original clips along with whatever effects are applied to them.

The lack of filtering in Motion is just fine, however, because you're only using the clip as a reference for creating an animated mask.

Create an Animated Shape in Motion

Using Motion, you'll next create a shape to isolate the area you want to color correct separately in Final Cut Pro. In this example, that means rotoscoping the background behind the actors. (*Rotoscoping* is a fancy name for tracing moving subjects frame-by-frame to isolate them for effects work.)

1   Choose Edit > Project Properties, and choose NTSC D1/DV Anamorphic from the Pixel Aspect Ratio pop-up menu in the Project Properties window.

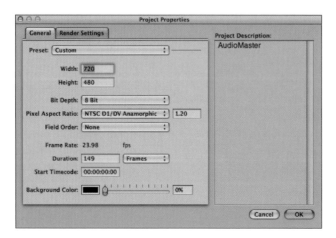

This ensures that the motion project will have the correct aspect ratio when you go back to the original project, which is an anamorphic project. This setting is not automatically made.

2   To start creating a shape, click the Create Shape tool in the toolbar at the top of the Canvas. For this example, choose the Bezier Shape tool.

You have the choice of creating either Bezier or B-Spline shapes. Each has its advantages: you may find that Bezier splines are more intuitive for creating detailed shapes that combine corners and curves, and B-spline shapes are sometimes faster for tracing curvy, less detailed regions. These are only generalizations, of course, animators often have different preferences depending on their experience.

NOTE ▶ For more information on creating shapes in Motion, see the chapter "Using Shapes and Masks" in the Motion user's manual, available from the Help menu.

3   Click anywhere in the Canvas to start drawing control points, and loosely trace the two actors to isolate the background behind them. Be sure to include part of the off-frame area to make sure you don't leave out any of the background.

Using the Bezier Shape tool, clicking once creates a corner point; clicking and dragging creates a curve. If you've used any other spline-based drawing programs, such as Freehand or Illustrator, you should already be familiar with the tool.

You can adjust existing control points by moving the Pen tool over the control point; when it changes to a pointer, drag the point wherever you need it. Moving the pointer off of the control point returns it to the Pen tool. You can even make these adjustments while you're in the middle of drawing.

4 When you're happy with the shape, click the first point you created to finish it. It immediately turns into a solid white shape.

NOTE ▸ If you don't see the control points going around the outside of your shape once it's finished, make sure that Show Overlays, Handles, and Lines are turned on in the View pop-up menu of the Canvas.

5   If necessary, press F7 to show the Dashboard. With the shape you've just drawn currently selected, drag the Feather slider to the right to blur the edge of the shape.

The Dashboard shows a short list of the most important parameters available for the currently selected object. F7 toggles the Dashboard off and on.

6   If necessary, readjust the outside of the shape so that the feathered edge isn't overlapping too much over the actors, but there isn't too much of a background halo around them, either.

NOTE ▶ If you want to see the outline of the shape without the white fill while you make adjustments, you can turn off the Fill parameter in the Dashboard. Make sure you turn it back on before finishing the project and going back to Final Cut Pro.

If the automatic snapping behavior is getting in your way while you make your adjustments, press the N key to toggle it off. (This is the same shortcut as in Final Cut Pro).

7   With the initial shape of the mask complete, click the Play button to see the clip in motion.

You should observe that the actors shift around a bit. You need to animate the shape you just created to move with the actors.

8   Scrub the playhead in the Canvas to the first frame that occurs just before the man begins to move (frame 45), and click the Record button (or press A).

By default, this step sets Motion to record keyframes for parameters corresponding to anything you manipulate in the Canvas. However, simply turning this control on doesn't record any keyframes for any parameters by itself.

NOTE ▶ Double-clicking the Record button opens the Recording Options window, where you can turn on the Record Keyframes on Animated Parameters Only option. For simplicity, leave this option off.

9 To place an initial keyframe as simply as possible, move one of the onscreen control points one pixel or so.

Doing so freezes the shape you just drew in its current state at this frame by creating a keyframe for that shape's Shape Animation parameter. You can't see it, but it's been recorded.

If you don't see the control points of a selected shape that you want to edit, you may need to choose the Adjust Control Points tool from the tool pop-up menu in the upper-left corner of the Toolbar. You can also press the Tab key repeatedly until the onscreen control points for the selected shape appear.

Whether you realize it or not, you've just started rotoscoping the actors in this scene. One of the nice things about rotoscoping for purposes of color correction is that, depending on the operation, you don't necessarily have to create the world's tightest and most accurate mask to get the job done. On the other hand, making it as good as you can never hurts.

10 Scrub through the clip, and make adjustments to the shape whenever one of the actors starts or stops moving. Every time you make an adjustment at a new frame, you'll be adding a keyframe to the shape's Shape Animation parameter.

When you're rotoscoping moving subjects, begin by making adjustments to your shape at frames where the subject begins moving into a particular direction and frames where the movement in that direction ends. The goal is to let Motion do as much of the work as possible by automatically animating the frames in-between these key shapes. When you play the result to see how well your shape matches the motion of the subject, you can make further manual adjustments at any frame where the movement of the subject deviates from the automatically animated shape.

For example, playing the clip shows that from frame 45 to frame 72, the man on the left lowers his head and pauses, while the woman shifts to the left and pauses. Because you've already established a keyframe at frame 45, frame 72 is a good frame at which to make the next adjustment to the shape.

At frame 95, the woman pauses after shifting to the right, so that's another good frame at which to adjust the shape. Frame 118 is also a likely frame for adjustment.

11 To see the keyframes you've just created, click the Timing button in the Toolbar to reveal the Timing area, which contains the Timeline, Keyframe Editor, and Audio Editor.

There are two places you can work with keyframes. You can view and edit them directly in the Timeline by turning on the Keyframe button (located in the lower-left corner).

This reveals the shape's keyframes underneath the shape clip in the Timeline, where they can be selected, moved, and deleted.

You can also use the Keyframe Editor, which is what you'll do in this exercise.

12 Click the Keyframe Editor tab, which is where you can expose and edit keyframes and curves for various parameters. Choose Animated from the Show pop-up menu to automatically reveal every parameter in your project that has been keyframed.

The Shape Animation parameter appears. Every change you make to a shape while the Record button is turned on creates a single keyframe for that shape in the Shape Animation parameter, which now appears in the keyframe graph to the left.

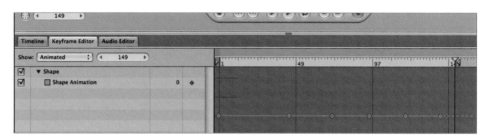

Here, you can delete or move keyframes. To change the timing of your animation by moving a keyframe, simply drag it to the left or right. (You can Shift-click or drag a bounding box to select multiple keyframes.) To delete one or more keyframes, select them and press the Delete key.

NOTE ▶ For more information on keyframing in Motion, see the chapter "Keyframes and Curves" in the Motion user's manual, available from the Help menu.

13 Click the Timing button again to close the Keyframe Editor.

14 Continue playing through your clip and adjusting the shape until you feel that the shape's animation follows the movement of the actors naturally.

15 When you're finished, click the Record button to turn it off, and then click the Project button in the Toolbar to reveal the Layers tab.

16 In the Layers tab, click the checkbox next to Layer 1 to turn it off. Layer 1 contains the clip that was sent over from Final Cut Pro.

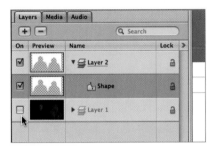

All of the work you've just done was solely to create an animated shape to be used as a matte back in Final Cut Pro. By turning off the imported clip you've been rotoscoping, you end up with the white-on-black image necessary for masking.

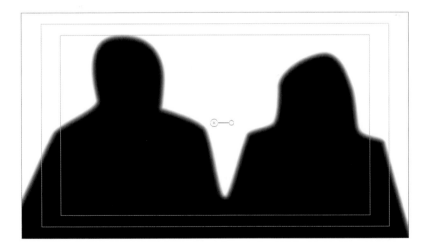

At this point, you're finished with Motion.

17 Save the project, and then go back to Final Cut Pro. Make sure that you always save your Motion project *before* going back to Final Cut Pro. After all that hard work, you wouldn't want to lose it! Also, wait until after Motion has finished saving the project before going back to your Final Cut Pro project.

Use the Motion Project as a Matte in Final Cut Pro

Back in Final Cut Pro, take a look at the Timeline; you'll see the .motn project clip has replaced the original clip that you had selected in track V2. You should also notice that the .motn clip has appeared in the Browser, along with an identically named sequence that contains the original clip that was originally sent.

Now the reason for creating two duplicated superimpositions should be clear. The V1 layer is to be the foreground of the masked correction, the V2 layer is the mask (where white identifies the area of adjustment, and black the area to be made transparent), and the V3 layer is to be the correction to the background that you're intending to make.

1 To see the image you'll be using as the matte, disable track V3.

The white shape you created should be superimposed above the clip in track V1. If it looks distorted, make sure you follow step 1 on page 300 before proceeding.

In the next two steps, you're going to use the shape in track V2 as a matte to isolate the background of the clip in track V3.

2   Enable track V3. Control-click the clip in track V3, and choose Composite Mode > Travel Matte Luma.

At the moment, nothing seems to have happened, but that's because you haven't made any changes to the Color Correctoion filter that's applied to the now isolated background of the clip in track V3.

3   Open the clip in track V3 into the Viewer, click the Color Corrector 3-Way tab, and drag the Whites contrast slider to the left to lower the highlights in the background.

You should immediately see the difference, isolated to the background of the actors.

If you render the resulting clip and discover changes you want to make, you can always reopen the Motion project by Control-clicking the .motn project clip and choosing Open in Editor in the shortcut menu.

When to Use This Technique

As powerful as this technique is, it can be time-consuming, especially when you need to animate the matte. Also, playback of the resulting clip won't be in real time on your video output monitor, so you'll have to render the result to see it at full resolution.

Unless you have no pressing need for speed, be judicious. Before going into Motion to mask every correction you want to make, make sure that a secondary key won't do the job, or that you can't achieve what you need with one of the simpler masked color correction techniques. With experience, you'll quickly get the hang of when this tool is indispensable, and when you're better served by simpler solutions.

Monitor Calibration

OVERVIEW ▶ The practice of adjusting your monitor's brightness and color to an objective standard to ensure the video signal is accurately represented in your viewing environment.

SEE ALSO ▶ color temperature, IRE and millivolts

Why Calibrate Your Monitor?

Your effectiveness as a colorist depends on having a color-critical broadcast monitor that's connected to your computer via a high-quality video interface (preferably outputting an SDI or component Y'CbCr signal). All the high-end equipment in the world won't help you, however, if your monitor isn't calibrated correctly.

You must calibrate your monitor so that it represents the video signal as accurately as possible within your viewing environment. You do this by matching your monitor's brightness and color to an objective standard, which is, conveniently, the standard color bars image output by Final Cut Pro, which has color bars generators for NTSC, PAL, and various high definition video formats in the Viewer's Generator pop-up menu (more on this in a bit).

When Should You Calibrate Your Monitor?

Checking the calibration of the client monitor the first time you walk into any edit suite is a good idea. You can never be sure of the last time it was adjusted, and checking the calibration can't hurt. Also, the settings of analog monitors may drift over time, so make periodic readjustments.

Furthermore, you should recalibrate the brightness and contrast of your monitor whenever the ambient lighting of the room changes, because the level of light in the room has a direct effect on the monitor's apparent contrast.

Menu and calibration controls found on a professional Sony broadcast monitor.

Important Monitor Menu Settings

Depending on which monitor you're using, it may have some or all of the following menu options. Make sure these options are correctly set to the standards for your region and video format before you follow the monitor calibration procedure.

Color Temperature

Professional broadcast monitors should have the option of changing the color temperature between D65, D93, and in some cases a user-definable setting:

▶ Select the D65 option for NTSC in North and South America and for PAL in Europe and Australia.

▶ Select the D93 option for NTSC in Japan and Korea and for PAL in China.

Color Temperature and Televisions

Consumer televisions operate the same way that broadcast monitors do (after all, a tube is a tube), and yet there are significant differences. In an ideal world, every television's color temperature would be set to the broadcast standard, and every picture would have the same quality of white. However, consumer televisions in the United States are usually set to a color temperature of 7100K, and sets in China, Japan, and Korea are set to 9300K. Why the difference? Because bluer whites can give the impression of "whiter, brighter" light, and everyone, from the electronics store on down to the viewer in the living room, wants their monitors to look "whiter."

Although there's nothing you can really do about this, it's useful to know, and it's always a good idea to watch your final program on a consumer-grade television to double-check what the audience might be seeing.

Component Level

If your monitor has a component level option, set it according to the video interface you're monitoring, using the following general standards:

▶ N10/SMPTE—For monitoring SDI (serial digital interface) and component Y'CbCr signals that don't require 7.5 IRE setup.

▶ Beta 7.5 and Beta 0—For monitoring component Y'CbCr signals with setup that is compatible with Sony's Beta and Beta SP videotape formats.

NTSC Setup

The NTSC Setup option allows you to adjust your monitor's black setup for the region you're in if you're monitoring an analog signal. NTSC in North America uses a setup of 7.5; NTSC in Japan, and PAL in all countries, use a setup of 0.

Calibrating Using Color Bars

You can easily adjust your monitor according to the standard color bars reference pattern output by Final Cut Pro.

1 Turn your monitor on, and let it sit for 30 minutes to warm up.

Some manufacturers recommend outputting a white signal to the monitor during this warmup period. White causes the CRT to run using higher voltage, which literally warms up the circuits more quickly.

NOTE ▶ If you do output a white signal, and it appears discolored in any way, this could indicate the need to degauss your monitor in order to demagnetize the CRT. Push the Degauss button, if your monitor has one, and wait for the image to stop bouncing on the screen. If such discoloration persists, do not use the Degauss button repeatedly, or you risk damaging your monitor. Instead, see a video technician.

2   If you're using Final Cut Pro to output your color bars, choose the appropriate color bars format from the Generator pop-up menu, located in the Video tab of the Viewer.

NOTE ▶ The Video tab will not appear in the Viewer if you don't have a video clip open, preventing you from accessing the Generator pop-up menu. To reveal the Video tab, open a video clip in the Viewer.

NOTE ▶ You can also calibrate your monitor using a dedicated signal generator that provides a color bars signal of the type (SDI, Y'CbCr) you'll be monitoring.

For example, if you select the Bars and Tone (NTSC) generator, you'll see the following image on your broadcast monitor when the Viewer is selected.

This image simulates the way the color bars look on a monitor with the brightness turned up far too high, in order to reveal the PLUGE (Picture Lineup Generating Equipment) bars at the bottom right.

3   (Optional) Turn the Chroma control all the way down to observe the color of the now desaturated color bars.

If they appear overly tinted, consult a video technician to see if your monitor needs to be adjusted.

4   If you're calibrating a PAL monitor, skip ahead to step 6. Because PAL color is effectively self-correcting, you don't need to adjust the color of your monitor.

If you're calibrating an NTSC monitor, turn on the Blue Only feature of your monitor in preparation for adjusting the chroma and, if necessary, phase.

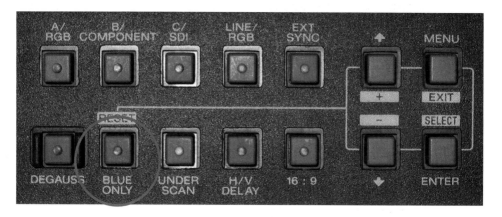

The Blue Only feature disables the red and green guns, which turns the color bars at the top of the image into an alternating pattern of gray and black bars that allow you to more precisely adjust the color of your monitor.

NOTE ▶ If your monitor doesn't have a setting for blue only, you can also perform these adjustments while looking at your monitor through a dark blue Wratten 47B filter.

The following image shows the color bars of a properly calibrated monitor with the Blue Only feature turned on. Notice how the alternating gray bars that occupy the top two-thirds of the image are of uniform brightness.

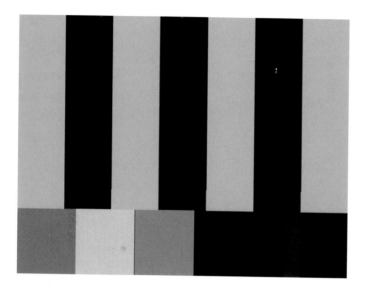

In the next image, chroma and phase are both improperly set: Notice the varying levels of the alternating gray bars that occupy the top two-thirds of the image, as well as in the split between the tops of the gray bars and the short segments that you can now see at each bar's base. On a properly calibrated monitor, the tops and bottoms of each gray bar should be indistinguishable from one another.

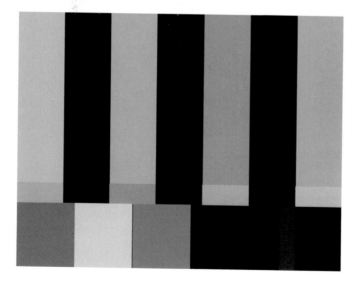

5 How you make these adjustments depends on what type of video signal you're monitoring.

▶ If you're monitoring an SDI or component Y'CbCr signal, you'll only need to adjust the Chroma control so that the tops and bottoms of the alternating gray bars (formerly the colorful bars at top) match. After you do this, continue to step 6, because the Phase control has no effect with SDI or component signals.

▶ If you're monitoring a Y/C (also called S-Video) signal, it's being run through an RGB decoder built into the monitor. In this case, adjust *both* the Chroma and Phase controls. The chroma affects the balance of the outer two gray bars; the phase affects the balance of the inner two gray bars. Adjustments made to one of these controls affects the other, so continue to adjust both until all of the gray bars are of uniform brightness at top and bottom.

NOTE ▶ The step in the second bullet also applies to the monitoring of composite signals, but you shouldn't be monitoring a composite signal if you're doing color correction.

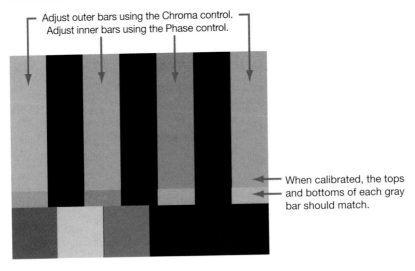

Adjust outer bars using the Chroma control.
Adjust inner bars using the Phase control.

When calibrated, the tops and bottoms of each gray bar should match.

6 When you're finished with these adjustments, turn Blue Only off.

Now it's time to adjust the brightness and contrast.

You'll adjust brightness by referring to the three PLUGE bars at the bottom right of the color bars image.

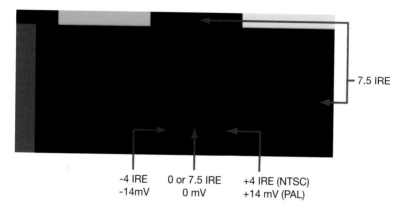

NOTE ▶ PAL users often use a different test signal that consists of only the PLUGE bars to set brightness, and a group of white, gray, and dark gray rectangles for adjusting contrast. Final Cut Pro does not generate this signal, but the PAL color bars output the correct PLUGE for this procedure.

Each color bars image has PLUGE bars appropriate to a different signal, with bars of differing levels depending on whether the bars are for NTSC, PAL, or HD. If you're viewing these color bars on a Waveform Monitor, the levels vary according to which format of video and what kind of signal you're outputting:

▶ When outputting a composite or component Y'CbCr NTSC color signal with a black level (setup) of 7.5 IRE for NTSC, the PLUGE bars correspond to one blacker-than-black bar of 3.5 IRE on the left, a black bar at 7.5 IRE in the center (which matches the black areas to the left, right, and top of the PLUGE bars), and a lighter-than-black bar of 11.5 IRE.

▶ When outputting a digital (SDI) or component Y'CbCr color signal with a black level (setup) or 0 IRE for NTSC, the PLUGE bars correspond to one blacker-than-black bar of -4 IRE on the left, a black bar at 0 IRE in the center (which matches the black areas to the left, right, and top of the PLUGE bars), and a lighter-than-black bar of +4 IRE.

▶ When outputting a digital (SDI) or component Y'CbCr color signal with a black level (setup) of 0 Volts (PAL), the PLUGE bars correspond to −14mV, 0mV, and +14mV.

7 Adjust the Brightness control so that the two PLUGE bars to the left merge together. The left and middle IRE bars should be indistinguishable from one another. The third PLUGE bar at the right should be visible, but faint, similar to the following image.

NOTE ▶ The Brightness control is also sometimes referred to as Setup, because it is really adjusting the black level of the monitor, similar to how you'd adjust the black level of a clip using the Blacks slider of the Color Correction filter.

8 Turn up the Contrast control so that the white square at the bottom left of the color bars image starts to bloom, or bleed, into the adjacent squares. (The white square corresponds to 100 IRE, the maximum legal brightness for analog video.) Finally, turn down the Contrast control until the blooming subsides.

The brightness controls the black level of the image, and the contrast control adjusts the overall luminance. Contrast should *only* be adjusted after brightness.

NOTE ▶ If you have a spot meter, a more objective way of adjusting the contrast of your monitor is to point it at the white square at the bottom left of the color bars image and adjust the Contrast control until this square reads 35 foot candles.

QC (Quality Control)

OVERVIEW ▶ Discussion of the process of checking a program submitted for broadcast, duplication, or projection to ensure it meets a predetermined set of signal requirements.

SEE ALSO ▶ broadcast legality

What Is QC?

Before you begin color correcting any program that's destined for broadcast, it's crucial that you obtain the technical requirements for the specific broadcaster you'll be submitting to. After you've finished with the program and submitted it to the broadcaster, a video engineer will put your submitted program through a final QC (quality control) process, checking to make if your program's video signal contains any deviations from the network's standards.

A network's technical requirements are typically wide-ranging, covering aspects of the submitted program including but not limited to:

▶ Approved mastering tape formats

▶ Approved methods for multiple reel submissions

▶ Approved video formats and aspect ratios

▶ Approved bars, tone, slate, timecode, and countdown requirements

▶ Closed captioning and audio requirements, including specific audio track assignments

▶ Video signal requirements (see Broadcast Legality)

Even the labeling of the tape and tape case may have specific requirements, and woe to the studio that hands off the media incorrectly. Although all of this may sound draconian, it's just to make sure that the process of accepting your program for broadcast, a stressful and time-critical affair, goes as smoothly as possible. To avoid a possible rejection of your program by the broadcaster, it's in your best interest to take the time to make sure that you're adhering to the requirements as closely as possible.

The following is a list of example QC violations that you as the colorist are directly responsible for:

- Video level (white level)
- Black level
- Chroma level
- Image clarity (is the image distinguishable to the viewer?)

Additional QC violations may arise from the video format itself:

- Tape dropouts
- Compression artifacts
- Aliasing
- Bad video edits

On top of all that, there are some QC violations that come from the way the project was originally shot:

- Focus
- White balance
- Black/white clipping
- Moire

Audio goes through its own process, but as a video colorist you typically won't have to worry about that part of the program.

For all of these reasons, many large post-production facilities have both an incoming QC and outgoing QC process of their own. All material coming into the facility is checked for focus, white balance, clipping, and other issues that might be rectified while the shoot is still going on. This also serves to give the editor and colorist a heads-up for things to keep an eye on when they start working. An editor might want to avoid a particular take, for example, or a colorist may need to allocate additional time for a particular scene that is known to be problematic.

On the way out, the post facility may also put the finished program through an outgoing QC process of its own, preemptively checking for problems that the broadcaster's own QC process would reveal before handing it off. Regardless, after handoff broadcasters do a QC look of their own at the program, just to triple-check.

> **NOTE** ▶ In some cases, broadcasters charge a fee for programs that are kicked back, so it's ideal to catch problems before they go out the door.

Once upon a time, an individual had to sit and watch the entire program using a set of scopes with alarms that indicated every error as it came up. These days, a variety of hardware- and software-based digital video scopes have the means to do an automatic QC pass, scanning the entire program automatically and logging any detectable QC violations in a list, along with the timecode at which it occurred.

Either way, once you're presented with a list of QC violations, you'll need to go through the finished program one more time, adjusting your corrections further so that the program passes muster.

Saturated Looks

> **OVERVIEW** ▶ Methods for controlling the intensity of color to create highly saturated images that are both broadcast legal and aesthetically interesting.

> **SEE ALSO** ▶ broadcast legality, limit effect (splitting corrections into regions)

Adjusting Saturation

The saturation in an image is the intensity of its color. Your images may contain all levels of saturation, which is measured by the Vectorscope and the Waveform Monitor with Saturation turned on (see Broadcast Legality).

In order to create different looks, correct for broadcast legality, and perform scene-to-scene color correction, you frequently have to adjust saturation, sometimes of the entire image and sometimes just a limited portion. In Final Cut Pro, three filters enable you to control color saturation.

The Saturation Slider

The Saturation slider in the Color Corrector and Color Corrector 3-Way filters lets you boost or lower the saturation of a clip. Every pixel of the image is adjusted by a uniform amount. Center the slider for the clip's normal saturation level; move it to the far left for 100 percent desaturation and to the far right for 200 percent saturation.

The Desaturate Filter

If you want to adjust a clip's saturation only, or you want to make a dedicated saturation adjustment at a particular point in a stack of filter operations, you can use the somewhat misleadingly named Desaturate filter. It actually works the same way as the Saturation slider in the Color Corrector filters, except in reverse (right is 100 percent desaturated, center is normal, left is 200 percent saturated). The default position of the slider is 100 percent desaturated, hence the name.

The Desaturate Highlights and Desaturate Lows Filters

For fast control of saturation at the extremes of a clip's tonal range, you can use either the Desaturate Highlights or Desaturate Lows filters. Each possesses the functionality of the other, but for convenience both are provided with the appropriate section of parameters turned on by default.

Each section has the following parameters:

▶ Enable turns on either the Highlight or Lows sets of controls.

▶ Apply Above/Below defines the threshold (as a percentage) at which desaturation begins.

▶ Softness lets you blur the transition from the fully saturated threshold and the completely desaturated portion of the picture.

▶ Amount of Desaturation determines the maximum amount of desaturation to be applied.

Creating a Super-Saturated Look

If you're trying to create a super-saturated look, do not simply crank up the Saturation slider and leave it at that. You'll get lots of color, but you risk loss of detail due to color bleed, reduced color contrast, artifacts, aliasing in video formats with low color sampling, edge ringing, and, of course, broadcast illegality.

Saturation works hand-in-hand with contrast in shaping the look of your clips. Controlling saturation in the shadows and highlights of your images is the key to creating a sophisticated look when increasing the saturation of your images, not to mention maintaining broadcast legality with more stringent broadcasters.

You'll also find that excessive saturation is a bit more successful in darker images, where the distribution of midtones is weighted more towards the lower end of the digital scale, from about 10 to 60 percent. Describing the difference in terms used by the HSB color model, colors with a lower brightness value appear richer than those with a higher brightness value, which can easily appear artificial and excessive when in abundance.

When you increase the saturation of images, it's even more important than usual to make sure that neutral areas of the image don't have an incorrect color cast. If you're deliberately warming or cooling the image, you may need to ease off the correction.

In the following exercise, you'll safely boost the color intensity in this image for an even more richly saturated look.

There is already plenty of saturation in the picture, which shows a peak of approximately 55 percent saturation in the Vectorscope, with significant saturation in the highlights (shown in the Waveform Monitor with Saturation turned on).

1   Open the *01 Raising Saturation* sequence, located in the Saturated Looks bin of the **Color Correction Exercises** project.

2   Apply a Color Corrector 3-Way filter to the first clip in the sequence. (The second clip is the finished correction, provided for comparison.) Open the clip into the Viewer, and click the Color Corrector tab to expose the graphical controls.

3   As with any other clip, adjust the contrast sliders first. Slightly crush the blacks, and lower the Whites slider to legalize the highlights so there are no superwhite values.

   These adjustments darken the image a bit, which is ideal.

4   Boost the saturation as much as you dare, being careful to keep the red spike underneath the R target in the Vectorscope.

   You should notice some red highlights appearing in the man's shirt.

5   Neutralize the red highlights by dragging the Whites color balance control towards a blue/cyan split.

   At this point, the clip's looking pretty intense, and there are definitely some saturation spikes above 100 percent and below 0 in both the Waveform Monitor and RGB

Parade scope, but addressing the clip's artificial intensity in the next few steps will take care of those spikes.

6   In the Viewer, click the Filters tab, and apply a Desaturate Highlights filter to the clip underneath the Color Corrector 3-Way filter.

7   Select the Enable checkboxes to turn on both Highlights and Lows. In the Highlight Desaturation section, lower the Apply Above parameter to desaturate most of the glowing highlights in the man's shirt, as well as reduce the color of the glowing red book spines on the book shelf (around 66 percent). Raise the Softness so there isn't a hard edge to the desaturated area (around 34), and keep Amount of Desaturation at 100 percent.

Adjusting the Highlight Desaturation parameters eliminates the saturation spikes rising over 100 percent in the Waveform Monitor. Highlights are bigger triggers of broadcast illegality than shadows are, so desaturating them is a priority.

8   Adjust the Lows Desaturation parameters. Raise the Apply Below parameter until the shadows no longer glow (around 38 percent), then raise the Softness to elimi-nate the hard edge to the desaturated area (around 38), and reduce the Amount of Desaturation to let a bit of color back into the shadows (around 55 percent).

And you're finished. Toggle the clips on (right) and off (left) to see the effect on your broadcast monitor:

One of the advantages of this technique is that it's fast but still leaves lots of room for variation. In an actual program, you'd probably want to apply the Broadcast Safe filter in a later step to make sure you catch every little spike so that everything's legal. When boosting saturation, you're always playing with fire.

Desaturating a Portion of the Spectrum

Another way you can achieve uniquely saturated looks is by using the Limit Effect > Hue control all by itself to lower or boost the saturation within a specific range of the spectrum.

This level of control has long been exercised by cinematographers through their selection of film stocks. A frequently made generalization is that Kodak color negative stocks yield excellent warm tones, with vivid reds and oranges, and Fujifilm color negative stocks are slightly cooler, with great sensitivity to greens and blues. These are generalizations—specific stocks vary—but they're useful nonetheless because many of the directors and DoPs you'll be working with may refer to them.

You may be thinking that with all this talk of warm and cool tones, why not just use the color balance control to warm or cool the images? Recording more or less saturation from different parts of the spectrum is not the same thing as a color cast, because selective saturation adjustments won't have any effect on the neutral tones in your images. This is a wholly different technique for your bag of tricks.

In this exercise, you'll selectively increase the saturation of the green and blue tones in the image.

1   Open the *02 Adjusting Specific Hues* sequence, located in the Saturated Looks bin of the **Color Correction Exercises** project.

2   Open the clip into the Viewer, and click the Color Corrector tab to expose the graphical controls.

     This clip contains the full spectrum of color.

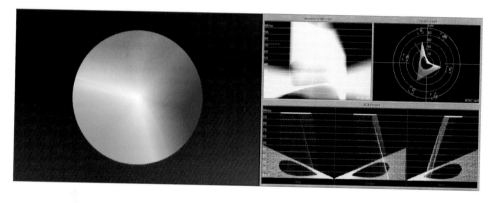

3   Open the Limit Effect controls, and drag the top Hue handles to include the green and yellow portions of the spectrum. (The Hue control turns on automatically whenever you make an adjustment.) Drag the bottom handles so that the tolerances are wide to create a soft transition at the edge of the area being adjusted.

When you make adjustments like this, keep the tolerances as soft as you can, so that the corrected area is nice and smooth, with no harsh border.

4   Lower the saturation.

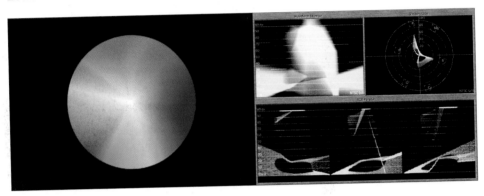

The greens and yellows become desaturated in all portions of the picture, regardless of the amount of saturation and the brightness of the color. If you drag the inside of the Hue control in the Limit Effect area, you can change the portion of the spectrum that falls within the selection handles. Experiment with lowering and raising saturation in different parts of the image until you get the hang of it.

In this next exercise, you'll use this technique to selectively control the saturation in a real-world clip:

1   Open the *03 Raising Greens and Blues* sequence, located in the Saturated Looks bin of the **Color Correction Exercises** project.

2   Open the clip into the Viewer.

This clip already has a Color Corrector 3-Way filter applied to it to adjust the contrast of the entire clip.

3   Apply a second Color Corrector 3-Way filter to the first clip in the sequence. Click the Color Corrector 3-Way - 2 tab in the Viewer, open the Limit Effect controls, and drag the top Hue handles to include the blue and green portions of the spectrum. Drag the bottom handles so that the tolerances are wide to create a soft transition at the edge of the area of being adjusted.

4   Boost the saturation to pour more color into the greenery and the woman's blue vest and sleeping bag.

As you make this adjustment, you'll notice other details in the image with blue/greenish hues turn a bit, as well, which is good, and part of the look (unless you want to narrow the Limit Effect selection). Compare the original frame (left) with your result (right):

This is also a pretty fast technique to use, and it plays in real time on most systems. The only catch is that when you're working with video formats that have limited color sampling (4:2:2, 4:1:1, or 4:2:0), the image may acquire artifacts when you make extreme corrections since you're adjusting the portions of the image with the least amount of data. This issue can be partially addressed by applying the Color Smoothing 4:1:1 or 4:2:2 filters prior to the Color Corrector filters.

> NOTE ▶ Alternately, you could try one of the G Nicer family of plug-ins (from Graeme Nattress), which use different methods to partially reconstruct color information in the Cb and Cr components of the image.

Boost the Saturation of Specific Objects

Another technique for creating the illusion of high saturation is to use the Limit Effect controls to increase the saturation of only specific subjects in the frame, rather than boosting the saturation of the entire image.

For example, the following image has plenty of saturation but not a lot of contrast:

One strategy might be to boost the contrast in the clip and slightly desaturate the overall color, but preserve and increase the saturation in the two men's ties with an inverted Limit Effect key.

Then, in a second operation, duplicate the first Color Corrector filter, turn off the Invert Selection button, and boost the color in the ties to provide greater color contrast with the rest of the image.

See Limit Effect (Splitting Corrections into Regions).

By using this strategy, you get to have your cake and eat it too: You can desaturate an image, but by selectively boosting the color of one or two objects, make it appear as if it's even more colorful.

Secondary keys in situations like this tend to be really tricky when you're trying to isolate small areas of specific color. As a result, this is one of the more time-intensive operations discussed here, and it's not suitable if your client is in a hurry.

Also, if you're working with a video format with a 4:2:2 or 4:1:1 color space, pulling a key that doesn't jitter and buzz can be even harder. Applying the Color Smoothing 4:1:1 or 4:2:2 filters prior to the Color Corrector filters can sometimes help subdue the noise if you're having too much trouble.

> **NOTE** ▶ Alternately, try one of the G Nicer family of plug-ins (from Graeme Nattress).

If you'd like to take a hands-on look at the preceding example (those ties were a really tricky key with DV footage), open the *04 Targeted Saturation Boosts* sequence, in the Saturated Looks bin of the **Color Correction Exercises** project.

Saturation (Reducing Oversaturated Hues)

> **OVERVIEW** ▶ A technique for desaturating only hues above a specific level of saturation in your program.

> **SEE ALSO** ▶ broadcast legality, limit effect controls

When to Control Specific Hues

Every once in a while, you'll have a clip or two (or an entire program) with a stubborn hue that insists on being oversaturated. The hue to blame is usually red, although yellow and cyan are also repeat offenders. If you try to lower the saturation of the overall clip to correct this, you'll end up with an unhappily desaturated image, not what you want.

In the following image, the background has a pleasant late-afternoon glow, but the jacket that the man is wearing is completely out of control. Not only is it unlikely to pass any broadcaster's QC, it's probably going to be an eyestrain for the viewers.

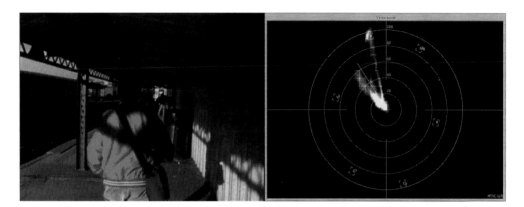

Lowering the overall saturation would bring the jacket into line, but at the expense of eliminating the overall look of the shot. Fortunately, there's an easy way to address these trouble spots using the Color Correction filter's Limit Effect controls.

Creating the Fix

In the following exercise, you'll learn how to selectively reduce the saturation of a specific area without affecting the rest of the image:

1   Open the *Limiting Jacket* sequence, located in the Saturation, Reducing Specific Hues bin of the **Color Correction Exercises** project.

   This is the same clip shown in the preceding screenshot. It already has a single Color Corrector 3-Way filter applied to it, creating the current look. This exercise focuses on the jacket itself.

2   Apply a Color Corrector 3-Way filter to the first clip in the sequence. (The second clip is the finished correction, provided for comparison.) Open the clip into the Viewer, and click the Color Corrector 3-Way - 2 tab to expose the graphical controls.

3   Open the Limit Effect controls, and toggle the View Final/Matte/Source control to Matte (a black key against a white background.)

4   Turn on Sat control, and adjust the handles to include all oversaturated values in the jacket. Make sure the tolerance (the bottom handles) is wide enough to create a nicely feathered selection.

It's OK if you catch some other highlights in the picture, chances are they're probably oversaturated, too.

In this example, keying all areas of the picture above a certain saturation is the fastest and most effective fix. In other instances, you may also choose to enable the Hue control to limit the correction to a specific color.

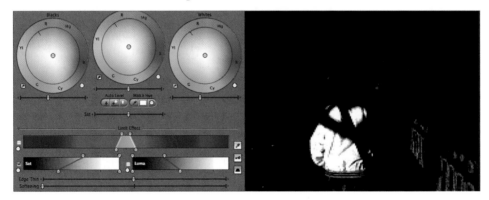

5   Toggle the View Final/Matte/Source control back to Final (a red key against gray).

6   Drag the Saturation slider to the left to reduce the saturation of the jacket.

Don't desaturate it too much, or it'll start to look strangely dark.

As you make this adjustment, you should notice that more detail emerges from the folds of the jacket. Oversaturated colors can overwhelm fine detail similarly to overexposed whites. Compare your results (right) to the original (left).

Expanding the Technique

You can use this technique as a video legalizing measure in any program with hues that are consistently brighter than the average saturation you want for your clips. You can apply a Color Corrector filter with these settings to a nested version of your edited sequence in order to correct the entire program at one fell swoop.

A further expansion of this technique would be to restrict this correction to oversaturated values above a certain luminance by enabling and adjusting the Luma controls as well, although at that point you might also consider using the Desaturate Highs filter, which does essentially the same thing. As mentioned elsewhere, high saturation in bright areas of the picture is risky if you're submitting your program to a broadcaster with stringent QC requirements.

Sepia Filter (Image Control Group)

OVERVIEW ▶ Explanation of a filter that adds either a monochromatic or blended tint to an image using a single filter; similar to the Tint filter but has one extra control for adjusting highlights. *Related terms:* Color cast, tint.

SEE ALSO ▶ color control, color temperature, tint filter (image control group), tinting methods, tinting (optical filters and gels)

How Does the Sepia Filter Work?

The Sepia filter fills the color channels of a clip with the Tint Color, while retaining the image's original luma channel. The Amount parameter lets you evenly blend the tinted result with the original colors to create a mix.

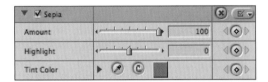

The Tint Color and Amount controls work exactly the same as those of the Tint filter. By default, Tint Color is a sepia tone (H=23.08, S=68, B=75), however, and the Amount is 100, which replaces the original color with a strong sepia tint.

With Amount set to 100, the result is a monochromatically tinted image. Reducing the Amount progressively blends more of the original color back into the image, with 0 showing all of the image's original color.

NOTE ▶ For a detailed look at how the Tint Color and Amount controls work together to tint an image, see **Tint Filter (Image Control Group)**.

The Effect of Highlight

At its default of 0, the Highlight parameter has no effect, but you can change it:

▶   Raise Highlight to a positive value to boost the midtones and the highlights together, while pinning the black point. Highlights become easily overexposed, so if you're going to use this parameter, also apply a Broadcast Safe filter to the clip.

▶   Lower Highlight to a negative value to lower the mids and crush the blacks, while pinning the white point.

Although the Highlight parameter lets you stretch the contrast of a clip to compensate for the washed-out look that tinting with some color values may produce, the parameter has a tendency to overexpose the whites or crush the blacks with relatively small adjustments.

This exercise demonstrates how drastically Highlight adjustments affect the contrast of an image.

1   Open the *Using the Sepia Filter* sequence, located in the Sepia Filter bin of the **Color Correction Exercises** project.

2   Choose the Color Correction window layout, and select the Waveform layout in the Video Scopes tab of the Tool Bench.

3   Apply the Sepia filter to the Elevator Scene clip, open the clip into the Viewer, and click the Filters tab.

The clip appears with the default sepia effect.

4   Raise the Highlight parameter to 40.

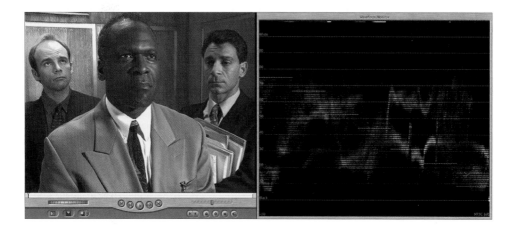

In the Waveform Monitor, you can see that the midtones of the image are all stretched up, with the whites jumping off the scale, resulting in illegal, and even clipped, whites.

5   Lower the Highlight parameter to –10.

This time, the mids are all stretched down, with the result being extremely crushed blacks, as evidenced by the bunched-up clusters of points along the 0 percent line of the Waveform Monitor.

As you can see, you should use Highlight with extreme care, if you use it at all. For more detailed adjustments to a clip's contrast, use one of the Color Correction filters instead.

Skin Tone (Ideals)

OVERVIEW ► Guidelines for monitoring and evaluating hue, saturation, and contrast for idealized skin tones.

SEE ALSO ► contrast adjustments, skin tone (isolated adjustments), video scopes

Why Is Skin Tone So Important?

If you want to sell a shot to the audience, you must strike a careful balance between the overall look of the program and the skin tone of the subjects. In fact, many colorists rely on the skin tone of subjects within the frame as their primary benchmark for the color balance of the scene. Before looking at different approaches for judging and adjusting the skin tone of subjects in Final Cut Pro, you should understand a little more about what makes skin tones so special.

Years of looking at one another have made us extremely sensitive to healthy skin tones, and even slight variations may create unwanted audience reactions. Too much yellow or green from a color cast may make someone look unintentionally sick; too much red may indicate the character spends more time getting sunburned (or in bars) than you want the audience to think.

One of the nice things about skin tone is that the complexion of everyone on earth falls within a fairly narrow range, as indicated on the Vectorscope. In some instances when color casts may be difficult to spot, the distribution of hues that are plotted in the Vectorscope graph can guide your correction by their relative distance from the Flesh Tone line, which indicates this ideal range.

The following screenshot has a blue color cast (exaggerated for print) that may be due to incorrect white balance, but there's no one part of the picture that leaps out as blatantly incorrect. Looking at the Vectorscope, however, reveals that the distribution of hues is offset from the Flesh Tone line at approximately 11 o'clock. This should set off warning bells, because the image is a close-up of a man's face.

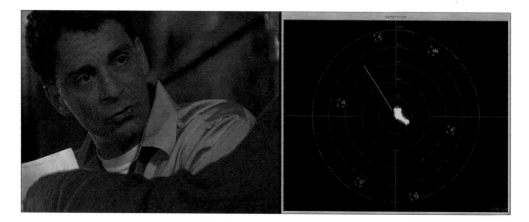

Making a correction such that the distribution of hues falls along this vector reveals clear, rich skin tones that are a clear improvement.

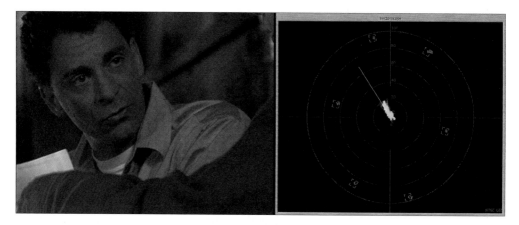

How Much of a Correction Should I Make?

It's always a good idea to be aware of the original skin tones of the actors and subjects that were recorded, so you don't overcorrect them. As long as skin tones look healthy and are recognizably human, however, the exact hues and saturation levels that may be considered *ideal* are fairly subjective. Some clients will want you to make adjustments towards more golden, kissed-by-the-sun skin tones, while others will prefer pinker, paler complexions.

Don't underestimate the effect that makeup has on an actor's complexion. On programs with an adequate budget, the desired skin tone of the actor may already have been decided upon, and the actors carefully made up to reflect the desired complexion. In this case, your job will be to preserve and balance the original skin tones in the shoot.

In lower-budgeted programs, where less time was spent on makeup and lighting, you'll have considerably more leeway and may find yourself making substantial adjustments to balance everyone out.

As always, a client who was involved with the original shoot will be one of your best sources of information regarding what everyone's skin tone should be. If there are inconsistencies in the makeup, or if an actor is more or less ruddy or tan from one shot to the next, you'll need to determine which was the preferred look for the program before balancing the individual clips in the scene.

What Gives Skin Its Color?

Skin, as any 3-D animator will tell you, is an incredibly complex surface in terms of color and reflection. The more you understand the characteristics and causes involved, the better you can understand how people's complexions react to light, giving you more control over the look you want to create.

Skin is actually translucent, and our complexions are a mix of colors from two layers of skin:

▶   Melanin is found in both light and dark complexioned people. This pigment adds color to the *epidermis* (upper layer of skin). There are two forms of melanin: *pheomelanin*, which ranges from red to yellow, and *eumelanin*, which ranges from brown to black. This is the pigment that differentiates the skin tone from people in different regions of the world.

▶   Blood flowing through capillaries in the *dermis* (lower layer of skin) also contributes a significant amount of red to the overall hue of skin tone. This tone is identical regardless of one's epidermal coloring, which accounts for the similarity in hue of people from all over the world.

The combined color of both of these layers gives skin its color.

Makeup

Makeup plays a vital role in narrative filmmaking, and it's interesting to note that makeup artists use tinted foundations to make color corrections to a subject's skin, similar to the way you might rebalance hues in the midtones of the video image to do the same thing. For example, applying yellow tones to fair-complexioned subjects or warm tones to dark-complexioned subjects gives the skin a healthy color that's tailored to the subject. Several layers of makeup contribute to the skin tones found in the face:

- ▶ Foundation is a layer of makeup applied to the overall face, and it performs the main "color correction" for the subject's complexion.

- ▶ Powder is added over the foundation to prevent shine, although some powders are formulated to create a subtle glow.

- ▶ Blush is added in the area of the cheeks both to accentuate (or de-emphasize) the cheekbones and to add targeted warmth to the face. It simulates the natural blush response, and in fact a common technique for choosing the appropriate blush is to pinch the cheeks and match to the resulting color. If you're sampling a hue from someone's face with one of the eyedropper tools, it's probably not a good idea to click on an area that has blush, as it's not representative of the overall skin tone.

In general, there's nothing special you need to do when correcting a scene in which the actors are wearing makeup, but you may notice some differences between people with and without makeup. Subjects wearing makeup may have slightly different skin tones on their face than on other parts of their body (although this is also true of subjects who get a lot of sun). Depending on the makeup scheme, features such as cheekbones and the sides of the nose might be warmer, and possibly darker, than the rest of the face regardless of the lighting.

Evaluating Skin Tones

Now that you know the elements responsible for creating skin tones, you can break them down into hue and saturation for purposes of analysis and correction. Of course, deviation of overall skin tones from what are considered the "norm" is also dependent on the color balance of the overall scene. If, due either to lighting or deliberate grading, there's a color cast in a clip, the ideal skin tones will be relative to the color cast that's been introduced.

Hue

Skin tone is weighted most heavily towards reds and greens. With a few exceptions, the blue channel is generally the weakest. Cropping the face out of an uncorrected clip and examining the Parade scope shows this clearly. (For a collection of clips showing people with different complexions both uncropped and cropped, open the *Skin Tones Compared* sequence, located in the Skin Tone, Ideals bin of the **Color Correction Exercises** project).

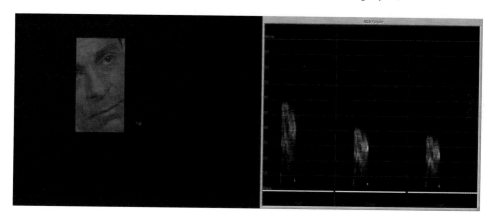

As just noted, everyone's skin tones fall within the same range of hue. When using the Vectorscope to judge skin tones, the average complexion of a neutrally balanced scene should fall within 20 degrees of the Flesh Tone line. Where individual subjects deviate from the Flesh Tone line, the following illustration indicates which complexions typically fall to which side of this line:

Within a single subject's face, the hue will vary slightly. When looking at the same cropped face in the Vectorscope with a magnified view, you can see that the man's face forms a wedge of values—hue in the highlights and shadows typically vary as much as 5 degrees.

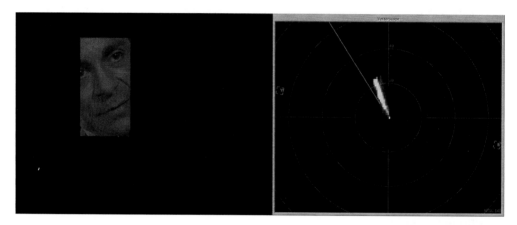

With clips of average exposure, skin tones usually fall solidly within the midtones. Because color casts are frequently correctable with a simple adjustment to the Whites color balance control, you can usually use the Mids color balance control to fine-tune the skin tones.

Saturation

The ideal saturation of a subject's skin tone is always going to be relative to the rest of the scene. That said, skin tones in a normally saturated image will generally fall between 20 to 45 percent saturation (as seen in the Vectorscope), depending on the person's complexion and relative to the overall saturation of the image.

Complexion Combines Hue and Saturation

Everyone's complexion is different, and you're generally not going to want to park everyone's skin tone directly on the Flesh Tone line. When allowing or creating variance among the subjects in a program, keep in mind that people tend to fall into five general categories:

▶   Ruddy/pink/mahogany-skinned—This skin type tilts towards the red target, falling to the right of the Flesh Tone line, and tends to be more saturated than the others. Both light- and dark-skinned people may fall into this category.

- ▶ Pale/fair-skinned—Generally fair-skinned people tilt just a bit more towards the red target, but they can be quite desaturated. Some extremely fair skinned people may even have a bit of a blue cast to their skin (which can be extremely confusing if you're basing the correction of the entire image on the deviation of their skin tones from the Flesh Tone line).

- ▶ Olive-skinned—These individuals typically appear just to the right of the Flesh Tone line. They don't have as much red as ruddy or pale individuals, but they have more than medium-skinned or golden-skinned folks. They have a tendency to stick out when they're in a two-shot with another subject that you're trying to correct, because they fall in-between everyone else. A single mids correction may have a significantly different effect on both subjects. If it's a real problem, you might have to do a secondary or masked correction on one of the subjects and create a separate correction.

- ▶ Medium/dark-skinned—Average skin for virtually anyone, falls right on or immediately to the left of the line, and their skin will be more or less saturated depending on how much sun the individual gets.

- ▶ Tanned/gold/Asian-skinned—Whether Caucasian or Asian, these complexions fall a bit further towards the yellow target. Tanned subjects will be more highly saturated; generally golden-skinned subjects will be less so.

The following examples show these principles applied to a secondary correction of the woman's face. (See Skin Tone (Isolated Adjustments).) To begin with, the woman in the following clip has fairly neutral skin tones that fall just to the right of the Flesh Tone line. To see these examples on your computer, open the *Manipulating Skin Tones* sequence, located in the Skin Tones, Ideals bin of the **Color Correction Exercises** project.

> **NOTE** ▶ The corrections in the *Manipulating Skin Tones* sequence are meant to be displayed on a broadcast monitor, and they may look wrong when viewed in the Canvas on your computer's monitor.

By adding a bit of yellow to the midtones with the Mids color balance control, slightly lowering the Mids contrast slider, and slightly boosting the Saturation, you can give the woman a tan.

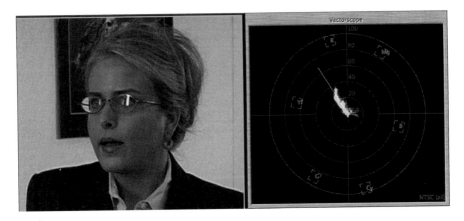

On the other hand, by adding a bit of red using the Mids and Whites color balance controls, lightening the image using the Mids and Whites contrast sliders (raising brightness), and slightly lowering the Saturation, you can give the woman a paler complexion.

These are extreme examples, and you're typically not going to perform isolated corrections for the skin tone in every clip (typically an adjustment to the Mids color balance control is sufficient), but they illustrate the point that a general familiarity with the interactions of hue and saturation within skin tones gives you much more control over your ability to correct them.

Exposure for People in the Shot

Recommendations for exposure are always highly subjective, but one generalization is probably safe to make. In every shot, the overall contrast and exposure should be optimized to keep the most important subject in the picture clearly visible.

If you think of exposure adjustments in the same terms as mixing sound, you want to set the levels of each element in the mix so that the most important subject, such as the vocals, is the clearest. In color correction, the skin tones of subjects in the frame are your vocals. If they're too similar in color and exposure to other elements in the background or foreground, your actors won't stand out (assuming you want them to). People in the shot need not be brighter or darker than everything else, they should simply be *distinct*.

The photographer Ansel Adams articulated this with his zone system, which is discussed in his book, *The Negative* (from Bulfinch Press; highly recommended reading). Dividing the tonal range of an image into 10 zones, Adams advocated exposing images so as to distribute detail throughout the available tonal range to maximize contrast. (The idea is similar to expanding contrast. See Contrast Adjustments.)

On the scale published in his book, he puts the shadows for Caucasian skin lit by sunlight into Zone 4, midtones for dark complexioned skin into Zone 5, average Caucasian skin into Zone 6, light Caucasian skin into Zone 7, and highlights on Caucasian skin into Zone 8.

If you're considering an ideal set of overlapping luma ranges for the highlights, midtones, and shadows of a subject's skin tone, the following may be used as a starting point for images of average exposure, with the higher portion of each range reserved for lighter complexions:

▶   Highlights from 60 to 90 percent; ideally there should be no overexposed areas on the skin except for occasional specular highlights on the face and head.

▶   Average midtones from 40 to 70 percent

▶   Shadows from 10 to 50 percent

This somewhat abstract set of guidelines is illustrated in the following screenshot. The contrast ratio of the entire uncorrected image ranges from 10 to 110 percent, which is good despite the lack of absolute blacks that may or may not be necessary, and the illegal superwhite values (from the highlights of the white shirt) that will need to be legalized. However, it's difficult to make out the exposure of the skin tones alone among all the other detail in the shot.

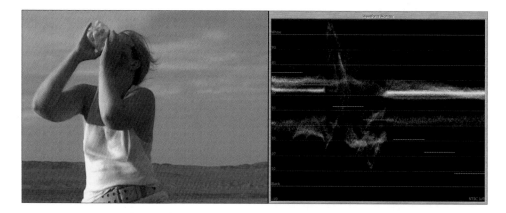

By cropping out everything except for a narrow slice of the highlights and shadows falling on the woman's skin, you can get a good look at the contrast ratio of the skin tone itself, which falls from 20 to 90 percent digital. It's nicely spread out relative to the tonality of the rest of the scene and, as predicted, falling squarely within the midtones.

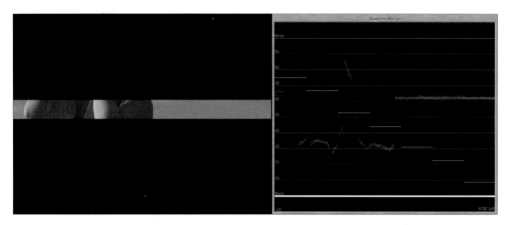

People with darker complexions absorb more light and will be potentially 10 to 20 percent darker than lighter complexioned people within the same shot. This is normal and doesn't ordinarily require correction.

In the following uncorrected clip, the three men in the elevator are lit similarly.

By isolating the men's faces and examining them on the Waveform Monitor, you can see that the man in the middle falls lowest, with average luma levels 10 percent below those of the other two men.

 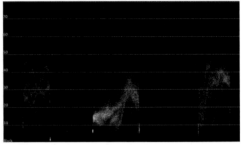

Further Considerations

The recommendations within this section are simply guidelines to help get you started. Every program has its own look, requirements, exposures, and subjects, and it's difficult to generalize about every possible case. Furthermore, with experience (and a well-calibrated monitor) you'll find yourself relying more and more on your eyes to make accurate judgments about skin tone. When in doubt, however, know that you always have the scopes to fall back on.

Skin Tone (Isolated Adjustments)

OVERVIEW ▶ Methods for making targeted adjustments to the skin tone of subjects within a clip.

SEE ALSO ▶ limit effect (optimizing secondary keying operations), limit effect (splitting corrections into regions), saturated looks, skin tone (ideals)

The Simplest Skin Tone Adjustments

When you're making adjustments to the color balance of an image, keep in mind that skin tones usually fall within the midtone range of an image. So if you're deliberately rebalancing an image to create a specific look, either correct or introduce a color cast by using the Whites color balance control first. Then, if the skin tone of the subject in the frame is adversely affected, you may be able to bring the skin tones back to normal by making a reverse adjustment to the Mids. Of course, whether or not this is really a simple fix depends entirely on the tonal range of the image, but it's the best place to start.

In this exercise, you'll put this adjustment into practice by introducing an extreme color cast and then rebalancing the skin tone of the actor within the same filter:

1   Open the *01 Simple Skin Tone Adjustments* sequence, located in the Skin Tone, Isolated Adjustments bin of the **Color Correction Exercises** project.

2   Apply a Color Corrector 3-Way filter to the first clip in the sequence. (The second clip is the finished correction, provided for comparison.) Open the clip into the Viewer, and click the Color Corrector tab to expose the graphical controls. Set the Video Scopes to display the Vectorscope only.

   The Vectorscope is an extremely useful tool for evaluating skin tones, along with all of the other saturated hues in your image.

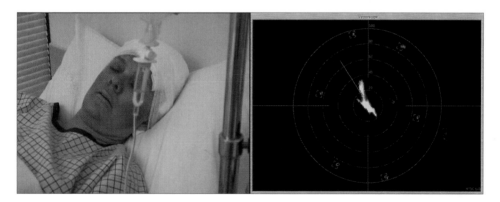

This clip is generally well exposed, but the lack of any real blacks, shadows, or highlights gives it a low-contrast look. The overall colors are a bit warm, but the image is otherwise fairly neutral. Given the hospital environment, the client wants the clip to be bright, bordering on the overexposed, and to have a very cool bluish-white look within abundant highlights.

3   Adjust the exposure for a nearly overexposed look, boost the highlights to the edge of legality using the Whites slider (you'll need to consult the Waveform Monitor for

that), and lower the Mids just a bit, in order to stretch the contrast at the upper 50 percent of the image.

These adjustments should bring more detail out of the woman's face, while creating the necessary bright highlights.

4   To cool off the white light, make a bold adjustment to the Whites color balance control, dragging it towards blue.

Don't be afraid of introducing a somewhat bluish color cast—that's what the client wants.

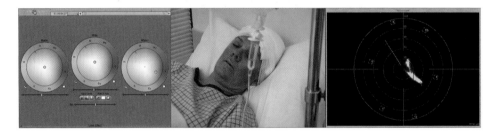

The highlights are definitely cool (cold, even), but because the woman's face is so close to the highlights, she's gone blue, too. Fortunately, this is an easy fix, and you don't even have to use a secondary.

5   Drag the Mids color balance control back towards orange/yellow in order to neutralize the color bleeding into the woman's face, and then keep dragging a bit further to warm it up.

As you make this adjustment, keep your eye on the Vectorscope graph to make sure her face is in the ballpark relative to the Flesh Tone line.

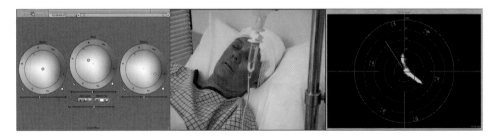

The result should be a fairly targeted correction to the woman's face, although some of the blues in the darker portions of the highlights may have been muted, as well.

You could stop here, but if the client wants more blue in the image, you can easily add a secondary without having to try to isolate the woman's face.

6   Add another Color Corrector 3-Way filter to the first clip in the sequence. Click its tab in the Viewer, open the Limit Effect controls, and drag the top Hue handles to include the blue portion of the spectrum. Drag the bottom handles so that the tolerances are wide to create a soft transition at the edge of the area being adjusted.

7   Boost the saturation to pump up the blue that's already in the picture, without doing anything to the other hues.

See **Saturated Looks**.

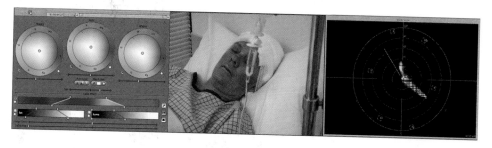

With this last correction, you may want to add a Desaturate Highlights filter at the end of the filter stack to desaturate any illegally oversaturated highlights, but otherwise you're finished.

Make sure that you've exhausted the possibilities of the three color balance controls before turning to secondary color correction to solve your skin tone problems. Often, you can simply rebalance the mids and whites. Also, because red is such a ubiquitous color, pulling well-isolated secondary keys on skin tone can be tricky, especially with highly-compressed video formats with low color-sampling ratios.

Adjusting Skin Tone with Secondary Corrections

If you can't get the look you want with the color balance controls, or if the look you're creating is such an extreme grade that you *know* the skin tone will be affected, sometimes throwing on a secondary is the best solution.

In particular, with tricky lighting setups, such as a mixed lighting scenario where one actor is illuminated by a fixture with a very different color temperature than that of the rest of the room, it's sometimes faster to just adjust the skin tone separately.

A somewhat more rare instance where skin tone is more easily adjusted with a secondary is when you have two actors with very different complexions in the same shot. In this situation, correcting or introducing a color cast may have very different effects on each of the actors, so you may be forced to attempt to pull a secondary key on one actor or the other to create an independent fix.

In this exercise, you'll create an extreme grade to significantly alter the look of the image, while protecting the skin tones of the woman in the shot with a secondary color correction:

1   Open the *01 Secondary Skin Tone Adjustments* sequence, located in the Skin Tone, Isolated Adjustments bin of the **Color Correction Exercises** project.

The clip has muted color, somewhat warm, but not overly so. In this instance, the client wants a higher-contrast, cooler, almost desaturated look to the desert environment but wants to maintain and enhance the tanned skin tone of the sitting woman. Because the other features that you'll be manipulating fall within the same tonal range as the woman's arms, it's a good bet that you'll need to protect them with some sort of secondary operation.

See Limit Effect (Splitting Corrections into Regions).

2   Apply a Color Corrector 3-Way filter to the first clip in the sequence. (The second clip is the finished correction, provided for comparison.) Open the clip into the Viewer, and click the Color Corrector tab to expose the graphical controls.

Because you know that you're going to be setting up a secondary color correction operation in advance, you can take a few steps to optimize the overall order of operations for the best effect.

3   In this first color correction operation, you'll begin by boosting the contrast, lowering the blacks, lowering the whites to legalize them, and boosting the mids to compensate for the whites adjustment. Then, boost the saturation to enhance the overall color of the clip.

These adjustments warm up the shot, and you can explain to your client that by boosting the saturation of the clip, you've enhanced the skin tone already in the shot, and you've also made the color values easier to separate and key in a secondary operation.

4 Add another Color Corrector 3-Way filter to the first clip in the sequence, click its tab in the Viewer, open the Limit Effect controls, then click the limit effect eyedropper button, and click on a midtone on the woman's arm in the Canvas. Then, click the limit effect eyedropper button again, and Shift-drag across the woman's arm, dragging across the highlights, midtones, and shadows.

When you release the mouse button, you'll find that the Limit Effect controls have expanded to include more of the image.

5 Toggle the View Final/Matte/Source button to Matte, and adjust the Limit Effect controls to isolate as much of the woman's arm as possible, while minimizing the areas of the background that are included in the key. Use the Edge Thin and Softening controls to fine-tune the key. (It may not look very good, but as long as the noise and irregularities aren't noticeable at full resolution, you can probably get away with a fairly ragged matte.) When you've isolated the arms, click the Invert Selection button so that the arms are excluded from the color correction operation in the next step.

NOTE ▶ You may be able to reduce the noise in your secondary key by applying the Color Smoothing 4:1:1 or 4:2:2 filters prior to the Color Corrector filters. Alternately, you could try one of the G Nicer family of plug-ins (from Graeme Nattress), which use different methods to partially reconstruct color information in the Cb and Cr components of the image.

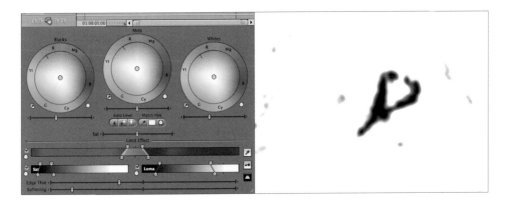

Since the overall contrast of the image and the flesh tones of the woman's arms were adjusted in the previous color correction operation, all you have to do now is to adjust the color quality of the background.

6   Toggle the View Final/Matte/Source button to Final, then drag the Mids color balance control towards a blue/cyan split to cool off the background, and lower the saturation to create the steely-gray granite look that the client wanted in the background.

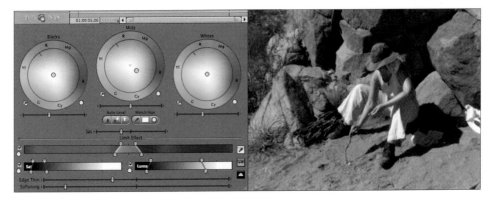

See Limit Effect (Optimizing Secondary Keying Operations).

Tanning and Sunburn Effects

Secondary color correction is also useful when you're trying to create tanning or sunburn effects. To a limited extent, you can warm or cool a subject's skin tone with simple Mids adjustments, but if you're making a significant alteration, you really don't want it to affect the background if you can help it.

In this example, you'll use a secondary color correction to simulate the effect of a severe sunburn, enhancing makeup that was already applied.

1   Open the *03 Tanning and Sunburn Sequence*, located in the Skin Tone, Isolated Adjustments bin of the **Color Correction Exercises** project.

2   Apply a Color Corrector 3-Way filter to the first clip in the sequence. (The second clip is the finished correction, provided for comparison.) Open the clip into the Viewer, and click the Color Corrector tab to expose the graphical controls. Lower the blacks to create more shadow detail, and then lower the whites to legalize them.

The clip becomes more contrasty, and the colors themselves intensify as they darken—a nicely dramatic look. Although the woman's makeup is pretty convincing, the client wants a more intensely painful look.

3   Add another Color Corrector 3-Way filter, and use the Limit Effect controls to isolate the woman's exposed skin.

   The makeup is a lucky strike, as the increased saturation it provides makes this a fairly easy key to pull.

4   Once you've isolated the subject, boost the saturation to intensify the skin tone. Make a small adjustment to the Mids color balance control to give just the right lobster-like burn tone.

   As an added touch, you might raise the Mids contrast slider just two or three points to lighten the woman relative to the background, so that she stands out a bit more.

Secondary keys can be tricky, and they are definitely time-consuming with highly compressed media, but in certain situations they can be essential to adding just the right touch to actors within a scene.

Skin Tone (Reducing Shine)

OVERVIEW ▶ Technique for minimizing shine on a subject's skin by selectively darkening facial highlights.

SEE ALSO ▶ skin tone (ideals), skin tone (isolated adjustments)

What Causes Shine?

Human skin, because of its texture and translucency, has a natural matte finish that's not ordinarily reflective. Skin shines when the presence of oils, sweat, or other cosmetics reflect light.

Shine is the result of specular highlights that are whiter and brighter than ordinary facial highlights. Shine occurs when reflected light on the face is bright enough to overpower the natural color of the subject's skin tone. In the following image, the white highlights on the woman's face are a clear example of shine.

Ordinarily, makeup artists use powder to eliminate shine, but warm conditions, hot stage lighting, or stressful situations can create a challenge, and from time to time you'll find yourself with a shiny actor. Of course, it's always good to inquire as to whether or not the subject is *supposed* to be shiny, because it could be a deliberate makeup effect.

Much of the time, this kind of shine is not desirable. Although it's usually not possible to eliminate it altogether, you can take steps to minimize it.

Reducing Shine

In this exercise, you'll practice minimizing shine using the face of the actress shown in the preceding image:

1   Open the *Subduing Shine* sequence, located in the Skin Tone, Subduing Shine bin of the **Color Correction Exercises** project and move the playhead to the marker in the first clip.

2   Apply a Color Corrector 3-Way filter to the first clip in the sequence. (The second clip is the finished correction, provided for comparison.) Open the clip into the Viewer, and click the Color Corrector tab to expose the graphical controls.

3   Open the Limit Effect controls, click the eyedropper, and then click a shine highlight on the woman's cheek in the Canvas.

Which highlight you click on has a dramatic effect on the quality of this correction. You want to make sure that the secondary key includes a wide portion of shine that's not too wide, but not too narrow.

4 Set the View Final/Matte/Source button to Matte (a black key against a white background) to examine the included section of shine. The portion of the image you're isolating will now appear as a white key against black. In this view, drag the Softening slider to the left to blur the secondary key so that the edges are nice and feathered.

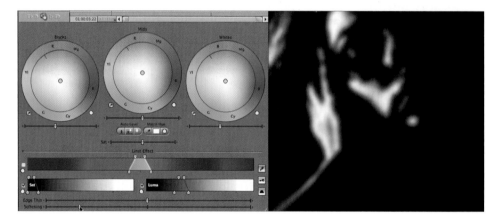

5 Set the View Final/Matte/Source button to Final (a gold key against a gray background), then drag the Whites slider to the left to lower the brightness of the shine, but not so far as to visibly discolor that area of her face. Adding a bit of yellow using the Mids color balance control might help keep her complexion even.

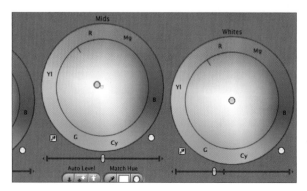

Compare the original shot (left) with the results (right):

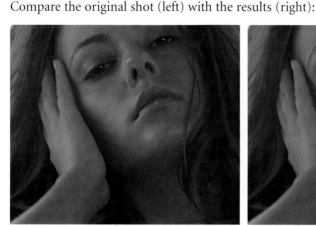

Further Considerations

Always be careful to avoid overdoing such targeted contrast adjustments because the results can be unflattering. This correction usually ends up being very subtle, and it won't always do the trick. Other times it can be highly effective; you may even want to remove the shine using two or even three secondary corrections, with each successive correction darkening a smaller region of slightly brighter shine. By suppressing highlights with multiple passes, you can sometimes avoid an inadvertent flattening of the image. You just have to be careful to soften the secondary keys enough to avoid posterization of the image.

Sky Corrections and Enhancements

OVERVIEW ▶ Explanation of and techniques for mimicking sky color during various times and conditions, as well as other atmospheric phenomena.

SEE ALSO ▶ limit effect controls, vignettes (creating shadows)

Enhancing the Color of the Sky

One of the most common corrections to nearly any exterior shot is to make the sky more blue. It's often difficult to capture the sky as we perceive it with either film or video, because haze, overexposure, and uncooperative weather all conspire to rob filmmakers of the rich blue skies they desire. In these cases, you can employ a variety of techniques to put the color back in. To do so most realistically, however, it's useful to learn a few things about how color is distributed through the sky.

The Clear Blue Sky

The Earth's atmosphere creates the sky's blue color by scattering a large proportion of the shorter blue wavelengths of light from the sun in all directions. This is referred to as *Rayleigh scattering*, after Lord John Rayleigh, an English physicist who described this phenomenon.

When making sky corrections of different kinds, bear in mind that skies are gradients, which in broad daylight are darkest at the top of the frame, lightening towards the horizon. This is because air doesn't just scatter the blue wavelengths; the other visible wavelengths of light are also scattered in lower proportions. The farther light travels towards the horizon, the more scattering takes place, and eventually enough of all wavelengths are scattered so that the sky appears white.

What this means to you as you contemplate different strategies for grading a sky is that on a typical clear blue sky, the hue of the sky remains consistent from the top of the frame to the bottom, but the saturation peaks at the top, and gradually diminishes the closer to the horizon the sky falls. The brightness, on the other hand, is lowest at the top, and highest at the horizon.

Rayleigh scattering also explains why mountains and other distant features of the landscape get bluer and then whiter the farther away they are, even in the absence of smog. Light is scattered between a viewer and a mountain the same way it's scattered between a viewer and the outer atmosphere. This is referred to as *airlight* (which is a different phenomenon than haze).

The Sky's Hue

The average color of a blue sky varies widely in brightness, saturation, and hue, ranging from light cyan to dark blue, because

- The color of the sky is intensified at higher altitudes; a thinner amount of atmosphere makes for a darker, more saturated shade of blue.

- At lower altitudes, the overall color of the sky tends to be less saturated and considerably lighter.

- The height of the sun in the sky affects its color, depending on your latitude and the time of the year.

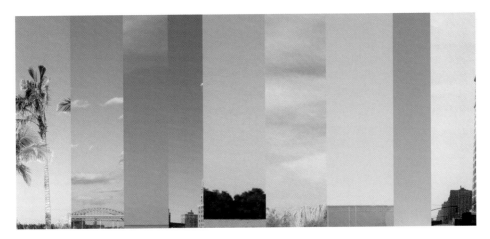

Expressed in the HSB color space, the hue of an average uncorrected sky clip (without accounting for atmospheric effects such as pollution) ranges from about 200 (towards cyan) to 220 (towards primary blue). Examining this range (depicted in the previous image by multiple slices of sky gradients) on a Vectorscope yields the following wedge of hues:

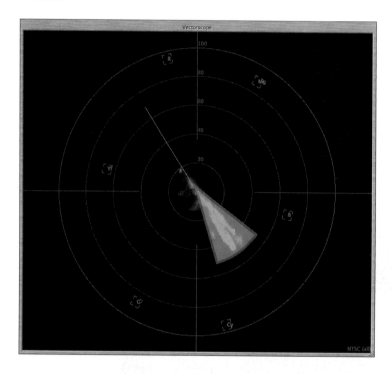

Because the saturation decreases as it nears the horizon, the light that's right at the horizon when the sun is high in the sky is generally white. However, it may be tinted by reflected light from the surface of the Earth. In their excellent book *Color and Light in Nature* (Cambridge University Press), authors David K. Lynch and William Livingston make the following observations:

▶   Over water, the sky near the horizon is dark.

▶   Over lush vegetation, the sky near the horizon is slightly green.

▶   Over the desert, the sky near the horizon is a brownish-yellow.

This, along with other atmospheric effects such as sunrise and sunset lighting, weather conditions, and aerial particulate matter, account for the wide variation in hue that is seen at the horizon.

The Sky's Saturation

The color component with the largest variation from the top to the bottom of any sky gradient is the saturation, which varies from perhaps 50 to 60 percent at the zenith, going down to as much as 0 at a level horizon that's unobstructed by buildings or mountains.

The Sky's Brightness

Because of the nature of Rayleigh scattering, the variation in the brightness color component of the sky is inverse to that of its saturation, with the lowest brightness at the top of the frame and the highest brightness at the horizon. You can see this in a waveform analysis of the sky gradient comparison, shown earlier, which reveals the sky slices ranging as much as 35 percent from the zenith to the horizon.

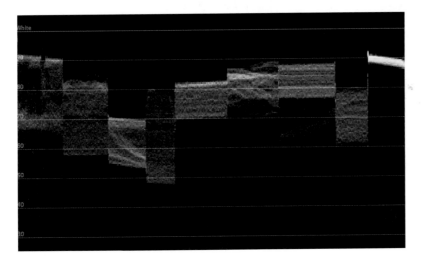

If a sky has a rich blue color, its brightness is not going to be at the very top of the luma scale at 100 percent. The white point is normally reserved for desaturated highlights (see Broadcast Legality).

The Angle of a Sky Gradient

The angle of a sky gradient depends on the position of the camera and of the sun. When the sun is high in the sky, or when the camera is pointed directly away from the sun, the gradient of the sky is pretty much vertical. (Check in the sky gradient comparison, shown earlier.)

However, when the camera is pointed in the direction of the sun, the gradient becomes more and more angled relative to the lower position of the sun, as shown here:

Sky Color Relative to Camera Position

When the sun is lower than its zenith, the darkest part of the sky is the portion that's farthest away from the position of the sun. In other words, when you turn your back to the sun, you're looking at the darkest and most saturated part of the sky. This can be a source of much consternation, depending on coverage of a scene with shot-reverse-shot sequences, because the sky in one direction looks very different than the sky in the other direction. In these situations, your sensibility will dictate the treatment. Leaving the sky levels alone is technically realistic, but if it's too much of a distraction, you may need to adjust the sky in one angle of coverage or the other to create a greater sense of continuity.

Other Sky Effects

Obviously, the sky isn't always blue. Given their cinematic value, here are some of the most common sky effects you'll end up working on.

Sunsets

As the sun gets lower in the sky, the increased atmospheric density between you and the sun filters out the blue and green light, leaving the longer red wavelengths

When the air is very clear, the sunset sky is generally yellow.

Particulate matter such as pollution, dust, and clouds catch and reflect the red wavelengths of light, resulting in the red/orange/peach sunrises and sunsets that photographers love.

This is illuminated most dramatically if there are translucent clouds in the sky, causing striated sunsets, with multiple levels of reds, yellows, and oranges that vary with the density of the cloud cover.

Brilliant red skies over the ocean are due to salt particles, which scatter the longer red wavelengths in greater proportions.

Clouds

Clouds appear white because water vapor and dust particles are significantly larger than molecules of air, so light is reflected off of these surfaces rather than scattered. This reflectivity explains the vivid desaturated white that clouds exhibit when catching the light.

Clouds, despite their ethereal nature, have volume that absorbs and reflects light. This accounts for the silver and gray lining that clouds exhibit, which is simply the shadowed half of particularly dense clouds. In all cases, clouds are desaturated, and the shadow areas are generally lighter and darker shades of gray. The exception is reflected sunrise or sunset lighting with a strong orange/red component.

Clouds also filter light, and the ambient color temperature of an overcast day (approximately 8000K) is significantly cooler than the color temperature of average north sky daylight (6500K). See Color Temperature.

Haze

Although Rayleigh scattering accounts for blue skies and airlight, *Mie scattering* is another phenomenon in which tiny particles scatter all wavelengths of light equally, resulting in a white glare and the absence of blue. This phenomenon accounts for the haze created by mist, fog, and the white glare that appears around the sun in certain atmospheric conditions. Mie scattering is also caused by aerosols—both natural (water vapor, smoke, dust, and salt) and man-made (pollution).

The effect is a diffusion and lightening of distant features of the landscape, which typically have low contrast as a result.

You can sometimes minimize haze by expanding the contrast of a clip.

Photographic Manipulation

Shooting skies can be tricky; depending on the overall exposure for the scene, it's easy to overexpose a bright sky. Furthermore, it's difficult to capture the rich blue colors that we perceive with unaided film and video.

In general, strong blues and distinct gradients are usually the goal when shooting exterior daylight scenes, unless specific weather conditions are called for. Two practical tools can help you enhance these aspects of the sky during shooting:

▶ Polarizer filters—Light from the sky is polarized, meaning that light waves traveling through the air are made to vibrate at one angle of orientation or another when scattered by the air. Light at the highest point in the sky is the most polarized. By rotating a polarizer filter, you can limit the light coming in through the lens to one orientation or another of polarization, which intensifies the color by darkening and saturating the sky. You can simulate this effect pretty well with secondary color correction (more on this in the next section). However, polarizing filters also mitigate the diffusing effect of haze and cut down on reflections from water and glass, and these effects are only possible at the time of shooting.

▶ Graduated neutral density filters—These filters have a neutral density (ND) coating on one half, with the other half left clear, with a soft transition between both halves. By orienting the ND half over they sky, you can lower its exposure to match that of the other subjects in the shot. This can sometimes result in a visible gradient in the sky (which also covers the subject, depending on the shot composition). This is especially true when using other kinds of graduated filters that actually apply color to the sky, adding blue or sunrise colors to an otherwise uninteresting sky. You can simulate this using vignettes.

Technical reasons for sky coloration aside, the color of the sky is ultimately a subjective decision. An awareness of natural phenomena provides a palette of choices that won't alienate the viewer, but how you choose to color the sky is subject to the requirements of the program, and the look the client wants to achieve. There is plenty of room for variation.

Correcting the Sky Using Secondaries

The simplest kind of sky correction to make is a secondary correction, basing the key on the color of the sky. This is a fast and easy way to add or alter color to an uncooperative sky shot.

1   Open the *01 Sky Correction* sequence, located in the Sky Corrections bin of the **Color Correction Exercises** project.

The first clip in the sequence already has a color correction applied to it that provides the overall grade. Although this primary correction does shift the sky color from cyan towards blue, the sky itself still isn't particularly amazing.

2   Apply a second Color Corrector 3-Way filter to the first clip in the sequence. (The second clip is the finished correction, provided for comparison.) Open the clip into the Viewer, and click the second Color Corrector tab to expose the graphical controls.

3   Open the Limit Effect controls, then click the limit effect eyedropper button, and click a midtone of the sky, somewhere underneath all the clouds that are higher in the sky.

4 Toggle the View Final/Matte/Source button to Matte (a black key against white), and adjust the Limit Effect controls to isolate as much of the sky as possible, without overlapping with the landscape or the woman. Once you've isolated the entire sky, drag the Softening slider to the right to blur the edges of the key a bit.

Bear in mind that because the range of luma throughout the sky is right in the midtones, the Luma control can be set to a fairly narrow band of midtone values and still isolate the entire sky.

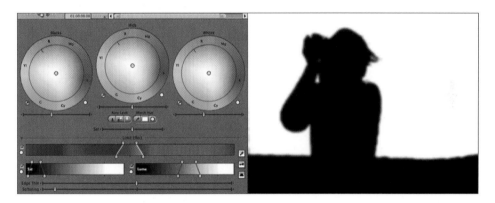

At this point, you have a creative choice. You could elect to apply a color correction to the *entire* sky (preceding figure), lightening and adding blue to the sky and the clouds all together, or you could choose to exclude the clouds by adjusting the Luma control of the secondary key (following figure). If the Luma control is isolating a narrow band, you can exclude the clouds by moving the entire luma selection to the left using the scroll wheel/ball of your mouse.

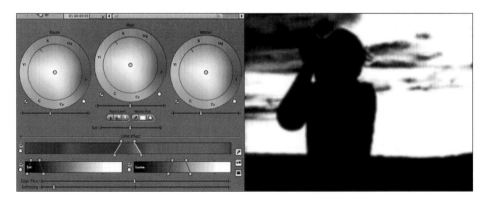

Excluding the clouds from the correction is technically more correct (clouds are typically desaturated). On the other hand, if the clouds are a dirty-looking gray, adding a bit of blue to the entire sky, clouds included, may look more attractive. The result will make them seem more diffuse and translucent. It all depends on look you're going for.

5 When you've isolated the portion of the sky that you want to correct, toggle the View Final/Matte/Source button back to Final (a gold key against gray).

Before making the actual correction, take a look at the Waveform Monitor, and notice the sky consists of a band of values that's solidly within the midtones. As mentioned in the previous section, this is pretty typical for a saturated blue sky.

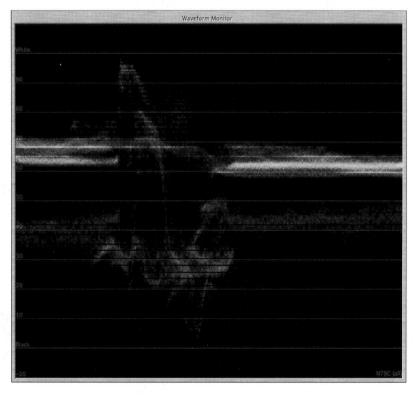

6 Drag the Mids color balance control towards a cyan/blue split. While you make the adjustment, drag back and forth from cyan to blue to see the difference this makes.

Skies range in saturation from 0 to 50 percent, depending on the time of day. You could push it even further, but you'll quickly spot when the sky starts becoming unrealistically neon.

After making the color correction, if you're dissatisfied with the gray tone of the clouds—they do start to look like storm clouds—relative to the newly juiced-up sky, you can readjust the Luma control to include the clouds in the correction, lightening up the sky considerably. The original (left) and result (right) are shown here:

This is a great technique to use when the sky already has a nice gradient, or shouldn't have one at all, because a single adjustment affects the entire sky uniformly. It's also useful when there is no color in the sky at all, such as when you're turning an overcast or hazy day into a brilliantly clear blue sky. It's also the fastest technique when there's camera movement in the shot.

Enhancing the Sky Using Vignettes

Another type of sky correction is needed when there's plenty of blue in the sky, but you feel that it's a little flat. As covered in Vignettes (Creating Shadows), gradients add a subtle depth cue that can help direct the eye towards the action, and sky gradients serve exactly the same function.

Often, the DoP will add depth to a flat sky, or add color to a white sky, using graduated filters placed over the lens. This effect is easily created in post, using colored vignettes. An added bonus of performing this step in software is that, unlike with optical filters, the color, brightness, softness, and width of vignettes added in post can be completely customized to suit the original color of the sky, the framing of the shot, and the grading needs of the program.

This technique is also useful in instances where intricate image detail prevents you from creating a successful secondary key. If there's not a lot of camera motion, your vignette's presence might go unnoticed; however, too much camera movement might be a little awkward.

As with all vignetting techniques, gradients benefit from being rendered out within Uncompressed 10-bit 4:2:2 sequences for completely smooth gradients that are free from the banding that's typically exhibited with 8-bit processing.

Simple Sky Vignettes

In this exercise, you'll use a simple vignette to intensify the gradient of the sky:

1   Open the *02 Sky Vignette* sequence, located in the Sky Corrections bin of the **Color Correction Exercises** project.

> NOTE ▶ This clip happens to have some lens vignetting in the outer action safe area at the upper- and lower-right corner.

The first clip has a primary correction, and although the client is generally happy with the color of the sky, it is a bit flat, and as a result the expanse of sky competes with the activity below. It's time to add a gradient.

2   In the Video tab of the Viewer, choose Render > Custom Gradient from the Generators pop-up, superimpose it in track V2 over the Dock LS clip, then open it up in the Viewer from the sequence and click the Controls tab in order to customize its parameters.

3   To turn the Custom Gradient generator into a vignette, Control-click the Custom Gradient clip in the Timeline and choose Composite Mode > Multiply to composite the two layers together. Then, move the playhead over both clips so you can see the results of your adjustments as you work.

4   Drag the rotation control in the Gradient Direction parameter so that the darkest part of the gradient originates from the top (0 degrees).

To create a gradient that's most compatible with the current color of the sky, you'll sample the darkest color value from the top of the sky within the clip in track V1.

5   Turn off the track visibility control for V2 to turn off the Gradient generator. Click the End parameter's eyedropper control, and click a dark blue value at the top of the Canvas.

6   Turn the track V2 visibility control back on.

The sky has become extra saturated, but it's a little *too* saturated. Because the highest part of the sky is also the darkest, it's time to adjust the brightness of the color used for the vignette.

7   Click the disclosure triangle for the End parameter, and raise the B (Brightness) slider until the gradient of the sky looks appropriate (around 38 or so, depending on what time of day it should be). Here the finished effect is exaggerated for print:

Masked Vignette

If there aren't any foreground or background elements sticking out into the sky, a simple vignette is usually sufficient. However, if a person or a tree is sticking out into the sky, the vignette will overlap with them, potentially tinting them a subtle shade of blue. This is actually what happens with optical filters, and if the amount of overlap isn't too much, it may be virtually indistinguishable unless someone is specifically looking for it (and somebody always will).

If you want to avoid this undesirable artifact, however, you can mask the gradient generator.

1   Open the *03 Masked Sky Vignette* sequence, located in the Sky Corrections bin of the **Color Correction Exercises** project.

NOTE ▶ This clip happens to have some lens vignetting in the outer action safe area at the upper-left corner.

The first clip has a primary grade applied to it, but the client wants to make an overall change to the colors making up the current gradient of the sky, lightening it and adding some more color to the left side. A horizontal gradient will do the trick, but while you could crop the bottom of it and feather it to fade it out, the irregular shape of the hills make the possibility of an awkward overlap fairly certain. However, you can use the mountains as a mask to hide the bottom of the gradient.

2   In the Video tab of the Viewer, choose Render > Custom Gradient from the Generators pop-up, superimpose it in track V2 over the Dock LS clip, then open it up in the Viewer from the sequence and click the Controls tab in order to customize its parameters.

3   To turn the Custom Gradient generator into a vignette, Control-click the Custom Gradient clip in the Timeline and choose Composite Mode > Soft Light to composite the two layers together and lighten the result. Then, move the playhead over both clips so you can see the results of your adjustments as you work.

4   Turn off the track visibility control for track V2 to turn off the Gradient generator. Click the End parameter's eyedropper control, and click a dark blue value at the top-right of the sky in the Canvas. Then click the Start parameter's eyedropper, and click a light cyan value at the lower-left of the sky in the Canvas.

5   Turn the track V2 visibility control back on to see the result.

As predicted, the overlap falling on the mountain is pretty severe, and it would look awkward even if it were cropped. For the moment, continue adjusting the color of the gradient to finalize the look of the sky.

6   Click the disclosure triangle for the End parameter, and raise the B (Brightness) slider all the way to 100 to lighten the right side of the sky. Then click the disclosure triangle for the beginning triangle, and lower the B slider to add more color to the sky.

The best way to limit the effect of the sky gradient is to key out the sky in a third superimposed layer and use the mountains themselves to mask off the bottom of the gradient.

7 Superimpose a duplicate of the Hiking ELS clip (along with the Color Correction filter that's been added to it) into track V3.

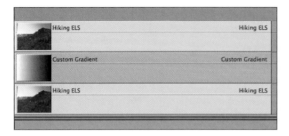

8 Apply the Chroma Keyer filter (in the Video Filters > Key bin of the Effects tab) to the duplicate Hiking ELS filter in track V3. Open that clip into the Viewer, and click the Chroma Keyer tab to begin isolating the mountains.

9 In the Chroma Keyer tab, click the eyedropper, and then click a pixel of the sky in the upper-right corner (the darker part). Click the eyedropper again, and then hold down the Shift key while dragging from a midtone blue all the way to the lighter cyan at the left side of the sky to expand the keyed area.

10 Click the View Final/Matte/Source control to view the key while you work (a black key on a white background), and adjust the Hue, Saturation, and Luma controls to make the sky completely transparent, while making the white mask over the mountain as solid as possible. Then raise the Softening slider until any chatter along the edge of the mask is blurred. Scrub back and forth through the clip while you're working to check the matte.

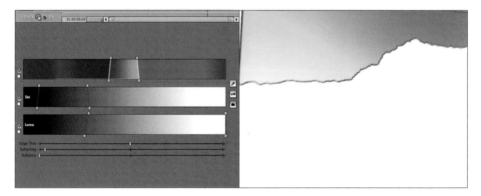

11 Toggle the View Final/Matte/Source control back to Final (a gold key against gray) when you're finished to see the final effect (shown on the right).

This technique also serves as the foundation for sky replacements, should you want to substitute an uncomposited gradient graphic or sky clip against the sky. If, however, your sky replacement is particularly involved (a moving camera, tricky key at the horizon, or a dozen other details that always need tweaking), you're probably better off working in a dedicated compositing environment such as Motion, Shake, or After Effects.

Enhancing and Creating Sunset Skies

This exercise involves putting sunset-like colors into the sky to create evening brilliance where before there was none:

1 Open the *04 Creating Late Day Sun* sequence, located in the Sky Corrections bin of the **Color Correction Exercises** project.

The first clip in the sequence has been graded to reinforce the late-afternoon look, but the client wants to punch up the sky with some pre-sunset color. Given the complex shape of the sky, secondary color correction is a good, fast approach. To provide a two-tone sky solution, you'll create two secondary corrections: one to add blue to the darker, upper-left portion of the sky, and a second one to add a red blush to the brighter, lower-right portion.

2   Apply a second Color Corrector 3-Way filter to the first clip in the sequence. (The second clip is the finished correction, provided for comparison.) Open the clip into the Viewer, and click the second Color Corrector tab to expose the graphical controls.

3   Open the Limit Effect controls, toggle the View Final/Matte/Source button to Matte (a black key against white), and adjust the Limit Effect controls to isolate a portion of the darker, upper-left corner of the sky. Lower the Edge Thin slider to smooth the matte, and raise the Softening slider to feather the edges.

4   When you're finished creating the matte, toggle the View Final/Matte/Source button to Final, then drag the Mids color balance control to add more primary blue to that part of the sky, and lower the Mids slider to darken it as well.

5   Add another Color Corrector 3-Way filter to the clip. Click its tab, open the Limit Effect controls, toggle the View Final/Matte/Source button to Matte (a black key against white), and adjust the Limit Effect controls to isolate a portion of the lighter, lower-right corner of the sky. As you create the secondary key, let portions of it overlap with the previous matte you created, because real sunsets often result in stripes of color reflecting off of different layers of clouds. Again, lower the Edge Thin slider to smooth the matte, and raise the Softening slider to feather the edges.

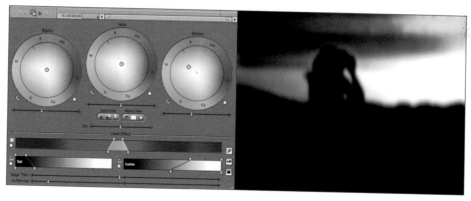

6   When you're finished creating the matte, toggle the View Final/Matte/Source button back to Final, then drag the Mids color balance control to add some magenta to the highlights of the sky.

Once you're satisfied with the balance and intensity of the color, you're finished! (See the image on the right.) As always, watch out for oversaturated colors in the highlights of the frame. When in doubt, turn on Saturation in the Waveform Monitor and check to see if any saturated portions of the graph rise above 100 percent.

Further Considerations

As you've seen, you have a lot of leeway when it comes to enhancing the skies of your programs. Still, reality is often hard to beat. It may sound obvious, but one of the best ways to get new ideas for color-grading is to pay closer attention whenever you're outside. Depending on the time of day and season of the year, and on your location (desert, forest, city, or beach), you're bound to notice significantly different looks, some of which you may be able to use in your color correction sessions. Carry a camera around with you and keep track. You never know when a reference photo might come in handy.

One last thing: beware of going overboard with your sky replacement. It's easy to either make the sky too saturated or to swing the hue to be too blue or too cyan, both of which may result in a neon-looking sky—problematic for the audience, if you're not working on a post-apocalyptic thriller. A little correction goes a long way.

Sunset and Morning Lighting

OVERVIEW ▶ The process of correcting and simulating the quality of light that falls on a scene during sunsets and sunrises.

SEE ALSO ▶ color temperature, limit effect (controls), sky corrections and enhancements

Simulating Sunset and Morning Lighting

From time to time, you'll be confronted with scenes supposedly taking place during sunset and sunrise. Depending on the nature of the shoot, you may have to perform a lot of balancing to account for changing light or significant correction to simulate the unique qualities of the desired light, because the footage was shot at other times of day. Why?

Shooting during a sunset or sunrise is always a tricky proposition. Shooting any scene takes a lot of time, and anyone in production will tell you that the light fades fast. If a crew is efficient, and things are set up well in advance, it's possible to shoot a variety of coverage, but the quality of light will change significantly from angle to angle as the sun moves along, and the resulting edited footage will inevitably need significant correction.

In other instances, the actual sunset will be used in an establishing shot only, with the rest of the scene shot at another time, with controlled lighting approximating the quality of light falling on the location.

Another reason that sunset and morning lighting is so tricky is that the camera (film or video) does not necessarily see what the eye sees. Sometimes, footage that was genuinely shot at these times in the day still isn't vivid enough, and needs it to be enhanced. An experienced DoP can account for this during the shoot, but in other, less controlled circumstances, you'll be called upon as a colorist to make adjustments to fine-tune the unique qualities of light that are found at these times. To do an effective job, you must understand why the light behaves as it does.

NOTE ► This entry does not cover the spectacular sky effects found in these conditions, instead focusing on the quality of light that illuminates the subjects and locations in these conditions. See Sky Corrections and Enhancements.

The Sun's Changing Quality of Light

The warmth associated with both sunset and morning lighting is caused by the same phenomenon. As the sun falls lower in the sky, its light passes through progressively denser sections of atmosphere. The thicker atmosphere absorbs more of the blue and green wavelengths of the sunlight, producing an increasingly warmer light that at the moment of sunset may be around 1600 degrees Kelvin. (For comparison to other light sources, consult the chart in Color Temperature).

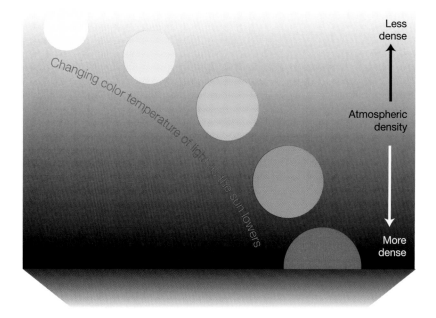

The warmth of late afternoon lighting begins with the so-called *golden hour*, which refers to the hour prior to sunset (also the hour *after* sunrise) during which the color temperature of light from the sun changes from approximately 5000K for afternoon lighting to around 3000K at the peak of the golden hour, down to 1600K at the moment of sunset. (All of these values are subject to atmospheric conditions such as cloud cover.)

Because this quality of light is considered flattering to actors and outdoor settings alike, shooting schedules (when budget permits) are often tailored to take advantage of this time of day.

The warmth of sunset and sunrise lighting can also be intensified by particulate matter in the sky. Smog, smoke from forest fires and volcanoes, and dust carried on seasonal air currents all intensify the reddish/orange light coming from the sun.

Furthermore, the lower the sun falls in the sky, the less light falls on the scene. There are many ways of compensating for this with camera and lighting adjustments, and typically the most noticeable result in recorded footage is higher contrast, as the shadows become progressively deeper. Another byproduct of these reduced light levels may be increased noise or grain, depending on the camera or film stock being used.

So that explains the overall quality of light falling on the subjects. This, however, is only part of the picture. An examination of an actual sunset image reveals other qualities that are just as important to creating a convincing sunset look. Study the following picture, and examine the quality of color in both the highlights and in the shadows.

A few things should leap out at you. In general, there are three important qualities to sunset and sunrise lighting:

▶ An extremely warm color cast in the highlights from the direction of the sun, which is progressively warmer as the sun comes closer to actual sunset. This is the key light in the scene, and the color cast in the highlights can be quite intense, overwhelming the natural colors in the subject. (White hot highlights will likely remain desaturated, however.)

▶ Warmer lighting in the midtones; however, the resulting color cast is not nearly so strong as in the highlights. This is the fill lighting that is still scattering in from other parts of the sky.

▶ Relatively normal color in the shadows. This is a key observation: The darker areas of the picture still have pure, fully saturated color that stands in stark contrast to the highlights. In the following picture of late morning light falling through a leafy canopy, observe how vivid the greens in the shadows of the leaves are, as opposed to the more golden color in the highlights. The last of the golden sunlight affects the highlights much more than the shadows.

These three observations provide a good start for analyzing sunset and sunrise scenes and adjusting them using the Color Corrector tools that Final Cut Pro provides.

Differentiating Morning from Evening

Although technically morning and evening lighting are identical, there are usually significant emotional differences between scenes meant to take place at the beginning and at the end of the day. For all the talk of degrees Kelvin and atmospheric conditions above, the bottom line is this: how intense is the spirit of the scene supposed to be?

Although it's always dangerous to make generalizations, here are a couple of things to consider. Your options for close-to-the-horizon light fall from a golden yellow, through orange, to a dark reddish-orange. By the time most characters are awake, fed, and at whatever early-morning appointment has dragged them into the program you're working on, the highlights probably have more of a more golden/yellow color quality to them because the sun has risen higher in the sky. Golden light indicates morning really well. It doesn't hurt that this color is a brighter, more energetic and optimistic sort of hue that usually fits well with scenes that take place at morning.

On the other hand, people are well used to blazing red sunsets, so warmer orange/reddish highlights indicate evening quite well. And because these warmer hues are more romantic and/or intense, this may also play right into the director and DoP's themes for the program.

Ultimately, atmospheric accuracy shouldn't preempt the look that's necessary for the program, but they can be a guide for different options that are available.

> **NOTE** ▸ For an excellent book on the effect of color on storytelling, see Patti Ballantoni's *If It's Purple, Someone's Gonna Die* (Focal Press).

Creating an Evening Look

With all of these observations in mind, it's time to apply them to correcting a clip. The following image was shot in the hour preceding the sun's dip behind a mountain range. The overall amount of light was being reduced by the mountain range, but the sun wasn't yet low enough in the sky to acquire the warmth of a true sunset. The director wants this scene to instantly read "sunset" to the audience, so it clearly requires some alteration.

1   Open the *Sunset Highlights* sequence, located in the Sunset and Morning Lighting bin
     of the **Color Correction Exercises** project.

2   Apply a Color Corrector 3-Way filter to the first clip in the sequence (the second clip
     is the finished correction, provided for comparison). Open the clip into the Viewer,
     and click the Color Corrector tab to expose the graphical controls.

     A look at the Waveform Monitor reveals no true blacks, a low average image bright-
     ness, but a few highlights stretching just to 100 percent. The image itself is well
     saturated but not too much so—overall a reasonable image to begin with, with no
     clipping and lots of detail.

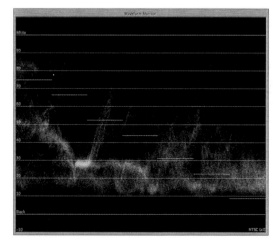

The first order of business is to create the overall look for the clip. The director wants a higher-contrast, warm, somewhat muted look for the image.

3   Boost the contrast by lowering the blacks such that the lowest point on the waveform just touches 0 percent.

If you wanted even higher contrast, you could opt to slightly crush the blacks, but for this image is isn't really necessary. Because the highlights are already hitting 100 percent, the best way to provide more image detail to contrast with the shadows is by boosting the mids slightly, just until you feel the contrast is suitably strong, but not so much as to create an inappropriately bright image. Remember, this is supposed to be the end of day, and the picture should be slightly darker.

4   To accommodate the warm but muted color tone for the image, drag the Mids color balance control towards orange until you feel the midtones are warm, but not glowing.

The goal is not to create the super-warm highlights described in the previous section, but to just warm up the overall image a bit to account for the slightly warmer fill.

5   Lower the Saturation slider just a bit to mute the colors, without eliminating them.

Slightly lowering the saturation of a clip sometimes allows you to "knock the edges off" of a clip, giving it a more subdued look. With the right image, this can look sophisticated. With the wrong image, the resulting look may be dull. Use your judgment.

Now that you've established the general look for the clip, it's time to really sell the sunset by manipulating the highlights in the image, to give that warm key-lit look.

You could try to warm up the highlights by using the Whites color balance control of the filter you just applied, but because of the extent that the filters overlap, you may end up warming the entire image much more than you want. Using a secondary color correction operation allows you to restrict the correction to a much more specific portion of the image.

6   Add a second Color Corrector 3-Way filter to the clip, then click the Color Corrector 3-Way - 2 tab, and open the Limit Effect controls. To see what you're doing, set the View Final/Matte/Source button to Matte (a black key against a white background).

The portion of the image you're isolating will now appear as a white key against black.

7   To isolate the highlights, turn on the Luma control, and drag the Luma handles to isolate the brightest parts of the image. Adjust the top handles to isolate the brightest highlights on the woman's face, arms, and clothing, and then adjust the bottom handles to keep the selection narrow, but keep a small falloff around the edges of the key. Lastly, drag the Softening slider to the right in order to soften the key, blurring the edges and preventing any buzz or chattering.

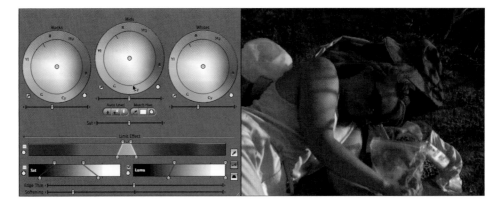

8   Set the View Final/Matte/Source button to Final (a gold key on a gray background) and drag the Whites color balance control towards orange to add more color and warmth to the highlights while viewing the result.

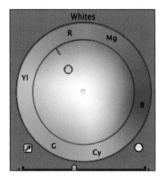

The intensity of the color in the highlights is directly proportional to how low the sun is in the sky. If you're unsure how to adjust the contrast and highlight color in a clip like this, ask the client what time it's supposed to be in the scene or how close it is to sunset.

When you're satisfied that the result (on the right) looks natural, you're finished:

Creating a Morning Look

In this exercise, you'll adjust a clip to create more of an early morning look:

1   Open the *Morning Highlights* sequence, located in the Sunset and Morning Lighting bin of the **Color Correction Exercises** project.

2   Apply a Color Corrector 3-Way filter to the first clip in the sequence (the second clip is the finished correction, provided for comparison). Open the clip into the Viewer, and click the Color Corrector tab to expose the graphical controls.

    As always, the first order of business is to create an overall look for the clip. In this case, the image is generally good, but the contrast could be expanded a bit and the midtones brightened.

3   Lower the blacks such that the lowest point on the waveform just touches 0 percent, and then crush the blacks by a couple more percent. Boost the mids a bit to brighten the image, for a well-lit, morning look.

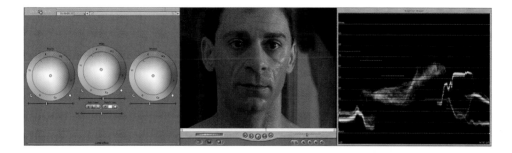

The color is fine, so next you'll be manipulating the highlights in the image, to create a golden morning key light.

4   Add a second Color Corrector 3-Way filter to the clip, then click the Color Corrector 3-Way - 2 tab, and open the Limit Effect controls. To see what you're doing, set the View Final/Matte/Source button to Matte (a black key against a white background).

The portion of the image you're isolating will now appear as a white key against black.

5   To isolate the highlights, turn on the Luma control, and drag the Luma handles to isolate the brightest parts of the image. Adjust the top handles to isolate the brightest highlights on the man's face, and then adjust the bottom handles to soften the edges of the key. Lastly, drag the Softening slider to the right in order to blur the key to prevent any buzz or chattering.

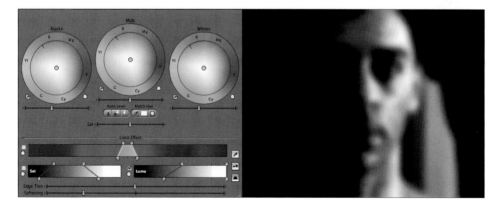

6   Set the View Final/Matte/Source button to Final (a gold key on a gray background) and drag the Whites color balance control towards a yellowish-orange to add more color and warmth to the highlights while viewing the result.

Be careful you don't go too much towards green, or the man will start to look ill.

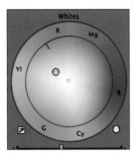

Make sure you don't overdo it, or you'll end up with neon highlights. When the effect looks natural on your broadcast monitor, you'll be finished (image on the right):

Further Considerations

Convincing sunset and morning looks involve targeted adjustments to the highlights. These techniques come in handy for many other situations where you want to make extreme changes to one luminance zone of an image without affecting the others.

Pulling secondary keys on the Luma component of a video clip is also a good way to get an extremely clean key, even with highly compressed media, because the Y channel of Y'CbCr video always has the maximum amount of data.

Television and Monitor Glow Simulation

OVERVIEW ▶ A method of mimicking the effect of lighting cast on a subject by a computer monitor or television.

SEE ALSO ▶ color temperature, limit effect controls

What Is Monitor Glow?

When someone is sitting near a computer display or a television, the monitor often serves as a light source itself, casting a soft cool light on the subject.

The distinctive blue glow of a computer monitor or television is caused by the cooler color temperature that these devices employ, relative to the tungsten lighting frequently used in most homes. Computer monitors are typically set to 6500K, whereas televisions may be set to 7100K or even 9300K (in Asia). According to the relative scale of color temperature for lighting sources, tungsten household lighting is around 2800K, and tungsten set lighting is around 3200K. In an environment with mixed lighting, the average television is going to appear quite a bit bluer.

NOTE ▶ For a thorough explanation of the color temperature scale, see **Color Temperature.**

The following reference photograph shows a subject (the author) illuminated solely by the 6500K lighting of two cinema displays and a broadcast monitor. The soft highlights that result are definitely on the cool side of the spectrum, relative to the skin tones of the subject.

Set lighting doesn't always account for this effect when two actors are shown sitting in front of a monitor. Perhaps the other lighting instruments are overpowering the practical light coming from the monitors. Or maybe the monitors are set up with tracking markers in preparation for being completely replaced by a composited image, and so they aren't turned on at all.

Depending on the aesthetic of your project, you may find you need to simulate this glow to "sell" the audience on the idea that the actors are sitting in front of a working monitor.

Creating Monitor Glow

This is one of several techniques that uses a single qualifier in the Limit Effect controls.

1   Open the *Monitor Glow* sequence, located in the Television and Monitor Glow bin of the **Color Correction Exercises** project.

   The first clip in the Timeline already has a color correction operation applied to it, creating a subdued interior evening look. Because of the practical lighting coming from a tungsten lamp on the desk, however, the highlights on their faces are still a bit warm. It's not obvious that the monitor they're looking at is turned on.

   NOTE ▶ The second clip in the Timeline is a finished version of this exercise for your reference.

Don't be tempted to add more blue to the highlights using the Whites color balance control of the Color Correction filter that's already applied. This results in all of the highlights going blue, which is *not* the desired effect. Because the light from the monitor is so soft, it falls off quickly the farther it travels from the source. To simulate this quality, you want to add only a bit of color to the highlights of whatever's closest to the monitor.

2   Apply a second Color Corrector 3-Way filter to the clip, open it into Viewer, and click the Color Corrector 3-Way - 2 tab to open the graphical controls of the second filter.

3   Open the Limit effect controls, click the checkbox next to the Luma control, and turn on the Matte view.

Now you're ready to use the handles in the Luma control to isolate just the highlights to which you want to add the blue cast. You'll be taking advantage of the fact that the practical lighting on the desk is illuminating the two actors similarly to how the monitor would be.

4   Drag the upper-right handle in the Luma control to include all of the highlights, and drag the top left handle to just below the halfway point of the mids to isolate only the brightest highlights of the image. Then drag the lower-left handle to create a smooth falloff at the edges of the selection.

The Limit Effect matte that's visible in the Viewer now shows the isolated highlights in white.

5 Drag the Softening slider at the bottom of the Limit Effect controls to the right to further soften the selection.

Softening the limit effect matte eliminates some of the animated "chatter" appearing at the edge of the matte that's a result of video noise, and it also creates a softer falloff for the blue highlights you're about to create.

NOTE ▶ Whenever you use the Limit Effect controls, scrub through the clip and see if the matte is too noisy. If so, continue to make adjustments until the isolated effect is seamlessly blended into the shot.

6   Set the View Final/Matte/Source button to Final, and then drag the Whites and Mids color balance controls towards a blue-cyan split to add the necessary cool cast to the highlights.

How much or how little blue you add to either the whites or the mids depends on how extreme a cast you want to create.

Further Considerations

This example was relatively easy, because the lighting supported a glow coming from the direction of the monitor that was quick to isolate with a luma key. If the on-set lighting isn't so accommodating, you might have to use a masked correction to create a similar effect.

Other things you could do to enhance this effect might include darkening the rest of the room with a reversed version of the secondary matte you created for the highlights (see Limit Effect (Splitting Corrections into Regions)), because people typically watch monitors in a darkened space.

Tint Filter (Image Control Group)

OVERVIEW ▶ Explanation of a filter that applies either a monochromatic or blended tint to an image using a single filter. *Related terms:* Color cast, tint.

SEE ALSO ▶ color control, color temperature, sepia filter (image control group), tinting methods, tinting (optical filters and gels)

How Does the Tint Filter Work?

The Tint filter fills the color channels of a clip with the Tint Color, while retaining the image's original luma channel. The Amount parameter lets you evenly blend the tinted result with the original colors to create a mix.

The default settings are black (H=0, S=0, B=0) for Tint Color, and 100 for Amount. Applying the filter with these settings replaces the original color with a black tint, which looks the same as the result of applying the Desaturate filter at its default settings.

For a monochromatically tinted image, set Amount to 100. Reduce Amount to progressively blend more of the original color back into the image; setting Amount to 0 shows all of the image's original color.

You can use the Tint filter as a color grade all by itself or as a "look" filter that you apply after other Color Corrector filters. Because the Tint filter has such limited control over the contrast of an image, it's typically best to use the Tint filter in conjunction with other filters to create your final look.

You'll get better results with the Tint filter if you remember these pointers:

▶   The Tint filter is very efficient and can play in real time on qualified systems.

▶   Colors with high saturation and brightness have the greatest effect on the image at low Amount settings.

▶ With Amount set to 100, reducing the saturation and/or brightness of the Tint Color only darkens the resulting monochromatic tint.

▶ With a high Amount value, Tint Colors with low saturation and/or brightness result in an image with reduced saturation.

▶ With low Amount values, Tint Colors with reduced saturation and/or brightness of the Tint Color create a more subtle tint.

As with all filters, you can save variations of this filter that you use often to the Favorites bin in the Effects tab of the Browser. If you do, be sure to name them descriptively.

> **NOTE** ▶ The Tint filter can introduce illegal chroma values into your image, so keep an eye on the scopes whenever you're using it. If necessary, you can also apply the Broadcast Safe filter to keep the signal legal.

Tint Filter Exercise

The best way to get a feel for the Tint filter is to take a tour of some of the effects you can create using it:

1   Open the *Using the Tint Filter* sequence, located in the Tint Filter bin of the **Color Correction Exercises** project.

2   Apply the Image Control > Tint filter to the Elevator Scene clip, open the clip into the Viewer, and click the Filters tab.

3   Click the disclosure triangle next to the Tint Color parameter to expose the H, S, and B sliders.

> **NOTE** ▶ This exercise relies on the H, S, and B sliders to show you how specific changes in color affect how the image is tinted. Although a more typical way of selecting color is with the eyedropper or color swatch control, the HSB sliders do provide you with an interactive way of seeing the Tint filter's effect on your clips as you adjust the color.

4   To add some color to the image, raise the S and B values to 50.

The picture becomes a monochromatic rust color.

This is a somewhat extreme effect, probably more suitable for a title sequence than for a scene in a movie. This shot would benefit from having some of the original color brought back into the picture.

5   Lower the Amount parameter to 35.

This change brings some of the original color back into the shot, and the Tint Color ends up creating a color cast over the entire image.

6   Change H to 227 to create a cooling blue tint.

The blue color cast, when mixed with the original values, actually neutralizes some of the warmth of the original lighting, so the effect isn't quite as pronounced as that of the dark red, which reinforced the warmth.

7   Raise the Amount to 80.

This creates a much more extreme color cast, yet there's still the barest hint of some of the original color showing through, mainly in the shirts and ties of the men standing in the back of the elevator.

8   Now lower the B slider to 25.

With this change, you can see that reducing the saturation and brightness of the Tint Color when the Amount is set to a high value creates a more desaturated picture overall. There's a bit of the original color left but not very much.

As you can see, the Tint filter is very useful when you want to add a simple wash of color over the entire image. Just remember that while the Amount parameter determines whether the colors in the image are completely replaced or not, the specific Hue, Saturation, and Brightness of the Tint Color you use makes a big difference in the final result.

Tinting (Duotones)

OVERVIEW ▶ The process of tinting so that the blacks become one color and the whites a second color.

SEE ALSO ▶ complementary colors

What Is a Duotone?

In a duotone, the darker portions of the picture are tinted with one color, and the lighter portions are tinted with another. This is not an effect you're going to use a lot, but it can useful for stylized imagery.

Creating Duotones with the Arithmetic Filter

Although Final Cut Pro doesn't come with an explicit Duotone filter, you can create a duotone effect by desaturating the image and then using two instances of the Arithmetic filter to selectively add color to the lighter and darker areas.

> **NOTE** ▶ There's a significant limitation to this technique: You can't create duotones with a pair of complementary colors. If you try, the interaction between the Screen and Multiply operations will neutralize the color being introduced by the first Arithmetic operation.

To create the duotone effect:

1   Open the *Duotone Example* sequence, located in the Tinting, Duotones bin of the **Color Correction Exercises** project.

2   Apply the Desaturate filter (in the Image Control bin of the Video Filters) and two copies of the Arithmetic filter (in the Channel bin of the Video Filters) to the first clip in the sequence.

NOTE ▶ The second clip in the sequence is a finished version of this effect, for your reference.

3   Open the clip you just added the filters to into the Viewer, and click the Filters tab. Make sure Screen is chosen (it's the default) in the Operator parameter of the first Arithmetic filter, and pick a color with which to tint the Shadows.

4   Set the Operator of the second Arithmetic filter to Multiply, and pick another color with which to tint the highlights.

For the best results, choose a color that's on the same half of the color wheel as the color you picked for the first Arithmetic filter.

NOTE ▶ To use the same colors as the example, choose Blueberry and Carnation from the crayons interface of the Colors Panel.

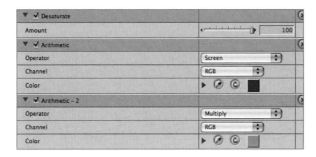

By lowering the Amount parameter of the Desaturate filter, and adjusting the Saturation and Brightness of the two Color values you're using for the tint, you can create different blends of the original and tinting colors.

Creating Duotones with the Gradient Colorize Filter

Starting with Final Cut Pro version 5.1.2, you can create duotones using the Image Control > Gradient Colorize FxPlug filter. This method has much more flexibility than the basic Final Cut Pro technique.

With the Gradient Colorize filter, the entire operation takes place within a single filter. More importantly, you can use any two colors you want to, you're not limited to non-complementary color pairs.

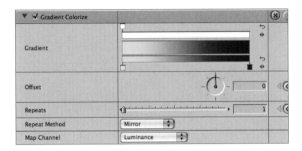

By default, the Gradient Colorize filter's Gradient parameter is set to a grayscale gradient (the filter shown above has been customized for this example).

You can right click on one of the squares underneath the gradient to reveal a color picker with which you can choose a tint color.

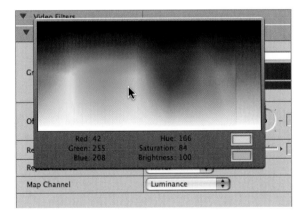

Remapping white and black results in a classic duotone.

You can also add more color definition boxes to the gradient by clicking the gradient itself. Creating more color definition boxes maps more colors to other parts of the image's tonal range, creating tri-tones or other multitonal variations.

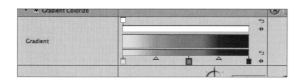

To remove a color definition box, drag it down past the border of the Gradient control, and it will disappear in a puff of smoke when you release the mouse button.

Using Third-Party Filters

Graeme Nattress' G Tint filter (from Nattress Set 1) is a third-party FXScript filter expressly for creating duotones. There are also many other parameters and options available to customize the effect. You can blend the tint with the original colors from the image, you can choose a composite mode with which to blend the two, and you can use a Luma mask to further control the tinted parts of the image.

Tinting Methods

OVERVIEW ▸ An overview of several methods of tinting clips in Final Cut Pro, using the Tint or Sepia filters, the Color Corrector 3-Way filter, superimposed color generators with composite modes, or the Arithmetic filter.

SEE ALSO ▸ sepia filter (image control group), tint filter (image control group), tinting (optical filters and gels)

What Is a Tint in Final Cut Pro?

The distinction between a tint and a color cast is a fine one, because both are caused by the same thing: the asymmetrical strengthening and weakening of an image's color channels above or below their original levels. For descriptive purposes, tints could be considered deliberately severe color casts.

Final Cut Pro offers several ways to tint clips in your projects. Which method you choose depends on the kind of visual effect you need. Do you want a subtle warming or cooling of the image, or do you need an extreme colored tint that replaces the original colors in the image?

The most obviously named filters for the job, Tint and Sepia (found in the Image Control group), create extreme effects, replacing the original colors in the image with the target color.

Other methods let you create more subtle washes of color over your images. In the following example, a superimposed color generator using the Overlay composite mode combines the original colors in the clip with the target color.

Using additional techniques, you can precisely control which parts of the image are tinted.

Which Method Should I Use?

When you want to create a tinted effect, ask yourself the following questions:

► How much of the image do I want to affect?

► How extreme do I want the tint to be?

Your answers will help you sort out which tinting method is best for your project:

► *To replace all of the original color in the image with a monochromatic tint*: Use the Tint or Sepia filters (Image Control group).

► *To create an extreme tint that still retains some of the original color:* Use the Tint or Sepia filters with a highly saturated color and the Amount parameter set to a lower value; or superimpose a color generator using the tint color, and use the Hard Light or Add composite modes to mix it with the image.

► *To tint a specific portion of the tonal range of the image*: Use the Color Corrector 3-Way filter to create an extreme color cast in the shadows, midtones, or highlights of the image as necessary. You can exercise further control using the Limit Effect controls.

▶ *To tint only the highlights and midtones:* Use the Arithmetic filter (Channel group) with the Operator parameter set to Multiply, or superimpose a color generator using the tint color, and use the Multiply, Overlay, or Soft Light composite modes to mix it with the image.

▶ *To tint only the shadows and midtones:* Use the Arithmetic filter (Channel group) with Operator set to Screen; or superimpose a color generator using the tint color, and use the Screen composite mode to mix it with the image.

▶ *To tint a range of clips in a sequence all at once:* Use one of the superimposed color generator methods, extending the duration of the superimposed matte to cover the entire range of clips. You could also nest a series of clips together, and apply a single group of filter operations to the entire nested sequence.

How to Compare Results

Guidelines are a good place to start, but nothing compares to seeing the results of each method. To compare each tinting method for yourself, open the *Tinting Methods Compared* sequence, located in the Tinting Methods bin of the **Color Correction Exercises** project.

The test clip used for each method combines a video image with a wide range of color (a blue sky, green foliage, yellow sign, and white highlights on the house) with a circular gradient underneath, with pure white at its center, a grayscale ramp off to each side, and pure black at the left and right sides.

This sequence allows you to clearly see the effect of each tinting method on the shadows, highlights, and midrange colors of your images, especially when combined with a look at the Waveform Monitor, Vectorscope, and Parade scope (visible by choosing WV + Parade from the Layout pop-up in the Video Scopes tab).

Beware of Illegal Levels

Many of the methods covered in this section can result in illegal luma or chroma values. As always, keep an eye on your scopes (software and hardware), and if necessary, adjust your Color Correction filters or add a Broadcast Safe filter to keep your video within specification.

Using the Tint and Sepia Filters

The most extreme tinting methods are the Tint and Sepia filters. These filters completely replace an image's existing color with a monochromatic version of the image in the tint color. The following image has the Sepia filter applied using the default setting.

Both the Tint and Sepia filters use the same method to tint the image, but the Sepia filter has an additional control (Highlight) that lets you either boost the whites or crush the blacks of the image.

Using these filters with the Amount parameter set to 100, the original color channels are completely overwritten with the tint color (as you can see both in the gradient and on the Parade scope). The color in the blacks and whites is significantly affected. You'll notice that the Vectorscope is displaying only a single point of color, reflecting the monochromatic nature of the tint.

If you examine the Waveform Monitor, you'll observe that the luma channel is relatively unchanged. The black and white points of the image remain more or less unaffected, although the blacks certainly seem washed-out due to the extreme color cast.

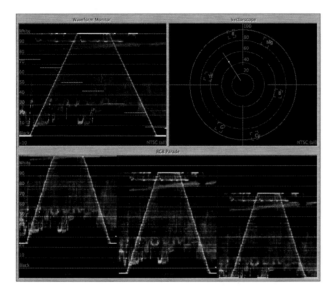

At the default settings, this is not a subtle effect, although you can mix the original colors back into the image by reducing the Amount parameter.

The Tint and Sepia filters have two significant advantages. First, they require a minimum of processing power and can play in real time. Secondly, you can create a library of different effects by saving different versions of these filters as Favorites.

See Sepia Filter (Image Control Group) and Tint Filter (Image Control Group).

Using the Color Corrector 3-Way Filter

The Color Corrector 3-Way filter is one of the best tools you can use to tint images in your project. It rebalances the colors in an image, rather than replacing them, so you can create far more subtle effects. It also gives you very precise control over the portion of the image being tinted—including the ability to include or exclude the highlights and shadows from the tint. The interface gives you terrific control over the tinting color.

For example, if you were to make an extreme adjustment to the Mids color balance control, but leave the blacks and whites alone, the result would be a targeted tint that has no effect on the brightest highlights and darkest shadows. This technique leaves the apparent contrast alone, while letting some of the original color of the clip show through, producing a more sophisticated look.

On the other hand, if your intention is to apply a less targeted tint to a wider portion of the image, or you want to apply a tint as an additional grade over a previously applied Color Correction filter, then the Color Corrector 3-Way may be overkill.

See Color Balance Controls.

Using a Superimposed Color Generator

Another method you can use to tint clips in an edited sequence is to superimpose a color generator set to the tint color over the clip to be tinted, and then use a composite mode to blend the color generator with the underlying clip.

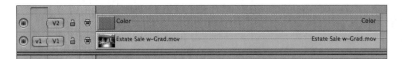

With this method, you can achieve unique color blends that would be difficult to create using other methods. Another advantage is that you can simultaneously grade multiple clips with a single superimposed color generator over them all. This method is fast to implement, and you can easily make changes by manipulating the color of the single superimposed color generator, as opposed to adjusting a series of individual filters applied to each clip in the scene.

Which Composite Mode to Use?

The composite mode you use on the color generator in track V2 determines which parts of the clip in track V1 are tinted. The various composite modes use math differently to combine the images together, in the process limiting the effect of the resulting tint to specific portions of your image.

In the following screen shot, a color generator is superimposed over the test image using the Multiply composite mode.

Using the same color generator, but changing the composite mode to Overlay, yields a very different result.

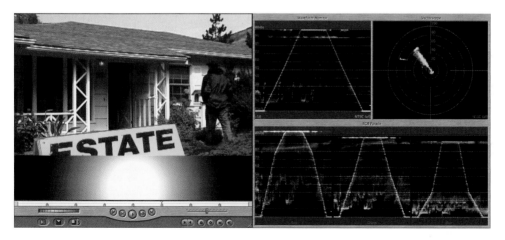

Of all twelve composite modes, you'll find five most useful for tinting: Multiply, Screen, Overlay, Hard Light, and Soft Light. See Tinting (Using Color Generators and Composite Modes).

Using the Arithmetic Filter

Another way of using the Multiply and Screen methods of tinting without using a super-imposed matte is to use the Arithmetic filter (Channel group). This filter allows you to select a color and then use one of a variety of composite modes to blend it with the image. An added feature of this filter is the ability to combine a color with a specific color channel of the image.

Of the wide range of composite modes available in this filter, only Screen and Multiply are really useful. The others, like the fascinating Xor operator shown in the following screen shot, are probably only good for rave videos and science fiction movies.

As with any other filter, you can create Favorites with custom settings, so if this is a technique you favor, you can create a range of ready-made tinting filters with all the colors you use most frequently.

This filter is also a good one to use if you want to combine this technique with other filters to create a filter pack in the Favorites bin.

Tinting (Optical Filters and Gels)

OVERVIEW ▶ The process of simulating the effects of optical warming and cooling filters.

SEE ALSO ▶ color control, color temperature, tinting methods

How Do Chromatic Lens Filters Work?

For years, cinematographers (and to a lesser extent, videographers) have been using optical filters to add a bit of color to images as they're recorded. To successfully re-create the effect of photographic filters in Final Cut Pro, it's helpful to understand how these filters—either chromatic or absorptive—affect the image.

Chromatic filters warm or cool the color temperature of the image. With these filters you can either correct for or create the quality of light as it appears at different times of the day. Absorptive filters increase the saturation of specific colors in the image; use these to emphasize a tone, such as the greens of foliage or the blues in the sky. When placed in front of the lens, absorptive filters block selected wavelengths of light while allowing others to pass. The result is a weakening of the color channels corresponding to the wavelengths being blocked, which introduces a deliberate color cast that affects the overall image as it's being recorded.

Seeing the effect is easier than describing it. For example, the following image was shot in afternoon daylight. The white balance of the video camera was manually set for daylight, but the overall image is still warm given the quality of light.

NOTE ▶ To more closely examine a collection of clips that were filtered in-camera, open the *Optically Filtered Clips* sequence, located in the Tinting, Optical Filters and Gels bin of the **Color Correction Exercises** project.

Now consider the same location, shot using the same white balance setting but with a Wratten 85C filter placed over the lens. The Wratten 85C is a "warming" filter, because it blocks blues to emphasize a combination of reds and greens that provide an orange cast, similar to the light produced by lower tungsten color temperatures.

> **NOTE ▶** Wratten filters are named for Frederick Wratten, the English inventor who developed this system for optical filtration and sold his company to Eastman Kodak in 1912.

In this image, the orange tones already in the image are reinforced, resulting in a more intense cast to the image.

This time the image was shot with the same white balance and a cooling Wratten 84 filter, which emphasizes blues, similar to higher daylight color temperatures. The light blue cast neutralizes the warm tones in the image and renders "whiter" whites.

For more information about the different qualities of light, see Color Temperature.

How Optical Filters Affect Color

There's more to optical filtration than "warm" and "cool," however. For example, the strength of the tint is nonlinearly applied across the tonal range of the image. This means that lighter portions of the image are more affected by the filter, while darker portions of the image are less affected. Regions of pure black are affected least of all.

> **NOTE** ▶ This effect is similar to superimposing a colored matte generator using Final Cut Pro's Multiply composite mode. See **Composite Modes**.

To see this, compare an unfiltered and filtered chip chart side by side in the Parade scope.

> **NOTE** ▶ To follow along with this demonstration, open the *How Optical Filters Work* sequence, located in the Tinting, Optical Filters and Gels bin of the **Color Correction Exercises** project.

In this example, a standard broadcast chip chart was shot twice, once with a neutral white balance (left) and once with a Wratten 85 lens filter over the lens (right). Portions of each chart were then cropped and superimposed side by side in the Canvas to produce the following image:

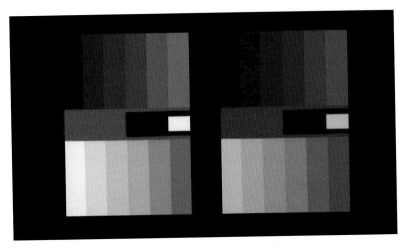

Examining this image in the RGB Parade scope provides the following graph:

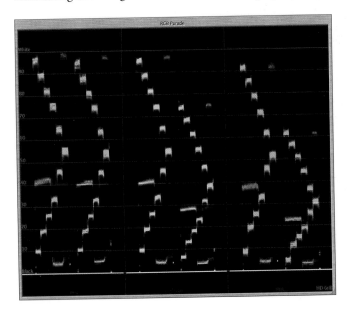

Look closely at the pairs of bars at the top of the graph (which represent the brightest parts of the chip chart). Notice that the left (unfiltered) and right (filtered) bars in the blue channel (the channel which is filtered the most) diverge quite widely, by approximately 29 percent. Meanwhile, the bottom pairs of bars don't diverge nearly as much, with a maximum difference of about 4 percent in the blacks of the blue channel.

You also can see that although the green channel is also filtered substantially, the red channel is virtually untouched.

How Optical Filters Affect Contrast

Because optical filters block light, they affect an image's contrast as well; how much depends on the severity of the tint and the quality of the optics involved. As with color, this darkening is nonlinear, affecting the whites differently than the blacks.

Examine the resulting graph in the Waveform Monitor, and you'll see that the white points of each image differ by approximately 18 percent. The midpoint (represented by the gray bar appearing all the way to the right of each series) differs by approximately 13 percent, and the black points differ by only 3 to 4 percent. Typically, however, the exposure is increased to compensate for this effect.

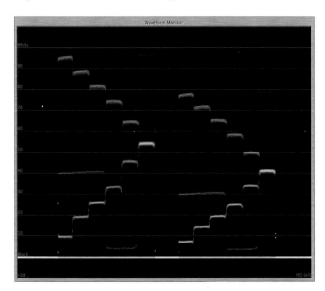

Unfiltered and filtered chip charts compared in the Waveform Monitor; notice how filtration reduces the overall amount of exposed light.

Colored Lighting Using Gels

Instead of applying a filter to the camera lens, you can tint images during recording by placing colored gelatin filters (called *gels*) directly in front of the scene's light sources. The result is a more limited color cast that affects only the portions of the image being lit by the filtered instrument. As with lens filters, filtration done with gels is a subtractive process. In simple lighting situations—all lights are filtered with the same color of gel to create a uniform color temperature—the effect on the scene is similar to that of lens filtration.

In Final Cut Pro, you can simulate mixed lighting, with different color casts in various parts of an image resulting from different lighting fixtures, using the Color Corrector 3-Way filter. Often, you'll get great results just using the Blacks, Mids, and Whites color balance controls to independently control the highlights, midtones, and shadows in an image. In other cases, you may need to isolate the lighting source more tightly using the Limit Effect controls.

Simulating Chromatic Filter Effects in Final Cut Pro

You can simulate the effect of chromatic filters in Final Cut Pro in several ways, most of which are summarized in Tinting Methods. Whatever method you use, you need to specify the color you're using to create the tint, and you should follow some general guidelines for tinting your clips with colors.

The values provided in the next section are approximations of some more commonly used Chromatic filters for adjusting color temperature. Bear in mind that for pure color correction, the Color Corrector 3-Way filter is your most versatile tool. When tinting an image, your ultimate goals are purely artistic: warming and cooling the images in your program to create an emotional effect.

Defining Color in Final Cut Pro

Each method used to tint images in Final Cut Pro relies upon the standard Final Cut Color control. (See Color Control.) When you click the disclosure triangle to the left of the eyedropper button, you'll reveal three numeric color sliders.

Color is defined within Final Cut Pro using the HSB model (hue, saturation, brightness).

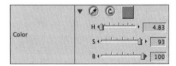

Every color that can be represented by Final Cut Pro is defined by these three parameters. For purposes of simulating chromatic filters, each parameter's use is covered here:

▶ Hue (H) defines the color of the filter (for example, whether it's orange/warming or blue/cooling).

▶ Saturation (S) determines how vivid a particular filter is. (Does it create an especially rich orange color cast, or is it very light?)

▶ Brightness (B) determines how dark or light a filter is. If you want to approximate the darkening effect of more intense optical filters, set Brightness somewhere around the low 90s. Otherwise, leave Brightness at 100 because you can filter images with no loss of light.

Using this method of describing color, you can approximate photographic cooling and warming filters, as well as lighting-correction gels, via the following guidelines.

Cooling filters
Hue = approximately 215
Saturation = 50 to 5
Black = 0

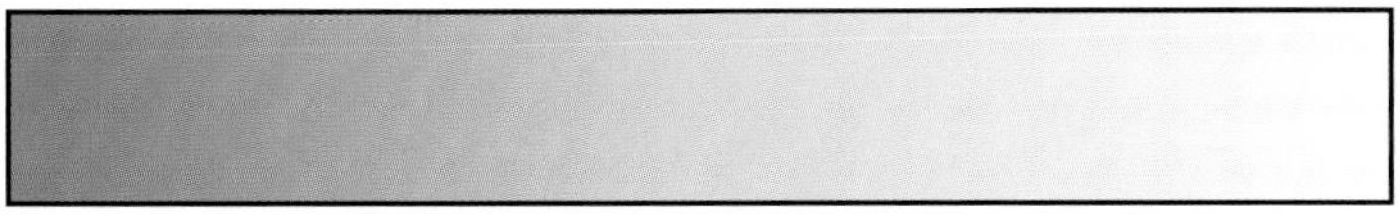

Warming filters
Hue = approximately 16
Saturation = 50 to 5
Black = 0

Green "fluorescent" filters
Hue = approximately 118
Saturation = 20 to 5
Black = 0

For example, to mimic a Wratten 85 warming filter use the following settings:

If you instead need a Wratten 80D cooling filter, use this combination of settings:

Finally, to approximate a PlusGreen gel, which simulates the chromatic spike fluorescent lighting causes when recorded, try the following settings:

Again, these values are only general guidelines, feel free to tweak them to discover your own looks.

If you use tinting techniques often, you can create a library of frequently applied colors using the swatch section of the Color panel.

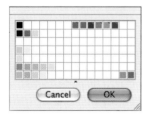

Whenever you find a value that you want to reuse as a filter later on, you can open the Color panel (by clicking a color swatch in Final Cut Pro) and drag your color down to the swatch section. See Color Control.

Using the Color Values That Approximate Filters

The values shown in the preceding section all assume you're using a multiplicative operation—either the Arithmetic filter set to Multiply or a superimposed Matte generator using the Multiply composite mode. Other tinting methods require modified colors to produce similar results. For example:

▶ When using the Tint or Sepia filters, reduce the saturation of the Tint Color. Alternately, you could reduce the filter's Amount parameter.

▶ When superimposing a Matte generator using the Overlay filter for more vivid colors and brighter whites, reduce the Brightness (B) parameter to achieve similar results.

See Tinting Methods.

Tinting (Using Color Generators and Composite Modes)

OVERVIEW ▶ The process of using superimposed color generators with composite modes to tint clips in specialized ways.

SEE ALSO ▶ color temperature, tinting methods, tinting (optical filters and gels)

Tinting with Color Generators

If other tinting techniques are not creating the effect you're after, you can try tinting with superimposed color generators, set to the tint color, using composite modes to blend the color generator with the sequence's underlying clip (or clips).

If you've never used them before, composite modes are special compositing operations (accessed by Control-clicking on a superimposed clip and choosing an option from the Composite Mode submenu in the shortcut menu or selecting a clip and choosing from the Modify > Composite Mode submenu) that use math to combine two or more superimposed images together in different ways.

Because composite modes are processor-intensive operations, this is not a real-time effect (although you can get a good preview on a fast computer using Unlimited RT). However, you can achieve unique color blends with this method that would be difficult to attain using other techniques.

To tint a clip using a superimposed color generator:

1 Open the *Creating a Superimposed Tint* sequence, located in the Tinting Methods bin of the **Color Correction Exercises** project.

2 Choose Matte > Color from the generators pop-up menu in the Video tab of the Viewer.

> **NOTE ▸** If the Video tab is not available, open a clip with a video track into the Viewer to make it appear.

3 Move the playhead over the clip in the Timeline, if necessary, and edit the color generator into the Timeline using a superimpose edit.

4 Open the color generator you've just edited into the Timeline back into the Viewer, and click the Controls tab.

5 Click the Color parameter's disclosure triangle, and set H to 23.08, S to 68, and B to 75. (This is the same color the Sepia filter uses as its default setting.)

6 Control-click the color generator in the Timeline, and choose one of the options in the Composite Mode submenu in the shortcut menu, such as Multiply.

> **NOTE ▸** The Color generator is the original Final Cut Pro FXScript generator. The Color Solid is an FXPlug generator. Both have identical controls, but different default colors.

The Effects of Different Composite Modes

Although the basic steps are the same for each tint, depending on which composite mode you choose, your results can be vastly different. The composite mode you use on the color generator in track V2 determines which parts of the clip in track V1 are tinted. How each mode uses math to combine the images determines how the tint applies and to which portions of your image it is limited. You don't need to understand the underlying math, but you should learn the effects some of the more common modes produce. Of the twelve composite modes, five—Multiply, Screen, Overlay, Hard Light, and Soft Light—are most useful for tinting.

> **NOTE ▸** As you read through each composite mode's effect, try experimenting with the different composite modes and color values in the *Creating a Superimposed Tint* sequence. To see a side-by-side comparison of all these blend modes, along with the tint filters, open the *Tinting Methods Compared* sequence.

Multiply

The Multiply composite mode is useful when you want the superimposed color generator to have the greatest effect on the whites of the image, with a diminished effect on the darker parts of the image and no effect at all on the black point. The white point literally becomes the tint color, and the midtones all become mixes of the original colors and the tint color. Absolute black is unaffected, as you can see by the bottom of the graphs in the Parade scope.

The Multiply composite mode literally multiplies the pairs of pixels from each image together. Any overlapping black areas remain black, and progressively darker areas of the clips darken the image. Overlapping white areas expose 100 percent of the opposing image.

This has a significant effect on the contrast of the image, with a tendency to darken that varies with the saturation and brightness of the color being superimposed. Unless your intention is to darken the image, the Multiply composite mode produces less extreme results when the superimposed color's saturation is reduced, and its brightness is raised.

Screen

The Screen composite mode is nearly the opposite of Multiply; it's useful when you want the superimposed color generator to have the greatest effect on the blacks of the image, with a diminished effect on the lighter parts of the image. The black point literally becomes the tint color, and the midtones become mixes of the original colors and the tint colors. Absolute white is slightly affected (as you can see in the slight dip at the 100 percent line of the red channel in the Parade scope).

Screen is essentially the opposite of Multiply. Overlapping white areas remain white, and progressively lighter areas lighten the image. Overlapping black areas expose 100 percent of the opposing image. Like Multiply, Screen also has a significant effect on the contrast of the image, with a tendency to lighten it that varies with the saturation and brightness of the color being superimposed. Reducing the brightness of the superimposed color is the best way to minimize this effect.

Overlay

The Overlay composite mode is one of the cleanest and most useful composite modes available for tinting an image. It combines the effects of the Multiply and Screen composite modes in an interesting way, screening portions of the image that are above 50 percent brightness and multiplying portions of the image that are below 50 percent brightness. The result is that the midtones of the image are affected the most, the white point is only slightly affected, and the black point remains unaffected.

NOTE ▸ Because of the way it works, using Overlay with a superimposed color generator with a neutral gray color (0 saturation, 50 brightness) results in a minimal change to the image.

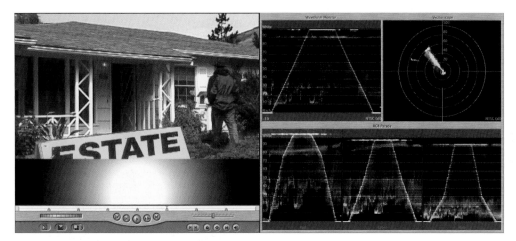

An added benefit is that the Overlay composite mode's effect on the contrast of the underlying image is largely limited to the midtones and, to a lesser extent, the white point.

Lowering the saturation and/or raising the brightness of the superimposed color generator boosts the midtones and whites, and raising the saturation and/or lowering the brightness lowers the midtones and whites. Making these changes results in a nonlinear change to the distribution of the midtones.

Hard Light

The Hard Light composite mode creates a more evenly distributed tint than the other composite modes, in that the tint has a significant effect on the whites, mids, and blacks of the image. It's most useful when you want to create an extreme tint. Unlike the Sepia or Tint filters, however, the tint color still interacts with the original colors from the underlying image.

The saturation and brightness of the superimposed color generator determine the degree to which different portions of the image are affected. Colors with higher saturation have a greater effect on the whites, and colors with higher brightness have a greater effect on the blacks.

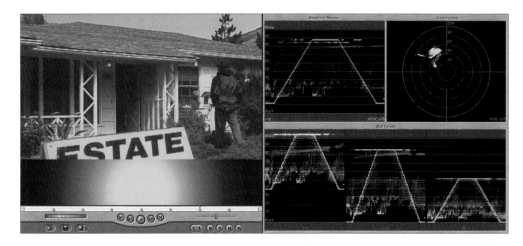

The Hard Light composite mode also affects the contrast of the image, both lowering the white point and boosting the black point, as you can see in the Waveform Monitor. How the whites and blacks are affected by the superimposed color depends on the intensity of the color.

Soft Light

The Soft Light composite mode is a milder version of the Hard Light composite mode, with a significant difference—it has no effect on absolute black. It's useful when you want a more even wash of color over the whites and mids, and down into the blacks, but you want the absolute blacks of your image to remain unaffected.

The Soft Light composite mode's effect on the contrast of your image is very similar to that of the Overlay composite mode.

Lightening Superimposed Tints

One of the best ways you can lighten a tint made with a superimposed color generator is to either lower the saturation or raise the brightness of the color being used.

Another method you can use is to lower the superimposed color generator's opacity, either using the Opacity overlay in the Timeline, or the Opacity parameter in the Motion tab.

Disadvantages to Using Superimposed Color Grades

There are some disadvantages to using superimposed color generators and composite modes to grade your clips. First, because composite modes are not real-time effects, they'll play only if you set Final Cut Pro to Unlimited RT playback, and even then they may drop frames on slower systems (this is because of the composite modes, and not the color generators). By comparison, ordinary Color Correction filters are real time, making them more efficient in most situations.

Another disadvantage is that none of the composite modes really accommodate pure, unsaturated whites (the Screen mode is probably too extreme for general color-grading). On the other hand, if your look involves rich washes of color, you can obtain looks this way that are difficult to achieve otherwise.

Lastly, dissolving to or from a clip with a superimposed color grade involves a few extra steps to get the color to dissolve along with the clip. You could nest the clip and its super-imposed color generator and then dissolve to the resulting nested sequence, or you could create the necessary transition in the Timeline for both layers. The steps are as follows:

1   Add the dissolve to the edit point between the two clips.

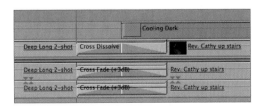

2   Extend the In point of the superimposed color generator to match the In point of the transition.

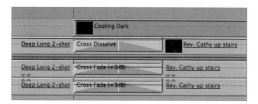

3   Add a transition of identical duration to the superimposed color generator that matches the duration of the transition below.

Creating a Library of Color Generators

If you use superimposed color generators a lot, you can create a library of frequently used color generators in one of two ways:

▶   You can open any generator into the Viewer and then choose Effects > Make Favorite Effect to place an instance of that generator into the Favorites bin of the Effects tab. This is a good method with which to create a library of generators for your own long-term use.

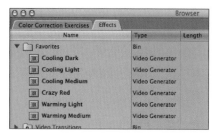

▶   You can also drag a generator from the Timeline into any bin of your project's tab in the Browser. In this way, you can organize a series of generators that are used repeatedly in a particular project so that they stay with the project file when it's given back to the client or when it's archived for long-term storage.

Tinting an Entire Scene with a Superimposed Color Generator

An advantage of grading with superimposed color generators is that you can simultaneously grade multiple clips with a single operation. For example, if you wanted to give a particular scene of four clips a cool blue look, you could accomplish it in the following way:

1   Adjust the contrast and relative color balance of each shot in the scene to a clean, neutral state using individual Color Corrector 3-Way filters, just as you would for any other scene.

2   For the final look, superimpose a single color generator over every clip in the scene, and choose the composite mode that blends the color most appropriately for your purposes.

Besides being fast to implement, another advantage to this technique is that when you need to make a change, you need only manipulate the color of the single superimposed color generator, rather then adjusting the filters applied to each clip in the scene.

Titles and Graphics (Choosing Legal Colors)

OVERVIEW ▶ Techniques for ensuring that colors and white levels of nonvideo elements are broadcast legal.

SEE ALSO ▶ broadcast legality, color control, gamma (imported and exported media)

Converting RGB Images into Y'CbCr

As you color correct your program, remember that the video clips aren't the only source of possible illegal video levels. Whenever you create a title card or graphic in another application for use in a Final Cut Pro project, you need to choose your colors carefully.

Typical 24-bit RGB images employ 8 bits per channel; in other words, there are 256 levels of color for each channel (0–255). When you import an image into a Final Cut Pro sequence that's set to a Y'CbCr codec, the color values are converted into the Y'CbCr color space (for 8-bit video, this range is 16–235, with higher and lower values reserved for other image data). When this happens, the RGB colors may be too bright and saturated, and they may translate into luma and chroma levels that are too hot for broadcast, especially when used as titles.

See Color Encoding Standards.

What's So Special About Titles?

Why do the luma and saturation of titles need to be so much more conservative than other portions of your video signal? Titles consist of pure regions of color and have sharp borders defining each letter of text. These borders translate into sudden changes in brightness as each line of video is drawn, and if these sudden changes are too high, they can cause problems for broadcasters.

Although the results may look perfectly fine on your broadcast monitor, they won't necessarily be broadcast legal. For this reason, you must be even *more* careful when choosing colors for titles and graphics than for other color-correction adjustments you might make.

Processing White and Superwhite

When you import any RGB image or .mov file (such as QuickTime movies compressed using the Animation codec), all of the RGB color values are scaled to corresponding Y'CbCr color values according to the Process Maximum White As setting of your sequence:

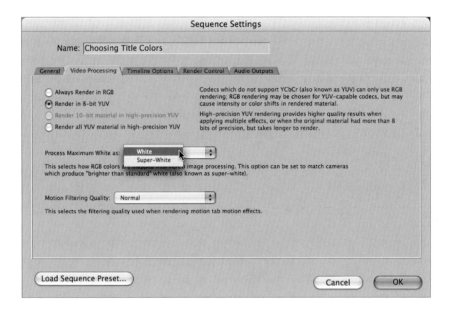

▶ White (the default setting)—Final Cut Pro remaps the white values in the imported image (255, 255, 255) to 100 percent digital, typically the maximum broadcast legal signal. This is the recommended setting for most projects.

▶ Super-White—Final Cut Pro maps white (255, 255, 255) to 109 percent digital, scaling the color values to extend up into the superwhite values supported by the Y'CbCr color space. This setting is only recommended if you're trying to match superwhite levels that already exist in other clips in that sequence, and you have no intention of making the program broadcast legal.

In either case, the program maps black (0,0,0) to 0 percent digital, and smoothly scales all of the values in-between to fit the appropriate range.

Keep in mind that you can change this setting at any time, and all of the RGB clips and Final Cut Pro generators (including Title generators) in the sequence will be automatically updated to fit into the new luminance range.

Making sure that Process Maximum White As setting is set properly is only the first step in ensuring that your title and graphics levels are correct.

NOTE ▶ One other thing to keep in mind when importing RGB images or .mov clips is the automatic gamma adjustment that Final Cut Pro makes. For more information, see Gamma (Imported and Exported Media).

Choosing an Optimal White Level for Titles Created in Another Application

Although Final Cut Pro conveniently maps the RGB white values of 255, 255, 255 to digital 100 percent when your sequence is set to Process Maximum White As > White, this isn't necessarily ideal for titles.

The maximum preferred white value for most broadcasters is 235, 235, 235, which sits at 93 percent digital in Final Cut Pro's Waveform Monitor. This is the brightest white you should use in your titles in order to be on the safe side when handing off your finished master to the client. If you turn on View > Range Check > Excess Luma, this level of white will trigger the green zebra stripes that indicate levels from 91 to 100 percent, but that's okay.

However, some broadcasters are more strict, preferring that no title exceed 90 IRE. To most easily accommodate these requirements, RGB color values of 224, 224, 224 create a white level that sits right at 90 percent digital in Final Cut Pro's scopes. You'll know that you're successfully hitting such a conservative mark, because you will not see any green zebra stripes when you turn on Range Check > Excess Luma.

The following screenshot shows an imported image from Photoshop with varying levels of white, with Range Check > Excess Luma turned on:

NOTE ▶ To see these examples within Final Cut Pro, open the Titles and Graphics, Choosing Legal Colors bin, in the **Color Correction Exercises** project, and open the *Choosing Title Colors* sequence.

Before you start working in your favorite image-editing application and worrying that your whites are going to look gray, remember that the viewer's perception of white is entirely relative to the brightness of the colors surrounding your titles. In the following image, the text at the left is exactly the same level of brightness as the text to the right:

Choosing White Values in Final Cut Pro

If you're creating titles or graphics using one of Final Cut Pro's title generators, the program scales the maximum white of your font to your Process Maximum White As setting. If your sequence is set to Process Maximum White As > White, then H = 0, S = 0, and B = 100 creates a white at digital 100 percent. To create a white at 90 percent digital, use the values H = 0, S = 0, and B = 88.

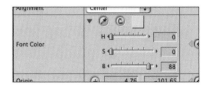

When you settle on a shade of white that you want to use consistently, you can save it as a swatch in the Colors panel. For more information, see Color Control.

Choosing Colors in Another Application

Choosing colors is a more complicated subject. When you're designing still or motion graphics for use in a broadcast program, remember that colors that look quite vivid when output to video often look dull and lifeless when viewed on your computer's display.

For example, consider the primary and secondary colors shown in the following figure. In each color pair, the bottom color is the most saturated RGB value (255 is the maximum value for any color channel), and the top is a muted version of the same color (all color patches are shown with their RGB values). Range Check > Excess Chroma is turned on, to indicate illegal chroma values.

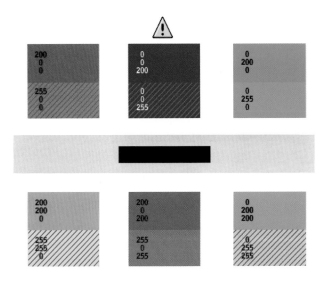

As you can see, the brightest colors are generally too hot. The pure red, blue, yellow, and cyan patches are all showing the red zebra stripes that indicate illegal values. The pure green and magenta patches are not, but you can bet they're on the edge. The muted versions of each color, on the other hand, are all perfectly fine. If you take a look at the Vectorscope reading for this image, you'll get a clearer idea of how close to legal the colors are. The outer clusters of color are the more saturated values, and the inner clusters of color are the muted values. Red and cyan are off of the scale.

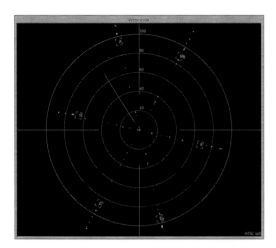

All of the levels are still a bit hot, but clearly the most saturated levels are well outside of the targets that indicate the conservative boundaries for safe chroma. As you can see from this example, red, blue, yellow, and cyan are the colors most at risk of producing illegal chroma levels, so make sure that you're using muted versions of these colors.

Many image editing applications have a video color safe filter of some kind. Photoshop has the Video > NTSC Colors filter, which automatically adjusts the colors in your graphics to create safe levels. See what happens when this filter is applied to the previous image; the modified color values are noted on each swatch.

NOTE ▸ These examples were created with Photoshop CS2.

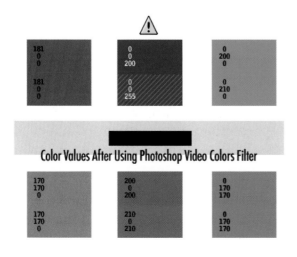

Color Values After Using Photoshop Video Colors Filter

The NTSC Colors filter modified all of the primary color swatches, except for the pure blue swatch (which is left alone, even though it's at an illegal level). Red, yellow, and cyan were muted the most, which makes sense because these are the most risky colors. Photoshop muted green and magenta much less, on the other hand. Evaluating these values on a Vectorscope shows that the red, yellow, and cyan values hit Final Cut Pro's targets squarely in the middle. Although the green and magenta values are still outside of the conservative targets, they are not so far as to be indicated illegal by range checking. Blue is the only color that slipped though the net completely, so you may want to keep your eye on those blue values in Photoshop.

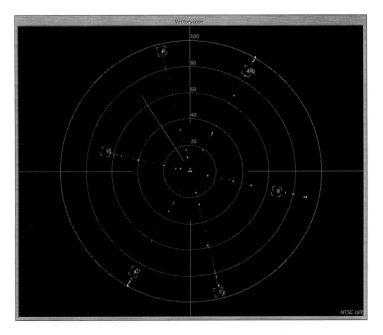

In general, when creating titles and illustrations in RGB-based image-editing and broadcast-design applications, keep in mind that you want to avoid very bright, very saturated colors, and that certain colors should be muted more than others. Lastly, although tools are available to help you manage the legality of your colors, it's never a good idea to rely on them to do all the work.

If you've been given a stack of graphics for your program, and you don't have the time to reprocess them all, keep in mind that you can always use the Color Corrector filters on them. After all, after they've been edited into a sequence, they're no different than any other clip.

Choosing Colors in Final Cut Pro

If you're creating titles or graphics using one of Final Cut Pro's title generators, readjusting your colors for legal chroma is quite a bit easier, because you can change the colors used by a generator interactively while watching the range-checking zebra stripes and the Vectorscope. Take a tour of your options:

1   Open the *Choosing Title Colors* sequence, located in the Titles and Graphics, Choosing Legal Colors bin of the **Color Correction Exercises** project.

    The first four clips provide hands-on versions of the examples provided previously in this section.

2   Move the playhead to the last clip in the sequence, choose Range Check > Excess Chroma, and set the Video Scopes to display the Vectorscope.

This is a Custom Gradient clip that uses two of the most troublesome colors for broadcast legality: red and yellow. The zebra stripes are showing a large strip of yellow and a narrow strip of red (which is hard to see in the screenshot, but should appear in the Canvas if you open up this exercise) that are too hot, both of which are well beyond the targets that indicate conservative legality in the Vectorscope.

3   Open the Custom Gradient clip into the Viewer, click the Controls tab, and open the Start and End color control parameters to reveal the HSB sliders.

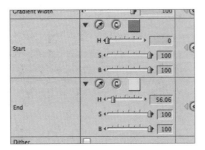

From these sliders, you can interactively change the color values while watching the zebra stripes and Vectorscope to make the colors legal.

4   In the Start color parameter, reduce the S parameter to desaturate the red until the zebra stripes disappear from the Canvas and the trace in the Vectorscope graph is within the R target.

5   In the End color parameter, reduce the B parameter to lower the brightness of the yellow, until the zebra stripes disappear from the Canvas and the trace in the Vectorscope moves within the Y target.

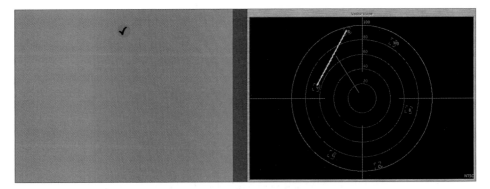

As you can see, for any given color with illegal chroma, you can either lower the saturation or lower the brightness. As with video legal signals in general, you get into trouble when a portion of the image is both too bright and too saturated. How much you'll have to adjust each color depends on its hue. As you've seen, some hues become illegal more easily than others. Just make sure to let your scopes be your guide, and remember to be *more* conservative with titles than you'd be with other images.

See Broadcast Legality.

Underexposure

OVERVIEW ▶ Explanation of how chroma subsampling affects your ability to adjust the contrast of clips that are too dark, as well as correction strategies.

SEE ALSO ▶ color encoding standards, contrast adjustments, saturated looks, video noise (matching), video noise (suppressing)

Chroma Subsampling Affects Underexposure Adjustments

When you're color correcting underexposed clips, the chroma subsampling of your media (whether it's 4:2:2 or 4:1:1/4:2:0; see Color Encoding Standards) has a significant effect on the extent to which contrast adjustments can be made without problems.

In particular, 4:2:2 encoded media can be adjusted much more aggressively and cleanly than can 4:1:1 or 4:2:0 encoded media, because 4:2:2 encoded media preserves more video data.

NOTE ▶ If you want to follow along, you can find this example in the *Chroma Subsampling Comparison* sequence, in the Underexposure bin of the **Color Correction Exercises** project. The first clip in the sequence, 422Clip.mov, has 4:2:2 chroma subsampling; the second clip, 411Clip.mov, is the same clip downconverted to 4:1:1 chroma subsampling. Both clips in the sequence have had their contrast adjusted for comparison.

Contrast Adjustments Compared

The following clip is exposed very darkly. As you can see in the histogram, the majority of the pixels in the image are under 10 percent, the midtones stretch from 10 to 50 percent, and what few highlights there are stretch in *very* small clumps all the way up to 95 percent.

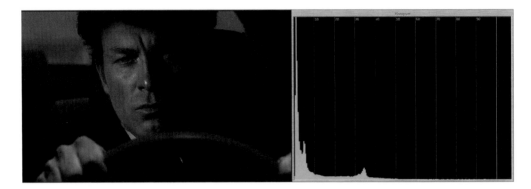

If you wanted to brighten the man's face, the easy fix would be to drag the midtones slider to the right to boost the midtones. Making a fairly aggressive adjustment (with the Midrange Level slider set to 141, as seen in the numeric controls in the Filters tab) to a clip with 4:2:2 color subsampling does the trick, and the results are quite clean.

Making an identical adjustment to a version of the same clip that's been downconverted to 4:1:1 chroma subsampling results in a much noisier clip. This is difficult to see in print, but it also manifests itself in the gaps that appear in the histogram below.

> **NOTE ▶** To see this noise, play each of the clips in the *Chroma Subsampling Comparison* sequence, in the Underexposure bin of the **Color Correction Exercises** project.

These separations in the histogram indicate that the image is being stretched beyond the available image data, which results in more visible noise in the image.

Saturation Adjustments Compared

Were you to increase the Saturation slider to compensate for the apparent lowering of saturation that occurs when you increase a clip's exposure (this happens no matter what the chroma subsampling is), you'll see a similar difference in the Vectorscope displays.

The following screenshots show vectorscope analyses of both of the clips with increased saturation (with the Saturation slider set to 173, as seen in the numeric controls in the Filters tab). On the left you can see the Vectoscope showing the 4:2:2 encoded version of the clip; the right Vectorscope showing the 4:1:1 encoded version.

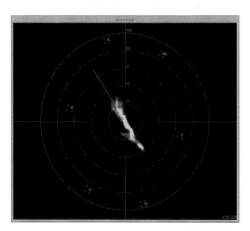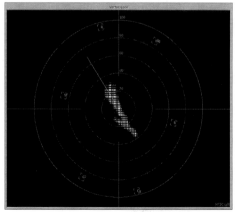

As mentioned elsewhere (see Chapter 2), the decision of which video format to use was made when the media was shot in the field. If it was shot with an uncompressed or minimally compressed format using 4:2:2 or better chroma subsampling, then you're in luck, and you should continue working in that format through postproduction.

If, on the other hand, you're working with media that was originally shot with 4:1:1 or 4:2:0 chroma subsampling, then you're going to have to work with what you've got. This doesn't mean that you won't be able to correct your footage; it just means that you're going to have to be a little more careful about how large a correction you make to underexposed clips. Noise is going to be a fact of life, and strategies for minimizing noise in situations where you need to increase the exposure no matter what will be important (see Video Noise (Suppressing)).

How to Handle Underexposed Clips

Underexposed clips usually suffer from two simultaneous problems after you've corrected them to add some brightness to the midtones:

▶   Excessive noise

▶   Undersaturation

These issues might not seem like much, but they can cause you some headaches, especially if you're working with highly compressed source media with 4:1:1 or 4:2:0 chroma subsampling. Consider the following example:

NOTE ▶ If you want to follow along, you can find this example in the *Correcting an Underexposed Shot* sequence, in the Underexposure bin of the **Color Correction Exercises** project. The example clip was recorded in the DV format, with 4:1:1 chroma subsampling.

The clip is pretty underexposed, but the color is rich, and this promises to be a nice sunset shot. Making a couple of simple adjustments with the contrast controls of the Color Corrector 3-Way filter to boost the midtones and lower the blacks makes the subjects more visible.

NOTE ▶ Boosting midtones is usually a better bet for trying to avoid noise than adjusting the whites, and it's generally more effective with severely underexposed clips.

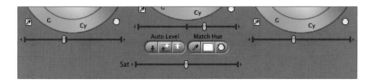

Suddenly, the image becomes noisy (this is easier to see when the image is playing), and the previously vibrant colors have become muted.

Unfortunately, these are the unavoidable consequences of pushing underexposed clips. It's important to note that increased noise when expanding contrast is a *much* more significant problem for video recorded with 4:1:1 and 4:2:0 chroma subsampling than with video recorded using 4:4:4 or 4:2:2 chroma subsampling. The latter two formats allow much greater latitude for contrast adjustments. See Color Encoding Standards.

> **NOTE** ▸ If your video was originally recorded with 4:1:1 or 4:2:0 chroma subsampling, converting it to a 4:2:2 or 4:4:4 subsampled format won't help. Incidentally, this is already done internally as part of Final Cut Pro's image processing pipeline. See Chapter 2.

Interestingly, a similar phenomenon occurs when you ask a film lab to "push" a roll of exposed film during development. Pushing film means having the lab develop the film for a longer period of time, raising its exposure at the expense of additional film grain and muddier shadows, very similar to what happens when you expand the contrast of underexposed video.

I mention this as reassurance that you're not doing anything wrong and that, when comparing a telecined video transfer to an originally recorded video clip with equal chroma subsampling ratios, film doesn't have any advantage over video when it comes to dealing with underexposure. In fact, you'll find that underexposed video typically has much more shadow detail than underexposed film (although film wins out when it comes to detail in overexposed highlights).

Although this is small consolation in post, the best solution is to make sure that the clips are properly exposed to begin with and to let your client know in advance that there are limits to what is correctable.

That said, the issue of saturation, at least, is a relatively easy fix. To put some zing back into the shot, you can raise the Saturation slider, pull the Mids color balance control towards red to add warmth to the highlights, and pull the Whites color balance control towards cyan to neutralize some of the mids adjustment to narrow the corrected area of the image.

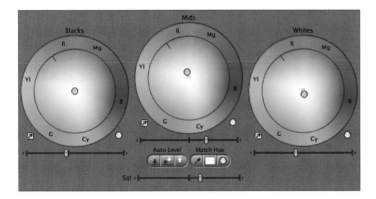

With the saturation taken care of, you have only the noise to contend with. See Video Noise (Matching) or Video Noise (Suppressing).

Hopefully, when you're in a situation where you're correcting a severely underexposed clip, the client will be so overjoyed at being able to see any detail at all that these problems will be forgivable, and you'll be showered with praise for saving the show. Otherwise, this is one situation where you'll have to carefully explain the limitations of the technology and find a way to split the difference for an acceptable compromise.

Video Noise and Film Grain

OVERVIEW ▶ Comparison of video noise and film grain, how they're related, and how they differ.

SEE ALSO ▶ video noise (matching), video noise (suppressing)

When Matching Color Isn't Enough

There will be times when, no matter how closely you've matched the contrast and color between two images, you still can't get the match quite right. Many times, it may be differences in video noise or film grain that's causing the problem. Frequently, the best solution may be to try to minimize objectionable video noise that's distracting to the viewer (see Video Noise (Suppressing)). Other times, you'll need to replicate video noise or film grain to match one clip to another series of clips (see Video Noise (Matching)).

Before you can do either of these things, you must first understand what video noise and film grain are, how to distinguish the differences between them, and how to identify differences in noise patterns from camera to camera. Once you're clear about what you're seeing, you can better decide how to deal with it.

What Is Video Noise?

Along with the individual pixels of detail inherent to any image, videocamera circuitry introduces video noise. The light-sensitive silicon chips at the heart of modern video recording cameras are, below a certain threshold of exposure, inherently noisy (CCD or CMOS chips are currently used). As with audio recording circuitry, there is a noise floor at which a certain amount of random electronic fluctuations always occur. The amount of this noise depends on the quality and size of the CCD used by a particular camera, and on the amount of light within the image being recorded.

When the signal-to-noise ratio falls below a certain threshold—in other words, the video image becomes underexposed—the noise becomes visible, appearing as an animated "buzzing" superimposed over your video.

Increasing a camera's Gain setting amplifies noise along with the rest of the video signal. Similarly, stretching the contrast of an underexposed clip using the Color Corrector filters in Final Cut Pro has the same effect, exacerbating video noise that's already latent within the image.

In general, video noise is something to be avoided, although it can sometimes be used to simulate film grain. (See the upcoming "What Is Film Grain" section.)

Noise, Chroma Subsampling, and Compression

The signal-to-noise ratio is only one factor that contributes to perceived video noise, however. The chroma subsampling of 4:1:1 and 4:2:0 formats (see Color Encoding Standards) also contributes to noise by decreasing the amount of data in the two color difference channels of Y'CbCr encoded video. This expresses itself as increased artifacting (blockiness) in the red and blue channels, when viewed individually in the Canvas.

Video compression also yields blocky and sometimes aliased artifacts that can appear similar to noise. Noise and compression together can result in some interesting effects. For example, consider this highly compressed noise taken from two successive frames of a HDR-HC1 camera recording a 1080i image in the HDV format.

As you can see, although the individual pixels have some differentiation due to camera noise, the MPEG-2 compression employed by the HDV format averages it into larger blocks of similarly toned noise. This is but one byproduct of aggressive compression in video acquisition.

Where Does Noise Appear?

Low light conditions increase video noise. In a video clip with both well-exposed and underexposed areas, noise is more likely to be visible in the underexposed areas of the picture.

Consider this image from an underexposed DV frame recorded with the Canon XL-1 camera that was set to record with increased gain. As you can see, there is discernable noise in both the lit and shadowed areas of the picture.

In the next image, a better-exposed high definition image is shown, where some colored noise appears alongside the natural details within the image.

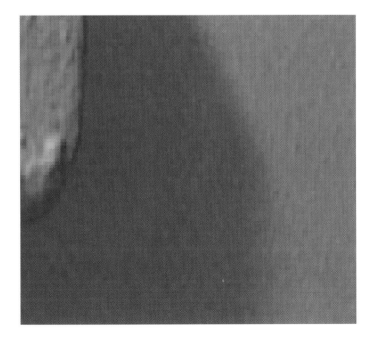

How Does Noise Look?

Video noise tends to be more colorful in darker areas and less saturated in brighter areas of the picture. This is an important characteristic to be aware of when you're trying to match noise in another clip.

Camera noise is comprised of individual pixels. When you zoom in, it's sharply defined, which contributes to its unpleasantness. Because of this, video noise is resolution dependent. In other words, individual pixels of noise in standard definition video appear larger than individual pixels of noise in high definition video.

Depending on the camera, individual color channels may have more or less noise. Compare the red, green, and blue channels recorded with a Canon XL-1 in the following image side by side. As you can see, the blue channel (right) has a significantly different noise pattern than the red (left) or green (center) channel.

Individual red, green, and blue channels of a frame recorded with the Canon XL-1 and enlarged for comparison.

To illustrate the differences between two different cameras recording with the same format, the following image compares the red, green, and blue channels of a frame recorded using Panasonic's DVX-100 camera. As you can see, the noise patterns in each of the channels are very different.

Individual red, green, and blue channels of a frame recorded with the Panasonic DVX-100 and enlarged for comparison.

Now consider the red (top), green (center), and blue (bottom) channels of an HDV image recorded with the Sony HDR-HC1 camcorder. The overall grain patterns are different, but the blue channel exhibits the greatest artifacting, assumably because of HDV's 4:2:0 chroma subsampling.

Individual red, green, and blue channels of a frame recorded with the Sony HDR-HC1.

Now that you know what to look for, you can decide what to do about it. See Video Noise (Matching) and Video Noise (Suppressing).

What Is Film Grain?

Although, to the untrained eye, the video noise and film grain may seem very similar, the origins of these phenomena are quite different. Unlike video noise, which is a spurious pattern of pixels that has nothing to do with the image itself, film images are *made* of grain. Understand this fundamental difference and you can better remove and replicate the effects.

Film stocks are comprised of three light-sensitive layers (nested within several other protective coatings), each of which is designed to selectively absorb the red, green, and blue components of light coming in through the lens of the camera. Each of these layers consists of microscopic silver halide crystals suspended in gelatin.

When exposed to light, these crystals stick together, becoming metallic silver. The more each layer is exposed, the more crystals become metallic, and the *denser* that layer becomes. Once developed, each layer's exposed silver grains are set, and the unexposed silver halide crystals are removed. Together, the three combined layers of dyed silver grains compose the final image.

Film colorists often discuss image *density*, which simply refers to how well exposed each individual layer of film is. The process just described results in a *negative* image, because the brightest areas of the picture create the most silver grains, while the darkest areas of the picture have little to no grain. The negative image is made positive either by printing onto another film stock to create a print for projection, or it can be made positive in the *telecine* or *datacine* process of transferring the image to an analog or digital video format.

Where Does Grain Appear?

Remember, with color negative film, the most well exposed parts of the picture contain all of the grains, and the darkest parts of the image have none. For this reason, film retains more information in the highlights than in the shadows (the exact opposite of video). As a result, grain disappears in the blacks, along with any other information in the picture.

The rest of the image, on the other hand, is all grain. Depending on the stock and exposure, it may be invisible. Most modern film stocks, even faster ones, are designed to produce extremely fine grain patterns.

In general, film grain becomes noticeable only when the animation of the individual grains attracts your eye, and even then film grain can be a desirable look. Although the grains within each frame of film change, consider that each frame's pattern of grains reveals different image detail, and the eye combines the detail from sequentially playing frames into a seemingly higher-resolution image.

How Does Grain Look?

Film grain varies with the stock that was originally exposed, the method of development, and the frame size and video format to which it's eventually transferred. For all of these reasons, film grain is tricky to profile and accurately reproduce.

Film stocks that are designed to be more sensitive to light (*fast* stocks) tend to employ larger individual grains that expose more quickly with less light. The resulting images are grainier than other stocks that require more light to expose (*slow* stocks) but have much finer grain.

When you transfer film footage to a high definition video format, you can see that film grains are not per-pixel, like video noise.

If you zoom into a per-pixel view, each grain is made up of a cluster of pixels that are naturally anti-aliased, providing a smooth transition from one grain to the next.

Individual film stocks exhibit differing grain patterns and sensitivities in each color channel, similar to the varying noise patterns in the red, green, and blue channels of recorded video.

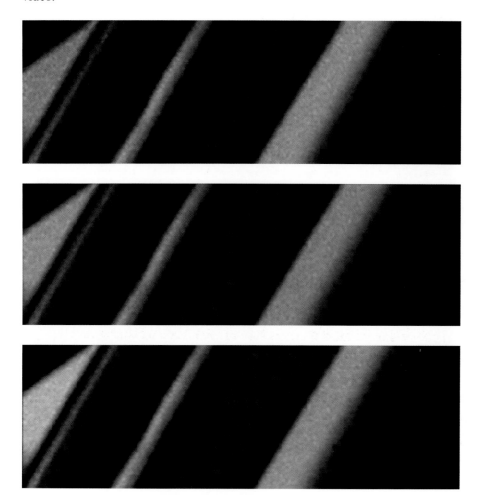

The grain patterns of the red, green, and blue channels of a film image.

Telecine—Combining Film Grain with Video Noise

Because telecine and datacine equipment use video technology to transfer film information to digital formats, it's worth discussing the intersection of film grain and video noise.

The imaging components of modern telecine equipment are made to automatically identify and correct noise and visual artifacts introduced by the telecine itself, so electronic noise is minimized from the start. In most cases, what little noise is introduced should be indistinguishable from the grain of the film being transferred.

Furthermore, many telecines and datacines have additional noise-reduction features that allow the operator to reduce film grain prior to recording to video, if so desired.

Finally, if you're spending the time and money to telecine film to video, you should master to an uncompressed video format with 4:4:4 or 4:2:2 chroma subsampling. This ensures maximum flexibility when making further corrections to your images, and that compression artifacts aren't contributing to the noisiness of the image.

Matching and Subduing Noise and Grain

Now that you've seen how to identify and differentiate noise and grain, see Video Noise (Matching) and Video Noise (Suppressing) for more information on matching, manipulating, or removing video noise.

Video Noise (Matching)

OVERVIEW ▶ Methods for adding video noise to your images for better matching with existing clips.

SEE ALSO ▶ video noise and film grain, video noise (suppressing), vignettes (creating shadows)

Why Would You Add Noise to a Perfectly Nice Image?

Most of the time, you do your best to *avoid* adding video noise to the clips you're correcting, so why a section on deliberately degrading your images?

There are many instances when you need to match a clip that's extremely well-exposed and clean to a noisy scene. This happens all the time with insert shots that were recorded much later than the original scene, or when editors get creative and mix clips from completely different scenes together unexpectedly.

You'll also find many instances of video noise increasing in subsequent angles of coverage as the daylight slipped away from the filmmakers, at which point you'll be forced to add noise to pristine footage shot at 4 pm so that it matches extremely grainy footage shot at 6:30 pm.

In other instances, you may be doing some limited compositing, such as a sky replacement, and the sky footage doesn't have the same noise pattern as the rest of the clip. In all these instances, you can use Final Cut Pro's built-in tools to apply noise to clips, either individually or in groups, to match the noise of other clips in the sequence.

It's important to know that noise isn't all bad. A limited amount of video noise also has some unexpected benefits:

▶   Noise reduces the visibility of banding artifacts in 8-bit video formats, since you're essentially dithering the entire image.

▶   Noise can also give still images that you're using as insert shots some life, so they look more like actual video footage.

▶   Adding a bit of noise to title text and other illustration-style graphics can take the edge off and further integrate the graphics with the background image.

Matching Video Noise in Another Clip

The following example guides you through the process of analyzing the video noise in one clip and attempting to match it as closely as possible in another. In this hypothetical situation, the first in a two-shot sequence has visible and unavoidable noise stemming from a contrast adjustment that lightens the image.

The second clip has been adjusted to match the general contrast and tone of the clip (although clearly it has highlights that the other clip lacks), but because it started out with better overall exposure, it lacks the grain of the first clip. When both are played together, the difference is subtle, but it stands in the way of a complete match.

If you've determined that removing the grain from the first clip would sacrifice too much detail (let's assume you have), your best option is to add grain to the second clip.

1   Open the *Adding Noise* sequence, located in the Video Noise, Matching bin of the **Color Correction Exercises** project.

Each of the first two clips in the Timeline have already been color corrected. If you play the clips together, you should notice the difference between the noise patterns of the two clips.

2   In the Viewer, choose the Render > Noise generator from the Video tab. Use the second one in the list; the first one is an FXPlug noise generator with fewer controls. (If you don't have a Video tab in the Viewer, open a clip with a video track into the viewer to force it to appear.)

By default, the Noise generator creates fairly harsh, grayscale, animated noise that's identical to static, although probably a bit sharper than you're used to seeing on television.

3   Superimpose the Noise generator over the second clip in the sequence.

If you take a close look at the light and dark areas of the first clip, you should notice that video noise is almost always stronger in the shadows than in the highlights. You need to composite the noise generator with the underlying clip to replicate this phenomenon, and the Screen composite mode simulates this well.

4 Control-click the Noise generator you edited into track V2, and choose Composite Mode > Screen.

The Screen composite mode essentially preserves the brightest portions of the super-imposed layer such that white pixels remain white, but black pixels become transparent, allowing the underlying image to come through. The initial result somewhat resembles a Seurat painting.

5 Lower the Opacity (to around 9) of the Noise generator until the video noise fades away from the brighter portions of the image and remains visible in the shadows and midtones.

This is a good time to zoom into a portion of the image and compare the image you're adjusting to a similar region in the previous clip. A little noise goes a long way.

You should notice that the translucent white noise that you've introduced into your clip has had the additional effect of lightening the shadows a bit. In the original clip (left), the darkest regions of shadow were fairly dense.

With the superimposed clip screened translucently against the image, the shadows have lightened a bit (right). This is actually a benefit, since the darkest shadows in the first clip were a bit washed out, as well. However, this change is a bit much, and the clips don't match as well as they did before.

Image before and after adding artificial video noise. The image is zoomed in to better see this effect.

6   Open the underlying clip in track V1 into the Viewer, and adjust the Blacks slider in the Color Corrector interface to lower the shadows a bit, so that the black level matches that in the previous clip.

There are filters that allow you to follow a similar process (see the upcoming section "Third-Party Options"), but the advantage of adding video noise to your clips with a superimposed generator is that you can cover an entire scene of clips with a single operation. On the other hand, if you only need to adjust one or two targeted clips, a filter could be more efficient.

Other Ways to Create a Closer Match

Grayscale video noise is a quick fix and often does the trick as is. If you have more time to spend on the shot, however, or the effect isn't matching as closely as you'd like, there are other adjustments you can make.

Preserving Noise-Free Highlights

Depending on the intensity of the video noise you're trying to match, it may become necessary for you to add noise to the shadows in one superimposed operation, and then add another layer to preserve the clean highlights in the original image using the same method described in the "Preserving Highlights in Vignettes" section at the end of Vignettes (Creating Shadows). This way, you can put more noise into the shadows and midtones without affecting areas of the picture such as skies.

Try Different Composite Modes

You can also try other composite modes to integrate the video noise into the image in different ways. If you'd like, use the previous exercise to experiment with the effects of the different composite modes on noise, following these guidelines:

▶ Multiply and Darken both emphasize noise in the highlights, instead of the shadows.

▶ Screen and Lighten emphasize noise in the midtones and shadows.

▶ Subtract applies a uniform layer of noise over the entire image, intensifying the midtones and blacks in the process.

▶ Overlay and Hard Light both apply a more uniform layer of noise over the entire image, but without intensifying the midtones and blacks as much.

▶ Soft Light emphasizes noise in the darkest shadows.

Add Color Noise

Sometimes the default black and white noise (on the left in the upcoming shots) works well, but sometimes adding color to the noise creates a better match (on the right). Different video cameras and film stocks can have different levels of noise on each color channel. You can attempt to match the resulting noise "color cast" by adding and adjusting color in the Noise generator.

1   Open the Noise generator into the Viewer. Click the Controls tab, and turn on the Color checkbox to create a random scattering of colored noise.

2   Zoom in on the clip you're trying to match, and use the View > Channels > Red, Green, and Blue viewing commands to determine if any one channel is noisier than the others.

    Blue channels of videocameras are often noisiest, so this is always a good channel to check.

NOTE ▶ By default, the View Red, Green, and Blue commands don't have keyboard shortcuts, but an easy way to use these commands is to assign custom buttons in the Canvas button bar. That way, you can simply click on the color channel you want to examine. Just be sure to also place the RGB button, so you can go back to the full image.

If you've determined that the noise from the preceding clip has a particular color emphasis, you could try adjusting the Red Tolerance, Green Tolerance, and Blue Tolerance sliders in the Control tab of the Noise Generator to match it, but it's faster and more intuitive to just add a Color Corrector filter with which you can adjust the color balance and saturation of the noise.

An image with superimposed monochrome noise (left) and the same image with colored noise (right).

Simulating Film Grain

If you're working with telecined film clips, and you're faced with having to match the grain in one clip to that found in another, you should be aware up front that this is not going to be a trivial operation, especially if you're working in standard definition. Video noise is very different from film grain. See Video Noise and Film Grain.

You can try to create a quick fix using the methods described in the preceding sections (if you're working at one of the 1080 HD resolutions, this may work better than if you're working in SD), but if the results are unsatisfactory, you may have a bit more work on your hands. Film grain is highly specific, but most often the grain pattern is smaller and tighter (on the right in the upcoming shots) than that of video noise (on the left in the upcoming shots). This difference makes sense, since film's native resolution is far, far higher.

Furthermore, the individual grains are softer, and their interactions with the image are much more specific.

Outside of third-party filters, one thing you can try is to create a custom film grain simulation clip of your own.

1   In Final Cut Pro or another compositing application, create a high-resolution clip of noise. (1920 x 1080, the high definition frame, is a good size.)

2   Blur the noise slightly to approximate film grain's smoother pattern, and then render the clip as a self-contained, uncompressed QuickTime file.

3   Import the grain clip into your project, superimpose it over the clip you're manipulating, and then shrink the grain layer to fit the frame size of your sequence.

4   Composite the superimposed grain layer by using the Subtract composite mode.

   With Subtract composite mode, the simulated grain darkens the image, rather than lightening it, in an effort to simulate film grain's relationship to image density.

5   If necessary, adjust the color and saturation of the grain clip.

Pay very close attention to the specific grain pattern you're trying to match, because film stocks vary widely. An example of this technique appears applied to the last clip at the end of the *Adding Noise* sequence; you can use it for experimentation.

Grain Matching in Shake

If you have a copy of Shake available, you can use its FilmGrain image processing node to analyze and reproduce grain patterns in other clips, or you can use one of its preset grain patterns available from the FilmStock pop-up menu. See the Shake documentation for more information on the FilmGrain node's use.

This is a good option if you have a handful of clips that have been difficult to match, and you want to create as precise a match as possible.

Adding Noise as Part of a "Film Look"

At the risk of editorializing, adding noise to your overall sequence as part of a film look often does more harm than good. Of course, this is entirely dependent on your creative goals, and if you're going for the degraded look of well-used 16mm educational films, then knock yourself out.

On the other hand, if you're trying to make your independent feature that was shot on video look more like film, you can try many other things to give your project a unique look that doesn't involve deliberately disfiguring your image, and chances are your video may have enough noise as it is. Deinterlacing, selective saturation adjustments, and specific contrast manipulations go a lot farther to create compelling imagery and preserve detail that will project extremely well.

Besides, if you're lucky enough to do a film print of your video masterpiece, you'll get all the grain you need then.

Third-Party Options

Several third-party filters allow you to add noise and simulated grain to your images in a single operation, which can be more convenient than the methods outlined previously.

Graeme Nattress

G FBM Noise—Nattress Set 2

www.nattress.com

This is a filter that uses a different sort of algorithm to create noise (see the docs for an explanation). Other features are a mode pop-up allowing you to select a composite mode for blending the noise with the original image.

Joe's Filters

Joe's Color Noise

Joe's Levels Noise

Joe's Saturation Noise

www.joesfilters.com

Three kinds of noise. The three filters offered provide a veritable smorgasbord of buzzing pixels, with a multitude of built-in options for pixel size, blur, color mixing parameters, contrast adjustments, and targeted saturation control.

CGM

Clone Grain—CGM Volume 3

www.cgm-online.com/eiperle/cgm_e.html

This filter lets you add noise to a specific portion of the image.

Video Noise (Suppressing)

OVERVIEW ► Techniques for minimizing video noise artifacts.

SEE ALSO ► video noise (matching)

Noise-Reduction Tradeoffs

When confronted with excessive video noise—say, from expanding the contrast of an underexposed clip—you naturally want to get rid of it. Unfortunately, Final Cut Pro (version 5.1.2 and earlier) doesn't come with any particularly good tools for doing so, but a couple of rudimentary techniques will help you minimize noise. Because noise is such a common problem, especially with projects shot with highly compressed video formats in available light conditions (imagine your favorite reality TV show), many third-party tools are available, which tackle the problem in a variety of ways.

Unfortunately, you don't get something for nothing. Eliminating noise from a region of your picture invariably softens detail in that same region. The techniques presented using Final Cut Pro's built-in filters are especially clumsy and should be considered tools of last resort. Even the more sophisticated third-party solutions (each of which poses different image-quality tradeoffs) will have an effect on the detail of your image.

Before you start applying noise-reduction techniques, make sure that the noise and grain in your images can't be minimized by simply easing off of whatever color correction you're making. Sometimes splitting the difference in your correction will be a better compromise than the detail you'll lose by attempting noise reduction.

Using a Fractional Gaussian Blur

If you're confronted with abominable noise, and you don't have any other options, you can always apply the Gaussian Blur filter and set the Radius to a small fractional value, from 0.2 to 0.8 for standard-definition clips (larger frame sizes can take more blurring).

For the following example, an extremely underexposed clip was corrected to bring out the midtones, add some color to the image, and generally brighten up the actors. The result is severe noise, which you need to reduce.

1   Open the *01 Blurring Noise* sequence, located in the Video Noise, Suppressing bin of the **Color Correction Exercises** project.

The first clip has already been color corrected. Playing it reveals significant noise that results from stretching the contrast.

2   Apply a Gaussian Blur filter to the clip, and type *0.2* into the Radius field to the right of the slider, and press Return.

The slider itself is only capable of selecting whole numbers.

Experiment with different values from 0.1 to 0.9 to see the results with values just below and above the recommended scale. In general, images with better-defined edge detail will hold up with higher fractional values, and images with less edge detail will require lower values for an acceptable result. The goal is to minimize the noise while keeping the overall image as sharp as possible.

The result is a slight softening of the image overall but an even more significant reduction in noise detail, which in many instances is an acceptable tradeoff.

One of the advantages of the Gaussian Blur filter is that on fast computers, these fractional value blurs are real-time operations.

Selectively Blurring Individual Color Channels

Another tactic you can try, although it's not often that much more successful, is to use the Channel Blur (found in the Channel bin of the filters in the Effects tab) instead of the Gaussian Blur. The Channel Blur has four sliders that let you simultaneously blur the Alpha, Red, Green, and Blue by different amounts.

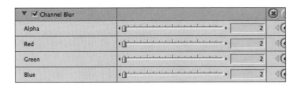

If you have a particular image with one or two color channels that are noisier than the others, you can try selectively blurring just the problem channels.

When you blur one channel only, you'll find that you may be able to use higher values (generally from 1 to 9, depending on the frame size of the image). If you overdo it, you'll notice a faint haloing around the edges of your subjects as the color channels start to soften and the boundaries enlarge.

NOTE ▶ This filter can be slow to process.

Blurring Shadow Areas

A slightly more targeted approach is to isolate the noisiest parts of your picture, typically the midtones and lighter shadows, and isolate those areas with a keying operation in a superimposed duplicate. Then, you can blur only the areas with the worst grain, leaving the details in your highlights and black details alone.

1   Open the *02 Keying Noise* sequence, located in the Video Noise, Suppressing bin of the **Color Correction Exercises** project.

The first clip has already been color corrected. Playing it reveals video noise and film grain in the shadows of the image, visible in the woman's hair and the legs of the man's trousers.

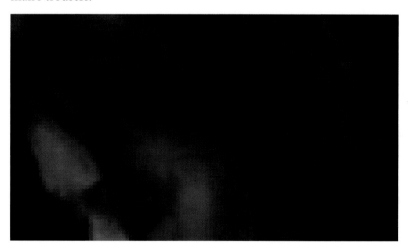

2   Superimpose a copy of the clip above itself in track V2 using one of these quick methods:

▶   In the Timeline, Option-drag the clip to track V2, holding down the Shift key to keep it locked to the same position on the Timeline.

▶   Drag the clip from the Timeline directly to the Superimpose target of the Canvas.

Keep in mind that this duplicate also has the same Color Correction filter. This is important, as it needs to match the clip below.

3   Open the superimposed clip in track V2 into the Viewer. Apply a Chroma Key filter (in the Video Filters > Key bin of the Effects tab) to it as the first video filter in the filter tab (before the Color Correction filter), and click the Chroma Keyer tab to expose its controls.

4   In the Chroma Keyer tab, turn off the Hue and Sat controls, and turn on the Luma controls. You're going to use the Chroma Keyer to perform a luma key, using the graphical controls this filter provides. Then, set the View Final/Matte/Source control to Matte to view the key while you work (a black key on a white background).

Viewing the key itself makes it easier to see which parts of the picture are being preserved and which parts are rendered transparent. In other words, the white areas show you the parts of the picture you'll be blurring, and the transparent areas (the unaltered parts of the image) are what's being held out.

5   Adjust the handles of the Luma control to isolate the darkest regions of the picture, including the man's suit and the woman's hair. Use the Softening slider to feather the edge of the selection, but only a small amount, to reduce any noise in the matte.

As you work, you'll see an exaggerated white area in the Canvas that covers the dark midtones and shadows. This is the matte that's showing the isolated area. The rest of the picture you see is the background image in track V1 showing through. When you apply the Gaussian Blur filter, it will affect only the areas currently showing as white.

6   Set the View Final/Matte/Source button to Final, then click the Filters tab, and apply a Gaussian Blur filter at the bottom of the filter stack. Make sure you set the Channel

pop-up menu to RGB (instead of the default, RGB+Alpha) so that you don't affect the matte being created by the Chroma Keyer filter.

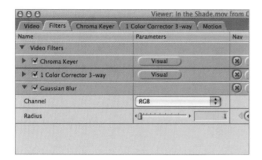

7 Increase the Radius until you've softened the noise, but not so much so there's a perceptible blurry halo (although that is a neat effect).

The finished example uses a Radius value of 1.

If you examine the darker details, you'll notice a softening of the noise and grain, while the details in the lighter areas remain sharp.

NOTE ▶ Because this combination of effects appears at preview resolution on slower machines, the color of the clip will be off until you render it.

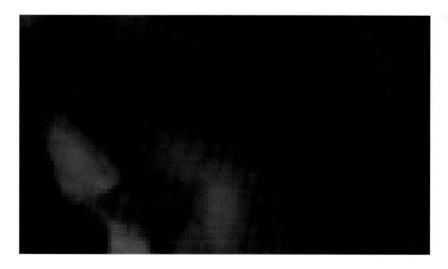

As you can see, this last technique is a little more targeted, but still fairly rough and time-consuming to set up.

Third-Party Filters

If your shot needs more help than you can give it with Final Cut Pro's built-in tools, consider one, or more, of the many third-party noise-reduction filters available for the program. Each has different advantages for specific situations, so the best strategy is to get your hands on a couple of them at least. Here is a cross-section of your options, arranged by developer.

Too Much Too Soon (TMTS)

Smart Noise Reduction

Noise Reduction

www.mattias.nu/plugins

Mattias Sandström is an exceedingly nice fellow who has created an extremely useful set of filters. Best of all, they're free! However, getting something for nothing isn't nearly as satisfying as the warm moral glow you'll get from making a donation via his Web site.

Smart Noise Reduction reduces noise by averaging adjacent frames together when there's no motion. Noise Reduction works by averaging pixels in areas where there's no detail.

Graeme Nattress

G Noise Reduction Chroma – Nattress Set 1

G Noise Reduction Spatial – Nattress Set 1

G Noise Reduction Temporal – Nattress Set 1

www.nattress.com

Graeme Nattress has three noise-reduction filters available. The Spatial reduction plug-in averages values within the frame, with options to reduce the noise of the luma and chroma components of the image by different amounts. The Temporal reduction filter is an adaptive approach that averages adjacent frames over time, with additional controls to preserve detail in areas where there is motion. The Chroma reduction plug-in is designed to improve images recorded with noisy chroma.

CGM

Noise Killer - CGM DVE Volume 3

www.cgm-online.com/eiperle/cgm_e.html

A plug-in that works to preserve edge detail while averaging noise.

CHV-Electronics

Noise Reduction – The Repair Collection

www.chv-plugins.com/collrepair.php

An adaptive noise-reduction filter with the virtue of simplicity: It has only four controls. Part of CHV's excellent Repair Collection, which includes tools for dirt removal, dropout elimination, and dead pixel replacement.

Joe's Filters

Joe's Noise Reducer

www.joesfilters.com

Combines edge masking with a median filter to smooth video noise in a more elegant way than using a garden-variety blur.

Algolith

http://shop.algolith.com

These aren't Final Cut Pro filters, but Algolith develops top-notch noise- and grain-reduction filters for Shake and After Effects. If you have noise problems that are too severe for any of the other filters to address, you may want to try processing the clips at fault in Shake or After Effects with Algolith's filters to see if you can get better results.

Video Scopes

OVERVIEW ▶ Technical explanation of the quality, performance, and options of Final Cut Pro's Vectorscope, Histogram, Waveform Monitor, and RGB Parade scope.

SEE ALSO ▶ broadcast legality

Examining the Video Scopes

Final Cut Pro's Video Scopes tab (located within the Tool Bench window) is your primary tool for analyzing the luma, chroma, saturation, color balance, and contrast of images in your program.

Prior to 5.1.2, the video scopes sampled only 16 lines of video, evenly distributed between the action safe areas of the picture. This was a decent approximation for purposes of general scene-to-scene comparisons, and the fact that the Histogram displayed a more accurate luma analysis throughout the image meant that you had a view into all the superwhite values that might have been in the picture.

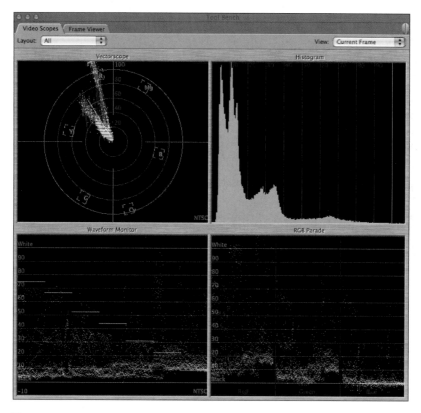

Video scope graphs displayed in Final Cut Pro versions 5.1 and earlier.

Starting with Final Cut Pro 5.1.2, the video scopes are capable of sampling every single line of video in your clips, and the resulting graphs look quite different.

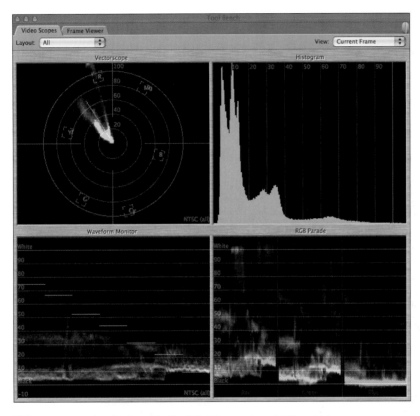

Video scope graphs displayed in Final Cut Pro versions 5.1.2 and later.

Furthermore, those of you who are accustomed to the old scopes may notice that the new ones display more of a grayscale image. The new ones present more information, because brighter pixels on the graph represent multiple overlapping pixels in the image that are at the same level of brightness. The fainter a pixel is in a video scope's graph, the fewer image pixels correspond to that particular value.

This feature can be somewhat problematic, because graph values corresponding to extremely small features, regardless of overall brightness, can be difficult to see. In the following example, the image to the left shows the Waveform Monitor's graph as you'll typically see it.

To the right, the contrast of the image has been pegged to show every single pixel of the graph within the image:

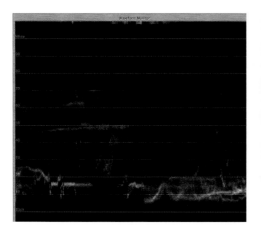 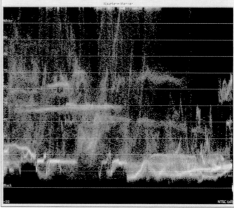

The Waveform Monitor graph as displayed by the Video Scopes tab on your monitor (left); a screen capture of the same Waveform Monitor graph that's been brightened in Photoshop to reveal detail in the graph that may be difficult to see (right).

The moral to the story? Make sure your monitor isn't too dark, otherwise you may not be able to spot valuable image data, even though it's there.

Differences Between Software and Hardware Scopes

The peaks and valleys of the graphs displayed in Final Cut Pro's software scopes should correspond to those displayed by a calibrated composite WFM (hardware Waveform Monitor) set to its LUM or LPASS mode (using a low-pass filter to display only the Luma component). If the Saturation option is turned on, this should be the equivalent of a composite WFM monitor in FLAT mode (displaying the luminance and saturation of chrominance together). If you look closely, however, you'll probably still notice a difference in appearance between the two.

CRT-based hardware scopes use an electron beam that sweeps over the phosphorescent coating on the screen from one point of data to the next as it draws an analysis of each sequential line of video in the image, creating the overall graph. The resulting series of overlapping *traces* serve to "connect the dots" and produce the graph that's characteristic of CRT video scopes.

Final Cut Pro's software scopes, on the other hand, don't need to draw a trace from point to point, instead drawing a more direct plot of all the values in the image. This plot resembles more a series of individual points than overlapping lines. (One exception is the Vectorscope, which simulates the traces of hardware scopes in order to render a more useful image.) As a result, individual points of data in Final Cut Pro's Waveform Monitor won't look exactly the same as the peaks on a hardware WFM scope. This doesn't mean that Final Cut Pro isn't displaying all of the information, it's just that the display is a little bit different.

> **NOTE** ▶ Some of the newer digital scopes from such companies as Videotek and Tektronix also have hybrid displays that try to integrate both types of graphs: plot and vector.

What Are Those Blacker-Than-Black Points?

Within the abundance of information that the video scopes in All Pixels mode provides, you may notice some things that aren't visible in older versions of the video scopes. One of the more unusual bits is the occasional appearance of pixels below 0 percent black.

The 0 percent baseline that Final Cut Pro calls black actually corresponds to the numeric value of 16 (in 8-bit video encoding) that's specified by the ITU-R BT. 601 and 709 encoding standards for standard and high definition video. The values of 1 to 15 correspond to the −300 to 0 mV range used for the sync portion of analog video signals, although digital video signals don't actually encode sync as part of the video.

However, that "superblack" portion of the signal is still there as a bunch of empty bits, even though it's not accessible to you (remember that all blacks adjustments you make are crushed at 0 percent). Videocameras generate noise, some more, some less, and depending on the make and model of camera, some cameras do record occasional noise in the 1 to 15 digit range, which appear within Final Cut Pro's video scopes as excursions below 0 percent black. It's always been there, you just haven't been able to see it until now.

To see if your camera generates noise in the superblack range, pop the lens cap onto your videocamera, and record a minute of black. Capture the result into Final Cut Pro, and take a look at the resulting waveform. This example of noisy black (enhanced to exaggerate every pixel of the waveform graph) was captured with the lens cap on a Sony HDR-HC1 camcorder.

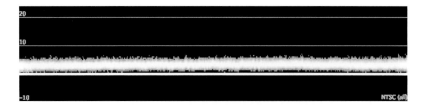

Notice two things in the example. First, absolute black isn't actually recorded by the camera at 0 percent. It's centered at about 3 percent, so it's actually lifted by default, which is good, because you'll notice secondly that there's about 3 percent excursion above and below the average center point of black. That's 6 percent worth of noise. By lifting the black point a bit, none of this noise is finding its way into the superblack region of the signal, which was probably by design. With other cameras, this might not be the case.

The point is not to pick on any one camera (the one used for this test is actually quite nice), because this is the case with lots of cameras, which is yet another good reason to make time for a color correction pass.

Superblack noise isn't going to cause any huge problems, and besides, the process of color correcting and rendering your clips usually results in those spurious pixels getting clamped to 0 percent prior to output.

Video Scope Analysis and Real-Time Playback

Beginning with Final Cut Pro 5.1.2, you can manually choose how much detail is shown in the video scopes from a group of options in the RT pop-up in the Timeline:

▶ All Pixels analyzes every pixel of every line in the video image.

▶ All Except Top & Bottom excludes the top and bottom nine lines of video, which typically contain other signal information, including closed captioning, eliminating unnecessary distractions from your analysis. This setting corresponds to the Clean Aperture setting of some hardware scopes.

▶ Select Pixels (fastest) provides a lower-resolution analysis of the image. As indicated by the red dashed lines (see the following figure), the video scopes analyze every other pixel of 32 lines evenly distributed between the upper and lower title safe area (as opposed to every pixel of 16 lines in Final Cut Pro 3 through 5.1.1).

As you can see in the following figure (on the right), Select Pixels (fastest) displays bolder and, in many cases, brighter representations of the video scope graphs than All Pixels mode (on the left). When you play through your sequence with the Video Scopes tab visible in Final Cut Pro 5.1.2 or later, the video scopes play along at this lower-resolution mode.

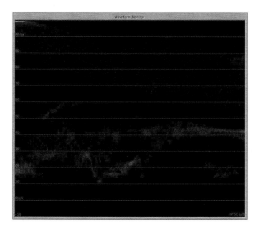 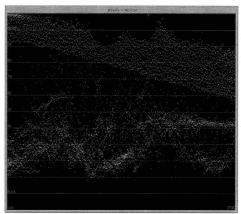

Just how real time the video scope's playback is depends on the processor power of your computer, on the real-time demands being made by your edited sequence, and on the performance of your computer's video card.

Also, when there's limited processor power available, video scope playback drops frames in favor of regular video playback, so you may notice that the scopes are slower to update. Real-time playback in the Canvas always takes priority.

Video scopes can play in real time only if the currently viewed sequence uses a supported real-time video format. Finally, the View pop-up menu in the Video Scopes tab must be set to Current Frame for real-time playback.

High-Quality Non-Real-Time Video Scope Playback

For a high-quality motion analysis of the video scope graphs, you can always use the Mark > Play > Every Frame menu command (Option-\ or Option-P). This option forces Final Cut Pro to step through each and every frame of video at high quality, similar to a continuous scrub, updating the Canvas, video scopes, and video output at high quality, as close to real time as possible. Most of the time, this should be more than sufficient for you to get a good look at how the video scope graphs are shaping up.

Video Scope Performance

Video Scope performance is also partially dependent on which video scopes are open, and on how many Tool Bench windows you have open displaying additional scopes simultaneously. Displaying multiple Video Scope tabs can be one way of showing multiple video scopes at larger sizes than the All option of the Layout pop-up allows. It's also the only way that you can have two versions of the Waveform Monitor open—one set to display Luma only, the other set to display Saturation (see **Broadcast Legality**).

In general, Final Cut Pro does one analysis of the video signal, and then processes the data for each type of video scope that's currently displayed. If you have two Tool Bench windows open with video scopes at the same time, the additional processor demands, although definitely increased, are not doubled. This means it doesn't hurt to have a couple of video scopes open at the same time. It also means that setting up an insanely detailed custom layout with six separate video scopes is probably not the best use of your computer's resources.

To optimize video scope performance, you can choose to restrict yourself to a single Tool Bench window, and even to a single video scope using the Layout pop-up menu. In most cases, the benefits should be negligible, unless you're on a system where every bit of additional performance helps. The following list presents the video scopes according to their processor demands:

▶   The Histogram is the fastest video scope.

▶   The Waveform Monitor showing luma only is the second fastest.

▶   The Vectorscope, Parade scope, and Waveform Monitor showing saturation are the most processor-intensive by comparison.

Differences Between Y'CbCr and RGB Sources

The scales displayed by the Waveform, Parade scope, and Histogram differ in two specific situations:

▶ A sequence is set to Always Render in RGB.

▶ You open a clip from the Browser into the Viewer and set the View pop-up menu of the video scopes to Viewer.

In both situations, there is no superwhite or blacker-than-black luma or chroma data in RGB encoding, so the areas of the displayed graticule (the scales that display different measurements) above 100 and below 0 are grayed out.

If you're editing Y'CbCr-encoded video into an RGB-rendering sequence, then waveforms corresponding to those clips extending into the superwhite are superimposed over the grayed-out area, letting you see which parts of the clip will be clamped when that clip is rendered (for example, if you applied a filter to it).

The Viewer's behavior bears a more detailed explanation. The Viewer displays clips opened from the Browser in RGB space even if the source media is Y'CbCr-encoded, so setting the Video Scopes View pop-up menu to Viewer results in an RGB analysis of the displayed clip.

On the other hand, if a clip is opened from the Timeline into the Viewer, the Viewer correctly displays the clip in Y'CbCr space, and you get a full Y'CbCr analysis in the video scopes.

Individual Scopes and Options

You can use the Layout pop-up menu to select which scope or combination of scopes is displayed in the Video Scopes tab of the Tool Bench.

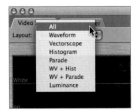

The video scopes have other options available from the shortcut menu that appears when you Control-click within any of the video scopes. Three options affect all of the video scopes at once:

▶   Targets—Use this option to toggle the targets corresponding to the 75% color bars in the Vectorscope and Waveform monitor. These are useful for making adjustments to video clips with color bars at the head or for identifying which hues correspond to which angles in the Vectorscope.

▶   High/Medium/Low/Off—With these options, you can change the intensity of the scope graticules.

▶   Green/White or Bright/Pale—These options both affect all scopes at once, toggling the Vectorscope, Histogram, and Waveform Monitor between green and white (white tends to be a little easier on the eyes), and toggling the intensity of the Parade scope between bright and pale (pale is similarly easier on the eyes).

Additionally, the Waveform Monitor, Vectorscope, and Histogram have individual options.

Waveform Monitor

The Waveform Monitor displays a left-to-right analysis of the luma levels in each line of video. Brighter pixels of video appear higher in the graph, where the vertical scale measures luma digitally from 0 (at the bottom) to 100 percent (at the top). The more pixels with identical luma values there are at a particular part of the graph, the brighter that portion of the graph appears; dimmer portions of the graph indicate fewer pixels in the image.

The default Luma-Only display of the Waveform Monitor is similar to that of a hardware WFM set to its LUM or LPASS mode (using a low-pass filter to display only the luma component). This mode is most useful for evaluating the overall contrast of the image, because you can clearly see the top and bottom of the luma portion of the waveform.

As you can see in the following figure, the top portion of the graticule (from White to the very top edge of the scope) indicates the superwhite portion of the image, corresponding to 101 to 110 percent luma and chroma (if Saturation is enabled). The bottom portion, from Black to −10 percent, indicates the blacker-than-black area. Although there aren't typically luma excursions at this low range, there may be illegally oversaturated values in the shadows that will extend below 0 percent.

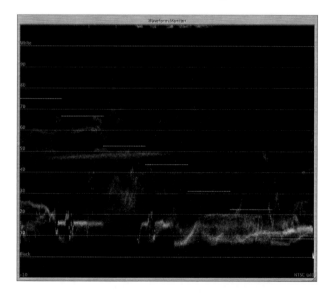

Control-clicking the Waveform Monitor and choosing Saturation from the shortcut menu is the equivalent of a composite WFM monitor in FLAT mode (displaying the luminance and saturation of chrominance together).

In this mode (see the following figure), each pixel in the graph has a vertical band super-imposed over it of which the height indicates how saturated that pixel is (taller portions of the graph are more saturated). This mode is most useful for evaluating saturation in the highlights and shadows of an image, where overly hot saturation values are most likely to cause video legal errors.

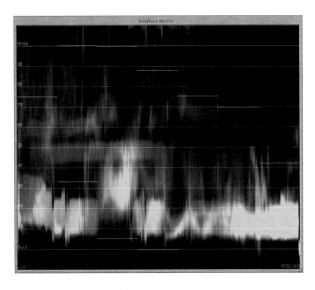

Histogram

The Histogram displays an analysis of an image's contrast. All the pixels corresponding to each percentage of luma are stacked up at that value on the scale. The height of the graph at any given percentage shows how much of the image falls into that percentage of luma. The red portion of the graph above the 100 percent line indicates the superwhite range.

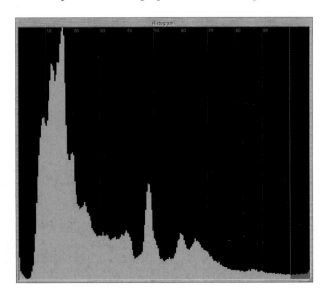

The graph's height is scaled relative to its tallest peak. If you're viewing an image with a lot of 0 percent black (such as graphics, video with letterboxing or pillarboxing, or video with extremely crushed blacks), the resulting spike in the graph at 0 percent may make seeing the rest of the Histogram more difficult because it's being shortened too much. Control-clicking the Histogram and deselecting Include Black prevents the graph from being scaled relative to 0 percent values.

Vectorscope

The Vectorscope shows the Hue and Saturation of values within the image. Hue is indicated by a portion of the graph's angle around the center, and saturation is indicated by a trace's distance from the center. The graticule is a series of concentric circles expanding outward, each of which represents another 20 percent of saturation.

The very center of this graph represents all desaturated, neutral values, from white to gray to black. If the graph is uncentered, and the image has neutral tones in it, a color cast may be present.

The targets (superimposed in magenta) include the color targets for the color bars test pattern (the outline of these patterns indicates the conservative broadcast legal limits for saturation), as well as the Flesh Tone line (corresponding to the I-bar on hardware scopes) that indicates the approximate ideal hue of skin tones (within 20 percent or so).

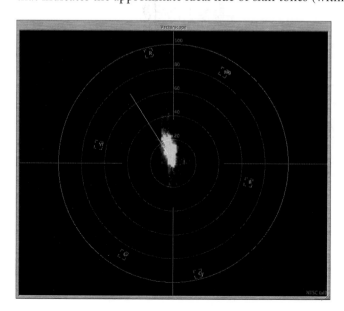

Control-clicking the Vectorscope lets you turn on the Magnify option, which magnifies the center portion of the scope (the zoomed portion can't be moved) to make it easier to see graphs from less-saturated images (a better description might be graphs of average saturation).

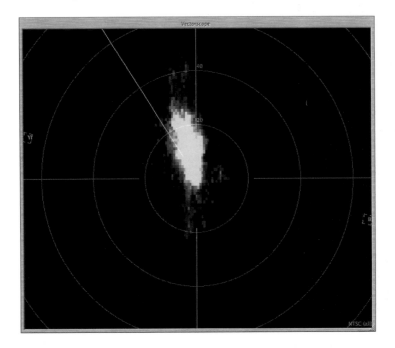

Parade Scope

The Parade scope shows separate waveforms analyzing the strength of the R, G, and B components of the video signal. This is a composite representation, even if the original video is Y'CbCr-encoded. By showing a comparison of the intensity of the red, green, and blue components of the image, you can detect and compare imbalances in the highlights (the top of the graph), shadows (the bottom of the graph) and midtones for purposes of idendifying color casts and performing scene-by-scene correction.

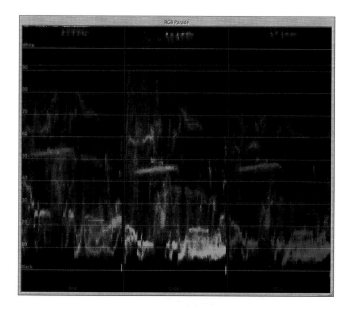

Learn Your Scopes

Mastery of the video scopes is extremely helpful to becoming an effective colorist. If you'd like more information and detailed tutorials for understanding the scopes, you can reference these other books:

▶ *Advanced Color Correction and Effects in Final Cut Pro*, by Alexis Van Hurkman with DigitalFilm Tree (Peachpit Press), provides additional tutorials and explanations for the beginner that are specific to Final Cut Pro.

▶ *Color Correction for Digital Video*, by Steve Hullfish and Jaime Fowler (CMP Books), gives a more general overview of how to understand video scopes across several platforms. This is a great book packed with tips and information about the color correction process.

▶ *An Introduction to Video Measurement*, by Peter Hodges (Focal Press), is a useful introduction to the use of hardware scopes.

You can also visit the Tektronix Web site (www.tek.com), where they provide many application notes, technical documents, and training PDFs that will help you to understand the arcane world of video measurement.

Vignettes (Adding Color)

OVERVIEW ▶ The process of using vignetting techniques to add color to features of a clip.

SEE ALSO ▶ color control, masked corrections, vignettes (creating shadows)

Adding a Splash of Color to a Shot

Sometimes you have a clip in which you'd like to enrich the color in a specific portion of the background, but the features you want to correct are too difficult to successfully isolate with a secondary key.

In the following shot, the client wants to intensify the green in the leaves, specifically those in the foreground to the right. Unfortunately, the media is highly compressed, and there's so much noise and detail in the greenery that any secondary key you try to create will buzz and chatter, exposing the effect.

In cases like this, you can try using a vignette to simply superimpose more color over the necessary region. This technique can be a great time-saver, *if* it looks convincing. The disadvantage is that you'll be adding a wash of color over every detail in that portion of the image, tinting other features that shouldn't necessarily possess that color.

Practice Superimposing Color

In the following exercise, you'll use a custom gradient generator to add a richer green to the branches to the right of the woman:

1   Open the *Coloring the Tree* sequence, located in the Vignettes, Adding Color bin of the **Color Correction Exercises** project.

The first clip in the Timeline has a color correction already applied to it, which is enhancing the contrast and muting the overall color saturation. (The second clip in the Timeline shows the completed effect, which you can refer to as you work.)

Unfortunately, this correction mutes the color in the trees along with everything else, but they're too difficult to exclude from the correction with a secondary key.

2   Choose Render > Custom Gradient from the Generators pop-up in the Video tab of the Viewer. Superimpose it in track V2 over the Hiking MS clip. Open it in the Viewer from the sequence, and click the Controls tab in order to customize its parameters.

3   To turn the custom gradient generator into a vignette, Control-click the Custom Gradient clip in the Timeline and choose Composite Mode > Multiply to composite the two layers together. Make sure that the playhead is over both clips so you can see the results of your adjustments as you work.

Before making any further adjustments, you need to change the black gradient to a shade of green that is compatible with the foliage you're trying to enhance.

4   Disable track V2 by clicking its Track Visibility control. Click the eyedropper button for the End parameter in the Controls tab of the Viewer, and click a well-saturated shade of green in the foliage showing in the Canvas.

Starting with a color that's already present in the image makes it much easier to make an enhancement that's compatible with the existing tones in the image. See **Sky Corrections and Enhancements.**

Next, it's time to put the color exactly where you want it.

5   Turn track V2 back on, and drag the rotation control in the Gradient Direction parameter so that the darkest part of the gradient originates from the upper-right corner and gently slopes to the right, covering the tree branches there. Then, click the Start parameter's crosshairs control, and drag the crosshairs in the Canvas to the right so that the green gradient is wide enough to cover the tree branches, but not too wide so that it covers inappropriate parts of the image (like the rocks).

Although these adjustments are best made while the gradient is superimposed over your image, the following screenshot shows the uncomposited gradient generator so that you can see the angle and width used in the final example.

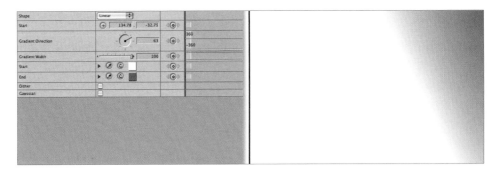

Bear in mind that this method is bound to put a bit of the vignette color in places it shouldn't necessarily be, but hopefully you'll be able to shape and position the vignette in such a was as to minimize this. What color does spill into other areas should look like moss, or more greenery.

Lastly, you may want to adjust the vignette color to further intensify or reduce the enhancement.

6   Click the disclosure triangle next to the color controls of the End parameter to reveal the HSB sliders, and adjust the S (saturation) and B (brightness) sliders until you're satisfied with the effect.

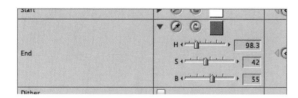

Because you chose the initial hue from the colors already within the picture, you should be able to raise or lower the saturation and brightness of the color within a limited range while maintaining the look of the shot. Compare the before (left) and after (right) versions.

NOTE ▶ There is a big difference between how this example looks on your computer monitor and how it looks on a broadcast display showing your video output. This example is designed to display well on a broadcast display, and it may look exaggerated on your computer's monitor.

If you scrub through the clip, you'll notice that the camera pans a bit. As with the other vignetting methods covered in this book, a bit of camera movement won't necessarily give away the vignette's position, but if the movement was more pronounced, you might need to animate the position of the superimposed generator clip to match the movement of the scene.

Further Considerations

Vignetting is a good technique to use to quickly put richer tones of color exactly where you want them. However, the indiscriminate way in which color is added means it won't always work. Another way of achieving a similar effect would be to use a masked correction, using the Hue control of the Limit Effects only in order to boost all of the greens in the image at once. See Saturated Looks.

As always, be careful about adding colors that are too saturated or bright, and always make your adjustments relative to Final Cut Pro's video output on a broadcast monitor in order to make sure the color is blending appropriately with the other colors in the image.

Vignettes (Creating Shadows)

OVERVIEW ▶ Techniques for selectively darkening outer regions of an image to control the viewer's focus, subdue lighting, or add depth.

SEE ALSO ▶ lens vignetting, sky enhancements, vignettes (adding color)

Vignetting as a Creative Tool

Vignetting is nothing new, and the technique's name actually comes from twin optical and mechanical phenomena that you should avoid while shooting: the appearance of a circular darkened region around the edges of a film or video image.

Once in Final Cut Pro, however, you can put an artificial version of this darkening effect to great creative use. For example:

▶ A shadowy vignette can call attention to a subject or region within a shot.

▶ A vignette can cut down on the ambient light in a shot, salvaging clips that are supposed to take place in the evening or at night but that appear over-lit when viewed in a darkened environment.

▶ The introduction of a shadow region can add dimension to evenly lit images that appear somewhat flat.

▶ Artificial vignettes can deliberately mimic the effect of optical or mechanical lens vignetting, matching effects already present in other shots of a scene or creating an old-fashioned film look.

Using variations on a handful of techniques, you can accomplish all these effects and more.

NOTE ▶ For more information about correcting and matching actual vignettes, see **Lens Vignetting**.

Vignettes to Call Attention to the Subject

Calling attention to a specific portion of the image through artificial vignettes is a technique that's been around since the days of silent film. Originally, filmmakers placed mattes in front of the lens to identify key subjects in longer shots or highlight close-ups of actors, such as in this still from 1925's *The Lost World*, featuring Bessie Love.

This technique is still in use today, although the effect is usually accomplished with more subtlety in post. In the following example, the image to the left has many elements that compete with the man sitting at the desk, such as the computer monitor, which dominates the screen, and the evenly lit wall. Using a simple oval vignette as in the right image, you can subdue the light level of the surrounding environment to emphasize the fully illuminated man at the center. (Note that the effect is somewhat exaggerated here for print.)

Control of the lighting ratio between the subject and the background is best exercised by the Director of Photography during the shoot. Controlling the viewer's attention with lighting is a powerful technique, and the best vignetting is but an imitation of the cinematographer's art. Nonetheless, many projects with limited schedules or budgets benefit greatly from the additional light control this technique affords.

To learn how to use vignetting to best effect, study the actual interplay of light and shadow in differently lit shots. An ideal vignette has the effect of subtly cutting down the ambient light in parts of the frame you want to deemphasize, while hopefully masquerading as shadows that are justified by features in the frame.

Making the subject brighter than its surroundings draws the viewer's attention more readily. If you angle and shape the vignette just right, the effect will have the appearance of deepening the shadows in the picture. The audience should never be able to detect the shape or presence of a vignette, unless it's for deliberate effect.

Vignettes to Create Depth

You can also use vignettes to create the perception of depth in an otherwise flat image. You can see how this works with a simple pair of gradients from black to white that meet at an imaginary horizon. These grayscale ramps alone give the impression of depth, without any other cues in the image.

You can exploit the same phenomenon using a vignette. In the following example, the image to the left is flatly lit, with no clear shadows and large expanses of similar color. As a result, it appears somewhat two-dimensional despite the inherent perspective in the shot. The image to the right has a superimposed gradient that vignettes the bottom of the image, falling off towards the subject of the trees and giving the illusion of depth.

You can add depth to shots of the sky with this same vignetting technique. (See Sky Corrections and Enhancements.)

In the following sections, you'll learn different techniques for creating vignettes to control light and focus in your programs.

Creating Vignettes with Generators

One of the fastest and easiest ways to create vignettes is to combine superimposed generators with gradients of different kinds using composite modes. This method has many advantages:

▶ Near real-time response—If you set Final Cut Pro to Unlimited RT on a fast computer, superimposing generators using the Multiply composite mode is a nearly real-time effect (you may drop a frame or two) at full image quality, which means you can make adjustments quickly, and your client will immediately see the results.

▶ Fast to use—Final Cut Pro's generators are fast to create and easy to customize without having to go to another application, which speeds up your coloring sessions.

▶ Easy to transport—Final Cut Pro's generators stay within the project file. If you move the project file around or give it to the client as one of the deliverables, there's no additional media to lose track of or manage.

▶ Leverages the Timeline—You can use the organization of the Timeline to your advantage. If you place every gradient you're using for vignetting on the same video track, it's easy to toggle them on and off all at once without affecting the other color corrections applied to the video clips in your program.

▶ Quick to identify—Because each vignetted clip has a superimposed gradient, it's easy to see which clips have this effect applied when looking at the Timeline.

The most useful generators for creating gradients include the Shapes generators (Circle, Oval, Rectangle, Square), Custom Gradient, and Highlight generators.

Using the Shapes Generator

In this exercise, you'll use the Oval generator to cut down the light surrounding the person in a scene, in the process drawing him to the viewer's attention. The Oval generator—one of the most flexible generators you can use—creates a classic round vignette.

1   Open the *01 Vignette Using Shape* sequence, located in the Vignettes, Creating Shadows bin of the **Color Correction Exercises** project.

    The first clip in the Timeline has a color correction already applied to it to give an after-hours office look. The second clip in the Timeline shows the completed effect, which you can refer to as you work.

2   In the Video tab of the Viewer, choose Shapes > Oval from the Generators pop-up.

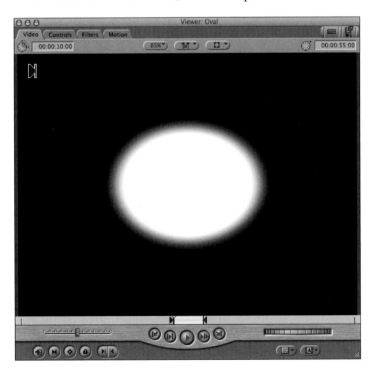

NOTE ▶ If the Video tab is not visible, open a clip with a video track into the Viewer to make it visible.

3   With the playhead over the first Desk MS clip in the Timeline, edit the Oval generator into the Timeline with a Superimpose edit so that it appears in track V2, above the Desk MS clip.

4   Control-click the superimposed generator in the Timeline, and choose Composite Mode > Multiply from the shortcut menu.

All of the generators you'll be using to create vignettes with in this section consist of radial or linear gradients of black to white, which lend themselves to being composited using the Multiply composite mode. Multiplying a generator with the clip underneath results in areas of 100 percent white becoming transparent, increasingly dark gray areas becoming increasingly opaque, and black areas remaining black.

5   Open the Oval generator you just edited into the Timeline back into Viewer, and click the Controls tab to reveal its parameters.

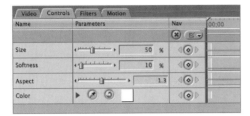

You can now customize this generator to create the desired effect.

6   Adjust the Softness parameter to the maximum value of 100.

You'll find yourself using high softness values for two reasons: you typically don't want viewers to be able to discern the edge of the shape, and you don't usually want to have any solid black in the shape you're using as a vignette.

After you establish the look of the vignette's edge, you're ready to adjust the size to best isolate the necessary parts of the image.

7   Shrink the size of the oval to 46 percent to tighten it up a bit.

8   Adjust the Aspect parameter (short for aspect ratio) to make the oval either taller or wider, depending on your needs. For this example, an Aspect value of 1.55 works best.

Larger values make the oval wider, producing more vignetting on the top and bottom of the image than on the sides. Large Aspect values usually work well with larger shapes.

Smaller values make the oval taller, producing more vignetting on the sides of the image than on the top and bottom. Small Aspect values usually work better with smaller shapes.

At this point, the vignette has the necessary softness and shape: The area immediately surrounding the man is untouched, and the walls, computer, and area behind the desk are darkened. The vignette itself is too dark, though, making for a not-too-subtle effect. You'll fix that in the last step.

9   Click the Toggle Clip Overlays button at the bottom of the viewer, and drag the opacity overlay of the Oval clip down until the tooltip reads 34.

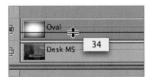

This creates an extremely subtle darkening that is almost imperceptible to the viewer, but that nonetheless draws attention to the brighter center of the image. If, at this point, you're unsure if the effect is really doing any good, toggle the Track Visibility control for track V2 off and on to compare the before (left) and after (right) shot. The results should now leap out at you.

Using the Custom Gradient Generator

If you need a vignette that covers only one side or corner of the image, try the Custom Gradient generator (in the Render submenu). The Custom Gradient generator differs from the Gradient generator in one important respect: You can customize the gradient. Using the Gradient Direction and Gradient Width parameters you can change the angle at which Final Cut Pro draws the gradient and the gradient's width, respectively.

 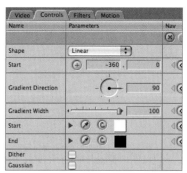

In this exercise, you'll use the Custom Gradient generator to darken a background wall:

1   Open the *02 Vignette Using Custom Gradient* sequence, located in the Vignettes, Creating Shadows bin of the **Color Correction Exercises** project.

The first clip in the Timeline has a color correction already applied to it to give a darkened evening look. (The second clip in the Timeline shows the completed effect, which you can refer to as you work.) The lighting is subdued, and the wall behind the man facing the camera has some shadow definition, but the overall scene still seems a little bright. You'll address this by adding some shadow to the upper-left corner of the frame.

2   Choose Render > Custom Gradient from the Generators pop-up in the Video tab of the Viewer, and superimpose it in track V2 over the Dining Room Over MS clip. Open it in the Viewer from the sequence, and click the Controls tab to customize its parameters.

3   To turn the Custom Gradient generator into a vignette, Control-click the Custom Gradient clip in the Timeline and choose Composite Mode > Multiply to composite the two layers together. Then, move the playhead over both clips so you can see the results of your adjustments as you work.

This is clearly not the effect that you wanted, so you need to customize the generator's parameters.

4   In the Gradient Direction parameter, drag the angle control so that the darkest part of the gradient originates from the upper-left corner (around 304 degrees).

5   The shadow isn't extending far enough into the picture, so click the Start parameter's crosshairs control, and drag the crosshairs in the Canvas to the left ear of the man sitting at the table.

At this point, the generator is positioned well, but it's too dark to plausibly be a shadow given the lighting elsewhere in the room. You could lighten the shadow by lowering the Opacity of the generator, but there's a more processor-efficient way of achieving the same effect: Change the colors the gradient uses.

6   In the End parameter click the color swatch, and using the Grayscale slider option in the Colors panel, choose a 75 percent gray.

The lighter the color, the more transparent it becomes when using the Multiply composite mode. By choosing a light gray instead of solid black for the end of the gradient, you've effectively made the shadow effect more transparent, without having to use another effect. Compare these before (left) and after (right) frames and notice how the shadows on the wall have deepened.

Besides cutting down on the ambient light in the scene, this vignette also gives a bit of depth to the shot. An additional benefit of the corner vignette is that it cuts down on the lighting of the foreground chair to the left of the frame, heightening viewer focus on the man sitting at the table.

Using the Highlight Generator

A third generator that's useful when you want to vignette two sides of the frame simultaneously is the Highlight generator (in the Render submenu of the Generator pop-up menu).

 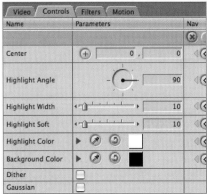

In the following exercise, you'll use the Highlight generator as a vignette to darken ambient light while preserving a streak of light from a handheld source (the lantern).

1 Open the *03 Vignette Using Highlight* sequence, located in the Vignettes, Creating Shadows bin of the **Color Correction Exercises** project, and play through the clip to find a frame where the man is halfway down the stairs.

The first clip in the Timeline has a color correction already applied to it to give a cool evening look. (The second clip in the Timeline shows the completed effect, which you can refer to as you work.) The scene is lit with a handheld lantern that throws a ring of illumination in all directions.

In this case, the client wants a darker, spookier look. Because the overall scene is already so dark, one solution is to darken some of the surrounding spill lighting, while leaving a splash of light on the walls alone, for dramatic effect.

2   In the Video tab of the Viewer, choose Render > Highlight from the Generators pop-up, superimpose it in track V2 over the Down Stairs MS clip. Open it in the Viewer from the sequence and click the Controls tab to customize its parameters.

3   To turn the Highlight generator into a vignette, Control-click the Custom Gradient clip in the Timeline and choose Composite Mode > Multiply to composite the two layers together. Then, move the playhead over both clips so you can see the results of your adjustments as you work.

4   To create an interesting angle to the shadowed effect, drag the angle control of the Highlight Angle parameter until the transparent part of the vignette is aligned diagonally, from the bottom-left to the top-right (about 41 degrees).

5 Drag the Highlight Soft slider to the right to increase the softness of the shadow, blurring the borders of the vignette and revealing more of the image.

At this point, the effect is complete. The light on the wall falls off much faster, creating a more inky blackness at the periphery of the frame. If you wanted to lighten the shadow to reveal more of the background, you could change the background color to a lighter shade of gray.

One detail you should notice, however, if you play the clip all the way through. At the very end of the clip, when the man walks off to the left of the frame, the lantern passes through the darkest part of the vignette and gets cut off.

You could correct for this by lightening the vignette, changing its angle, or even fading it out at that point to fully reveal the background clip. In the next section, you'll learn another way of preserving highlights that overlap vignettes.

Preserving Highlights in Vignettes

Sometimes a vignette you're creating to deepen the shadows in a clip overlaps with a practical light source. The result is that the level of the light source is artificially reduced, which may or may not be a bad thing. If the reduction is noticeably duller, and it's one of the only light sources in the frame, you probably want to raise that highlight to its original level.

This next exercise shows you how to raise such a light to the proper level by isolating just the highlights of a clip and superimposing them over the vignette.

1   Open the *04 Preserving Highlights* sequence, located in the Vignettes, Creating Shadows bin of the **Color Correction Exercises** project.

The first clip in the sequence is color corrected, and it also has an oval vignette applied to it to darken the shadows around the edges of the room. There's a light at the top of the door, however, that overlaps with the oval vignette.

2   Click the Track Visibility control for track V2 a few times to toggle the Oval generator on and off, and examine the light both in the Viewer and in the Waveform Monitor.

You can see that with the vignette on, the level of the light at the top drops quite a bit, dulling the light, and eliminating an important bit of dynamic range in the image. The result is not really flattering.

Looking at the light levels in the Waveform Monitor before and after the vignette is applied illustrates the effect even more dramatically. Notice how the light extends all the way to 100 percent when the vignette is off (left monitor), but after you turn on the vignette (right monitor), the level of the light drops to approximately 80 to 90 percent, an unflattering reduction.

 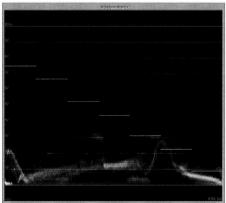

3 To bring back the highlights without eliminating or otherwise altering the vignette, superimpose a duplicate of the Basement LS clip (along with the Color Correction filter that's been added to it) into track V3.

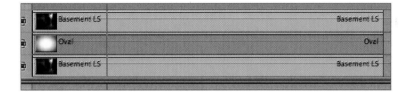

In the next four steps, you'll be using the luma controls of the Chroma Keyer manually to isolate the highlights.

4 Apply the Chroma Keyer filter (in the Video Filters > Key bin of the Effects tab) to the duplicate Basement LS filter in track V3. Open that clip into the Viewer, and click the Chroma Keyer tab to isolate the highlights.

5 In the Chroma Keyer tab, turn off the Hue and Sat controls, and turn on the Luma controls.

You're going to use the Chroma Keyer to perform a luma key, using the graphical controls this filter provides. Then, click the View Final/Matte/Source control (the key, which should turn into a black key on a white background when in Matte mode) once to view the key while you work. Viewing the key itself makes it easier to see which parts of the picture are being preserved and which parts are rendered transparent.

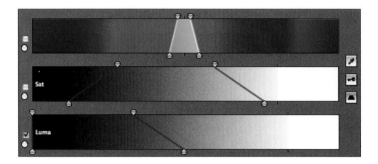

Immediately, you'll see an exaggerated white area in the Canvas that covers the highlights. This is the matte that's showing the isolated area. Because the Luma controls are set to the darkest areas of the picture, with a gradual falloff towards the midtones, the darkest areas of the superimposed clip in track V3 are turned transparent, leaving only the highlights.

6   The currently keyed highlights have rough edges, so drag the Softening slider to the right to blur the edges of the matte, just a bit.

7   Click the View Final/Matte/Source control twice to view the final effect.

The key changes to a red key against a gray background.

The isolated highlights are now superimposed over the oval vignette, allowing you to retain the deepened shadows that contrast nicely with the bright area of the picture.

Further Considerations

As you've seen, there are myriad uses for vignettes. This section focused primarily on reinforcing and deepening shadows in the picture to focus viewer attention, but you may have also noticed that all of the examples were scenes that take place in the evening. Vignettes can also be used to add color, to lighten areas rather than darken, and more. To find the entries that will show you how, consult the See Also listing at the start of this entry.

Index

in some places, one mistake can cost you everything

Official Selection
2006
BRECKENRIDGE
FILM FESTIVAL
Breckenridge, Colorado

Official Selection
2006
SALENTO
INTERNATIONAL
FILM FESTIVAL
Salento, Italy

Official Selection
2006
ReelHeART
INTERNATIONAL
FILM FESTIVAL
Toronto, Ontario

Official Selection
2006
FAIF
INTERNATIONAL
FILM FESTIVAL
Hollywood, California

Official Selection
2006
LONGBAUGH
FILM FESTIVAL
Portland, Oregon

Official Selection
2006
SAN FERNANDO
VALLEY
FILM FESTIVAL
Los Angeles, California

FOURWEEKSFOURHOURS

Judi BEECHER, Eric PIERPOINT, Kaylynn RASCHKE, and Scott ESCAMILLO

a film by ALEXIS VAN HURKMAN
www.fourweeksfourhours.com